EARLY POTTERY IN THE SOUTHEAST

Early Pottery in the Southeast

TRADITION AND INNOVATION
IN COOKING TECHNOLOGY

Kenneth E. Sassaman

A Dan Josselyn Memorial Publication

The University of Alabama Press
Tuscaloosa

Manufactured in the United States of America
designed by zig zeigler

The paper on which this book is printed
meets the minimum requirements of
American National Standard for Information
Science-Permanence of Paper for
Printed Library Materials,
ANSI Z39.48-1984

Library of Congress Cataloging-in-Publication Data

Sassaman, Kenneth E.
Early pottery in the Southeast: tradition and innovation in cooking technology / Kenneth E. Sassaman.
p. cm.
"A Dan Josselyn memorial publication."
Includes bibliographical references and index.
ISBN 0-8173-0670-6 (alk. paper)
1. Indians of North America-Southern States—Pottery. 2. Indians of North America—Savannah River Valley (Ga. and S.C.)—Pottery. 3. Indians of North America—Southern States—Antiquities. 4. Indians of North America—Savannah River Valley (Ga. and S.C.)—Antiquities. 5. Southern States—Antiquities. 6. Savannah River Valley (Ga. and S.C.)—Antiquities.
I. Title.
E78.S65S27 1993
730'.09758' 1—dc20 92-35435
CIP

ISBN 978-0-8173-0670-0 (alk. paper) ISBN 978-0-8173-8426-5 (electronic)

Contents

List of Tables

List of Figures

Acknowledgments

This book is a revised version of the doctoral dissertation I presented to the University of Massachusetts–Amherst in 1991. The members of my dissertation committee, Dena F. Dincauze, chair, H. Martin Wobst, Arthur S. Keene, and James K. Boyce, inspired me to think in new ways about old archaeological problems, and I thank them for the guidance, encouragement, and resources they provided over the course of this project. I was particularly influenced by Drs. Dincauze and Wobst; any success I have enjoyed in this endeavor is owed in large measure to their wisdom and care.

A number of individuals graciously provided access to the artifact collections I examined for this project. For this my gratitude is extended to Eugene Futato, Office of Archaeological Research at Moundville; David Hally, University of Georgia; Michael Taylor, Hilton Head Museum; Genevieve Fischer, Peabody Museum, Harvard; Dan Simpkins, Lewis Larson, and Ray Crook of West Georgia College; Martha Zierden, The Charleston Museum; Sharon Pekrul and George Lewis, South Carolina Institute of Archaeology and Anthropology; and Bob Carnes and Bob Neumann, Museum of Geoscience, Louisiana State University. My thanks also go to colleagues who provided data or copies of unpublished reports: Mark Brooks, David Anderson, Glen Hanson, Tommy Charles, George Lewis, Dan Robinson, Janice Campbell, Michael Trinkley, Fred Cook, Dan Elliott, Bob Johnson, Albert Goodyear, David Hally, Steve Davis, Jerald Ledbetter, and Read Stowe. I am also grateful for the theoretical insights of my fellow students at UMass, especially Michael Nassaney, John Cross, Bill Fawcett, Dean Saitta, and Elena Filios. Equally important in this endeavor was the wealth of substantive insight provided by David Anderson and Mark Brooks on matters of southeastern prehistory.

Funding for this research was provided by the Savannah River Archaeological Research Program (SRARP), under the direction of Glen Hanson until 1989, and through the offices of Bruce Rippeteau, South Carolina State Archaeologist and Director of the South Carolina Institute of Archaeology and Anthropology, and Ron Jernigan of the Savannah River Operations Office, United States Department of Energy. I can honestly say that this project, and perhaps my graduate career, would not have survived without the foresight and commitment of Glen Hanson to support student research, and for this I am especially grateful. The current SRARP managers, Mark Brooks and Richard Brooks, and its DOE contracting officer, Drew Grainger, also deserve credit for continuing in this same spirit.

I have several people to thank for their thoughtful comments on drafts of this book in its various stages of development: David Anderson, Mark Brooks, Chester DePratter, George Lewis, John Gero, David Dye, Ned Jenkins, and Trudie Calvert. My deep gratitude also goes to Judith Knight and the staff of the University of Alabama Press for their professionalism and patience. Finally, to all the others who helped to make this project materialize—to my parents, friends, and colleagues—I cast my wishes for all the best.

EARLY POTTERY IN THE SOUTHEAST

CHAPTER 1

Problem Orientation and Overview

Pottery is one of several technological achievements that was long believed to have been a consequence of, or precondition for, the transition from hunting and gathering to food production. As canonized in the works of V. Gordon Childe (1925, 1944, 1951), the "Neolithic Revolution" marked the point at which humans took control of nature, domesticating its plants and animals to provide a secure and abundant food base and to escape the environmental vagaries that constrained their technological and social development. Under agriculture, the story went, the requirements of processing and storing domesticated grain created a demand for vessel technology, leading to the widespread development of durable, heat-resistant pots. Childe (1951:76) believed that pottery technology had "great significance for human thought and for the beginning of science." It involved an appreciation of a host of chemical and physical processes, the control and use of heat, clay, and temper. Viewed this way, the concomitant developments of agriculture and pottery provided a strong technoeconomic basis for generating the surplus believed necessary to move humans along the pathway to "civilization."

The structural unity between agriculture and pottery denoted above, along with the teleological overtones of the model, have long been refuted by archaeological evidence to the contrary. Pottery is well documented in archaeological contexts that lack evidence for food production. Early pottery traditions in Japan, Denmark, Colombia, Ecuador, and the American Southeast are testimony to the development of ceramic vessel technology within economies of hunting, gathering, and fishing. In attempting to reconcile these anomalies with the prevailing Neolithic view of pottery, archaeologists initially suggested that the technology diffused from food-producing cultures elsewhere (e.g., Griffin 1952:357; Sears and Griffin 1950). Since then, refinements in chronology have demonstrated that hunter-gatherer pottery preceded the emergence of local agricultural communities by hundreds, even thousands, of years (e.g., Ikawa-Smith 1976; Stoltman 1966, 1972).

Despite the recognition that pottery was used by hunter-gatherer populations across the globe, vestiges of the Neolithic Revolution model prevail in the minds of archaeologists. For example, some researchers have noted a strong association between the earliest pottery and exploitation of coastal estuaries (Goodyear 1988; Stoltman 1972). Worldwide, the resource potential of these coastal zones appears to have supported relatively sedentary populations of hunter-gatherers (Ikawa-Smith 1976; Rowly-Conwy 1983). From either the demands or opportunities of settled life, pottery was developed, the argument goes, to take full advantage of the resource potential of coastal zones. In this regard, coastal resources, particularly shellfish, have assumed the role of plant domesticates in contributing to the development of ceramic vessel technology.

In contradistinction to this example, recent explanations for the use of pottery by hunter-gatherers have downplayed the sophistication of the innovation, denying it the technological status given to it by Childe. Using phrases such as "technologically unimpressive" (Smith 1986:30) and "simple and crude" (Brown 1989:208) to describe early pottery, archaeologists maintain a technological distinction between hunter-gatherers and agriculturalists. Experiments on the mechanical performance of early pottery have tended to support the notion that hunter-gatherer vessels were relatively unsophisticated "gadgets" designed for ease of manufacture and portability (Schiffer and Skibo 1987:608). Yet by bringing to these studies the a priori assumption that early pots necessarily reflect the life-styles of the people who made and used them, the results serve to support the notion that hunter-gatherers lived a simple, mobile life and that little demand was placed on their labor or time to produce more sophisticated technology, or that a life of mobility constrained their ability to make and use pottery.

In short, the fact that pottery was made and used by prehistoric peoples before agriculture developed has been obscured either by redefining *Neolithic* to include coastal hunter-gatherers or by redefining *pottery* to exclude less sophisticated forms of ceramic technology. Either way, the interpretations fail because they presuppose that variability in the organization of human societies is interpretable on the basis of technological and economic definitions (or redefinitions). Many archaeologists still maintain a boundary between societies acting upon nature and those interacting with nature, what Barbara Bender (1985a:21) calls the boundary between "hot" and "cold" societies. The problem in classifying human societies by their position above or below such a boundary is that other aspects of society, particularly social and political organization, are conflated with technology and economy. In the case of hunter-gatherer societies the tendency has been to reduce sociopolitical variation into categories—egalitarian, band, kin, and generalized reciprocity—that downplay the potential of such societies for internally generated conflict and change. Despite a growing recognition that hunter-gatherer societies embody a wide range of variation in technology, settlement organization, and subsistence economy (e.g., Price and Brown 1985), proportionately less attention has been given to sociopolitical variation. This is unfortunate because it can be argued that variation in the sociopolitical organization of production and exchange can explain much of the technoeconomic variation we observe in the archaeological and ethnographic records of hunter-gatherers (Bender 1981, 1985a, 1985b; Filios 1990; Root 1983, 1984; Saitta and Keene 1990).

Thus to deny the potential for sociopolitical variation among hunter-gatherers is to ignore a wide range of factors that may help to explain the emergence and spread of ceramic vessel technology. In the American Southeast, for example, pottery was used in three distinct subareas. The pottery traditions shared some technological traits, but they originated at different times and had different levels of acceptance within the respective areas. What is more, it took nearly two millennia for the innovation to become widely accepted throughout the Southeast. Although the earliest locations of pottery use each contain evidence for shellfish exploitation and semisedentary settlement (Peterson 1980), the existence of similar conditions at locations lacking pottery suggests that an economic or ecological explanation alone is insufficient. Instead, the social and political variation across the region during this interval provides a range of alternative explanations of why pottery was adopted where it was and why it failed to be more widely and rapidly adopted across the greater Southeast.

Social Variation and Early Pottery in the American Southeast

As should be evident by now, my theoretical approach to documenting and explaining variation in the archaeological record of early hunter-gatherer pottery in the American Southeast is explicitly social. I take as my guiding premise that technological change is the result of social demands on labor. I illustrate how hunter-gatherer economies varied with regard to the organization of production and exchange and how certain strategies of production and exchange created social obligations that could not be alleviated through fissioning. I see technological change as both the result of increased demands on labor and a source of new demands on labor. Although some strategies of production and exchange engendered technological change, others served to perpetuate the status quo and, consequently, acted as a fetter to technological change. I therefore aim to illuminate not only the social conditions of production and exchange that led to the development or adoption of pottery but also those that inhibited the spread of the innovation across the Southeast.

The social perspective on technological innovation I employ in this study is derived from the growing body of theory which exposes the wide range of sociopolitical variation among hunters and gatherers (Bender 1981, 1985a, 1985b; Cross 1983, 1990; Filios 1990; Keene 1986; Marquardt 1985; Root 1983, 1984; Saitta 1987; Saitta and Keene 1985, 1990; Testart 1982, 1988). My approach to technological innovation is strongly influenced by Bender's (1985a, 1985b) social models of the Late Archaic and Woodland periods of the American Midwest. Bender argues that the creation and maintenance of exchange alliances were the driving forces behind production in Late Archaic society. She points out that differential access to materials and information is inherent to all exchange alliances and that a potential always exists for individuals to control access. She further maintains that social differentiation, be it potential or real, is masked or validated in the context of ritual and ceremony and that ceremonial activities and the exchanges they underwrite make demands on time and labor. Technological change, Bender argues, can be understood as a response to these social demands. I adhere to this premise in this book but expand upon it to argue that similar processes can serve to inhibit or prevent the spread of technological innovations.

A social perspective on technological innovation does not preclude the need for detailed technofunctional analyses of early pottery. On the contrary, the technological manifestations of social variation will include not only patterns of differential acceptance but also variation in the manufacture and use of pots. Information on the functions of early pots is just now beginning to accumulate. Laboratory experiments (Schiffer and Skibo 1987; Skibo, Schiffer, and Reid 1989) and ethnohistorical data (Reid 1988) are important in this regard, but much more work needs to be done on archaeological collections of early pottery (e.g., Skibo, Hally, and Schiffer 1988). Unfortunately, the emphasis in analysis of early pottery in the Southeast has been and continues to be on typological and chronological variation. In lieu of functional data on early pottery, assumptions based on the uses of pottery from later periods are used with little regard for their appropriateness. It is often assumed, for example, that early pots had an advantage over preceramic alternatives because they could be used directly over a fire. The assumption carries with it a host of technical implications about the heating effectiveness of pottery that can be addressed only through detailed technofunctional analyses (e.g., Braun 1983; Hally 1986; Rice 1987). If we can strip away any preconceptions we have about the earliest uses of pottery, we may find that technofunctional data on early pottery reveal a variety of uses, some of which may appear counterintuitive or even maladaptive.

In this regard, it is also critical to collect detailed technofunctional data on the available alternatives to pottery (e.g., Brown 1989). A varied and long-lived set of preceramic cooking alternatives was available to southeastern hunter-gatherers. Because pottery was not uniformly adopted across the region, one might conclude that certain traditional alternatives were adequate to meet their food-processing needs. Yet it is equally likely that pottery had a significant advantage over traditional technology but was not so perceived. There is also little reason to assume that the use of pottery rendered traditional technology obsolete. Pottery may have been used in conjunction with alternative containers and techniques or simply relegated to special functions. To address these hypotheses we need to combine detailed technofunctional data on alternative vessel technologies with contextual information on the times and places such alternatives were used.

Bringing these data to bear on a social model of technological innovation presents the most formidable challenge to this study. Detailed archaeological information on the organization of hunter-gatherer production and exchange is not readily apparent, but the lack of these data is more a shortcoming of the questions asked of the record than it is of the record itself. Various configurations of production and exchange have specific implications for the distribution of people and materials that can be evaluated with archaeological data. For example, the level to which individuals interact with one another through relations of production and exchange should be evident in patterns of stylistic variability (Root 1984; Wobst 1977). Similarly, the context and distribution of raw materials and finished products are useful for examining patterns and modes of exchange. Each of these data sets will contain variation that is referable, theoretically, to variation in the use of ceramic vessel technologies.

Social Variation and Early Pottery in the Savannah River Valley Region

The data parameters I briefly mentioned in the foregoing paragraphs pose some stringent requirements on the selection of a study area for this project. Each of the three provinces of early pottery use in the Southeast—the South Atlantic Slope, peninsular Florida, and the Midsouth—is relevant to a social model of innovation, but only one offers an opportunity to conduct detailed technofunctional, distributional, and stylistic analyses on a large sample of well-documented sites. The Savannah River Valley region of the South Atlantic Slope has been the subject of nearly continuous archaeological investigations since the late nineteenth century. Major survey projects in the valley and on the coasts of Georgia and South Carolina have provided relatively thorough coverage of the region (Figure 1). Hundreds of Late Archaic sites spanning the preceramic and ceramic periods (5000-3000 B.P.) have been documented, and many have been excavated. Large artifact assemblages have been collected at dozens of the sites, and more than sixty radiocarbon dates are available.

Besides its superiority in archaeological sample size and quality, the Savannah River Valley region is an especially appropriate study area for this project because of the antiquity and variability of its earliest pottery. Fiber-tempered pottery in the region has been dated to nearly 4500 B.P., making it the oldest well-documented pottery in North America. Despite its great antiquity, pottery was not widely adopted in the region until about 2500 B.P. An overall trend of rapid and widespread use on the coast is contrasted with the slow and gradual adoption of pottery in the interior portion of the valley. Unlike the coast, cooking technology in the interior included the use

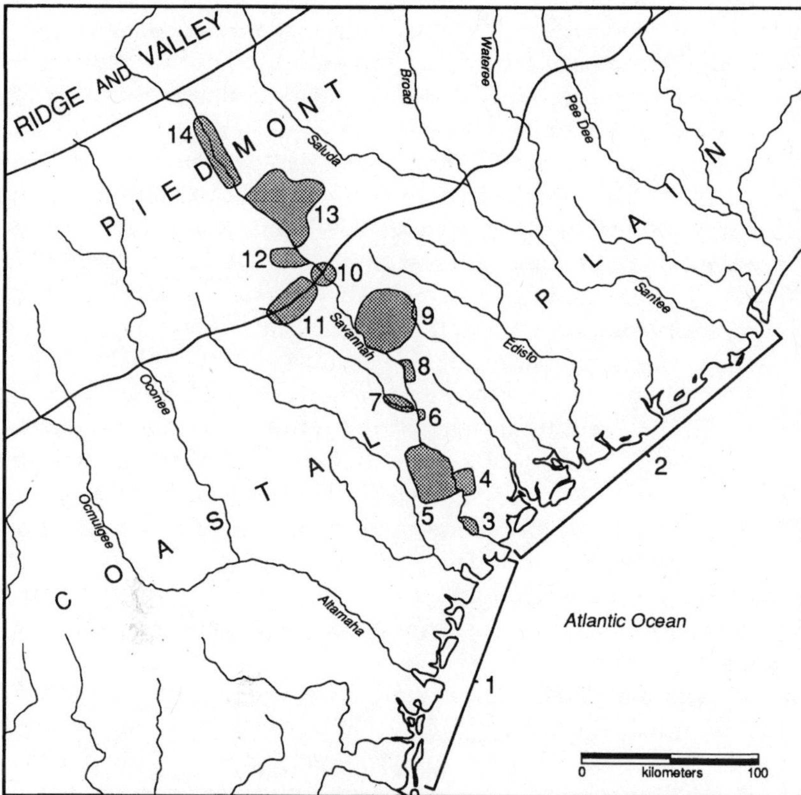

1. Georgia Coast (Crusoe and DePratter 1976; DePratter 1979b; DePratter and Howard 1980; Waring 1968a, b; among others).
2. South Carolina Coast (Garrow and Willams 1980; Hemmings and Waddell n.d.; Michie 1980; Trinkley 1980b, 1986; among others).
3. Savannah National Wildlife Refuge (Marrinan 1979).
4. Jasper County (Brooks and Sassaman n.d.).
5. Ebenezer Watershed (Fish 1976).
6. Groton Plantation (Peterson 1971b; Stoltman 1974).
7. Brier Creek (see Elliott and O'Steen [1987] for summary).
8. Allendale Chert Survey (Goodyear and Charles 1984).
9. Savannah River Site (Hanson et al. 1978, 1981; Martin et al. 1986; see Sassaman et al. [1990] for synthesis of work).
10. Various Augusta Projects (Cable et al. 1978; Crook 1990; Elliott and Doyon 1981; Elliott et al. 1992; Ferguson and Widmer 1976; Ledbetter 1988, 1991; among others).
11. Fort Gordon (Braley 1992a, b; Campbell et al. 1981; King and Braley 1992; Price and Braley 1990).
12. Tributary Survey (Smith 1974).
13. Sumter National Forest (see Elliott [1986b] for summary of some of the work).
14. Richard B. Russell Reservoir (see Anderson and Joseph [1988] for synthesis of work).

Figure 1. Savannah River Valley region with locations of major survey projects.

of soapstone for indirect "stone boiling." Soapstone was available in only limited areas of the interior, but the wider archaeological distribution of soapstone cooking stones suggests that these items were entered into local exchange networks.

I employ data on the distribution and use of soapstone and pottery to support the argument that soapstone exchange in the middle Savannah River Valley served to limit the adoption of pottery because its adoption represented a threat to existing exchange relationships. Initially, resistance to pottery prevented its spread into the interior; later, after being adopted in the interior, pottery was used only as a container for stone boiling. Simultaneously, coastal inhabitants outside the sphere of soapstone exchange were quick to use pots over fire, and they rapidly developed innovations to improve the thermal efficiency of pottery. I argue that socioeconomic organization on the coast was significantly different from that of the interior. Based primarily on economic arrangements that imposed constraints on the ability of individuals to fission, conditions were right for the development and rapid adoption of technological innovations that were responsive to the increased demands on personal time and labor.

My arguments about social variation in the Late Archaic period in the Savannah River Valley region hinge to a large degree on the reconstruction of social boundaries. I recognize that boundaries are political tools used by humans to define access to resources and that boundaries exist at all scales of human interaction, from personal to collective, from local to supraregional. The distribution of soapstone artifacts constitutes a boundary between those with social access to soapstone and those without. Similarly, the stylistic variation of pottery embodies evidence of patterns of interaction that can be used to infer boundaries around or between various groups. Early pottery in the Savannah River Valley region exhibits an extremely high degree of variation in surface decoration (Figure 2). Changes in design through time have been incorporated into pottery chronologies for the region (Anderson, Cantley, and Novick 1982; DePratter 1979a; Trinkley 1980a; Waring 1968a), and evidence for spatial patterning possibly indicative of sociopolitical boundaries has also been noted (Anderson 1975). Just what such spatial patterning reflects is beyond the scope of this book, though I do assume that stylistic variation is referable to variation in the types of interactions that took place, if not in the intensity or duration of interactions (cf. Hodder 1982; Plog

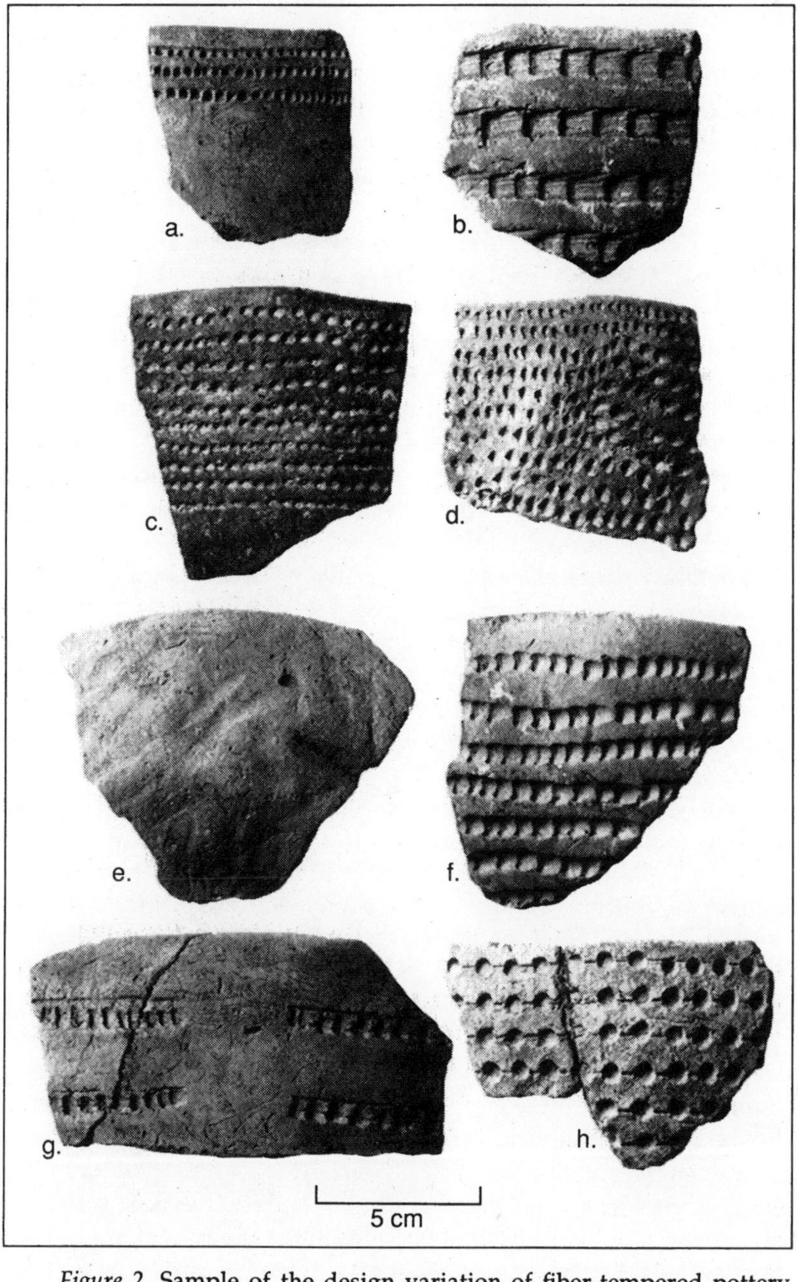

Figure 2. Sample of the design variation of fiber-tempered pottery from the Savannah River Valley region and coasts of South Carolina and Georgia (a. Cane Patch; b-d, f. Chesterfield; e. Daw's Island; g. Fish Haul; h. Theriault).

1978). Thus I expect that variation in the adoption and use of alternative cooking technologies will be paralleled in the stylistic variation of pottery inasmuch as this variation symbolizes the social interactions involved in the production and exchange of cooking technologies.

In its social variation and patterns of technological innovation, the Savannah River Valley is something of a microcosm for the greater Southeast. A detailed study of early pottery in the region sheds new light on the processes of technological innovation and diffusion in the Southeast. Interestingly, the pan-southeastern commerce in soapstone vessels that was part of the Poverty Point exchange network may have created a social barrier to adoption of pottery similar to that observed in the Savannah River Valley. The Poverty Point exchange has heretofore been viewed as the mechanism though which pottery spread to the Midsouth (Jenkins 1982; Jenkins, Dye, and Walthall 1986). Drawing on the empirical results of the Savannah River case study, I show how a social perspective on Poverty Point exchange illuminates alternative explanations for the westward spread of pottery.

Organization of the Study

This book is divided into three sections. The first section provides the empirical and theoretical background for the study. I begin in Chapter 2 with a review of the major early pottery traditions of the American Southeast and examine interpretations for their development and spread. I highlight the shortcomings of diffusionist and functionalist interpretations to show how extant models have masked potential sociopolitical variation that affected the rate and pathways of the diffusion of innovation. I then examine the broader social and political aspects of innovation and diffusion. The major points of my argument are that a chief demand on labor among hunters and gatherers is derived from the creation and maintenance of exchange relationships; that certain economic relations constrained fissioning and thus had the potential to become institutionalized social obligations; that changes in the organization of production and exchange caused by social demands on labor are often accompanied by technological innovation; and that inherent inequalities in certain modes of production and exchange strongly influenced the rate and direction of technological change.

The second section of the study consists of a detailed look at the innovation and adoption of pottery in the Savannah River Valley region. Archaeological background on the region is the subject of Chapter 3. I emphasize the contrast between the records of the coast and the interior, describing the environment, typology, chronology, and settlement-subsistence of these subregions to provide a context for interpreting their distinct technological histories. The review also emphasizes the shortage of detailed technofunctional information on early pottery and its nonceramic alternatives.

Technofunctional analyses of alternative cooking technologies form the major empirical contribution of this book. The methodological and chronological background for the analyses is described in Chapter 4. I discuss sample selection, variable selection, and methods of analysis and review stratigraphic data from key sites in the region to derive chronologically sensitive sorting criteria for pottery. I then adapt these criteria to a paradigmatic classification scheme for the purpose of sample chronology and verify and anchor the classification with available radiocarbon dates.

With a sample chronology in place, I turn to a study of the manufacture, distribution, and use of alternative cooking technologies in Chapter 5. Ethnohistoric, experimental, and archaeological data are reviewed to draw inferences about the functions of perforated soapstone slabs, baked clay objects, pottery, and soapstone vessels. Data on the formation of soapstone slab assemblages, including patterns of recycling and maintenance, are examined to determine their effects on the spatial distribution of these items in the region. The results show that soapstone slabs are widely distributed throughout the Coastal Plain, an area devoid of naturally occurring soapstone. I also show that soapstone cooking stones and baked clay objects co-occur at many sites in the Coastal Plain, and, on the basis of limited data on the mechanical performance of baked clay objects, I conclude that these alleged clay alternatives to soapstone could not have functioned as effective boiling stones.

The bulk of my technofunctional analysis is devoted to pottery. Combining the literature on mechanical performance of cooking pots with recent information on hunter-gatherer pottery, I identify design attributes that can be used to distinguish direct-heat vessels from those used in indirect-heat cooking (i.e., stone boiling). Observations of these attributes on archaeological data are evidence that ceramic vessels were used in both indirect- and direct-heat methods of cooking. Further observations on the use wear (soot) of vessels support this inference. I apply the sample chronology to these results and find that pots were used directly over fire on the coast throughout the Late Archaic period but that a technique of indirect-heat cooking persisted in the interior long after pottery was adopted and even after innovations appeared on the coast which improved the thermal efficiency of ceramic vessels.

Interpretations of the chronological and technofunctional patterns of pottery in the Savannah River Valley and the greater Southeast are the subject of Chapter 6. I begin by employing pottery surface decorations to reconstruct "stylistic boundaries" for the region. Using these bounded entities for comparative purposes, I reintroduce the theoretical parameters of production and exchange discussed in Chapter 2 to interpret observed patterns in the use of alternative cooking technologies. I propose that the organization of production on the coast was characterized by labor arrangements that constrained group fissioning and placed social demands on individual labor. Pottery was widely adopted throughout the zone in response to increased labor demands, and innovations to improve the functional efficiency of pottery soon followed. Simultaneously, soapstone cooking stones continued to be produced and distributed in the interior as a means of maintaining local exchange alliances. I argue that individuals with direct access to soapstone were able to channel the social surplus of local exchange into higher levels of exchange and that the prestige accrued from extralocal interaction was influential in persuading others to resist innovations in ceramic vessel technology and to maintain the technique of stone boiling with soapstone. Locations of social aggregation, ritual, and ceremony probably represent the arenas in which prestige leaders exerted their greatest influence on individuals to impede change.

In the remainder of Chapter 6 I extrapolate the results of the Savannah River Valley test case to the greater Southeast. I argue that the local process that impeded the spread of pottery innovations had an interregional equivalent in exchange of soapstone vessels. Emphasizing possible constraints on labor stemming from the production and exchange of soapstone vessels, I argue that pottery failed to spread rapidly via channels of Poverty Point exchange because the widespread use of pottery had the potential to decrease the exchange value of soapstone and thus undermine the prestige system of participating communities. I propose instead that certain pottery innovations were transmitted through peripheral exchange relations during seasons of settlement dispersal. I close by identifying some of the effects this process may have had on Late Archaic societies in the areas of exchange alliance, settlement integration, and gender relations.

CHAPTER 2

Early Ceramic Vessel Technology in the American Southeast

RETROSPECT AND PROSPECT

During the prehistoric period referred to as the Late Archaic (i.e., 5000–3000 B.P.), pottery was made and used in three major areas of the American Southeast: the South Atlantic Slope, peninsular Florida, and the Midsouth. Other than the use of fiber for temper, the pottery traditions of these areas are distinct from one another in vessel form and surface finish. In addition to their technological differences, the traditions originated at different times and had varying levels of acceptance within their respective areas.

Studies of early southeastern pottery have conventionally focused on typological and chronological issues (Bullen 1954, 1972; DePratter 1979a; Jenkins 1982; Jenkins, Dye, and Walthall 1986; Waring 1968a). In drawing inferences about the origins of early pottery, archaeologists have invoked diffusionist models to propose cultural-historical linkages between the noncontiguous areas of early pottery use (Crusoe 1972; Ford 1966, 1969; Marrinan 1975; Sears and Griffin 1950; Walthall and Jenkins 1976). In some cases, the interactions accounting for the diffusion of early ceramic technology were outlined (Jenkins 1982), but usually regional connections were postulated simply by comparing lists of traits.

In the 1960s, a break from the cultural-historical emphases of early research engendered functional interpretations of pottery. Working from an adaptationist perspective, archaeologists began posing explanations for early pottery that looked to indigenous causes for technological change (Peterson 1980; Stoltman 1972, 1974). Unfortunately, this was done with little empirical information on the actual functions of early pottery. Pottery was believed to have a functional advantage over nonceramic cooking technology, but the presumption suffered from a lack of data on the uses of pottery. In lieu of detailed functional data, the tendency has been to invoke archaeological or ethnographic analogues from the ceramic technologies of agriculturalists. Because the cooking pots of agriculturalists generally have superior mechanical performance over alternative containers such as baskets, skins, and pits, the use of such analogues in hunter-gatherer contexts has served to perpetuate the notion that pottery indeed represented a "container revolution" (Smith 1986:28). Greater technological and functional variation in the pottery of early hunter-gatherers might be exposed if we relax the assumption that pottery was inherently superior to its nonceramic alternatives.

Diffusionist and functionalist positions on early pottery have been equally poor in explaining the variegated pattern of technological change in ceramics in the Southeast. In concert with cultural-historical emphases, diffusionist approaches in archaeology have been particularly damaging to our perception of social variation. The tendency has been to treat archaeologically defined "cultures" as internally homogeneous entities in which individuals responded in like manner to the introduction or development of technological innovations. A similar problem exists in functionalist doctrine, and it is further biased by its tautological view of adaptation. Neither perspective accommodates variation in the motives, opportunities, and strategies of individuals or subgroups that affect the rates and pathways of technological change. Because they ignore social variation, these perspectives are unable to explain why it took nearly two thousand years for pottery to become widely adopted in the American Southeast. They are similarly weak in accounting for technological and functional variation in early pottery across areas of the Southeast that otherwise had similar cultural-historical and environmental situations.

In this chapter I lay a foundation for exposing variation in the sociopolitical organization of Late Archaic societies that helps to explain variation in the adoption of pottery and in its uses and contexts. First I review the major early pottery traditions of the Southeast, discussing briefly the locations, chronologies, and techno-functional data of each. I emphasize chronological data that document regional and local lags in the adoption of pottery, arguing that these patterns have been largely ignored in research on pottery and that they point to the need for revised theory and method on the subject.

In the balance of the chapter I review diffusionist and functionalist explanations for the development and adoption of pottery. I point out the weaknesses of these perspectives, particularly regarding their inability to account for variation in the adoption and use of pottery. An alternative, social perspective on early pottery is provided in the final portion of this chapter.

Early Pottery Traditions in the Southeast

The earliest ceramic vessels in the Southeast are variants of shallow, open bowls dating between 4500 and 2500 B.P. Common to most variants of these wares is the use of organic fiber for temper. Three series of fiber-tempered pottery are documented in the region (Figure 3): (1) Stallings and St. Simons, centered on the Savannah River Valley, South Carolina, and Georgia; (2) Orange, in the St. Johns Valley of east Florida and on the Gulf Coast of Florida above Tampa Bay, and (3) Wheeler, in the western middle Tennessee Valley region of the Midsouth (Griffin 1943; Sears and Griffin 1950; Bullen and Stoltman 1972). Fiber-tempered potsherds have also been recovered from fourth-millennium sites in Kansas and Missouri (Reid 1984), but because current information on the wares is very limited, a typological definition has not yet been established.

In addition to the fiber-tempered pottery series, early sand-tempered pottery is found along the Atlantic seaboard from southeastern North Carolina to the mouth of the Savannah River. This series, referred to as Thom's Creek (Griffin 1945; Waddell 1963), appeared as early as 4000 B.P. and persisted through the fourth millennium before present (Trinkley 1980a).

Stallings Series

Two dates from Rabbit Mount in the lower Savannah River Valley (Figure 3) mark the appearance of Stallings pottery by about 4500 B.P.

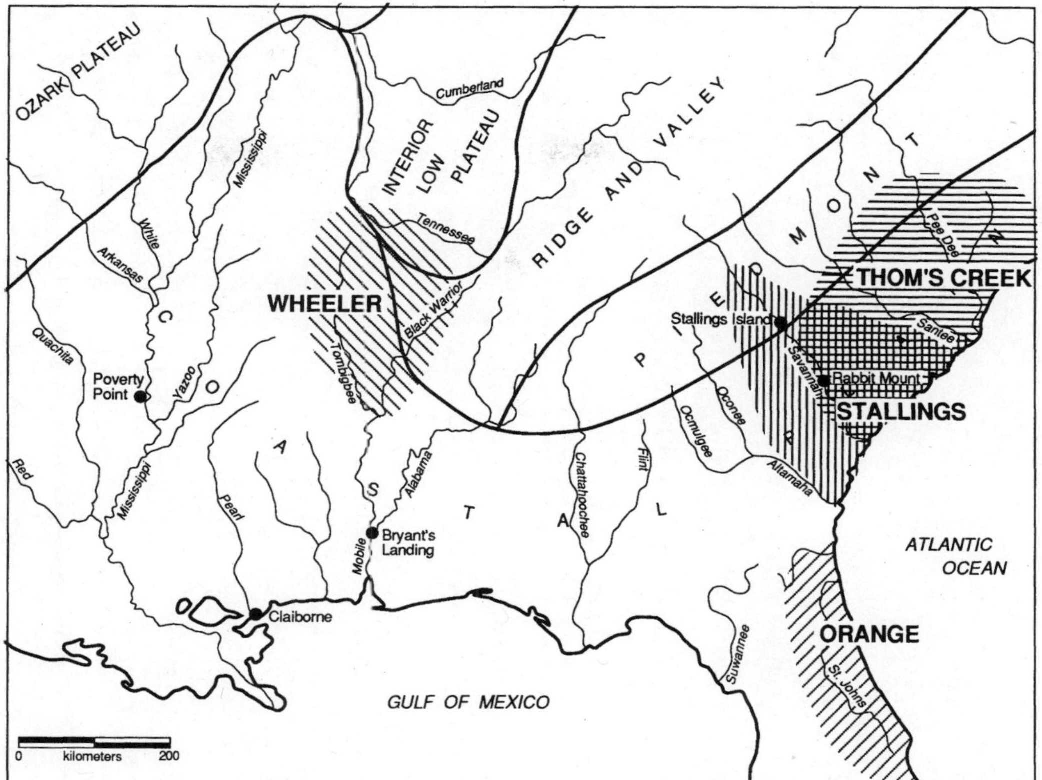

Figure 3. The American Southeast with locations of major Late Archaic pottery traditions.

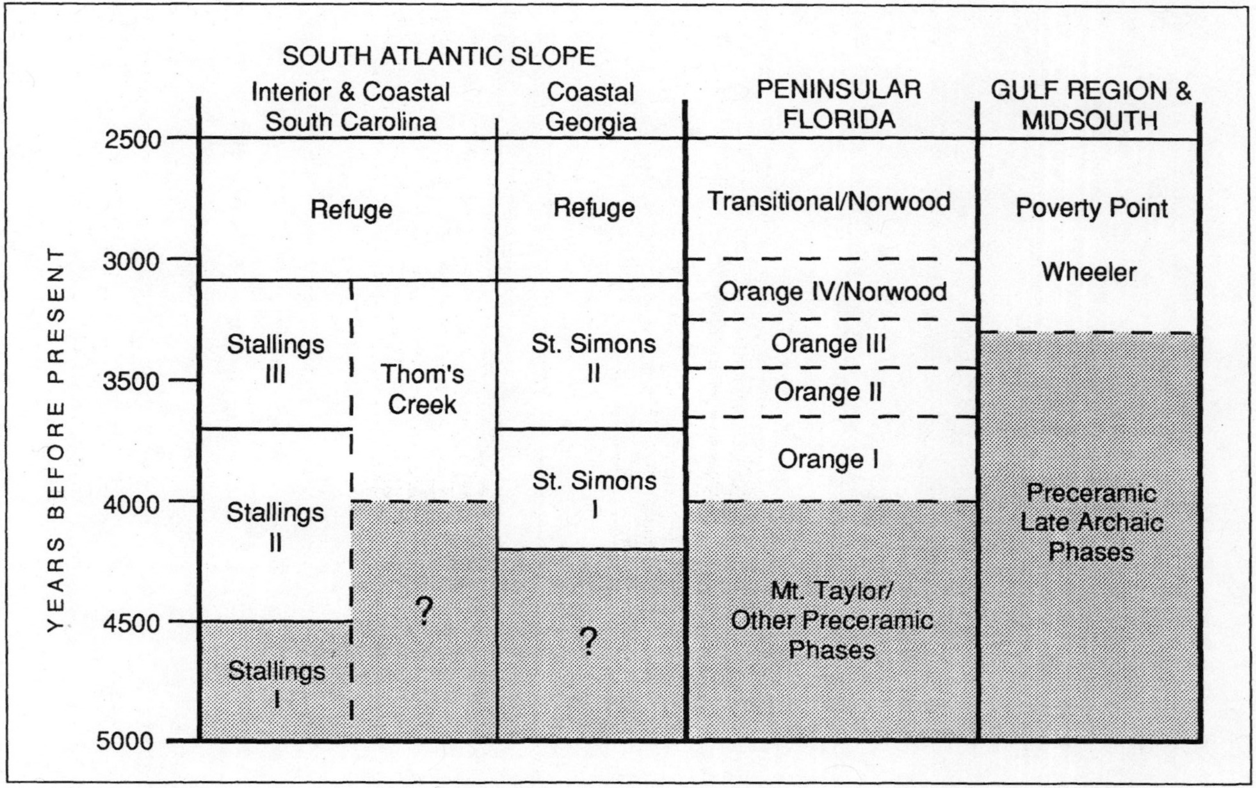

Figure 4. Chronological chart of ceramic Late Archaic phases in the South Atlantic Slope, peninsular Florida, and the Midsouth. Shaded portions represent preceramic phases.

(Stoltman 1966), making it the oldest documented ceramic vessel technology in North America (Figure 4). James B. Stoltman (1972:38) indicates that sites with Stallings components are distributed in the Savannah River Valley from the coast to the lower Piedmont and on the Atlantic Coast from the Santee River, South Carolina, to the Altamaha River, Georgia. Two other type series, Bilbo and St. Simons, have been defined for fiber-tempered wares on the coast (Caldwell and McCann 1941; Holder 1938; Waring 1968a). Although the Bilbo terminology has fallen into disuse, fiber-tempered pottery from sites on the Georgia coast and coastal plain is usually classified as St. Simons (e.g., DePratter 1979a; Marrinan 1975; Snow 1977) because of variability in surface treatment believed to reflect cultural-historical differences between the coast and the interior.

Radiocarbon dates (Appendix A) for Stallings pottery range from 4465±95 to 3110±110 B.P. (Calmes 1968; Stoltman 1966), while St. Simons, or coastal Georgia, dates range from 4190±90 to 3010±80 B.P. (Marrinan 1975:48; Thomas and Larson 1979:20). The range of St. Simons dates is shorter either because of truncation of the coastal record by rise in the sea level or ecological constraints on coastal occupation before 4200 B.P. (see Chapter 3). Despite the shorter record, the St. Simons phase is characterized by historical developments that parallel those of the Stallings phase. A reported shift from predominantly plain pottery to assemblages that include decorated vessels is the basis for subdividing the phases at 3700 B.P. (DePratter 1979b:18; Stoltman 1974; Waring 1968b; Waring and Larson 1968; Figure 4). Stoltman further divided the Stallings phase to include a preceramic Stallings I subphase. In the absence of a documented pre-4200 B.P. archaeological record, a preceramic subphase has not been defined for the coast.

The only documented form of Stallings/St. Simons vessels are shallow, open bowls with slightly rounded or flattened bottoms (Trinkley 1986:166; Waring 1968b:160, 192). Jars with more constricted orifices may be a minority vessel form on the Georgia coast (DePratter 1979b:17). Rims are usually straight or slightly incurvate, and examples of carinated rims are present at a few sites. Methods of vessel manufacture include pinching, slab modeling, and coiling (Griffin 1943:159; Trinkley 1980b:46–48, 1986:160–62). Surface treatments include plain, punctated, incised, and stamped. A high level of design variability is evident among punctated and incised vessels.

Thom's Creek Series

From the mouth of the Savannah River Valley extending up the Atlantic Coast into southeast North Carolina are fourth-millennium sites containing sand-tempered Thom's Creek pottery (Griffin 1945; Trinkley 1980a; Figure 3). Interior coastal plain distributions for Thom's Creek sites are also documented (Anderson 1975; Phelps 1968). The series overlaps with Stallings along the coastal area of South Carolina between the Savannah and Santee rivers and in the interior Coastal Plain of South Carolina. Thom's Creek pottery shares many of the design attributes of Stallings pottery, and the two wares co-occur at many sites north of the Savannah River. The lack of Thom's Creek or comparable sand-tempered pottery on the Georgia coast reflects distinct cultural-historical sequences of fiber-tempered and sand-tempered wares south of the Savannah River.

The Stallings and Thom's Creek phases have considerable temporal overlap, though it is widely recognized that the fiber-tempered ware preceded the sand-tempered variety by a few centuries (Trinkley 1980a, 1983; Figure 4). Radiocarbon dates for Thom's Creek pottery range from 4170±350 to 2885±175 B.P. (Southerland 1974; Trinkley 1980b:191–92). The oldest date, from Spanish Mount, is suspect for its poor association with Thom's Creek pottery in excavated context and for its large sigma. The next oldest date, 3890±110 B.P., from the Small Ford Shell Ring (Calmes 1968), provides a more secure beginning for the Thom's Creek phase at about 4000 B.P.

Three Thom's Creek vessel forms are described by Trinkley (1980a): a shallow bowl with a slightly constricted orifice; a shallow bowl with an unrestricted orifice; and a deep, open jar. Vessel bases are frequently flat, though some are slightly rounded. Coiling and modeling methods of manufacture were used. Thom's Creek pastes vary from "temperless" to gritty, and it is probable that aplastics were simply natural constituents of clays chosen by potters (Trinkley 1980a:8–9, 17–18). Punctated designs are similar to Stallings, and added to the repertoire are finger-pinched designs referred to as Awendaw (Williams 1968b:321; Waddell 1965).

Orange Series

To the south, fiber-tempered pottery of the Orange Series dates to about 4000 B.P. and lasted until about 3000 B.P., when it was replaced by sand- and fiber-tempered pottery of the Norwood Series of northwest Florida (Phelps 1965), by limestone-tempered ceramics along the Gulf Coast above Tampa Bay (Bullen 1972:26), and five hundred years later by the chalky, sand-tempered St. Johns wares of east and central Florida (Milanich and Fairbanks 1980:152).

Ripley P. Bullen (1954) divided the Orange period into four subperiods, later adding a "Transitional Period" (3200–2500 B.P.) to cover the time between the end of Orange and the beginning of Deptford (Bullen 1959, 1972; Figure 4). Primarily on the basis of stratigraphic excavations at the Bluffton Site on the St. Johns River, Bullen documented decorative and technological changes in Orange period pottery (Bullen 1955, 1972; Milanich and Fairbanks 1980:156). Plain shallow, flat-based and straight-sided circular bowls and rectangular trays characterize the Orange 1 subperiod (ca. 4000–3650 B.P.). Similar forms persisted in the Orange 2 subperiod (ca. 3650–3450 B.P.), and incised motifs consisting of concentric vertical diamonds (Orange Incised) and incised spirals with background punctations (Tick Island Incised) were added. Incisions in the subsequent Orange 3 subperiod (ca. 3450–3250 B.P.) are linear, and a decrease in the number of rectangular vessels is apparent. Soapstone vessels are also found at Orange 3 sites (e.g., Bullen and Bullen 1961), and a close resemblance between soapstone and ceramic vessels forms is apparent. The final subperiod, Orange 4 (ca. 3250–3000 B.P.), exhibits simple incised motifs, some mixture of sand and fiber tempering, and the appearance of a coiling method of manufacture.

Wheeler Series

Fiber-tempered pottery appeared in the Midsouth near the end of the Early period (4500–3000 B.P.) of the Gulf Formative Stage, as defined by Ned J. Jenkins (1982). Sites containing the early wares, defined as the Wheeler series (Haag 1939; Sears and Griffin 1950), are concentrated in the western Middle Tennessee Valley (Webb and DeJarnette 1942) and the central and upper Tombigbee Valley (Bense 1987; Jenkins 1975; Figure 3). Wheeler sherds are found in lesser numbers at sites along the lower Tennessee Valley in northern Tennessee and throughout western Alabama and Mississippi, but not west of the Mississippi River (Sears and Griffin 1950; Jenkins, Dye, and Walthall 1986). The total number of Wheeler sherds at a given site is generally small, indicating that ceramic vessels at this time were a minor component of the local subsistence technology.

Few radiocarbon dates for Wheeler pottery are available, and the phase definitions for Wheeler in the Middle Tennessee and Tombigbee River valleys are based on cross-dating with sites in the Poverty Point and Gulf coastal areas. The limited radiocarbon data base has a range of 3314 (averaged) to 3100 B.P. (Connaway, McGahey, and Webb 1977:107; Gagliano and Webb 1970:69), but researchers suspect that Wheeler pottery was made and used well into the third millennium (Figure 4). Arguing from additional evidence, Jenkins indicates that a conservative date range for the Broken Pumpkin Creek phase of the Wheeler variant is 3000 to 2500 B.P. (Jenkins and Krause 1986:43).

Wheeler vessel forms include wide-mouthed, flat-bottomed beakers and flat-bottomed bowls with slightly excurvate wall profiles (Jenkins and Krause 1986:33; Jenkins, Dye, and Walthall 1986:548). A coiling technique of manufacture was used. Most vessels were plain, although among the minority decorated specimens, punctate, dentate, and simple stamped designs were used.

Discussion

The time span of fiber-tempered pottery in the greater Southeast is 4500–2500 B.P. During the two-thousand-year period when knowledge of this pottery was available, the technology was intensively used in only a few limited areas. The generally poor preservation of fiber-tempered pottery may explain the limited record of early pottery use in some areas (Reid 1984) but is insufficient to account for the variegated spatial and temporal patterns of adoption. Regardless of the archaeological visibility of fiber-tempered pottery, well-fired sand-tempered vessels were being made very early on the Carolina coast (ca. 4000 B.P.) but were not developed or adopted in Florida until after 3000 B.P. and a few centuries later in the Midsouth. Only after sand-tempered pottery was present in all of the major fiber-tempered pottery areas (around 2500 B.P.) was ceramic vessel technology widely used throughout the Eastern Woodlands.

Fiber-tempered pottery was indeed accepted slowly in the Southeast. From its first appearance in the Savannah River Valley, several centuries elapsed before fiber-tempered pottery was used in peninsular Florida and another half-millennium elapsed before it was used in the Midsouth. Even at the local level the rate at which pottery was developed or adopted was slow. For example, within the Savannah

River Valley region pottery was widely used at sites in the Coastal Plain and on the coast for at least seven hundred years before it was used in the Piedmont portion of the valley (Figure 5). Moreover, pottery was not intensively used in the Piedmont until after 2500 B.P.

Researchers interested in the origins of ceramic vessel technology have ignored the local and regional lags in the use of pottery. Studies have addressed the reasons why pottery was used where it was but have failed to account for limitations or constraints in the spread of ceramic technology.

Interpretations of the Adoption or Development of Pottery

Interpretations of the emergence of early pottery in the Southeast fall into two basic camps: diffusionist and functionalist. Diffusionist interpretations are the more traditional, being derived in modern anthropology from comparative cultural analysis and in archaeology from the concern for time-space systematics. Diffusionist models are not usually explanatory but are simply descriptions of cultural similarities and differences, usually set within a temporal framework. Functionalist explanations refer to an array of materialist approaches that emphasize the dynamic relationships between behavioral and environmental variability, usually within an explicit adaptationist program.

Diffusionist Interpretations

Before radiocarbon chronologies were developed for the Eastern Woodlands, southeastern fiber-tempered pottery was believed to be the result of stimulus diffusion from the Northeast (Griffin 1952:357; Sears and Griffin 1950). It was hypothesized that pottery in the Northeast originated in Asia (McKern 1937) or Europe (Kehoe 1962), neither of which is seriously considered today (Snow 1980:242). Once the temporal priority of fiber-tempered pottery became known (Stoltman 1966), attention turned toward southern routes of diffusion.

Archaeological research on the coasts of Ecuador (Meggers, Evans, and Estrada 1965) and Colombia (Reichel-Dolmatoff 1965) led to the refinement of theories regarding transoceanic contacts between Asia, South America, and North America. Shortly after the publication of this work, James Ford (1966; 1969) proposed that a series of colonizing ventures from coastal South America led to the rise of early ceramic period cultures in Florida and Georgia. Ford's evidence consisted of a set of comparisons in settlement patterning, lithic technology, ornaments, and especially form and decoration of ceramic vessels. Regarding early pottery, the fiber-tempered wares of Puerto Hormiga, appearing around 5000 B.P. (Reichel-Dolmatoff 1965), were considered to be the stimulus for Stallings and Orange Series pottery, with Ecuadorian elements of form and style added through direct contact and diffusion. Subsequent ceramic comparisons by Donald L. Crusoe (1972) aimed to bolster Ford's arguments. William H. Sears (1977, 1982) contributed to the discussion by positing that peoples from the Orinoco Delta of Colombia colonized the St. Johns drainage. Beyond the work of these researchers, consideration of trans-Caribbean contacts has dissipated in the last twenty years. A recent notable exception is a paper by Donald W. Lathrap (1987), which reviews evidence for the introduction of maize in the Southeast. Lathrap (1987:349) contends that "Florida was established as an enclave of South American tropical forest culture" as early as 6000 B.P., and he regards fiber-tempered pottery as some of the strongest evidence for early contact.

The historical relationships among the various fiber-tempered series of the Southeast have been the subject of considerable discussion. Lacking benefit of radiocarbon chronology, Sears and James B. Griffin (1950:3) argued that Stallings, Orange, and Wheeler were "apparently contemporaneous and represent groups in contact with one another to some degree." Since the mid-1960s the Savannah River Valley region has been widely accepted as the hearth of fiber-tempered pottery in the Southeast. Diffusion from this region is often posited to account for the technology in Florida and the Midsouth.

On the basis of analyses of Georgia coastal sites, Rochelle Marrinan (1975:103) suggested that "influences from the South Carolina-Georgia area will ultimately be shown responsible for ceramic developments in Florida. These skills were spread coast-wise continuing along the Florida coast and up the St. John's drainage."

Figure 5 (opposite).Uncorrected radiocarbon dates and ranges (± one standard deviation) for Late Archaic sites in the South Atlantic Slope, Florida Atlantic, and Gulf regions of the American Southeast. Dates for aceramic/preceramic contexts denoted by open triangles. Shaded areas in the Georgia-Carolina coastal and Savannah River Valley regions illustrate local lag in the adoption of pottery.

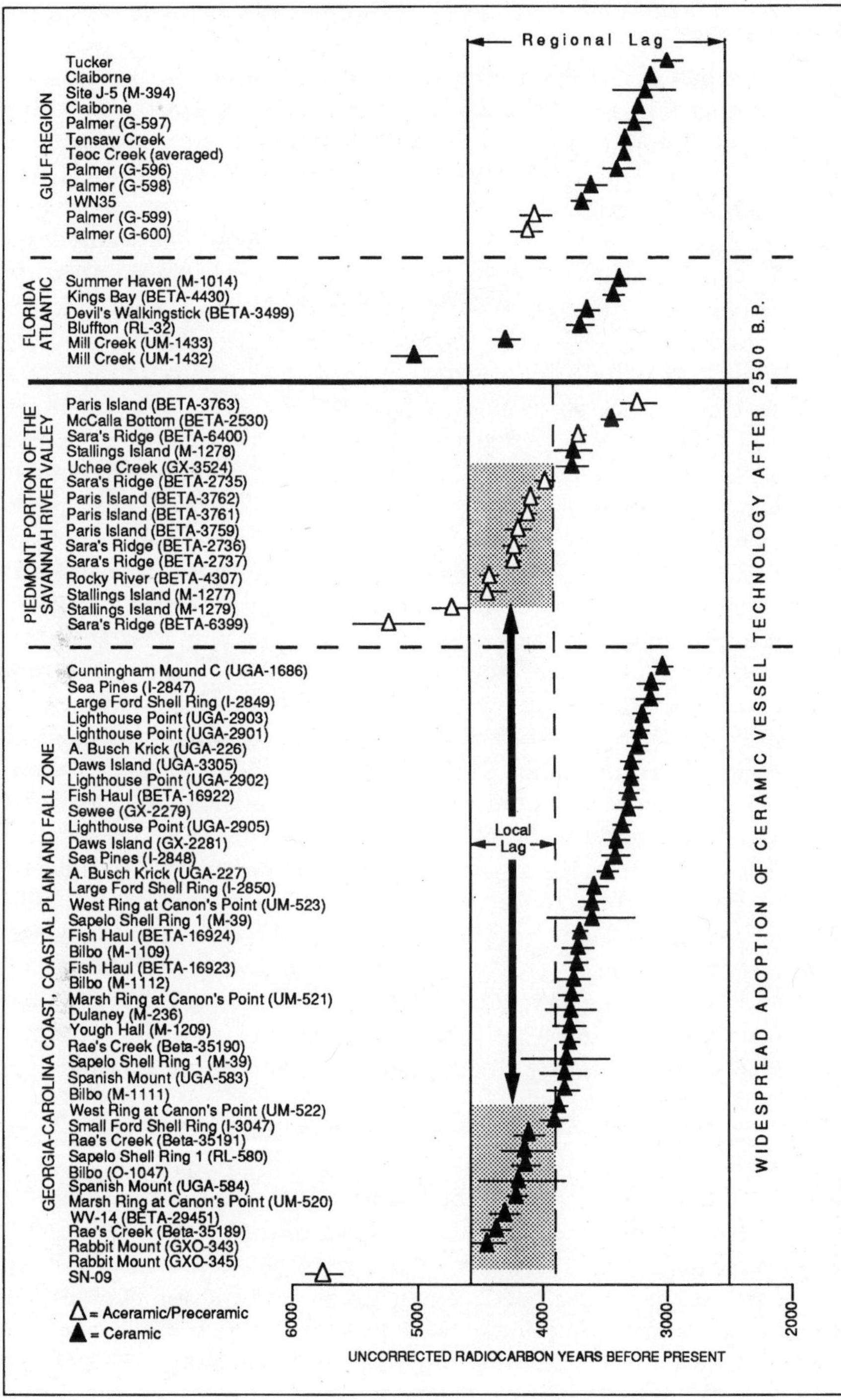

Regional Lag
GULF REGION
Tucker
Claiborne
Site J-5 (M-394)
Claiborne
Palmer (G-597)
Tensaw Creek
Teoc Creek (averaged)
Palmer (G-596)
Palmer (G-598)
1WN35
Palmer (G-599)
Palmer (G-600)
FLORIDA ATLANTIC
Summer Haven (M-1014)
Kings Bay (BETA-4430)
Devil's Walkingstick (BETA-3499)
Bluffton (RL-32)
Mill Creek (UM-1433)
Mill Creek (UM-1432)
PIEDMONT PORTION OF THE SAVANNAH RIVER VALLEY
Paris Island (BETA-3763)
McCalla Bottom (BETA-2530)
Sara's Ridge (BETA-6400)
Stallings Island (M-1278)
Uchee Creek (GX-3524)
Sara's Ridge (BETA-2735)
Paris Island (BETA-3762)
Paris Island (BETA-3761)
Paris Island (BETA-3759)
Sara's Ridge (BETA-2736)
Sara's Ridge (BETA-2737)
Rocky River (BETA-4307)
Stallings Island (M-1277)
Stallings Island (M-1279)
Sara's Ridge (BETA-6399)
GEORGIA-CAROLINA COAST, COASTAL PLAIN AND FALL ZONE
Cunningham Mound C (UGA-1686)
Sea Pines (I-2847)
Large Ford Shell Ring (I-2849)
Lighthouse Point (UGA-2903)
Lighthouse Point (UGA-2901)
A. Busch Krick (UGA-226)
Daws Island (UGA-3305)
Lighthouse Point (UGA-2902)
Fish Haul (BETA-16922)
Sewee (GX-2279)
Lighthouse Point (UGA-2905)
Daws Island (GX-2281)
Sea Pines (I-2848)
A. Busch Krick (UGA-227)
Large Ford Shell Ring (I-2850)
West Ring at Canon's Point (UM-523)
Sapelo Shell Ring 1 (M-39)
Fish Haul (BETA-16924)
Bilbo (M-1109)
Fish Haul (BETA-16923)
Bilbo (M-1112)
Marsh Ring at Canon's Point (UM-521)
Dulaney (M-236)
Yough Hall (M-1209)
Rae's Creek (Beta-35190)
Sapelo Shell Ring 1 (M-39)
Spanish Mount (UGA-583)
Bilbo (M-1111)
West Ring at Canon's Point (UM-522)
Small Ford Shell Ring (I-3047)
Rae's Creek (Beta-35191)
Sapelo Shell Ring 1 (RL-580)
Bilbo (O-1047)
Spanish Mount (UGA-584)
Marsh Ring at Canon's Point (UM-520)
WV-14 (BETA-29451)
Rae's Creek (Beta-35189)
Rabbit Mount (GXO-343)
Rabbit Mount (GXO-345)
SN-09
Local Lag
WIDESPREAD ADOPTION OF CERAMIC VESSEL TECHNOLOGY AFTER 2500 B.P.
△ = Aceramic/Preceramic
▲ = Ceramic
6000
5000
4000
3000
2000
UNCORRECTED RADIOCARBON YEARS BEFORE PRESENT

Bullen (1974) and Jenkins and John A. Walthall (Jenkins 1982; Jenkins, Dye, and Walthall 1986; Walthall and Jenkins 1976) outlined hypotheses of regional exchange to account for the westward spread of fiber-tempered pottery from Florida. Walthall and Jenkins (1976:46) describe Wheeler as "a combination of attributes from the Stallings Island and St. Johns complexes which coalesced between 1200 and 1000 B.C." They note that this process coincided with the florescence of Poverty Point culture in the lower Mississippi Valley (Broyles and Webb 1970; Webb 1968, 1982). The Poverty Point site (Ford and Webb 1956) was the center of an expansive trade network that reached as far as the Great Lakes, the eastern Piedmont, and peninsular Florida. Jenkins maintains that pottery of the Wheeler series may have been a by-product of trade funneled through and managed by Poverty Point traders stationed at outposts near the Gulf Coast (1982; Jenkins, Dye, and Walthall 1986:548). One such outpost may have been the Claiborne site at the mouth of the Pearl River (Gagliano and Webb 1970). Both Wheeler and St. Johns sherds were found in the Claiborne Poverty Point midden dating 3200–3100 B.P. Also found were soapstone vessels, a popular Poverty Point trade item. Trace-element analysis of soapstone from Poverty Point sites indicates that it originated in the Piedmont of western Georgia and eastern Alabama (Smith 1981). Citing this evidence, Jenkins and co-workers (1986:550) propose that soapstone (and with it pottery or the idea of pottery) was brought out of the Alabama-Georgia Piedmont down along the Chattahoochee, then westward across the Gulf Coast to Poverty Point trade outposts like Claiborne (see also Bullen [1974:82], who suggests that the Bryant's Landing site in Alabama [Wimberly 1960] was a Poverty Point "way station" between Florida and Louisiana). After being introduced to the western Gulf Coast, fiber-tempered pottery, John Griffin argues (1972:36), probably reached the Tennessee River area through the Tombigbee drainage.

Functionalist Interpretations

Developments in archaeological method and theory in the 1960s and 1970s turned attention away from diffusionist models and toward functional explanations. The rise of functionalism in archaeology was in some respects explicitly antidiffusionist (Kehoe 1978). Nested within evolutionary and ecological theory, the "processual" or "new" archaeology that unfolded over two decades ago viewed culture as "adaptation": a series of behavioral responses to environmental conditions mediated through the process of natural selection (Binford 1962, 1968). One manifestation of this perspective in ceramic analysis is to regard pots as tools that embody technological solutions to contingencies of pottery manufacture, use, and distribution (Braun 1983). Examples of this approach are David P. Braun's (1983, 1987) analysis of Woodland pottery, which links changes in vessel wall thickness to increased dietary reliance on starchy seeds, Doreen Ozker's (1982) discussion of midwestern thick wares and nut oil processing, and Alan Osborn's (1988) argument relating shell-tempered pottery to nutritional limitations of a maize diet.

Explicit functionalist explanations for early pottery in the Southeast are lacking, though some broad interpretations have been offered. Stoltman (1972:54) was among the first to suggest that fiber-tempered pottery in the Savannah River region appeared as "a late and non-disruptive additive trait (origin unknown) in an on-going shellfish-based economy." He speculated that pottery may have been developed to meet the need for shellfish storage and cooking (Stoltman 1974:233; see also Peterson [1971a:7]). Drexel Peterson (1980) contributed to this line of reasoning by first emphasizing the importance of shellfish in subsistence at interior sites in the Southeast and then arguing that similar ecological conditions and subsistence strategies existed along interior Coastal Plain rivers (including the southern loop of the Tennessee) at which fiber-tempered pottery was used. Emphasizing instead the subsistence demands of semi-sedentary coastal populations, Albert C. Goodyear (1988) suggests that pottery was adopted to increase the efficiency of boiling foods, especially small shellfish such as marsh periwinkle, coquina, and pond snail.

Materials science approaches have recently been used to explore functional and technological dimensions of fiber-tempered pottery (Schiffer and Skibo 1987; Skibo, Hally, and Schiffer 1988; Skibo, Schiffer, and Reid 1989; Reid 1989). In experiments by Michael B. Schiffer and James M. Skibo (1987), performance characteristics of pottery such as ease of manufacture and heating effectiveness were tested for fiber-, sand-, and nontempered ceramic samples. They showed that fiber-tempered pottery was not effective in heating properties but that it was easy to manufacture and transport. They conclude that fiber-tempered pottery was "made expediently by a society that was mainly hunter-gatherer in subsistence base. . . . The resource base is thought to have been broad-spectrum, including seeds, shellfish, and small terrestrial animals, the exploitation of which required a variety of 'gadget technologies' (Hayden 1981). While cooking in pots was part of the repertoire of food preparation techniques, we doubt that it was in any way central. Most likely, ceramics were adopted because cooking in a pot—even if it took the form of stone boiling—would require less attention than cooking in skins or with hot rocks in baskets" (Schiffer and Skibo 1987:608).

The passing reference to "stone boiling" in the above quote suggests that the addition of pottery did not necessarily entail a dramatic change in food-processing techniques. Accordingly, the persistence of a stone-boiling technology coupled with a hunting-and-gathering subsistence base makes the addition of ceramic technology problematical. To claim that the use of pots would require less attention than cooking with stones presumes that increased time or labor efficiency was desired. Like functionalist interpretations that assume a priori that early pots were used directly over fire, this interpretation implies that pots had an adaptive advantage over aceramic alternatives. Such interpretations are weakened by a lack of empirical information on actual pot functions, though some studies have begun to improve this situation (e.g., Skibo, Hally, and Schiffer 1988).

The Shortcomings of Extant Interpretations of Early Pottery

The extant interpretations of early pottery in the Southeast show when and where and, to a lesser extent, how and why ceramic vessels were adopted. They have not adequately considered variation in the spatial and temporal patterns of adoption or in the functions pottery may have filled. The theoretical reasons for these shortcomings are outlined below.

Diffusionism

In a comparison of diffusionist and functionalist doctrine, D. Bruce Dickson (1988) portrays diffusionism as a model of "Geographical Epidemics," that is, the idea that cultural traits are spread through contact in a manner similar to disease spreading through the contact of affected and unaffected persons. Continuous distributions of cultural traits are accepted as prima facie evidence of cultural contact. Further, diffusionism emphasizes the accumulative nature of culture, its ability to absorb outside influences and change.

Because diffusionism serves to describe but fails to explain cultural contact and change, it lacks explanatory power (Binford 1968; Davis 1983; Osborn 1988). Diffusionist models of early pottery, such as Ford's (1966, 1969) South American model described earlier, lack an explanatory framework to account for the reasons why pottery diffused. The shared trait of pottery between the American Southeast and Colombia is cited as evidence for cultural contact, but the process of contact and change is not considered. More recent models of diffusion, such as Jenkins's (1982; Jenkins, Dye, and Walthall 1986) account of the western spread of fiber-tempered pottery, outline processes through which contact occurred (e.g., exchange), but they do not incorporate theory about the constraints or limitations of diffusion (i.e., reasons for differential acceptance or use of pottery).

Approaches to the study of innovation and diffusion in the social sciences are more sophisticated than archaeological applications would lead one to believe (e.g., Brown 1981; Hägerstrand 1967; Rogers 1962; Rogers and Shoemaker 1971). Everett Rogers and F. F. Shoemaker (1971), for instance, point to factors that affect the rate of innovation diffusion, including the degree of interpersonal communication, the compatibility of innovations within existing systems, the complexity of the innovation, the perceived relative advantage of using an innovation, attitudes toward change in a society, and the social complexity of the adopting group. They also emphasize that many of these factors will vary from individual to individual, resulting in differential rates of adoption and rejection within a given community. Unfortunately, few archaeological studies of innovation diffusion have attempted to model possible variation between communities, let alone individuals (for exceptions, see Davis [1983] and Prentice [1986]). By ignoring such variation, archaeologists have deflected attention away from the differential rates and degrees of change, technological or otherwise, that surely exist beneath the imposed temporal and spatial boundaries of prehistoric "cultures."

Functionalism

Functionalism offers an explanatory framework for technological change in the form of evolutionary theory. But like diffusionism, functionalism suffers from some fundamental theoretical flaws. Critiques (Friedman 1974; Jochim 1983; Keene 1983; Levins and Lewonton 1985; Sahlins 1976) show that three flaws of functionalism are relevant to a rethinking of early pottery: the tautology of adaptive behavior, the reductionist scale of analysis, and the use of energy as a basic and universal currency of the selection process.

The tautological problem of functionalism is best understood as an overzealous belief in the adaptive prowess of organisms. Simply put, the tautology is that behaviors or biological structures that survive are adaptive, thus adaptive behaviors or biological structures are ones that survive. This problem is especially acute in archaeology and paleontology because of the coarse-grained nature of the chronology employed. In essence, the fossil and archaeological records are composed of behaviors and structures that survive long enough to become well represented. Archaeological "phases" and "periods" defined through comparative artifact analysis and chronology are records of relatively long-term, surviving human behaviors. It is the goal of the adaptationist program to explicate the relationships between environment and behavior/structure that account for survival and to explain changes in such relationships that brought particular adaptations to an end. Each component of an adaptive system is subject to such scrutiny so it is not surprising that an adaptive role is found for every component. What is not generally entertained in adaptationist models of human behavior is the possibility of nonadaptive or neutral components of the system (e.g., Levins and Lewonton 1985). As regards early pottery, there is no inherent reason why the use of a ceramic vessel would confer a selective advantage over the use of any other sort of vessel or no vessel at all. Functional analyses that pose the adoption of pottery as problematical might indeed demonstrate the adaptive advantages of ceramic containers for cooking or storage, but this should not be construed as a foregone conclusion.

The second problem to address is scale. Functionalist approaches in anthropology are reductionist in that they divide the range of observable phenomena into parts of a system that can be related to one another through function, or adaptation. For an adaptation model to be implemented, normative criteria of human behavior, such as the optimization criteria of subsistence models (Keene 1983:146), must be imposed upon the possible range of variation. Individual variation is ignored, explicitly or otherwise, by focusing on the averages or modes of behavior in populations. In Dickson's portrayal, functionalist models are "Anthropological Utopias" in which cultures are viewed as closed, homeostatic systems "characterized by isolation, uniformity or consensus in values, social stability or immobility, and the absence of structurally generated conflict" (Dickson 1988:54). The "culture" concept enables humans to organize behavioral and ideological variation into categories or types for a variety of political, social, and economic purposes (Wolf 1984). At the scales of analysis at which most social scientists operate, however, "cultures" are rarely, if ever, made up of individuals with identical beliefs, aspirations, politics, statuses, abilities, and the like. By ignoring such intracultural variation, functionalist perspectives deflect attention away from major factors that affected the acceptance and use of early pottery.

The third problem of functionalism is the use of energy as the basic currency of selection in the adaptationist program. The natural selection process of neo-Darwinian theory sorts out from a range of behavioral and structural variation those behaviors and structures that confer the greatest reproductive success (fitness). In operationalizing analyses of this process, most analysts have attempted to relate reproductive fitness to energy flow. Energetic efficiency has proven to be a useful measure of fitness because it can be related to food search, food capture, mate search, nurturing, defense, and other aspects of behavior that determine the success of reproduction and survivability of offspring (Smith 1979). Energy studies in archaeology have been generally limited to subsistence models, perhaps because they can be readily described in energetic terms. But unlike the individual decision making that characterizes such models, energy is not always an appropriate currency for measuring social interactions (Keene 1983:143–45). Additional variables need to be considered. For instance, choices of food or technology may fail to make sense in energetic terms, but they may reflect social relations of production in the areas of sharing, prestige, equality, or social resistance. In considering the processes and patterns of early pottery adoption, then, it will be necessary to expand the purview of decision making to include social currencies, particularly those that might contradict the expectations of an energetic efficiency model.

Prospectus for Alternative Interpretations of Early Pottery in the Southeast

In the recent literature on early pottery in North America only two models have been advanced to account for its spotty spatial and temporal distributions. One is a taphonomic model for the preservation of low-fired ceramics in general (Skibo, Schiffer, and Reid 1989) and fiber-tempered pottery in particular (Reid 1984). As argued by Kenneth C. Reid (1984), fiber-tempered pottery diffused rapidly across the American Southeast and Midwest, being adopted and used in areas that today lack substantial archaeological evidence for the ware. He proposes that fiber-tempered pottery was eliminated by freeze-thaw processes that distorted the archaeological record of pottery in the midlatitude zones where frost action was appreciably destructive. If proven to be the case, Reid's hypothesis would force a complete revision of our views on early pottery in North America.

Goodyear (1988) has pointed to two sound reasons why Reid's hypothesis fails to account for the distribution of early pottery in the Southeast. The first is that pottery is not uniformly distributed within subregions of the Southeast. Goodyear cites the Savannah River Valley as an example, noting, as I have, that pottery was widely adopted early on in the coastal zone but virtually ignored in the interior portion of the valley until late in the Late Archaic period. Because the zones of frost penetration do not appreciably differ between the coast and interior, a taphonomic explanation for the contrasting records is unlikely. Second, the Thom's Creek tradition is proof that during most of the period of fiber-tempered pottery, well-fired sand-tempered pottery was subject to diffusion throughout the Southeast. That this ware did not diffuse widely is problematical, but a taphonomic process cannot be blamed because this type of pottery was not susceptible to freeze-thaw destruction. In short, although Reid's freeze-thaw model may explain the spotty occurrence of fiber-tempered pottery in the Midwest, it cannot account for the southeastern distribution of early pottery, and we must seek other explanations.

A recent economic model of technological innovation by James A. Brown (1989) provides one alternative explanation. Interested in the failures as well as the successes of pottery adoption, Brown considers economic factors that influence the supply and demand of containers in general. He rejects the notion that pottery was inherently superior to preceramic alternatives. Focusing instead on the economics of producing alternative cooking containers, Brown suggests that pottery was adopted in response to an increased demand for containers in combination with labor constraints in meeting this demand. Sedentism is cited as the source of these conditions and is thus considered to be "a prerequisite for the earliest cases of [pottery] adoption" (Brown 1989:216). A stable residential pattern provided the time schedule and labor conditions necessary to reap the benefits of pottery production. Accordingly, pottery could respond better to increased demand for vessels than its alternatives because of cheap labor and material costs and because its production could be expanded in sedentary situations with proportionately less investments in labor (i.e., economy of scale). Conversely, when there were no constraints in meeting the demand for vessels, even with increased demand, the adoption of pottery was not likely.

Brown's economic model is valuable for identifying labor constraints in the supply and demand of vessels and for including nonceramic vessel technologies in his consideration of pottery innovation. He unfortunately does not address the processes that caused labor constraints, that is, the causes of sedentism. In the lack of an explicit process for the economic conditions Brown identifies, his model is subject to the conceptual conflation of economy and society that is apparent in other functionalist explanations of early pottery. Social relationships that define and redefine the way humans produce, distribute, and consume resources are not epiphenomena of economic behavior; they are the essence of economic behavior. Thus relationships that people enter into willingly, unknowingly, or otherwise, create debts and dependencies that bind people together economically. Certain relationships obligate people to one another and to particular places, and through their creation and maintenance, sedentism results. Knowledge of the social variation of production and exchange in any economy not only provides an explanation for the rise of sedentism, but it also exposes a range of processes through which social demands on labor contribute to technological change. A social perspective on technological innovation also exposes processes that act to impede technological change.

Social Demands on Labor

I suggest that the apparent neglect of social process in models of early pottery stems from the conventional belief that hunter-gatherer societies are internally homogeneous, egalitarian social formations. Described as the "domestic mode of production" (Sahlins 1972), hunter-gatherer economy is portrayed as a kin-based system with labor weakly divided along lines of age and gender and involving simple, portable technology available to all individuals. Combined with the ability to maintain small, mobile, and flexible social formations, the economic organization of hunter-gatherers thus enables individuals to produce for themselves without expending an inordinate amount of labor. As an example, Richard B. Lee's (1968, 1969) data on the !Kung San show that the actual amount of time the San devoted to subsistence needs amounted to only about seventeen hours per adult per week. With this light work load, it is hard to imagine technological change resulting from the demands on subsistence labor alone.

Yet the conditions of "underproduction" (Sahlins 1972:41) apparent in many hunter-gatherer societies are not without cost. As others have emphasized (Filios 1984; Root 1984; Wiessner 1977, 1982), underproduction is a social process whereby the reciprocal obligations that individuals create and maintain through food sharing and other social exchanges enable them to work well below their capacity. For this system to operate, a good portion of the hunter-gatherer work schedule is devoted to social production (as opposed to subsistence production).

The fundamental form of social production (or reproduction) in hunter-gatherer societies is sharing. Reciprocal sharing, along with other forms of exchange, establishes the patterns of and rules for appropriating social labor. Individuals accrue prestige through sharing, but they do not want to be too successful in this respect because the obligation to share leads to an accumulation of unwanted social debts. It is fissioning or, more accurately, the ability of individuals or groups physically to disengage from obligations (Woodburn 1982) that allows individuals to avoid the potential conflict of undersharing as well as the potential of being exploited from oversharing. Because of their impermanence and flexibility, short-term labor commitments enable individuals to avoid social demands on their labor. Ironically, the ability to maintain flexible settlement and labor options is underwritten by a network of social exchanges that require time and energy to maintain. The point here is that hunter-gatherer social life contains an inherent contradiction: strategies employed to avoid undue demands on individual labor embody the potential for increasing the work load of individuals. It is at this level—where social demands on labor may result in economic solutions that put constraints on individual autonomy—that technological innovation and change will arise.

Bringing this concept to bear on Brown's (1989) model of pottery innovation, the emphasis on social demands on labor shifts the analytical focus to factors that prevent individuals from exercising the option to fission as a means of alleviating demands on their labor. Thus rather than viewing sedentism as a cause of labor demand, we must ask why individuals or groups were unable to maintain the mobile settlement strategies that supported an economy of underproduction. Put another way, how is sedentism the result of continuing obligations of individuals to each other (Woodburn 1968)?

The answer to this question is beyond the immediate scope of this research, but studies by Dolores Root (1984) and Elena L. Filios (1990) examine a variety of social processes that account for the development of sedentism. For now I emphasize that the causes of sedentism can be traced to increasing reliance on social, economic, and political strategies that bind individuals and groups into long-term obligations and to particular places (Woodburn 1980, 1982). Examples of such strategies include storage (Testart 1982), task specialization (Cross 1983, 1990), and the use of facilities (Fawcett 1984, Root 1984). None of these has to be considered a dramatic departure from the traditional "domestic mode of production" perspective if we consider that each can result from the efforts of individuals and groups to maintain egalitarian relationships. Further, although sedentism may appear to be a precondition for the development of pottery, we must pay closer attention to the economic strategies that obligated people to specific sites and productive processes. The issue, then, as Brown (1989) alludes to, is not what people were doing with pottery but rather what they were doing with the time and energy gained from using pots instead of preceramic alternatives.

Resistance to Innovation

The strategies hunter-gatherers employed to assert egalitarian relationships served to inhibit the development and spread of technological innovations. For the American Southeast, this assertion rests on two factors. First is the nature of underproduction. As long as individuals and groups were able to maintain options to relocate and therefore avoid long-term, binding obligations, demands on labor should not have surpassed the ability to meet all subsistence and nonsubsistence needs. This is not to say that mobile groups did not experience social demands on labor, though we must assume that the ability to relocate at will alleviated any tendency for (social) labor demands to exceed the immediate supply of labor. Ethnographic examples of pottery use by mobile people are not uncommon (Arnold 1985) so we cannot attribute the differential acceptance of pottery to settlement pattern alone. As Brown (1989) has argued, differences in the supply and demand of alternative vessel technologies and of labor are more critical than settlement pattern, and although he cites sedentism as a necessary factor for the adoption of pottery, he does not consider it to be a sufficient cause for the innovation.

The second factor affecting the differential adoption of pottery in the Southeast is the production and use of soapstone cooking technology. In the Savannah River Valley region, perforated soapstone slabs were apparently both an important preceramic cooking technology and an important medium of exchange among local inhabitants. I argue that the network of reciprocal exchanges involving soapstone provided individuals and groups with a variety of options for fissioning. As long as the supply of soapstone was good, technological alternatives were unnecessary. This is true not only because an effective cooking technology was in place but also because the social network created and established through soapstone exchanges allowed individuals to alleviate undue demands on social labor through fissioning.

Eventually, as I will show in Chapter 6, the circulation of soapstone in the Savannah River Valley became restricted to the central portion of the valley. Other lines of archaeological evidence show that the regional landscape of Late Archaic societies was in a state of flux. The establishment of long-distance exchange networks reflected higher levels of economic and political organization than ever witnessed before in the region. Although the Savannah River Valley was apparently peripheral to much of this activity, a parallel set of processes was contributing to intensified levels of settlement permanence, ceremonialism, and nonsubsistence production. All of the trappings of sedentary life were well established by the time pottery was widely adopted in the Savannah River Valley.

Although the conditions were right for the rapid spread of pottery elsewhere in the Southeast, the innovation moved at a slow and erratic pace. To propose one explanation for this apparent lag, we must again look to soapstone exchange. Yet unlike the reciprocal exchanges I alluded to for the Savannah River Valley, the regional trade in soapstone was undoubtedly better organized. For instance, the Poverty Point commerce in soapstone bowls that Jenkins (1982) cites as the mechanism for the diffusion of pottery could not have been possible without the creation of formal, binding obligations between individuals or groups. It is also reasonable to suggest that not all individuals or groups participated equally in Poverty Point trade. Those directly involved in such trade probably enjoyed greater prestige and perhaps power in Late Archaic societies, and they were no doubt influential in shaping the direction and pace of technological change in the region.

Any innovation perceived by soapstone traders as a threat to the perpetuation of exchange relations was probably resisted. Accordingly, if it was perceived as a substitute for the soapstone bowls of the Poverty Point trade network, pottery could have weakening constraints on fissioning by undermining the obligations of soapstone exchange. Traders standing to lose the ability to appropriate labor may have felt the greatest threat, though anyone involved in exchange may have been similarly affected, especially if soapstone was imbued with special meaning. An illustration of this effect is found among the Yanomamö of Brazil. Individuals in all Yanomamö villages have a knowledge of pottery, and suitable clays are ubiquitous. Yet pottery manufacture is restricted to certain villages, which export it to nonproducing villages through reciprocal exchange alliances (Chagnon 1977:100–101). Apparently, the need to maintain exchange alliances outweighed any desire for economic autonomy. In an example closer to the Late Archaic case, the Chumash of California are said to have resisted the imposition of ceramic vessel technology by neighboring groups so they could maintain their traditional basket and soapstone vessel industries and exchange networks (Hudson and Blackburn 1983:207–9). I suspect that in both the Yanomamö and Chumash cases, certain individuals exerted influence or pressure on others to resist the adoption of pottery technology and that the outcome of this decision had differential effects on individuals.

That the widespread adoption of innovations can undermine the prestige and power of privileged individuals is well documented in the anthropological literature. For instance, snowmobile use in northern Alaska redefined the prestige structure of local Eskimo groups. Because the skills necessary to operate a snowmobile effectively are not the same as those needed to drive a dog sled, men of previously low prestige found new opportunity for accumulating status (Hall 1978:211–12). The introduction of steel axes to the Yir Yoront of Australia had even stronger effects on extant social relationships. The traditional stone ax was an important symbol of masculinity in Yir Yoront society. This value was manifested in patterns of trade among males and by prohibiting females from owning axes. When contact with missionaries in the early twentieth century led to widespread access to steel axes by men and women alike, trading partnerships weakened, sex roles became confused, and a new set of leadership roles emerged based on participation in the outside economy (Sharp 1952).

Archaeological examples of similar transformations can be cited. Bronze Age Europe underwent substantial social and economic reorganization with the spread of iron metallurgy in the seventh century B.C. Bronze Age wealth was much dependent on access to copper and tin. Because these resources were relatively restricted in distribution, individuals with direct access to them gained power and wealth from control over the extraction and distribution of the ores. Iron ore was more widely available in Europe so individuals at the local level were able to produce iron products as long as technical information on iron production was available. Because information is more difficult to control than matter, iron metallurgy spread quickly through local channels of communication. The new technology essentially undermined the power structure of Bronze Age Europe by redefining patterns of individual access to important resources (Sander van der Leeuw, personal communication 1987). Similarly, the introduction of bow and arrow technology and Late Woodland cooking innovations in eastern North America may have undermined the prestige structure of exchange networks by lessening the economic interdependency of households (Blitz 1988; Muller 1986:148).

The foregoing examples serve to show that individuals in privileged positions may need actively to maintain their positions by discouraging the widespread use of certain innovations. When social differentiation is institutionalized, access to innovations may be regulated through economic control or authority. For instance, Homer J. Barnett (1953:305) has shown that the upper class in Chamorro society of Guam actively resisted the lower class's adoption of Christianity because their own exclusive use of it validated their elite position. Similarly, in a study of agriculture and irrigation in Bengal, James K. Boyce (1987) argues that the largest constraint to rural development of irrigation technology was the resistance to institutional change posed by the self-interests of the rural elite. The development of effective irrigation depended on the creation of institutions for collective action in water control. Despite the incentive for growth, the rural elite "forgo the possibility of increased production [because] the institutional changes which are its precondition threaten to undermine their own positions" (Boyce 1987:254).

In situations of noninstitutionalized social differentiation, limits or controls over the adoption of innovations are not likely to be supported through authoritative structures. Instead, individuals along the entire spectrum of social status may serve to maintain the status quo. This is not to say that all individuals will respond in like manner to the availability of innovations but only that the position an individual occupies will be a precondition for his or her response to an innovation, and the response will feed back into the legitimation of that position. Thus individuals or groups on the social periphery of trading may resist adopting an innovation they perceive as a constraint on fissioning. Individuals or groups more central to exchange networks might be expected to resist an innovation if its adoption is perceived as a threat to the continuation of exchange relations. As an example, the exchange value of a material or service may be diminished by an innovation that makes obsolete the productive process in which the material or service is used. Social rules about the use and exchange of traditional materials or services can certainly change to accommodate an innovation, but there is bound to be some inertia when a large number of individuals benefit from the maintenance of existing exchange networks.

Conclusion

Compared to extant interpretations of the origins of pottery in the American Southeast, a model that emphasizes variation in the social composition of hunter-gatherer production and exchange is better equipped to explain the variegated early ceramic record. Inasmuch as my perspective is materialist and based on the issues of production and reproduction, it is essentially functionalist. But I do not assume that the use of pottery conferred an adaptive advantage over the use of its alternatives. Furthermore, I avoid imposing normative criteria of human decision making in explaining the acceptance or rejection of pottery, and I reject the concept of energetic efficiency as the basic criterion of decision making.

Instead I suggest that differences in the perceptions of the relative advantage of pottery can be related to social production, that is, to the strategies of cooperation, appropriation, and reciprocation that define hunter-gatherer social life. I further suggest that social demands on labor—the labor required to create and maintain social life, as opposed to biological life—are the ultimate cause of technological change. Thus I suspect that pottery was developed and spread when the organization of production and exchange obligated individuals and groups to one another to the extent that fissioning could not alleviate demands on individual labor. I do not mean to imply that pottery was adopted only under sedentary conditions. Rather, the key is simply the inability to disengage from any obligation that influenced the allocation of one's time and labor.

Regarding the slow and erratic pace of pottery diffusion, I maintain that the production and exchange of soapstone cooking technology put constraints on the adoption of pottery. These constraints operated at different levels. I argue that at one level reciprocal exchange in soapstone was one among many forms of material exchange in which individuals participated to establish and maintain a regional network of social relations. These relations provided settlement and economic options to alleviate local demands on individual labor; they thus prevented the buildup of social obligations that might have led to technological change. Simultaneously, the maintenance of a regional social network required time and labor that may have impinged on an individual's or group's ability to meet local labor demands. New technological solutions would be expected, but rather than adopting pottery as a substitute for soapstone (and undermining the exchange value of soapstone), people may have adapted pottery for alternative uses. Thus uses of pottery for traditional stone cooking or for nonutilitarian purposes may signify strategies for mediating the contradiction between increased work load and the need to maintain exchange networks.

Later on, when soapstone was entered into the Poverty Point exchange network, production and exchange were probably influenced, if not driven, by select individuals or groups. I propose that soapstone traders perceived pottery as a threat to the perpetuation of exchange relations and that they actively thwarted its spread. Thus I do not view Poverty Point exchange as a major conduit of pottery diffusion. Indeed, the volume of early pottery recovered from sites along the major routes of Poverty Point exchange is very low. As an alternative, I propose that pottery also spread among individuals and groups on the social and geographic peripheries of Poverty Point exchange. This hypothesis is brought to the fore by considering the social contexts of soapstone exchange and rejecting the notion that contact alone accounts for the diffusion of an innovation.

Finally, a social model of pottery innovation begs the issue of gender relations. If we assume that pottery is a gender-specific technology, attributable to women, in hunter-gatherer societies, then the social variables I point to for understanding the development and spread of pottery must include gender relations. For example, the contradictions I spell out regarding individual work and social demands on labor have specific consequences for women's production. If control over the distribution of soapstone extended to the manipulation of women's labor, there was probably a social value placed on women's production that inhibited the adoption of pottery. It is possible that women may have mediated this contradiction by adopting pottery for use in contexts outside the immediate control of soapstone traders. Thus the use of pottery in areas peripheral to the core of soapstone exchange may indicate an arena of personal power that had the potential to transform gender relations in Late Archaic society and led to the widespread adoption of the innovation.

The ideas set forth in this chapter will no doubt be difficult, if not impossible, to evaluate with archaeological data. At a minimum, data are required on the spatial, temporal, and technofunctional variation of early pottery and its alternatives. This information then needs to be coupled with detailed information on the spatial, temporal, and organizational variation of human populations in the study area. Of the three major areas of early pottery use in the Southeast, only the Savannah River Valley offers the quality and quantity of data needed to address these questions. In the next three chapters I provide the background, method, and analysis of Savannah River Valley Late Archaic archaeology and technology, returning in Chapter 6 to evaluate my social model for the adoption of and resistance to pottery with the available data.

CHAPTER 3

Archaeological Review of the Late Archaic Period in the Savannah River Valley Region

The Late Archaic period is usually depicted as a time when population, sedentism, and organizational complexity increased among the hunting and gathering economies of eastern North America (e.g., Dragoo 1976; Griffin 1967; Ford 1974; Smith 1986; Stoltman 1978). Joseph R. Caldwell (1958) described the Late Archaic as the culmination of increasing efficiency in exploiting seasonal food resources during the Archaic period, the attainment of "Primary Forest Efficiency." It was through this success, Caldwell maintained, that Archaic period populations were afforded a degree of settled life that enabled the development of horticulture, social complexity, and pottery. Although this explanation is generally rejected by contemporary archaeologists, the emergence of "settled life" is a persistent theme in characterizations of the Late Archaic period.

The subsequent Early Woodland period is traditionally defined by the widespread adoption of pottery technology in the Eastern Woodlands, coupled again with increasing sedentism and organizational complexity (Griffin 1967). The conceptual boundary between the Late Archaic and Early Woodland periods at a pan-eastern level is argued to be most strongly marked by the addition of pottery, for changes in other material realms are not so obvious or considered to be as "revolutionary" (Smith 1986). Clearly, pottery was differentially adopted across the Eastern Woodlands. Hence the boundary it represents is neither spatially nor temporally coterminous. Moreover, the earliest uses of pottery were not accompanied by other changes in material culture and economic organization in a structural, unified way. The timing, locations, and contexts of early pottery varied at the regional level, making it difficult to draw any boundary for Eastern Woodlands prehistory on the basis of this trait alone. As I maintain in this study, early pottery use at the local level was equally variable.

The oldest documented pottery in eastern North America was found in the Savannah River Valley. In contemplating the significance of this early pottery, archaeologists have been divided between two camps. One has argued that pottery was added to the Late Archaic technological inventory without abrupt change in settlement and subsistence or in other forms of material culture (e.g., Fairbanks 1942; Miller 1949; Stoltman 1974). In opposition, others have pointed to a distinct break in the material inventories and behavioral adaptations of early pottery-making peoples (e.g., Crusoe and DePratter 1976).

It is no coincidence that archaeologists perceiving continuity in Late Archaic prehistory tend to be more familiar with sites and assemblages in the interior than with those on the coast. The interior of the Savannah River Valley contains a complete, unbroken record of Late Archaic occupations. The period is signified primarily by the broad-bladed, stemmed hafted bifaces typical of Late Archaic technology throughout much of the Eastern Woodlands. In the Carolinas the form is referred to as the "Savannah River Stemmed" hafted biface (Coe 1964:44). This type and its local variants (e.g., Keel 1976:196) have been securely dated to the fifth and fourth millennium before present (Alterman 1987:22–26; White 1982:45–50), and this interval (5000–3000 B.P.) is widely accepted as the duration of the Late Archaic period.

Although pottery was known to Late Archaic inhabitants of the Savannah River Valley region by 4500 B.P., there is little evidence to suggest that it was widely used in the interior until late in the period, that is, until after 3500 B.P. Documented uses of pottery in the interior before 3500 B.P. are not uncommon, but evidence documenting other changes in the material culture and organization of interior pot users is ambiguous. In particular, lithic assemblages, the primary means of dating Late Archaic sites in the interior, have not been useful in discriminating between preceramic and ceramic period assemblages (Alterman 1987:247; Anderson and Joseph 1988:195–98), despite earlier suggestions to the contrary (Bullen and Greene 1970; Crusoe and DePratter 1976).

In stark contrast with the interior, the coastal archaeological record of the Late Archaic period is entirely ceramic. Components lacking pottery have not been documented, and lithic artifacts are rare in coastal assemblages. Two explanations for the lack of preceramic components have been offered. The first is that exploitation of the coastal zone was not possible until 4200 B.P., when marsh-lagoon systems matured in response to a slowing in the rate of sea-level rise (DePratter 1979b:7; DePratter and Howard 1980). Groups moving to the coast to take advantage of these newly productive habitats brought with them the pot-using and shellfish-eating traditions that were established in the middle Coastal Plain by 4500 B.P.

The counterexplanation for a lack of preceramic sites on the coast is that sites predating 4200 B.P. are buried under marsh sediments deposited during subsequent transgressions of the shoreline (Brooks, Colquhoun, and Sassaman 1990; Marrinan 1975). Such early sites, if they exist, may or may not contain pottery, and they may or may not include shellfish refuse. In any event, the coastal archaeological record is viewed as truncated; that which is observable or accessible is exclusively a ceramic period record and is hence perceived as being distinct from the interior record.

In sum, the interior and coastal archaeological records of the Savannah River Valley region contain contrasting elements that have important ramifications for explaining technological change. In the conventional, now anachronistic sense, the Savannah River Valley region was occupied simultaneously by Late Archaic and Early Woodland populations. At the heart of this distinction is the differential adoption of pottery and, to a lesser extent, the exploitation of shellfish. Secondarily, differences in the local availability of lithic raw materials influenced other technological decisions and led to distinct technological records for the interior and coast. Unfortunately, the recognition of technological differences between the interior and coast has generally remained a typological exercise directed toward chronological concerns. I aim to improve this situation with a technofunctional analysis of the alternative cooking technologies of interior and coastal groups. But as I indicated in the preceding two chapters, an explanation for technological variability in the Savannah

River Valley region requires more than detailed technofunctional information. We must consider the economic, social, and political contexts in which technological innovations arise and spread. The combination of technofunctional data and contextual information provides a strong empirical basis for explaining the lag in adoption of pottery at both local and regional levels and thus the reasons why the Late Archaic-Early Woodland "boundary" is so temporally and spatially variegated.

As a foundation for the technofunctional and contextual analyses in Chapter 5, I present in this chapter an archaeological overview of the Late Archaic period in the Savannah River Valley region. The temporal boundaries of the overview are 5000–3000 B.P. The study region is the area encompassing the Savannah River and all its tributaries, and the Georgia-South Carolina coast at the midpoints between the Savannah and its two adjacent counterparts: the Altamaha to the southwest and the Santee to the northwest (Figure 6). The coastal range therefore extends roughly from St. Catherines Island to the city of Charleston and includes several smaller drainages: the Edisto, Salkahatchie, and Coosawhatchie in South Carolina and the Ogeechee and Canoochee in Georgia.

The content and organization of my presentation are intended to highlight the contrasting archaeological records of the interior and coastal zones. I begin with brief descriptions of the environment of these zones and follow with a historical review of the archaeological research and key sites in the region (Figure 6). The presentation thereafter is divided into coastal and interior sections. Subsections on cultural-historical sequence, settlement-subsistence organization, cooking technology, and other subsistence technology are provided for each of the sections.

Environmental Background

Coastal Zone

The coastal zone is a combination of islands, mainland coast, intervening marshes, lagoons and tidal creeks, brackish water marshes of river channels, and the maritime forest communities of the mainland perimeter. Thorough discussions of the physiography, geology, soils, climate, flora, and fauna of the coastal zone are provided by DePratter (1979b:5–15) and Trinkley (1986:8–38). My brief review of this information is drawn primarily from these sources.

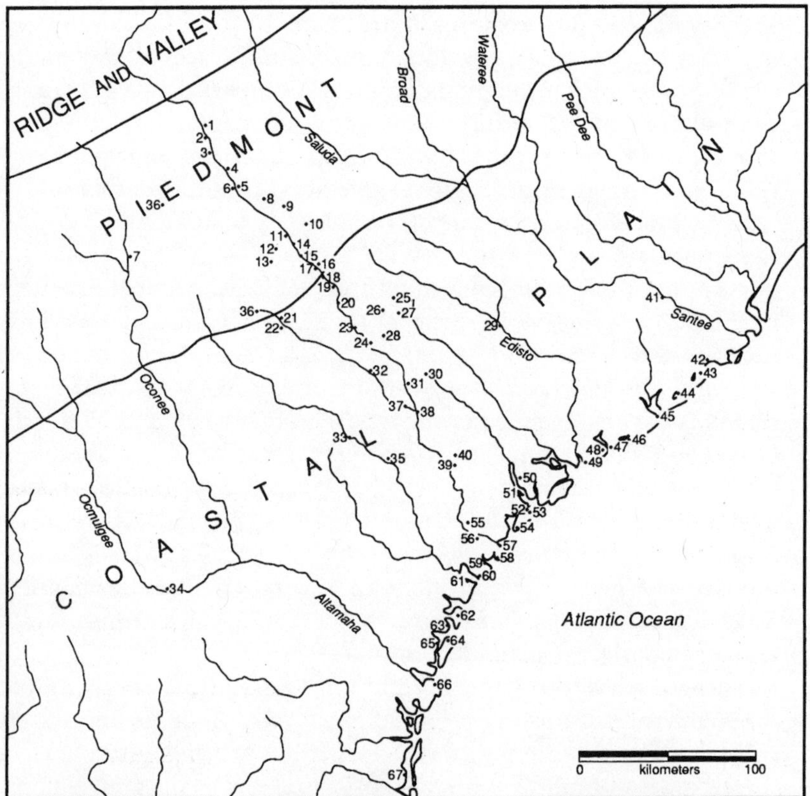

1. Sara's Ridge
2. Gregg Shoals
3. Rucker's Bottom
4. McCalla Bottom
5. Rocky River
6. Paris Island
7. 9GE145
8. 38MC428
9. 38MC479
10. Moody
11. Lake Spring
12. 9CB23
13. 9CB12
14. Kiokee Creek
15. 9CB15
16. Mims Point
17. Stallings Island
18. Pig Pen, Rae's Creek
19. Lover's Lane
20. White's Mound
21. 9RI137
22. 9JF21
23. G.S. Lewis
24. Pen Point
25. 38AK288
26. 38AK158/159
27. Tinker Creek
28. L-Lake Sites
29. Cal Smoak
30. Love
31. Fennel Hill
32. Theriault
33. Rocky Ford
34. Lowe
35. Ogeechee I
36. Mill Branch Sites
37. SN-05,08,09,15
38. Rabbit Mount
39. WV14,23
40. WV18
41. Mattassee Lake Sites
42. Sewee
43. Venning Creek
44. Stratton Place, Yough Hall
45. Charles Towne, Lighthouse Point
46. Bass Pond
47. Fig Island
48. Horse Island, 38CH61
49. Spanish Mount
50. Chesterfield
51. Daw's Island
52. Ford Rings
53. Fish Haul
54. Sea Pines
55. Refuge
56. Deptford, Delany, Bilbo
57. 9CH14a
58. 9CH114
59. Pagan Plum
60. 9CH111
61. Cane Patch
62. Cunningham
63. 9LI41
64. Sapelo Ring 1
65. A. Busch Krick
66. Canon's Point
67. 9Cam167

Figure 6. Savannah River Valley region with locations of Late Archaic sites mentioned in text and/or included in the assemblage samples used in analyses in Chapters 4–6.

The Georgia and South Carolina coasts have different morphologies, the former consisting of a chain of barrier islands interrupted by occasional sounds, the latter consisting of an unbroken arcuate strand to the north, a small eroding cape in the middle, and a chain of low-lying barrier and sea islands to the south. The area of interest to this study is characterized by nearly continuous island formations.

Coastal processes that formed the present shoreline and island morphology can be attributed to changes in sea level during the Quaternary. Pleistocene episodes of sea-level transgression led to the successive development of the Talbot, Pamlico, Princess Anne, and Silver Bluff shorelines, each lower and farther east than its predecessor. Remnants of the older two shorelines are preserved as sand ridges on the mainland, while the younger two comprise portions of the present-day coastal islands.

After the Silver Bluff shoreline formed 25,000 to 35,000 years ago, sea level dropped because of the Wisconsin glaciation. After being stranded on the mainland for nearly twenty thousand years, the Silver Bluff shoreline was reflooded by seawater during the mid-Holocene. The rate of sea level rise slowed considerably after 6000 B.P. (Colquhoun and Brooks 1986) and set in motion a series of processes that led to the development of coastal habitats conducive to human exploitation. By this time the flooding of the low-lying areas behind the Silver Bluff islands began to form a salt marsh-lagoon system, which gradually began to fill with sand and clay deposited by interior rivers, eventually leading to brackish water marsh drained by tidal creeks. This process created superior oyster habitat in the intertidal zone.

Oyster beds and associated marsh-lagoon resources were being exploited on the coast of Georgia by about 4200 B.P. The marsh-lagoon system may not have developed or matured until this time so earlier settlement of the Georgia coast, if it depended on this coastal habitat, was perhaps limited (DePratter 1979b:7; DePratter and Howard 1980). Because of differences in coastal morphology which affect tidal range, salt marshes behind the Silver Bluff islands should have developed slightly earlier to the north. Development of back-barrier marshes along certain portions of the South Carolina coast may have been under way by 6000 B.P. Occupations of small marsh islands in the broad, seaward areas of South Carolina's larger tidal flats should have been made possible by salt marsh development by at least 5000 B.P. Unfortunately, marsh infilling accompanying the rise in sea level between 5000 and 4200 B.P. (net increase of two meters) suggests that such locations would now be buried by about one meter of sediment (Brooks, Colquhoun, and Sassaman 1990). Occupations during subsequent periods of low sea level would also be buried under recent marsh mud. The Late Archaic coastal archaeological record as it now stands consists of sites with maximum elevations at or above the current low tide level. Many of these sites are currently accessible because they were established during times of relatively high sea level (especially 4200–4100 B.P. and 3800–3700 B.P.) or because they have tall shell middens that have not been completely covered by marsh infilling.

For the broader resource potential of the coastal zone, microenvironments other than the marsh-lagoon system were important to human occupants. Chester B. DePratter (1979b:8–15) identifies four other microenvironments: open sea, beach and dune, maritime forest, and pine forest.

Paleoenvironmental data on the floral and faunal composition of these microenvironments are limited. Archaeological evidence (reviewed in the section on settlement-subsistence below) indicates that a variety of fish, shellfish, and turtles were taken from the aquatic habitats and that acorn, hickory nuts, deer, and smaller mammals were important terrestrial foods. The contemporary maritime forests cover most of the high ground of the coastal islands and mainland fringe and consist mainly of oak. Pine forests exist in lower portions of the coastal zone, but they are more prevalent west of the mainland fringe in the adjacent Coastal Plain. Among the aquatic microenvironments, the marsh-lagoon system was undoubtedly the most important. Not only were abundant shellfish available, but the many fishes that inhabited the tidal creeks and rivers were easier to catch than those of the open sea. Migratory waterfowl, small mammals, and numerous reptiles were also present.

The combined resources of the intertidal marsh-lagoon system and the maritime forests offered Late Archaic residents year-round subsistence. Under the influence of nearby warm ocean air, the seasonality of the coast is minimal. Winters are short and mild, summers are long, hot, and humid. The only major climatic constraint for humans is the tropical storm season from late summer to early fall. High tides, torrential rains, and damage to near-shore food resources are dangers of tropical storms.

Perhaps the biggest shortcoming of the coastal zone was the lack of lithic resources. The closest substantial outcrops of flakable rock were those of the Flint River and Black Mingo formations of the middle Coastal Plain. Coastal inhabitants either had to travel or trade to obtain materials or scavenge the channel beds of rivers draining the Coastal Plain for cobbles. River cobbles were not abundant, but ancient marine deposits of exposed Pleistocene ridges might have provided a source of small cobbles. Mostly the coastal residents developed alternatives to lithic technology in bone, antler, and shell media.

In contrast to hard rock resources, clays were abundant in the former lagoons of old barrier islands (Trinkley 1986:18) and were no doubt exploited for pottery and other ceramic technology. For example, baked clay objects of various sizes and shapes have been argued to be substitutes for stone atlatl weights (South 1970) and cooking stones (DePratter 1979b).

Interior

The Savannah River drains a major watershed of the South Atlantic Slope that is over 350 kilometers in length and covers about 27,500 square kilometers. Like other rivers of the South Atlantic Slope, the Savannah traverses three major physiographic provinces, with headwaters in the ridge and valley, then flowing perpendicularly across the Piedmont and Coastal Plain provinces. Compared to adjacent watersheds, the Savannah is relatively narrow. Large tributaries enter the Savannah along the upper two-thirds of the drainage, but the largest run roughly parallel to the main channel because of the constricted physiography of the basin.

The Coastal Plain consists of a series of ancient marine terraces formed by old shorelines of Tertiary and Quaternary age (Colquhoun and Johnson 1968; Cooke 1936). In the Savannah watershed, the province is about 200 kilometers wide, with elevations just above sea level near the coast to over 100 meters at the fall line. Fluvial dissection has created sharp topographic relief within the higher terraces, but in lower areas relatively mild, featureless terrain is prevalent.

The topography and resource potential of the lower Coastal Plain depend to a large extent on the degree of channel switching and swamp development within floodplains of rivers and tributary stems. The floodplain and swamp zone vegetation is presently dominated by southern floodplain forest, primarily tupelo and cypress (Kuchler 1964). Fluvial terraces overlooking floodplains and swamps are better-drained landforms which support mixed hardwood and pine forests. Interriverine ("upland") areas between major drainage channels consist of well-drained sandy soils with mixed forests dominated by pine in the driest areas (generally corresponding to the "pine barrens" described by Larson [1980]). On the South Carolina side of the middle to lower Coastal Plain, channel switching within active and ancient floodplains has created extensive ridge and swale topography that supports a mosaic of hydric, mesic, and xeric vegetation. In stark contrast, the Georgia side consists of steep bluffs along the active floodplain margin, which creates a sharp contact between hydric and xeric communities and has a relatively low potential for intermediate or transitional communities.

The upper third of the Coastal Plain consists of the Sandhills formations. The Aiken Plateau is the geographic division of the Sandhills located between the Savannah and Congaree rivers (Cooke 1936). The surficial deposits of the Aiken Plateau consist of unconsolidated sand of marine origin (Plio-Pleistocene), dissected by major rivers flowing from the Piedmont and by numerous dendritic tributaries of these rivers.

Interfluvial ridges of the Aiken Plateau are characterized by relatively xeric vegetation dominated by pine (Shelford 1963:86–87). More mesic communities with abundant oak are found on terminal ridge noses and slopes adjacent to active tributary stems (Barry 1980:97–116; Hanson, Brooks, and White 1981:31). Major tributary streams in the Aiken Plateau, such as Upper Three Runs, have formed broad floodplains that support hydric flora in regularly flooded areas, as well as diverse mesic communities along floodplain margins and terraces. Thus the topographic gradients of the Aiken Plateau created by tributary dissection support vegetative gradients consisting of xeric, mesic, and hydric communities (Hanson, Brooks, and White 1981:28–36; Langley and Marter 1973; Whipple 1978; Whipple, Wellman, and Good 1981). Dotting xeric ridges in some areas are shallow, undrained depressions referred to as Carolina bays (Johnson 1942).

The food resource potential of Coastal Plain environments has been discussed by various researchers (Anderson 1979; Anderson, Lee, and Parler 1979; Blanton, Espenshade, and Brockington 1986; Brooks and Hanson 1989; Cable and Cantley 1979; Hanson, Brooks, and White 1981; Larson 1980) and need not be repeated in detail here, although a couple of general points should be emphasized. First, a basic contrast between bottomland and upland resource potential is important. Bottomland zones contain resources not available in the uplands, notably aquatic resources, and they are associated with mesic habitats of fluvial terraces which support a wide range of flora and fauna. Because of the generally xeric nature of much of the upland habitat, the subsistence potential of the Coastal Plain depends in large part on the availability of bottomland zones. The abundance of these zones increases in a downriver direction as the gradient of the Savannah decreases, the floodplain widens, and topographic relief of the coastal terraces decreases.

Second is change in the abundance and resource potential of bottomland zones through time. Mark J. Brooks discusses fluvial responses to sea-level changes in the mid-Holocene as a factor in the decreased potential for freshwater shellfish productivity and a stimulus to increased upland resource potential (Brooks and Hanson 1989; Brooks et al. 1986; see also Hanson 1982). The onset of modern floodplain development after 5000 B.P. was an upriver, time-transgressive process which diminished the ecological potential for freshwater shellfish while simultaneously contributing to subsequent hydrologic changes in upland tributaries. This resulted in increased biomass of aquatic plant and animal resources as tributaries adjusted to a low energy flow and mature floodplain regime. These newly productive stream-associated resources constituted spring and summer resources that were previously limited to mesic terrace zones of the main river channel. Given this new resource potential, along with attendant improvement in deer habitat associated with tributary changes, Brooks posits that in the upland strict fall resource procurement of deer and nuts changed to seasonal habitation along upland tributaries during the Late Archaic period, leading eventually to multiseasonal habitation within upland zones by the Early Woodland period. In the upper Coastal Plain, this process occurred after 4100 B.P., when the modern floodplain of the Savannah was in place (Stevenson 1982).

The contact between unconsolidated sediments of the Coastal Plain and crystalline formations of the Piedmont is referred to as the fall line (Fenneman 1938). The contact is more of a transitional feature (Fall Zone) with respect to hydrology, consisting of low falls, shoals, and rapids in a twenty-kilometer stretch of the lower Piedmont-upper Coastal Plain. In ecological terms, the Fall Zone is an ecotone that affords access to resources of the Piedmont and Coastal Plain, as well as those unique to the ecotone. The Fall Zone shoals support freshwater shellfish beds, and they afford ideal conditions for capturing anadromous fish. Presumably, the bottomland resource potential of the Fall Zone was not affected by the Holocene hydrologic changes.

The Piedmont is an eroded peneplain that slopes from the northwest to the southeast, roughly 120 to 240 meters above mean sea level (amsl) within the Savannah basin. The Savannah River, constrained by resistant bedrock that in some locations of the inner Piedmont produces shoals and rapids, has cut a deep and narrow valley into the Piedmont. Bluffs rising 30 meters or more above the floodplain are common on both sides of the valley. Tributaries of the Savannah have cut smaller but similar valleys in the adjacent uplands. In general, relief in the uplands consists of gently rolling hills interrupted by perennial and intermittent streams. Significant changes in the fluvial regime and upland topography have occurred in the historic era. Particularly significant has been the extensive erosion of cleared land, which has removed most of the upland soils (Trimble 1974) and led to deep levee and terrace deposition downriver.

The Piedmont is presently covered by pine-oak scrub communities, but throughout most of the Holocene oak forests dominated the province (Delcourt and Delcourt 1987). The widespread occurrence of mast producers coupled with the relatively limited occurrence of bottomland has led to the suggestion that upland and bottomland resource potential in the Piedmont was not dramatically different (e.g., Ward 1983:63). The apparently undifferentiated land use of the Piedmont during the (Middle Archaic) Morrow Mountain phase (Sassaman 1983, 1985) lends support to this supposition, as does the existence of habitation sites in upland and bottomland zones alike during the Late Archaic period (see below).

There is distinct lithology in the Piedmont, Fall Zone, and Coastal Plain provinces. The major raw material exploited in the inner Piedmont was quartz, which was and still is widely available as float in the soil, in ridgetop veins, and in cobble beds of streams. The Piedmont also contains minor quantities of quartzite, basalt, and metachert (Overstreet and Bell 1965; Ledbetter, Kowalewski, and O'Steen 1984; Wood et al. 1986).

The Fall Zone is characterized by metamorphic formations crosscut by intrusive volcanic flows. The major raw materials exploited from these formations were rhyolite, argillite, and tuff, rocks collectively referred to as metavolcanics. Basalt occurs in intrusive formations and was used occasionally. Vein quartz was also available, as were a variety of Piedmont materials in the shoals of the Fall Zone.

Unlike the upper portion of the valley, the Coastal Plain contains comparatively little lithic raw material. The Savannah does, however, crosscut two underlying sedimentary formations that contain chert and other siliceous rock. The larger of the two is the Flint River Formation in the middle Coastal Plain. This formation contains localized outcrops of chert, technically silicified grainstone (Upchurch 1984), in Allendale County, South Carolina, and Burke County, Georgia. Albert C. Goodyear and Tommy Charles (1984) surveyed these outcrops and found that the more siliceous and isotropic sources were quarried prehistorically. Lower-quality cherts are also found in the Barnwell Formation of the upper Coastal Plain (Upchurch 1984). Sources known to have been used in Aiken County, South Carolina, are highly fossiliferous (Sassaman 1987), although small pockets of isotropic rock are present today and may have been important local sources of raw material in the past.

Soapstone is found in many locations of the Piedmont and Fall Zone. Within the Savannah watershed, soapstone outcrops have been identified in Pickens, Oconee, Abbeville, and Edgefield counties of South Carolina and in Stephens, Elbert, Wilkes, Lincoln, and Columbia counties of Georgia (Wood et al. 1986:305). Among these, the only sources presently known to have been quarried prehistorically are those in Oconee County, South Carolina, and in Elbert and Wilkes counties, Georgia (Elliott 1981:18; Wood et al. 1986:305). This indicates a fairly wide, albeit patchy, pattern of soapstone procurement in the valley above the fall line.

Clay is present throughout the Savannah River Valley, and much of it is suited to pottery manufacture. Oxidized residual clay is abundant throughout the Piedmont and Fall Zone, and lesser sources of alluvial clay are exposed in cut banks and levees of the Savannah River. The Coastal Plain contains deposits of ancient marine clay which are exposed in the cut banks and slip faces of upland tributaries. Surficial alluvial clays in the Coastal Plain are the result of historic erosion in the Piedmont, but older deposits in the infilled swales of the Savannah River floodplain may have been an important source of alluvial clay for pottery manufacture.

Investigative History and Key Archaeological Sites

Serious archaeological investigations in the Savannah River Valley region can be traced to the late nineteenth-century explorations of

Charles C. Jones, Jr. (1873) and Clarence B. Moore (1897, 1899). Field investigations waned over the ensuing decades but resumed in the late 1920s and 1930s when several expeditions were conducted on the coast and in the interior.

Building upon earlier tests by Jones (1873) and William Claflin, Mr. and Mrs. C. B. Cosgrove mounted a massive excavation program in 1929 at the Stallings Island shell mound (9CB1) near Augusta, Georgia (Claflin 1931). A few years later, Woldemar Ritter and Warren K. Moorehead conducted test excavations at the Chesterfield shell ring (38BU29) near Beaufort, South Carolina (Flannery 1943), and a sample of sherds from the site was used by James B. Griffin (1943) to propose the Stallings fiber-tempered pottery series. Test excavations at the Bilbo site (9CH4) near Savannah, Georgia, by Antonio Waring (1968b) and at sites on St. Simons Island, Georgia, by Preston Holder (1938) were made in the 1930s.

In addition to his work at Bilbo, Waring conducted key excavations at sites in the vicinity of Savannah during the 1940s. Tests of the deeply stratified Deptford site (9CH2) provided the basis for the Woodland ceramic sequence that he and Joseph Caldwell formulated (Caldwell and Waring 1939). More detailed information on the pre-Deptford Early Woodland Refuge complex was collected in Waring's tests of the Refuge site (Waring 1968c). Fiber-tempered pottery in the basal strata of both of these sites provided proof that this ceramic tradition predated the stamped, sand-tempered wares of the Woodland period. Finally, a surface collection of the Dulany shell midden (9CH54) included a large sample of plain fiber-tempered sherds, which, on the basis of subsequent testing by Lewis Larson, is purported to be among the oldest fiber-tempered pottery in the coastal region (Williams 1968b).

Among the few interior projects conducted in the 1940s was the survey of the area now inundated by Clarks Hill Lake. A massive shell midden known as the Lake Spring site was tested during the survey by Carl Miller (1949) and found to contain a cultural sequence similar to that of Stallings Island. Earlier in the decade, Charles Fairbanks (1942) had conducted additional testing at Stallings Island, primarily to document the preceramic component.

Archaeological work in the 1950s moved at a slow pace. Waring and Lewis Larson (1968) conducted test excavations in 1950 at Shell Ring No. 1 on Sapelo Island, a site Moore had investigated in 1897 (Moore 1897), and William G. Haag revisited Bilbo for test excavations in 1957 (Dye 1976), but little else involving Late Archaic components was accomplished.

The 1960s brought a flurry of archaeological research to the Savannah River Valley region. James Stoltman's 1964 investigations at the Rabbit Mount shell midden (38AL15) on Groton Plantation, Allendale County, South Carolina, resulted in the documentation of the earliest known fiber-tempered pottery assemblage in the Southeast (Stoltman 1974). A similar fiber-tempered component at a site immediately downstream from Augusta, Georgia, White's Mound (9RI4), was investigated in 1963 as part of a larger testing program by David Phelps (Phelps and Burgess 1964). Sporadic testing at the Fennel Hill site (38AL2; a.k.a. Cox and Milberry Mound), twenty kilometers upriver from Rabbit Mount, was also under way in the 1960s (Trinkley 1975; Fred Cook, personal communication 1988), as was excavation at the Theriault site in Burke County, Georgia (Brockington 1971).

On the coast in the late 1960s, Alan Calmes (1968) conducted test excavations at three shell rings on Hilton Head Island, South Carolina. The nearby Daws Island shell midden (38BU9) was discovered by James Michie in 1968 and discussed in several reports (Hemmings 1969; Michie 1973, 1974). Among other coastal field investigations was testing of the Sewee Shell Ring in northern Charleston County, South Carolina, by William Edwards (1965). Also during the 1960s, Eugene Waddell (1965) reported a radiocarbon date from the Yough Hall Plantation Shell Ring (38CH41) near Charleston, a site investigated by Waring but not reported.

The 1970s witnessed a series of survey efforts by Donald Crusoe, Chester DePratter, and others that led to the identification and testing of many fiber-tempered components on the Georgia coast (Crusoe and DePratter 1976; DePratter 1979a; DePratter and Howard 1980). Among these, the Pagan Plum (9CH61), Cane Patch (9CH35), and A. Busch Krick (9McI87) sites are especially noteworthy for the quality of test excavations conducted as well as the large samples of fiber-tempered pottery recovered. The expeditions of the American Museum of Natural History to St. Catherines Island (Thomas and Larson 1979), Rochelle Marrinan's (1975) testing at St. Simons Island, and the revisit to Sapelo Island led by Lewis Larson (Simpkins 1975; Simpkins and McMichael 1976) also contributed to the growing data base on early ceramic period sites. Meanwhile to the north, test excavations were being made at the Spanish Mount shell midden (38CH62;

Sutherland 1973, 1974) on Edisto Island, South Carolina, at the nearby Fig Island Shell Ring (38CH42; Hemmings 1970a, 1970b), and at the Stratton Place and Lighthouse Point (38CH12) shell rings in Charleston County (Trinkley 1980b, 1985).

The growth of federally mandated archaeology in the mid-1970s led to a burgeoning of field research and contract reports. In the interior, major survey projects were conducted in the interriverine Piedmont of South Carolina (e.g., House and Ballenger 1976; Goodyear, House, and Ackerly 1979; Rodeffer, Holschlag, and Cann 1979), in the vicinity of Augusta, Georgia (Bowen 1979; Elliott and Doyon 1981; Ferguson and Widmer 1976), in the Richard B. Russell Reservoir of the inner Piedmont (Taylor and Smith 1978), in the upper Coastal Plain at the Department of Energy's Savannah River Plant (Hanson, Most, and Anderson 1978), and in the Wallace Reservoir of the Oconee River Valley (DePratter 1976). Key aceramic and ceramic phase Late Archaic components identified in these projects include Sara's Ridge (38AN29), Paris Island (9EB21), Rocky River (38AB91), McCalla Bottom (38AB288), Rucker's Bottom (9EB91), and Gregg Shoals (9EB259) in the Russell Reservoir area (Anderson and Schuldenrein 1985a, 1985b; Anderson, Schuldenrein, and Cantley 1985; Schuldenrein, Anderson, and Cantley 1985; Tippitt and Marquardt 1984; Wood et al. 1986; see Anderson and Joseph [1988] for a synthesis of the Russell investigations); Lover's Lane (9RI86) and 9RI88 in Augusta (Elliott and Doyon 1981); and Tinker Creek (38AK224), Pen Point (39BR383), 38AK158, the L-Lake sites, and Lewis-East (38AK228) on the Savannah River Plant (Brooks and Hanson 1989; Hanson 1980; Hanson and Sassaman 1984; Sassaman 1987; see Sassaman et al. [1990] for a synthesis of the SRP investigations).

Other key interior sites documented in recent contract work include those of the Brier Creek survey and testing program (Blanton and Espenshade 1986; Elliott 1986c; Espenshade 1986; Joseph 1985; Wise 1986); the Rae's Creek (Crook 1990), Pig Pen (9RI158; Ledbetter 1988), and Lover's Lane (Elliott, Ledbetter, and Gordon 1992) sites in Augusta, Georgia; the Mill Branch sites at the headwaters of Brier Creek, Georgia (Ledbetter 1991); and several sites in the Sumter National Forest of South Carolina (Elliott 1986b). Recent and ongoing survey on Fort Gordon near Augusta continues to add to the inventory of Late Archaic sites in the middle Savannah River Valley (Braley 1992a, 1992b; Campbell, Weed, and Thomas 1981; King and Braley 1992; Price and Braley 1990).

Some important Late Archaic sites have been documented in contract projects on the coast. Noteworthy among them are the Bass Pond site (38CH123) on Kiawah Island (Michie 1979) and the Fish Haul site (38BU805) on Hilton Head Island (Trinkley 1986). In addition, excavation of the Mattassee Lake sites on the Santee River provided a wealth of data on Thom's Creek and Refuge components in the interior lower Coastal Plain (Anderson, Cantley, and Novick 1982).

Finally, the recent and ongoing research projects of professional and avocational archaeologists alike add to the large body of data on the Late Archaic period. Among these are revisits to Stallings Island by H. Bruce Greene (Bullen and Greene 1970) and Crusoe and DePratter (1976); testing at the Albert Love (38AL10; Trinkley 1974), Moody (38ED31; Moody et al. 1979; Moody, Carter, and Beard 1985), and Cal Smoak sites (38BM4; Anderson, Lee, and Parler 1979); Frankie Snow's (1977) survey of the Ocmulgee Big Bend area; the middle Savannah River Valley survey conducted by Richard Smith (1974); ongoing survey and testing in Jasper County, South Carolina (Brooks and Sassaman n.d.); studies of Late Archaic assemblage and settlement variability in the South Carolina Piedmont (Canouts and Goodyear 1985; Sassaman 1983; White 1982); and Daniel T. Elliott's (1981) distributional study of soapstone in the Wallace Reservoir area of Georgia.

In sum, the Savannah River Valley region contains an abundant record of Late Archaic sites. Archaeological investigations span a century, and there are no major geographical gaps in the survey coverage of the region (Figure 1). In the earlier decades of investigation emphasis was placed on the obtrusive shell middens and shell rings. The growth of contract archaeology since the 1970s has improved the representativeness of the documented Late Archaic record by including small, mundane sites associated with shell middens and by providing survey coverage in areas lacking shell midden sites.

Coastal Archaeological Record

Cultural-Historical Sequence

Late Archaic chronology and typology on the coast are well established and relatively straightforward, though they suffer from some inconsistency in the use of type and phase nomenclature.

The term *St. Simons* was first used by Holder (1938) to identify fiber-tempered pottery from St. Simons Island, and it later became the type name for coastal Georgia varieties of the ware (Caldwell and McCann 1941; Caldwell and Waring 1939). Some preferred to use the Stallings Island terminology (Griffin 1943); others embraced the St. Simons terminology, drawing on additional stratigraphic data to refine the emerging cultural-historical sequence (Waring 1968a). To confuse matters, Waring subsequently used the term *Bilbo Plain and Incised* to describe fiber-tempered pottery from the Bilbo site and the greater Savannah area (Waring 1968d:216; Williams 1968a:104). Waring drew upon the Bilbo nomenclature to propose a cultural-historical phase made up of an early (Bilbo I) and a late (Bilbo II) subphase (Waring 1968d:216–17).

Use of the Stallings type descriptions and phase designations on the coast as first proposed by Griffin (1943) and advocated by Stephen Williams (1968a:105) has not been accepted by many archaeologists (cf. Anderson 1975; Trinkley 1986:159). The reluctance to use nomenclature attributed to the interior site of Stallings Island stems from the belief that interior and coastal technologies were divergent. Waring was an early proponent of distinct traditions, and he made some preliminary suggestions about the historical relationships and interactions of neighboring populations (e.g., Waring 1968a, 1968b). Conversely, Stoltman (1974:19) and Michael B. Trinkley (1986:159) point out that differences between interior and coastal pottery assemblages are not sufficient to separate Stallings from either Bilbo or St. Simons.

Following Waring (1968b:191), Crusoe and DePratter (1976:13) argue that coastal marsh sites were used by people who moved to the coast from the interior. Viewing the ensuing adaptations as divergent, they maintain that the Bilbo terminology is a useful means to delineate coastal derivatives from interior manifestations that predated, coexisted with, and postdated the Bilbo phase. Crusoe and DePratter further maintain that sites given to the Bilbo phase extend from Cumberland Island to the South Carolina marsh, around Hilton Head (basically, the Georgia coast), and that groups occupying this area restricted their interior movements to the brackish zone. The Bilbo phase is said to have lasted twelve hundred years, from 4200 to 3000 B.P., with the Bilbo I subphase spanning 4200–3700 B.P. and the Bilbo II subphase spanning 3700–3000 B.P. (Crusoe and DePratter 1976:14).

Working later with additional information, DePratter (1979a) proposed some changes to the Georgia coastal sequence. Returning to the use of St. Simons nomenclature, DePratter recognized two phases of the St. Simons period: St. Simons I and St. Simons II. The earlier phase is marked by the exclusive use of plain fiber-tempered pottery and dates from 4200 to 3700 B.P. (DePratter 1979a:114). Punctation, including both random and linear, began sometime around 3800–3700 B.P. and marks the onset of the St. Simons II phase (DePratter 1979a:114–15). Incised decoration is also said to have begun in this phase but perhaps slightly later than punctation (DePratter 1979a:115).

DePratter's cultural-historical sequence has gained widespread acceptance by coastal researchers, and it does not deviate markedly from previous models for the Georgia coast, although anomalous data are evidence that refinements in the sequence are needed. For instance, radiocarbon dates from the West Ring at Cannon's Point suggest that pottery decoration, particularly incised motifs, was introduced no later than 3900 B.P. Also, late dates associated with plain fiber-tempered pottery assemblages have been obtained at Pagan Plum and Cunningham Mound C, suggesting that assemblages lacking decorated sherds can be expected to continue well into the late St. Simons phase. Taking these anomalies into account, I draw on stratigraphic and radiometric data in Chapter 4 to refine the extant cultural-historical sequence to provide a more detailed chronology of the Late Archaic period.

Whatever the sequence of events or processes that led to distinct coastal and interior histories, coastal assemblages from sites south of the Savannah River are markedly different from those to the north. Compared to South Carolina assemblages, fiber-tempered pottery from the Georgia coast is predominantly plain. Among the few assemblages with abundant decoration, incising, punctation over incising, and shell punctation are common, and drag and jab reed punctation is rare. At the mouth of the Savannah River, decorated assemblages are more common, with examples of linear punctation being most abundant. North of the Savannah River the incidence of decoration increases. In this portion of the coast, drag and jab punctation is very common, shell punctation is an appreciable minority decoration, and incising is rare. Finger-pinching, primarily limited to sand-tempered or nontempered pottery, is concentrated in the Charleston area, where the incidence of fiber-tempered pottery is low.

Lacking the benefit of an extensive radiocarbon chronology, Waring believed that differences in pottery along the coast reflected the movement and gradual development of the same group through time (Waring 1968a:255). This view helped to engender the belief that fiber-tempered pottery preceded sand-tempered pottery (e.g., Stoltman 1974:78, 84). It is now accepted that the Thom's Creek phase began at least as early as 4000 B.P. and was established by 3500 B.P. (Trinkley 1980a, 1980b). This apparent contemporaneity, or at least considerable temporal overlap, suggests to Trinkley (1980b:284) that an argument for the linear development of Thom's Creek from fiber-tempered pottery is unwarranted.

Geographically, the distribution of Thom's Creek and Stallings pottery is distinct, though considerable overlap is obvious in the lower coastal area of South Carolina. Fiber-tempered pottery is not usually decorated north of the Edisto drainage. Instead, Thom's Creek pottery dominates the early decorated wares between the Edisto and North Carolina. If 3700 B.P. is accepted as the time of the onset of abundant decoration of fiber-tempered wares, fiber-tempered pottery was apparently replaced by Thom's Creek wares by this time along the northern half of the South Carolina coast, and the two persisted for a long time (ca. 4000–3000 B.P.) along the lower half of the South Carolina coast. Thom's Creek pottery was never used along the Georgia coast below Wilmington Island. In this area, fiber-tempered pottery persisted until it was supplanted by sand-tempered Refuge pottery around 3100 B.P. (DePratter 1979a).

In sum, the extant Late Archaic cultural-historical sequence of the Georgia-Carolina coast is characterized by two major divisions, one temporal, the other spatial. In an initial phase (Bilbo I or St. Simons I) beginning no later than 4200 B.P. pottery was plain. Sometime before 3700 B.P. punctation and incising appeared, as did sand-tempered or temperless pottery. Decoration became more elaborate and diverse at about 3700 B.P., marking the beginning of a second phase on the coast (Bilbo II or St. Simons II). Certain forms of decoration appeared and increased in popularity during this phase, including shell punctation and finger-pinching and perhaps drag and jab punctation. Spatially, the coastal assemblages of Georgia and South Carolina exhibit marked differences. The proportions of fiber-tempered pottery surface treatments vary along the coast. A more significant contrast is the development and use of Thom's Creek pottery north of the Savannah River and its virtual absence in coastal Georgia assemblages.

Finally, I must stress that preceramic Late Archaic shell middens have not been documented on the coast, nor has a preceramic component been discovered beneath the dozens of ceramic-bearing deposits investigated to date. Some investigators have discounted the possibility that shell middens predating 4200 B.P. exist on the coast, basing their arguments primarily on the supposition that productive oyster beds were not present before the most recent advance of sea level (Crusoe and DePratter 1976; DePratter and Howard 1980). A more moderate stance is that early shell middens may have existed but could not have survived the erosion of sea-level transgression (Chester DePratter, personal communication 1988). No one has mounted an intensive search for buried sites, which, on the basis of sedimentological data (Colquhoun and Brooks 1986), should be buried by eighty centimeters or more of marsh sediment (Brooks, Colquhoun, and Sassaman 1990). Until an intensive search is carried out, the coastal record remains limited to a ceramic period beginning around 4200 B.P.

Settlement-Subsistence Summary

In the earliest model of coastal Late Archaic settlement-subsistence, Waring (1968a:253) identified three types of sites along the Georgia-Carolina coast: scattered occupations along marsh edges and bluffs, marsh middens, and shell rings. His "scattered occupations" apparently include nonshell sites that have yet to be adequately documented. The marsh middens are interpreted as "primary fishing stations from which weirs were tended and where oysters were opened" for transport back to dwellings (Waring 1968a:253). The location of dwellings is not specified, but presumably they were adjacent to marsh shell middens. Waring described shell rings as communal centers but was unable to provide any detail about what activities may have occurred there.

Michie (1979) offers a similar typology of coastal sites, drawing a functional distinction between amorphous shell middens and rings on the basis of assemblage content. He argues that amorphous shell middens such as Bilbo, Daws Island, Venning Creek, and Bass Pond represent base camps located in estuarine locations that afforded access to both marine and terrestrial habitats. Assemblages from these sites are described as the most diverse of coastal sites, particularly in regard to the lithic inventory, a large portion of which is believed to have been employed in the manufacture of bone and antler tools (Michie 1979:93–95). Shell rings are associated with each of these sites. The assemblages of shell rings, Michie argues, are less diverse than base camps, suggesting a more restricted function. Similar to Waring, Michie proposes that shell rings served communal functions, perhaps as ceremonial centers. Marrinan (1975:95) also assigns social significance to shell ring sites, though she does not specify the relationship of rings to other types of sites.

Primarily on the basis of his excavations at Stratton Place and Lighthouse Point, Trinkley (1980b:311–12) posits an alternative to Michie's model. Trinkley's primary objections to Michie's model are that shell rings contain solid evidence for intensive habitation, they are located to take full advantage of both terrestrial and aquatic resources, and the "artifact assemblage from the postulated 'base camps' is no different from that found at shell rings" (Trinkley 1980b:312). On the first two counts, Trinkley's evidence is compelling (see below), but the assemblage argument is weak. Trinkley and Michie both employ an unconvincing trait list method. Because they do not provide quantitative comparisons of "base camps" and shell ring assemblages, possible functional differences between the site types cannot be resolved.

One of the more valuable results of Trinkley's research on shell rings is his documentation of intrasite patterning. Trinkley has found that shell ring sites consist of four distinct activity areas: exterior edge of ring, shell midden, interior edge of ring, and interior of ring (Trinkley 1985:108). Refuse is accumulated at the exterior edges of rings. The amount of pottery and shell refuse rapidly decreases in an outward direction, and there is virtually no evidence of aboriginal activity beyond thirty meters of a ring's edge. Ring middens consist of adjacent primary house middens deposited in a circle and gradually accumulating to form a contiguous ring of varying height and width. Large shellfish steaming pits are located under the midden, and to some extent, refuse accumulated in the midden from construction, use, and abandonment of pits. Post holes are also present under the rings and are suspected to be present throughout the midden, though no clear structures have been identified. Along the interior edge of the ring, roasting pits and hearths containing hardened ash, burned shell, and fish bone are common. There is no evidence of habitation, though this portion of the ring appears to have been an important food preparation area. Ring interiors contain very few artifacts or features, suggesting limited activity, perhaps communal activities with no refuse accumulation. Finally, Trinkley speculates that the circularity of the rings can be related to the egalitarian nature of the resident populations, "where a circular clustering of habitations would promote communication and social interaction" (1985:118).

Subsistence data from Lighthouse Point indicate that the shell ring there was occupied year-round (Trinkley 1980b:175). Trinkley (1980b:306) estimates that the site could represent the remains of a band of twenty adults living year-round at the site for twenty to thirty years or thirty adults for thirteen to twenty years.

Noting that all of the Georgia shell middens and rings contained roughly similar artifact and faunal assemblages, DePratter argues that coastal populations "practiced a concentrated pattern of settlement" (1979b:35). Settlements were relatively permanent, with nearly all activities taking place at a single location. DePratter implies that several sedentary communities coexisted along the Georgia coast by suggesting that site selection was to some extent influenced by the location of neighbors. He estimates that individual communities were small because only a few structures could have fit on the average shell midden and concludes that shell middens and rings were occupied by small bands consisting of two to six families. He dismisses nonshell scatters as limited occupations in marginal areas and argues that the total population of the Georgia coast was small at any given time (DePratter 1979b:37–38).

Many writers agree that shell rings formed through the accumulation of individual household middens (see also Reichel-Dolmatoff [1972:2] and Waring and Larson [1968:273]), and research emphasis has been focused on the secular aspects of ring occupations. Comparatively little attention has been given to the social and ceremonial significance of shell rings. For instance, an Archaic period midden outside of the Sapelo Island shell rings (Simpkins 1975; Simpkins and McMichael 1976) may reflect a two-tiered settlement pattern indicative of a "more complex social organization than the egalitarian nature commonly attributed to pure hunting/gathering cultures" (Simpkins and McMichael 1976:99). Moreover, nearly all shell rings and other shell middens on the coast have yielded human skeletal remains (see listing by Trinkley 1980b:322), albeit usually small fragments. These are sometimes recovered from basal shell strata that lack artifacts or food remains other than shell. Perhaps shell was accumulated at certain sites for the purpose of human interment, a hypothesis proposed by Cheryl Claassen (1988) to account for Shell Mound Archaic sites across eastern North America. Such a function does not preclude habitation but rather offers an alternative or supplemental explanation for why rings and large amorphous midden sites were revisited or occupied for long periods of time.

The significance of shellfish to the subsistence of Late Archaic populations has long attracted attention among southeastern archaeologists, with opinions ranging from shellfish being central to the subsistence economy (Caldwell 1958), to it being merely a supplement (Parmalee and Klippel 1974), to nonsubsistence or indirect subsistence (e.g., fish bait) alternatives (Claassen 1988). The relative contribution of shellfish to Late Archaic diets on the south Atlantic coast remains unknown, but we can probably safely conclude that shellfish were not collected throughout the year on the coast. Claassen (1986) indicates that with minor exceptions, Atlantic shellfish were collected from the late fall to spring, coincident with the fastest rate of growth among oysters and the time when carbohydrates peak in oysters but protein is low. Conversely, protein is maximized during periods of slow growth in summer. Thus, consumption of shellfish on the coast had to be complemented by other sources of protein.

Coastal shell middens and rings contain the remains of foods other than shellfish, as various projects by Trinkley have demonstrated. At Lighthouse Point, for example, deer, raccoon, turtle, duck, and turkey were important terrestrial resources (Trinkley 1980b:236–45, 300–305). Fish remains consisting chiefly of sea catfish, mullet, and black drum are evidence that fish were likewise important. Other species represented by more than one individual include opossum, rabbit, gray squirrel, mink, mud turtle, cooters and sliders, and snapping turtle. The ranked importance of species on the basis of potential kilocalories is deer, fish, birds (primarily turkey), raccoon, and turtle. On the basis of kilocalories represented per unit excavated, deer constitute 40 to 50 percent, shellfish 32 to 39 percent, small game 12 to 15 percent, and birds, turtle, and fish combined 6 percent of total caloric yield. Trinkley suspects that fish are underrepresented (1980b:305) and postulates that they could have been as important as shellfish. Marrinan's (1975:101) analysis of the Cannon's Point faunal assemblage shows that fish (menhaden, marine catfish, drum, and mullet) and crustaceans were more important than molluscs. Mammals in the Cannon's Point assemblage represent more meat by weight than fish and crustaceans, but the number of individual mammals was small (Marrinan 1975:77).

Sites lacking substantial shellfish remains on the coast suffer from poor preservation so they have limited potential for supplementing information on subsistence from shell midden sites. For example, shellfish at Fish Haul were not abundant and were restricted to pit features. Because of the favorable preservation of these features, the 178.2 kilograms of shellfish recovered (most from one feature) yielded a biomass estimate (21.1 kilograms) that exceeded all other resources combined. The nonshellfish remains at Fish Haul were dominated by mammals (deer, raccoon, rabbit, fox, squirrel), followed in biomass by fish (drum, sheephead), aquatic reptiles (diamondback terrapin), birds (turkey, loon, and duck), and snakes (rattlesnake, copperhead/moccasin, mudsnake) (Wilson and Wilson 1986:292). Calculations of minimum number of individuals (MNI), diversity, and equitability suggest that though few species account for the bulk of biomass, primarily deer, terrapin, and drum, a diverse subsistence pattern is evident (Wilson and Wilson 1986:295).

The only plant food remains found with any regularity at coastal sites are hickory nut shells (Trinkley 1976). Acorn has been observed at a lower frequency than hickory at some sites (Marrinan 1975:94; Trinkley 1976; cf. Waring and Larson 1968:267, who placed greater emphasis on acorn). Hawthorn seeds were reported at Fish Haul (Trinkley 1986:318), and hackberry was found at Cannon's Point (Marrinan 1975:94). Trinkley (1986:319) suggests that the ubiquity of hickory at Fish Haul indicates that its nuts were a major food source. A fall-winter occupation is implied, although the nuts may have been stored.

Some interesting data on Late Archaic diet were obtained from coprolites at Lighthouse Point (Trinkley 1980b:225–32). Most of the coprolites contained digested animal and plant remains, a few with unusually large quantities of fish remains. Excepting one sea catfish, the live weight of fish consumed was small, weighing from two to fifteen grams. Some otoliths in the specimens suggested larger fish, perhaps over two hundred grams. Overall, the size and weight of the stools reflect a diet low in fiber but high in protein (Trinkley 1980b:231).

Finally, information on subsistence practices can be gleaned from the condition and context of food remains. A lack of damage to bivalve shells (e.g., Lawrence 1986:332; Marrinan 1975:94) suggests that meats were removed from shellfish through the application of heat. From an analysis of oysters from Fish Haul, Lawrence (1986:332) suggests that some shellfish were roasted over fires or hot coals. Excessive heat alteration on smaller individuals further suggests that fire was part of the culling process. An alternative method of preparation is exemplified by the steaming pits at Lighthouse Point (Trinkley

1980b:184–89) and numerous other sites. This latter technique was apparently common, as was the subsequent infilling of pits with shellfish and other refuse. Small gastropods such as the marsh periwinkle had to be prepared in some container, perhaps pots (Goodyear 1988). Similarly, animal bone pounded into little bits at many sites (e.g., Bilbo, Daws Island, Lighthouse Point) suggested to Waring that bone was boiled to render fat (Waring 1968b:156, 191; see also Goodyear [1988], Trinkley [1980b:245]).

Little evidence for preparation of plant food is available, but the general lack of lithic materials might suggest that hickory and other nut species were processed in wooden mortars. The sweet, live oak variety of acorns so abundant in maritime forests was probably easy to prepare for consumption because it does not require leaching of tanins (Waring and Larson 1968:267). Other coastal varieties, such as the laurel oak, would have required leaching to be palatable.

Cooking Technology

Ceramic cooking vessels are the hallmark of Late Archaic subsistence technology on the coast. Information on the manufacture, form, and use of fiber-tempered and sand-tempered Late Archaic pottery is summarized in this subsection, as are the enigmatic baked clay objects that are generally believed to be important clay substitutes for stone cooking on the coast.

Fiber-tempered Pottery. Fiber-tempered vessels were shaped from pinched slabs of clay containing variable proportions of organic fiber. One of the more common fibers used was Spanish moss, a material with properties believed to be helpful in binding clays during shaping and in facilitating drying of the clay (Simpkins and Allard 1986). Fibers were usually burned during the firing process, leaving behind vesicles in the paste. These are often visible on sherd surfaces, but when vessel walls were smoothed while the clay was still moist, a relatively common process, clay particles floated to the surface and masked the presence of fiber. The paste of fiber-tempered sherds is usually contorted, owing to poor mixing and the molded or pinched technique of shaping. Paste texture is usually very fine and friable, lacking visible sand inclusions, although occasional grains are present depending on the local source of clay. Inorganic temper was apparently not added to clay. The incomplete state of oxidation common to fiber-tempered pottery indicates that pots were fired in open pits at temperatures below 1000° C (Trinkley 1986:161).

Long ago, Griffin observed evidence of possible coiling on fiber-tempered sherds from the Chesterfield shell ring (1943:159). Others have since explicitly noted a lack of evidence for coiling on sherds from other coastal sites (e.g., DePratter 1979b:17; Waring 1968b:160). Trinkley (1980b:46–48; 1986:160–62) has added to this argument by pointing out that coiling does not always result in coil fractures so that evidence for coiling must be sought elsewhere. To this end, Trinkley employed radiographic techniques on sherds from Fish Haul to document orientation in fiber vesicles indicative of coiling. He suggests, based on the Fish Haul dates, that this technique was probably added toward the end of the Stallings phase, perhaps by 3750 B.P. (Trinkley 1986:334).

No comparative analyses of fiber-tempered vessel forms have been undertaken, but some general assemblage descriptions are available. The Fish Haul assemblage described by Trinkley (1986:166) consists of large, wide-mouth bowls with orifice diameters ranging from twenty to fifty-one centimeters. One vessel was twenty centimeters high. Rims are straight to slightly incurvate. Bases are slightly rounded to flat and thickened. Vessel walls range from six to sixteen millimeters in thickness, with rims tending to be slightly thinned. Waring (1968b:160, 192) provides similar dimensions for pots from Bilbo, with bowl heights up to thirty centimeters. DePratter (1979b:17) indicates that other coastal sites contain sherds suggestive of jars with more constricted orifices, though this has never been quantified.

There has been much speculation about the function of fiber-tempered vessels (e.g., Marrinan 1975:93–94; Schiffer and Skibo 1987; Stoltman 1974:233–34; Waring 1968b) but no detailed functional analyses. Some writers have suggested that baked clay objects and perforated soapstone disks were used in indirect boiling and that pots were one among several containers used to hold liquids (e.g., Anderson, Lee, and Parler 1979; DePratter 1979b:19). Others have either explicitly or implicitly assumed that pots were used directly over fire (e.g., Goodyear 1988), but evidence for this was only recently identified. Hally noted a high incidence of exterior sooting on sherds from Cane Patch (Skibo, Hally, and Schiffer 1988). Trinkley made similar observations on sherds from Fish Haul, in addition to finding carbonized material on the interiors of some sherds (Trinkley 1986:166). In other assemblages sooting appears to be the exception rather than the rule, although a lack of sooting may be attributed to preservation bias.

Thom's Creek Pottery. Thom's Creek pottery has been traditionally regarded as the sand-tempered descendant of fiber-tempered pottery (e.g., Stoltman 1974:78, 84). Now that it has been demonstrated that the two wares were contemporaneous over much, if not all, of the fourth millennium (Trinkley 1980a, 1980b), a great deal of technological and stylistic overlap is obvious, and distinguishing the two wares is not always easy. Most decorative elements of fiber-tempered pottery are shared with Thom's Creek wares so surface treatment alone is an unreliable indicator. Obviously, the two wares differ in the type of temper used, but it is not always apparent whether fiber was an intentional temper. Sherds containing one or a few fiber vesicles probably were not tempered with fiber. Thom's Creek paste varies from temperless, to a very fine sandy paste, to one with grit-sized quartz grains. Trinkley notes (1980a:8–9, 17–18) that clays available in the coastal zone of South Carolina contain variable amounts of sand and grit, suggesting that variation in the aplastic components of Thom's Creek paste depends on the clay source. Apparently, inorganic temper was not added to the clays of early pottery. In contrast, pottery of the subsequent Refuge phase (dating as early as 3500 B.P. in the Santee drainage [Refuge Punctate; Anderson 1982:268] and 3100 B.P. on the Georgia coast [DePratter 1976, 1979b]) contains an added inorganic temper, either grog or sand/grit.

On the basis of his analysis of more than eight thousand Thom's Creek sherds from fourteen coastal South Carolina sites, Trinkley (1980a:8–13) provides detailed information on vessel manufacture and morphological variation. Basal portions of vessels were started with pinched slabs of clay. Bases were frequently flattened, though some sherds indicate slightly rounded bottoms. Vessel walls were then formed through two methods, coiling and modeling. Wall thickness ranges from 4 to 13 millimeters with a mean of 8.5 millimeters. Vessel wall interiors were often scraped with a bivalve shell or other hard object when the clay was plastic or leather-hard. The exterior was usually wiped while still plastic. Most vessels appear to have been rapidly fired, resulting in incomplete oxidation, especially on the interior, which suggests that vessels were inverted during firing.

Three shapes of Thom's Creek vessels are described by Trinkley

(1980a:10): a shallow bowl with an unrestricted orifice, a similar form with slightly restricted orifice, and a deep jar or pot with unrestricted orifice. Vessel diameters range from ten to forty-five centimeters with a mean of thirty-five centimeters. Bowl capacities are about two liters, and jars hold ten times that amount. Six basic lip forms are identified by Trinkley (1980a:10–13). Rounded lips are most common (46 percent), followed by flat lips (35 percent), exterior rounded (8 percent), interior rounded (4 percent), interior (2 percent) or exterior (3 percent) flanges, and other minor types (2 percent). Rims are straight, slightly incurving, or slightly outcurving. Sharply incurving and S-shaped rims occur in less than 2 percent of the sample.

Because Thom's Creek vessels exhibit a wider range of forms than fiber-tempered pottery, it seems reasonable to assume that they fulfilled a broader range of functions. Unfortunately, functional analyses of Thom's Creek pottery are lacking. Interior residues are noted for Thom's Creek sherds (Trinkley 1980a:13), but I know of no reports of exterior sooting. Admittedly, the sandy, poorly fired wares characteristic of the southern half of the Thom's Creek distribution (Trinkley 1980b:285–86) are not conducive to preservation of sooted surfaces. The better-fired wares at the north end of the distribution should, however, exhibit evidence of sooting if these vessels were used over fire.

Decoration of fiber-tempered and Thom's Creek pottery was done with reeds, shells, or fingers. Donald R. Sutherland (1974) replicated most nonshell punctation designs found on the coast with marsh reeds (*Spartina* spp.). Shell punctations were usually produced with the point of a marsh periwinkle and less often with the edge of other varieties such as cockleshells and angel wings (Trinkley 1980a:7). Sometimes the side of a periwinkle shell was used to make shallow punctations. Incising was accomplished with reeds, sticks, or perhaps bone, antler, or stone implements.

Baked Clay Objects. Baked clay objects are small spherical or amorphous items shaped from nontempered clay, sometimes bearing traces of finger and palm impressions and sometimes with perforations, punctations, or incisions (South 1970). These items resemble the Poverty Point objects (Ford, Phillips, and Haag 1955) from Louisiana and the Gulf Coast, though they are not nearly so elaborate. At some of the Georgia sites, baked clay objects are present in the deepest portions of shell deposits together with plain fiber-tempered pottery, but they gradually diminish in number in levels containing decorated pottery (e.g., DePratter 1979b:19, 44; Dye 1976:42, 44; Waring and Larson 1968).

Two interpretations are proposed for the function of baked clay objects: they are described as clay substitutes for either boiling stones or roasting stones (DePratter 1979b:19). To evaluate the boiling stone hypothesis, Trinkley (1986:211–12) compared the phosphate content of three fiber-tempered sherds and one baked clay object from Fish Haul. Following the argument of G. Duma (1972), contact with organic materials would enrich the phosphate content of the clays used. Trinkley found that the pottery sherds had a high phosphate content, consistent with organic enrichment, but the baked clay object did not. He concludes that the object was not used in stone boiling but may have been used in roasting.

That baked clay objects served as roasting stones at Jaketown was first suggested by James A. Ford, Phillip Phillips, and William G. Haag (1955). DePratter (1979b:19) provides support for this interpretation in noting that baked clay objects were found in pits beneath the middens at Sapelo Island and Pagan Plum Point. That baked clay objects would be found in pits where they were heated seems reasonable regardless of whether they were used to boil or roast foods. That these objects appear to have become obsolete with the introduction and refinement of pottery technology argues for a boiling function, assuming that early pottery was used over fire to heat liquids.

Other Subsistence Technology

Compared to inland locations close to sources of rock, coastal Late Archaic sites contain relatively few lithic artifacts. Notably lacking within the flaked stone inventory on the coast is evidence of tool manufacture (i.e., debitage, cores, hammerstones). Hafted bifaces usually exhibit an advanced degree of edge maintenance, and debitage is usually limited to small retouch flakes (Michie 1979:60; Oliver, Claggett, and Novick 1986). Ground and polished stone tools are either scarce or absent from coastal sites.

In contrast to stone, artifacts made from bone and antler are well represented at coastal Late Archaic sites. The abundance of these items is in part owed to the favorable preservation conditions of shell middens. Tool forms made from bone and antler include projectile tips, punches, awls, pins, chisels, basketry fids, and netting tools (DePratter 1979b:18; Dye 1976:35–36; Marrinan 1975:62–64; Michie

1979:63; Trinkley 1980b:218–19; Waring 1968b). Modified shell, primarily whelk (*Busycon* spp.), was also drafted into use as scrapers, picks, hammers, and adzes (DePratter 1979b:20; Simpkins 1975:27–34; Trinkley 1980b:174, 209–12, 296).

Other organic media used in subsistence technology have not been documented, but indirect evidence for basketry and net technology is available. For instance, the polish of bone pins may have been produced from use as fids in basket coiling (Marrinan 1975:92) or weaving nets and other fabrics (DePratter 1979b:19; Trinkley 1980b:218–19). Baskets or nets would have been necessary for capturing the small fish so common to many coastal shell middens (DePratter 1979b:16, 19; Trinkley 1986:210) and for transporting shellfish and other foods to locations of consumption.

Interior Archaeological Record

Cultural-Historical Sequence

Stoltman (1974) issued the first comprehensive nomenclature for organizing the temporal variability of Late Archaic manifestations in the Savannah River Valley. He defined three phases of the "Stallings Culture": Stallings I, a preceramic phase; Stallings II, a ceramic phase dominated by plain fiber-tempered pottery; and Stallings III, a ceramic phase characterized by plain and decorated fiber-tempered pottery (Stoltman 1974:19). Absolute dates for these phases were not provided, but the dates for plain fiber-tempered pottery at Rabbit Mount showed that Stallings II began no later than about 4500 B.P. Fiber-tempered assemblages with abundant decoration at Stallings Island and Bilbo date to around 3700 B.P., the date used to mark the beginning of the Stallings III phase. Though the coastal record lacks preceramic and early ceramic components, the Stallings II and III phases mesh fairly well with the Bilbo/St. Simons I and Bilbo/St. Simons II phases, respectively.

The most significant feature of Stoltman's formulation is the formal recognition of a preceramic Late Archaic phase separate from its ceramic period successor. Earlier work at Stallings Island and Lake Spring documented preceramic components, but attempts to describe the sequences emphasized continuity between preceramic and ceramic occupations (Caldwell 1958; Fairbanks 1942). Bullen and Greene (1970) and Crusoe and DePratter (1976) later dispelled the notion of continuity, citing changes in lithic artifact classes that distinguished preceramic and ceramic components at Stallings Island.

The value of stemmed hafted biface morphology in delineating phases of the Late Archaic period has been the subject of lengthy discussion (Alterman 1985; Anderson and Schuldenrein 1985b; Ledbetter 1991; Oliver 1981; 1985; Sassaman et al. 1990; White 1982). The "Savannah River Stemmed" was first recognized by Claflin (1931) at Stallings Island and formally defined by Joffre L. Coe (1964) from excavations in North Carolina. Bullen and Greene (1970) later noted a trend for decreasing size among stemmed bifaces at Stallings Island. Large specimens, which they called Stallings Type 1, were chiefly associated with preceramic levels of the site. Smaller varieties (Types 3 and 4) were common to levels bearing Stallings fiber-tempered sherds. The Type 1 variety from Stallings Island is morphologically and chronologically equivalent to the Savannah River Stemmed. Many equate smaller stemmed forms in the region with the Otarre type defined in North Carolina by Bennie C. Keel (1976:194–96). Dates for Otarre contexts in the region are coterminous with or postdate the Savannah River Stemmed phase. On the basis of observations of Piedmont North Carolina assemblages, Billy C. Oliver agrees that a small stemmed biface is a viable temporal marker for the latter part of the Late Archaic, but following Coe (1964; see also South [1959:153–57]), he chooses to refer to the diminutive forms as Small Savannah River Stemmed (Oliver 1981, 1985:204). Despite the disagreement over what the smaller forms should be called, there is general agreement that they fall at the latter end of the Late Archaic stemmed biface tradition (cf. Anderson and Schuldenrein 1985b:324). Two points that remain equivocal are whether classic (i.e., large) Savannah River Stemmed forms were completely replaced by smaller forms, and if this is true, whether it coincides with the inception of pottery manufacture.

In the absence of an unequivocal hafted biface sequence corresponding to preceramic and ceramic phases, a lack of pottery is usually assumed, often implicitly, to be indicative of early Late Archaic sites. This is an unfortunate bias of the interior record. In using the lack of pottery to define preceramic assemblages, the assumption is made that all assemblages of pottery-using people will contain pottery. Little consideration has been given to the possibility that early pottery may have been a seasonal or site-specific technology.

A more troubling bias is the assumption that once pottery was available in the valley (by ca. 4500 B.P.) it was widely adopted.

Radiocarbon dates on Piedmont sites in the Russell Reservoir area indicate that pottery was not used there until after 3700 B.P., perhaps not until after 3500 B.P., a full millennium after it was being used in the Coastal Plain. Further, an early fiber-tempered pottery component at Stallings Island has not been substantiated, and the date for inception of pottery use at the site is only 3730 B.P. Obviously, the earliest fiber-tempered pottery, that believed to be indicative of a Stallings II phase, was not widely distributed in the valley. Accordingly, the applicability of the Stallings I–II–III phase sequence at the valley-wide level remains suspect.

Sufficient radiometric and stratigraphic data are available to suggest that the Stallings I phase persisted in the Piedmont well into the fourth millennium and a Stallings II phase is not recognized in the Piedmont, nor has it been definitively documented in the Fall Zone. Much more work needs to be done to resolve the spatio-temporal relationships of the various Stallings phases, but for now it remains a useful heuristic for the Coastal Plain and, in more limited fashion, the Fall Zone and Piedmont.

The cultural-historical relationship between fiber-tempered and Thom's Creek pottery in the Savannah River Valley is not well understood. Thom's Creek assemblages are represented in the lower half of the valley (Phelps 1968). No radiometric dates for them are available, and stratigraphic data are ambiguous. Fiber-tempered pottery is slightly deeper than Thom's Creek pottery at some sites (Phelps and Burgess 1964; Phelps 1968; Stoltman 1974) but not at others (Brockington 1971). Unfortunately, deep, stratified sequences containing both wares have not been located in the interior. Arguments thus far have rested on superpositioning of the wares within shallow, sandy strata and on spatial co-occurrence in surface or non-provenienced collections. The Savannah River Valley, like the lower coast of South Carolina, is an area where the two traditions overlap, and undoubtedly the traditions also overlapped temporally. As it now stands, the development of non- or sand-tempered pottery appears to have greater antiquity on the coast than in the interior (Hanson 1982:14) so we should expect in the Savannah a longer phase of exclusively fiber-tempered pottery (i.e., Stallings II).

Settlement-Subsistence Summary

At least five types of Late Archaic sites can be defined in the Savannah River Valley on the basis of location, internal structure, and assemblage context: riverine habitation sites with shellfish refuse;

riverine habitation sites lacking shellfish refuse; riverine limited-activity locations; upland habitation sites; and upland limited-activity locations.

Large shell middens are exemplified by Stallings Island (Claflin 1931) and Lake Spring (Miller 1949). Small shell middens are present at Rabbit Mount, Fennel Hill, and numerous Fall Zone sites in the Stallings-Lake Spring area. All of the inland shell middens appear to have formed during ceramic phase occupations. Preceramic shell middens have not yet been adequately documented. Investigative emphasis on the larger shell mounds in the first half of this century contributed to the biased view that a shellfish-based economy existed in the interior. A widening of the research purview in recent years has steered attention away from shell mounds, allowing a more representative view of Late Archaic settlement-subsistence to emerge.

Recent excavations at floodplain or terrace sites along the Savannah River prove that nonshell habitation sites (Type 2) were an important aspect of Late Archaic settlement in the valley. These sites include Paris Island and Rocky River in the Piedmont, Lover's Lane and Rae's Creek in the Fall Zone, and Lewis-East and WV-14 in the upper Coastal Plain. These sites yielded midden deposits, pit features, hearths, relatively diverse and dense artifact assemblages, structural remains, and, at two sites, evidence of specialized tool production. Examples of preceramic or aceramic and ceramic phase sites are included in this category.

Smaller riverine sites in the Piedmont reflect less intensive use, but they often contain indirect evidence of hearths, relatively diverse tool assemblages, and possible structural remains (e.g., Piedmont sites such as Sara's Ridge and, to lesser extents, Gregg Shoals and Rufus Bullard [Anderson, Cantley, and Schuldenrein 1985]). Finally, many sites along the Savannah River consist of small, low-density, low-diversity assemblages (Type 3) indicative of resource extraction activities launched from base camps (Goodyear, Montieth, and Harmon 1983; Taylor and Smith 1978).

Sites in upland or interriverine zones (i.e., uplands between major drainages) include a surprising array of dense and diverse Late Archaic assemblages (Type 4) indicative of seasonal, possibly multiseasonal habitation. Exemplifying these are the Moody, Love, and Mill Branch sites and, to a lesser extent, 38AK158 and Tinker Creek. Of course, small "lithic scatters" (Type 5) are dominant in the uplands, especially at locations distant from permanent water

(Canouts and Goodyear 1985; Hanson, Brooks, and White 1981; Sassaman 1983; White 1982).

In sum, the Late Archaic archaeological record of site types and locations is characterized by considerable variation. Differences among sites can be attributed to such factors as function (both subsistence and nonsubsistence production activities), length of occupations, size of coresident or task groups, and degree of reoccupation. Because habitation sites are located in both riverine and interriverine zones, Late Archaic settlement choices by no means focused exclusively on large river channels. Instead, dispersed habitation along upland tributaries, as well as large riverine terraces or floodplains, is indicated. Large sites on the Savannah River may reflect locations of aggregation or, more simply, locations that were more regularly reoccupied.

Subsistence data from Late Archaic components in the interior are generally limited to a few riverine sites. Shell midden sites contain the largest and most diverse faunal assemblages. Besides freshwater bivalves and other varieties of shellfish, these sites contain abundant white-tailed deer along with lesser numbers of smaller mammals, reptiles, birds, and fish. More specific faunal information can be extrapolated from the assemblage at Rabbit Mount (Stoltman 1974:137–50). White-tailed deer was dominant among mammal remains, which included beaver, opossum, raccoon, muskrat, rabbit, gray fox, skunk, and bobcat. Bird remains chiefly consisted of turkey; fish bones were predominantly catfish; and turtles were numerous and diverse. A similar variety of resources is described for Stallings Island (Claflin 1931:12), but quantitative and provenience data are not presented. Stallings Island also produced "quantities" (Claflin 1931:12) of sturgeon and gar.

Nonshell riverine sites in the Piedmont and Coastal Plain upland sites contain few faunal remains, but they often yield hickory nut shell and occasional acorn and walnut (Gardner 1986:387; Moore 1985; Trinkley 1974). An isolated maypop seed and a possible tupelo seed were found at Sara's Ridge (Gardner 1986:387). Seed remains are typically scarce or absent in other soil or flotation samples that have been examined.

Inferences about seasons of occupation based on available subsistence remains from interior sites are not usually strong. Claassen (1986) reports that freshwater shellfish in the Southeast were collected from spring to fall but not in the winter. Presence of sturgeon remains, an anadromous species, indicates that Stallings Island was occupied during the spring when these fish migrated inland to spawn (Dye 1976:71). Nut remains from other sites imply that they were occupied in the fall, but if the nuts were stored or used for fuel, their seasonal specificity is diminished. Models developed for the Piedmont (House and Ballenger 1976) and upper Coastal Plain (Hanson, Brooks, and White 1981) indicate that upland sites were occupied or most intensively used during the late fall and winter when nuts and deer were available.

Recent models of Late Archaic settlement-subsistence in the interior converge on a pattern of seasonal mobility, usually described as an aggregation and dispersal pattern (Alterman 1987; Brooks and Hanson 1989; Sassaman 1983; White 1982). One model proposed for the middle Savannah area includes two levels of riverine social aggregation and seasonal upland household dispersion (Sassaman 1988; Sassaman et al. 1990). The higher level of aggregation is represented by Fall Zone sites such as Lake Springs and Stallings Island. These sites contain evidence of intensive occupation by relatively large groups engaged in diverse subsistence pursuits, nonsubsistence production, and ceremonialism. These aggregates probably consisted of all or most social entities occupying the upper Coastal Plain and Fall Zone portions of the Savannah River watershed.

Evidence of sturgeon (early spring migration) and shellfish procurement indicates aggregation during spring. Sites also contain abundant deer remains, but not enough is known about the condition and representation of this species to derive seasonal inferences. Fall Zone locations are ideal freshwater shellfish habitat and effective locations for harvesting anadromous fish using weirs. Modern data on range and periodicity of anadromous fish migrations in the Savannah (e.g., Rostlund 1952) are biased by human alterations of the river (Goodyear, House, and Ackerly 1979:141–42) so we cannot be sure if sturgeon, shad, and other species regularly migrated as far inland as Stallings Island. Under certain conditions it is presently possible for these fish to climb the Fall Zone rapids and penetrate as far as Stallings Island (Robert Wolfe, personal communication 1988). If anadromous species were similarly available in prehistoric times, their procurement may have required a coordinated communal effort involving delayed-return investments on nonportable facilities (weirs) and considerable information and decision-making organization. Such investments place constraints on fissioning (see Chapter 2), encouraging individuals to remain aggregated through a period of return. Conflicts and contradictions that arise out of constraints on fissioning were probably negotiated through ritual.

Mortuary ritual was certainly a key aspect of Stallings Island occupations. The political and economic reasons for social aggregations were probably embedded in burial ceremonialism. In this regard, all of the subsistence pursuits associated with ceremonialism (i.e., provisioning) may be explained as a consequence, not a cause, of aggregation.

A lower level of settlement aggregation is represented by sites such as Lewis-East and Lover's Lane, located at the mouths of major tributaries of the Savannah River. Each of these locations may represent staging areas for residential groups that dispersed in fall and winter throughout the respective tributary watersheds. They may also represent the locations of specialized subsistence activities (e.g., fish processing) related to larger-scale aggregation. In any event, these locations contain evidence for multi-household occupations and nonsubsistence production. If they functioned as staging areas for large-scale aggregation, they would have been important for consolidating environmental information, solidifying social relations, and preparing for aggregation rituals.

People were likely to disperse to the uplands in fall and winter (Brooks and Hanson 1989; Sassaman 1987; Sassaman et al. 1990). During that time households engaged in relatively autonomous subsistence pursuits, primarily procurement of deer and nuts. Such a dispersed settlement pattern constituted a wide catchment of social interaction with groups in adjacent drainages. Nonlocal raw materials (soapstone, Fall Zone "slates") flowed through these upland exchange channels, and information probably also flowed through them. Because the channels of information and nonlocal materials were dispersed in accordance with the settlement pattern, no one individual or group of individuals would have been able to sustain control over the access to these resources. The items and information obtained during times of seasonal dispersion would have been important playing cards in the social interactions that took place during times of aggregation.

Cooking Technology

Cooking technology in the interior includes a wider array of artifact classes than on the coast. The chief additions to the inventory of interior assemblages are the ubiquitous cooking stones. Among these are perforated soapstone slabs or disks, items believed to be used in so-called stone boiling. Soapstone was also used to manufacture vessels.

Soapstone Cooking Technology. Perforated and grooved soapstone objects are commonly found in Late Archaic assemblages of the Savannah River Valley. Both have been referred to as "netsinkers" (e.g., Claflin 1931:31–33), but the more common perforated slab was apparently used as a cooking stone (Anderson, Lee, and Parler 1979; Dagenhardt 1972; Ferguson 1976; Trinkley 1974; Wood et al. 1986; see detailed discussion in Chapter 5). Perforated slabs are common in the Savannah River Valley and adjacent watersheds but scarce elsewhere in the Southeast. More than twenty-five hundred are reported from Stallings Island (Claflin 1931:32), and considerable quantities are known from other Fall Zone and Piedmont sites, especially near outcrops of soapstone. Slab fragments are present in the Coastal Plain (e.g., Stoltman 1974; Trinkley 1974; Waring 1968b), though in lesser numbers than in the Piedmont (a pattern consistent with Elliott's [1981] review of Georgia distributions).

Soapstone vessels were made and used in the Savannah River Valley but not to the extent that they were in other regions of the Eastern Woodlands. In northern Alabama and western Tennessee, soapstone vessels predate, or are coeval with, pottery. In the Savannah region pottery seems to have preceded soapstone vessels (Wood et al. 1986:333). No stone vessel fragments were found at Stallings Island and Lake Spring, but they occur with fiber-tempered pottery at smaller sites upriver (Schuldenrein, Anderson, and Cantley 1985; Tippitt and Marquardt 1984:7–22) and in Stallings, Thom's Creek, and Refuge assemblages in the Coastal Plain (Sassaman 1988). Soapstone vessel fragments make up a higher proportion of soapstone artifacts in parts of the Coastal Plain than in the Piedmont, a pattern that also characterizes soapstone distributions in Georgia (Elliott 1981:16).

Studies of Late Archaic use of soapstone in the area have focused on production and exchange. Elliott has provided the most thorough investigations of soapstone use based on work in the Oconee Valley, Georgia (Elliott 1981) and the Savannah River Valley (Elliott and Doyon 1981; Wood et al. 1986). He describes patterns of soapstone procurement, organization of production, techniques of manufacture, and models of exchange. From analyses of the Paris Island assemblage, Wood and colleagues suggest that perforated slab production may have been an activity of specialists (Wood et al. 1986:326; Wood and Elliott 1983).

On the basis of a falloff in distribution in the nearby Oconee River Valley, Elliott argues that soapstone exchange was facilitated by local reciprocal relationships that lacked a more complex level of sociopolitical organization (Wood et al. 1986:326; see also Elliott [1981:61]). A quantitative study of soapstone in the Savannah River Valley has not been conducted, however, so inferences based on distributional data elsewhere are suspect. Soapstone distribution in the Coastal Plain appears to have modal tendencies that deviate from a monotonic decrement pattern of reciprocal exchange (e.g., Renfrew 1977) but instead suggests asymmetrical exchange relations (e.g., formal exchange alliances; Sassaman, Hanson, and Charles 1988). Furthermore, soapstone items are found in human burials (Waring 1968b:187) and unusual caches (e.g., Spell Cache; Blanton 1979:47) in the South Carolina and Georgia Coastal Plain, contexts that preclude straightforward comparison to Piedmont distributions of items in more mundane (utilitarian) contexts.

No excavations of soapstone quarries have been conducted in the Savannah River area, but Roy S. Dickens and Linda R. Carnes (1983) and Elliott (1986a) have reported on work at Soapstone Ridge near Atlanta, and T. A. Ferguson (1976) and others (Lowman and Wheatley 1970; Overton 1969) document quarries near Spartanburg, South Carolina. Their work provides detailed information on quarry technology, stages of bowl production, and vessel forms. Comparable information on quarrying and producing perforated slabs has not been collected.

Pottery. With some exceptions, the descriptions given above of fiber-tempered and Thom's Creek pottery in the coastal section generally apply to interior ceramic assemblages as well. Waring cited four traits of fiber-tempered pottery at Stallings Island that separated it from Bilbo pottery (1968b:160): thinner, more uniform vessel walls; small, neater, and more varied punctations; simple stamping; and flanged, carinated bowl forms. A systematic investigation of these differences employing more assemblages has not been made. Casual observations indicate that the carinated bowl form (Claflin 1931:14) may be a unique aspect of interior assemblages, with Chesterfield the only coastal exception. Simple stamping is found on lips of fiber-tempered pottery on the coast and interior, but its use on vessel walls may be limited to interior assemblages. Differences in punctation between the coast and interior are indeed evident and can be used to infer stylistic boundaries in the study area (see Chapter 6).

Analysts working in the Coastal Plain have repeatedly noted difficulty in separating fiber-tempered pottery from Thom's Creek pottery (Brooks and Hanson 1989; Sears and Griffin 1950; Elliott and Doyon 1981:104). The problem is that so much fiber-tempered pottery contains sand but little fiber. Sherds from upland sites in the upper Coastal Plain are especially difficult to classify. Brooks and Sassaman (1988) suggest that these sites were occupied late in the Stallings period, when Thom's Creek and Refuge pottery was beginning to be widely used. This chronological explanation accounts for some of the typological ambiguity, but it is also true that early fiber-tempered pottery (Stallings II) often has a sandy paste. The sandy paste helps to distinguish Stallings II pottery of the interior from contemporaneous coastal pottery, especially that of the Georgia coast, which lacks sand.

As with coastal assemblages, the functions of Late Archaic pottery from the interior are poorly understood. Some stratigraphic data have been used to suggest that pottery replaced a stone-cooking technique (Crusoe and DePratter 1976; Elliott and Doyon 1981), implying that early pots were used directly over fire or coals in moist cooking. Fiber-tempered sherds from Stallings Island were recently examined by Hally for evidence of direct-heat cooking, but none was observed (Skibo, Hally, and Schiffer 1988).

Other Subsistence Technology

The material assemblages of Late Archaic sites in the interior are dominated by lithic artifacts. Sources of flaked and ground stone were accessible in all parts of the valley except the lower Coastal Plain. Large stemmed bifaces (Savannah River Stemmed, among others), drills, flake cores, unifacial scrapers, flake tools, and debitage are common items of flaked stone assemblages. Hammerstones, anvils, manos, and grinding basins are among the more common ground-stone or cobble tools. Miscellaneous cracked rock, or "fire-cracked rock," is likewise common at Late Archaic sites and is usually attributed to cooking activities (e.g., Sassaman 1987; Tippitt and Marquardt 1984:7–47).

Polished stone subsistence technology includes atlatl weights and grooved axes. Although utilitarian, these items were labor-expensive to make and, because of their costs of manufacture and often nonlocal origin, probably entered into the nonsubsistence contexts or exchange and ritual. More obvious nonsubsistence items made of polished stone include gorgets, beads, and pendants (Claflin 1931:33; Sassaman 1988; Wood et al. 1986:279–80).

Subsistence technology made from organic media is not well represented at interior sites because of poor preservation conditions. Shell midden sites in the Savannah River Valley, however, have preserved examples of atlatl hooks, awls, pins, fish hooks, projectile tips, hafts, billets, flakers, and other tools made from bone and antler (Claflin 1931:22–23; Miller 1949; Stoltman 1974:131–36).

Summary and Conclusions

A complete, unbroken record of Late Archaic occupation in the interior of the Savannah River Valley region contrasts with the truncated record of the coastal zone. Limited to site components postdating 4200 B.P. and consisting exclusively of ceramic components, the coastal archaeological record is a biased sample of the regional range of Late Archaic technologies and behavioral strategies that existed in the fifth millennium before present. Whether this bias is an accurate reflection of the range of technologies and behaviors for the coast or is rather an artifact of poor archaeological visibility, the coastal record is nevertheless distinct from that of the interior in its predominance of shell midden sites, dearth of lithic artifacts, and evidence for relatively permanent settlement.

The site with the oldest documented pottery—Rabbit Mount—is located in the interior Coastal Plain, and similar assemblages of presumably equal antiquity are located throughout the Coastal Plain and perhaps into the Fall Zone. These sites and most interior Late Archaic sites lacking pottery contain fragments of perforated soapstone slabs, items used in indirect stone cooking. The functional relationship between the soapstone slabs and pottery is not understood, but some stratigraphic evidence suggests that pot cooking replaced stone cooking. If this indeed is the case, the change to pot cooking in the interior took at least seven hundred years to unfold.

In contrast, the lack of soapstone or alternative types of cooking stones on the coast may explain the rapid and widespread use of pottery by coastal inhabitants. The organizational demands of increasingly permanent settlements and exploitation of shellfish on the coast probably contributed to the fast pace and pervasiveness of technological change. Seemingly, the subsequent appearance of shellfishing and the organizational complexity at interior locations like Stallings Island and Lake Spring were accompanied by increased pottery use. Yet stone cooking technology did not disappear completely, and, rather than replacing stone cooking where they were adopted, early ceramic vessels may have been incorporated into traditional cooking practices. The actual uses of early ceramic vessels, their relationship to soapstone technology, and the social and economic contexts into which these technologies entered are the subjects of the remaining chapters.

CHAPTER 4

Sample Selection, Methods of Analysis, and Component Chronology

The technofunctional and distributional analyses I employ in Chapters 5 and 6 to document the histories of Late Archaic cooking innovations are based on interassemblage comparisons of soapstone artifacts and early ceramic vessel sherds from dozens of sites in the Savannah River Valley region. In this chapter I provide the methodological background for the analyses.

Selection of a Sample

The selection of a sample of artifact assemblages for this study was most strongly influenced by the need for broad geographical and temporal coverage. A series of assemblages that spanned the preceramic and ceramic periods was deemed essential, and because the interior and coastal areas of the region appear to have experienced distinct technological histories, site assemblages from throughout the valley and along the coast had to be included. Thus two complementary dichotomies—preceramic/ceramic and interior/coastal—are believed to embody the full range of technological variation important to this study and hence delimit the parameters of selection of an assemblage sample.

In drawing geographical limits for the sample, I considered the Savannah River watershed to be an absolute boundary for sites of the interior. Researchers working in the area have argued that the settlement ranges of resident hunting and gathering populations were roughly delimited by watershed boundaries (Anderson and Hanson 1988; Taylor and Smith 1978). Ranges obviously became smaller through time (Sassaman, Hanson, and Charles 1988), but major rivers presumably continued to be the primary conduits of group interaction and integration. It is likely that communication between or "across the grain" of watersheds was also an important means of group interaction (e.g., Anderson and Hanson 1988; Sassaman 1988), and I discuss the implications of such interaction on the pan-southeastern spread of ceramic vessel technology in Chapter 6. For the purpose of detailed technofunctional and distributional analyses, however, the sample of interior site assemblages is limited to locations within the Savannah River watershed and its adjacent, subordinate Coastal Plain watersheds.

The bounding of a sample of coastal sites was dictated by the documented distribution of Stallings and Bilbo/St. Simons fiber-tempered pottery (Anderson 1975; DePratter 1979b). Although coastal sites with these wares extend northward into North Carolina (Phelps 1983) and grade into the St. Johns area of northeast Florida, the core of the distribution is bounded by the Santee River to the north and the Altamaha River to the south (Stoltman 1972:38). North of the Broad River estuary in South Carolina, however, assemblages are usually dominated by Thom's Creek pottery. Because the temporal placement of early Thom's Creek pottery remains uncertain, I chose to exclude assemblages from sites located north of the Broad River estuary. This decision is in some respects regrettable because the development of sand-tempered or nontempered pottery in this area was a significant technological innovation, one seemingly attached to the rise of a well-defined cultural boundary between the Georgia and South Carolina coasts. Fortunately, the wealth of information on coastal South Carolina sites generated by Trinkley and others provides sufficient information to integrate the Thom's Creek data into the regional picture of technological change.

In addition to the geographical parameters outlined above, there were practical concerns over the provenience and context of assemblages. It was ideal to include only those assemblages either from deeply stratified excavation contexts or from single component sites of limited duration. Failing those, excavated assemblages with reliable site provenience and collection records were deemed sufficient. Last, I hoped to include all assemblages with associated radiocarbon dates.

In drawing up a list of potential candidates, I realized that despite the long history of Late Archaic investigations in the region, only about twelve sites met all or even most of these criteria. Thus, in the interest of obtaining a larger sample with broader geographic and temporal coverage, I added surface assemblages and others with indeterminate provenience.

Ultimately, assemblages from thirty-four sites in the study area were selected for analysis (Table 1). The sample encompasses coastal sites ranging from Sapelo Island, Georgia, on the south to the Broad River estuary just north of the mouth of the Savannah and interior sites westward along a three-hundred-kilometer stretch of the Savannah River. Several of the assemblages consist of minor samples of sherds and soapstone. These are not conducive to rigorous statistical analyses but are included because they provide coverage in areas of the valley that otherwise would be overlooked.

Regrettably, a few major assemblages could not be analyzed despite the good efforts of several individuals to locate the collections. Most unfortunate was the inability to locate many of the sherds of the Bilbo collection obtained by Haag in 1957 (Dye 1976) and the sherds recovered by the Crusoe expeditions to Stallings Island and Pagan Plum (Crusoe and DePratter 1976). The Albert Love collection, presumed to be housed at the University of North Carolina at Chapel Hill, was likewise unavailable.

In lieu of the Crusoe collection from Stallings Island, an analysis by Glen Hanson of sherds from two test units excavated by Greene (Bullen and Greene 1970) was useful, and soapstone artifacts in private Stallings Island collections stored at the South Carolina Institute of Archaeology and Anthropology were analyzed. A full listing of the assemblage samples with information on the source and type of collection, location where each is housed, and general assemblage characteristics is provided in Table 1.

Methods of Analysis

Soapstone artifacts and Late Archaic pottery from each of the assemblages listed in Table 1 were subjected to detailed techno-functional and stylistic analyses. In many cases all available soapstone and pottery was examined, though some large collections were sampled. These primary data, including information on the provenience of the collections examined, are provided in the original documentation of this research (Sassaman 1991).

Table 1.
Assemblage Samples Tabulated by Number and Name, Collection Source, Curation, Sample Type, and Assemblage Content

Sites with radiocarbon dates Number/Name	*Source*	*Curation*	*Sample type*	*Preceramic/ Aceramic Late Archaic component*	*Ceramic Late Archaic component*	*Soap-stone slabs*	*Baked clay objects*	*Soap-stone vessels*	*Fiber-tempered vessels*	*Other early vessels*
38BU9/Daw's Island	J. Michie	SCIAA	1		X	X	X	X	43	6
38AB288/McCalla Bottom	Schuldenrein et al. 1985	OAR	4		X	X		X	23	
9McI87/A. Busch Krick	Crusoe and DePratter 1976	UGA	2		X				22	
38BU805/Fish Haul	Trinkley 1986	MHH	4		X		X		49	1
9CB1/Stallings Island	Bullen and Greene 1970	FMNH	2		X	X			88	
9McI23/Sapelo Ring 1	Waring and Larson 1968	WGC	2		X		X		43	
9EB21/Paris Island	Wood et al. 1986	OAR	4	X		X				
WV14	Brooks and Sassaman n.d.	SCIAA	3		X	X	?		44	4
38AB91/Rocky River	Anderson et al. 1985	OAR	4	X		X		?		
38AL15/Rabbit Mount	Stoltman 1974	PM	4		X	X	X		212	34
9CB1/Stallings Island	Various	SCIAA	6	X		X				
Rae's Creek	Crook 1990	GSU	2		X	X	X		28	4
38AN29/Sara's Ridge	Wood et al. 1986	OAR	4	X		X				

Sites without radiocarbon dates Number/Name	*Source*	*Curation*	*Sample type*	*Preceramic/ Aceramic Late Archaic component*	*Ceramic Late Archaic component*	*Soap-stone slabs*	*Baked clay objects*	*Soap-stone vessels*	*Fiber-tempered vessels*	*Other early vessels*
WV23	Brooks and Sassaman n.d.	SCIAA	1		X				12	
WV18	Brooks and Sassaman n.d.	SCIAA	1		X				13	

9LI41	F. Cook	UGA	1		X				3	
9CH35/Cane Patch	Crusoe and DePratter 1976	UGA	2		X				123	7
9CH14a	DePratter 1979b	UGA	1		X				9	8
9CH111	DePratter 1979b	UGA	3		X		X		26	1
Chesterfield	Flannery 1943	CM	2		X				55	12
9RI137	G. Lewis		1		X			X	2	
9CH114	DePratter 1979b	UGA	1		X			X	18	3
38MC479	B. McConnell	SCIAA	1		X			X	8	1
38AK224/Tinker Creek	Hanson 1980	SCIAA	4		X	X		X	8	15
9RI4/White's Mound	Phelps and Burgess 1964	UGA	2		X	X	X	X	46	21
9JF21	G. Lewis		1		X			?	1	
Rocky Ford	G. Lewis		5		X	?			26	2
38AK288	SRARP Site Files	SCIAA	2		X	X			2	
9BUR2/Theriault	private collection	SCIAA	7	?	X	X		X	63	61
38BM4/Cal Smoak	Anderson et al. 1979	SCIAA	4	?	X	X		?	4	3
38AL2/Fennel Hill	F. Cook	SCIAA	2	?	X	X	X		64	4
9EB91/Rucker's Bottom	Anderson and Schuldenrein 1985	OAR	6	X	X	X		X	11	1
38AK158	Sassaman 1987	SCIAA	4	X	X	X		X	1	6
38ED31/Moody	Moody et al. 1979, 1985	SCIAA	2	X		X				
38AK228/G.S. Lewis-East	Hanson and Sassaman 1984	SCIAA	4	X		X				

Key to Curation Facilities:

CM: Charleston Museum (South Carolina)

FMNH: Florida Museum of Natural History, Gainesville

GSU: Georgia State University (Atlanta), Department of Anthropology

MHH: Museum of Hilton Head Island (South Carolina)

OAR: Office of Archaeological Research, Univeristy of Alabama (Moundville Museum)

PM: Peabody Museum of Archaeology and Ethnology, Harvard University, Cambridge, Massachusetts

SCIAA: South Carolina Institute of Archaeology and Anthropology, University of South Carolina

UGA: University of Georgia, Athens, Department of Anthropology

WGC: West Georgia College, Carrollton, Office of State Archaeologist

Key to Sample Type:

1: Surface collection 2: Test excavation 3: Surface collection and test excavation 4: Block excavation 5: Salvage test excavation 6: Various 7: Unknown

Soapstone Analysis

The analysis of soapstone artifacts was designed to address four questions: (1) What were the functions of subsistence tools made from soapstone? (2) Where were soapstone tools being used? (3) How important was soapstone to Late Archaic subsistence technology? (4) What was the functional relationship between soapstone technology and ceramic vessel technology?

With these questions in mind, I selected a series of formal and metric attributes relevant to the technology and function of perforated soapstone slabs and vessels. Data on these attributes were also collected to provide information on the spatial patterns of soapstone tool production, distribution, use, and discard.

For each of the soapstone assemblages, a count of the minimum number of perforated slabs was attempted. Few of the specimens were whole, especially at locations removed from sources of soapstone, so I began each assemblage analysis with a cross-mending effort. All whole, cross-mended, and remaining slab fragments were then coded for portion represented, planview shape, cross-sectional shape, edge morphology, surface condition, number and type of perforations, and length, width, thickness, and weight. Observations on size, shape, and reperforation of slabs were collected to assess the degree of recycling at each site and to predict the original volume of soapstone used within a given site area. Additional observations on the perforated slab assemblages included an assessment of the diversity of raw material present and evidence for heat attrition or other signs of alteration as a result of use.

Many of the assemblages contain soapstone slab fragments; half as many contain soapstone vessel sherds, most with only one or two small fragments of vessels. Accordingly, information on slabs was abundant, but there was only limited information on vessels.

Pottery Analysis

Pottery analysis was designed to address four basic questions: (1) What were the functions of early ceramic vessels? (2) Where and for what purpose were ceramic vessels first used? (3) What innovations appeared in the design and use of early ceramic vessels? (4) Where and at what rate did innovations in ceramic vessel technology spread? To address these questions, the pottery analysis was designed to obtain not only data on function but also chronological information from the stylistic variability of vessel surface finishes. The stylistic data likewise provide information on the spatial distribution of sociocultural entities across the study area.

Because of the technofunctional emphasis of the pottery analysis, a vessel unit of analysis was selected over the more traditional sherd unit of analysis. To be more specific, inferences about the functions of early pottery are to be drawn, in part, from observations about vessel form, so every effort had to be made to reconstruct individual vessels and to obtain information on the formal variation of vessel assemblages. The disadvantage of a vessel unit of analysis is that it limits quantitative comparisons with previous studies based on sherd analyses. This is less of a problem with respect to technofunctional properties, but it may potentially alter the results of chronological typologies based on surface finish. For example, the ratio of plain to decorated sherds has often been used to differentiate early from late assemblages. But decorations are sometimes limited to the rim portions of vessels so that more than half of the sherds of these vessels are plain. Accordingly, a sherd unit of analysis has been systematically biased toward plain sherd counts in assemblages containing partially decorated surfaces.

The procedure for analyzing vessels as opposed to sherds began by isolating all rim sherds in an assemblage as well as all body sherds with decorated surfaces. These sherds were then sorted into groups on the basis of lip form, rim form, paste, and surface finish. An effort was made to join pieces within each group of similar sherds. Eventually, groups of sherds, or individual sherds in many cases, were assigned vessel numbers, and analysis proceeded from there. A total of 1,222 "vessels" from thirty assemblages were analyzed.

Each vessel was coded for a series of technological, functional, and decorative variables. The technological and functional variables are derived from mechanical performance criteria specified in Chapter 5. In short, these criteria embody properties such as temper, vessel shape and size, and wall thickness, which serve to distinguish indirect-heat cooking vessels from direct-heat cooking vessels. Evidence for alteration caused by use—namely soot—is also employed to draw inferences about vessel function.

For observations of surface finish a hierarchy of variables was used which includes both general and specific attributes of decoration. The variables include general surface finish (plain, punctated, incised, finger-pinched, stamped); type of punctation stylus (e.g., hollow reed, bifurcated reed, shell, fingernail); orientation of punctations (e.g., right angle, oblique); design orientation (e.g., linear parallel to rim, rectilinear); location of decoration (e.g., entire vessel, rim only, zoned exterior). The first of these variables encompasses the surface finish categories used often in previous studies of fiber-tempered pottery. The other variables include attributes that likewise have been used in previous studies, but for the most part these variables were selected to generate a more comprehensive data base of surface finish variability than previous studies have provided. The strategy was meant to be inductive: my aim was to search for dimensions of temporal and spatial variability that have heretofore gone unrecognized. Some success was achieved, as data presentations below and in Chapter 6 will attest. Not unexpectedly, much of the collected data on design variability proved to be superfluous for the purposes of this study.

Chronology

Chronological control over variation among assemblages is essential to any analysis of technological change. Toward this end, radiometric and stratigraphic data are available for some site components selected for this study, though these alone are insufficient to construct a complete chronology for the sample. Thus, drawing on observations from sites with well-stratified deposits, I developed a paradigmatic classification of pottery assemblages for the purpose of building a relative chronology. I used the available radiocarbon dates to assess the validity of this classification and to provide absolute temporal anchors for phases inferred from the classification.

Preceramic or Aceramic Components

Five sites in the sample contain preceramic or aceramic Late Archaic components and no subsequent ceramic components. Three additional sites have both preceramic and ceramic components. Among the latter, only Stallings Island exhibits stratigraphic separation between preceramic and ceramic components, and radiocarbon dates from this site corroborate the observed superpositioning. Because I suspect that the adoption of pottery in the study area was neither uniform nor synchronous, I cannot assume that the other components lacking pottery necessarily predate the earliest occurrence of pottery in the region.

Fortunately, some of the preceramic or aceramic components in the sample are among the most securely dated in the region. Occupations at Stallings Island, Paris Island, Sara's Ridge, and Rocky River have been dated to 4700–3700 B.P. by a series of eight radiocarbon assays (Appendix A). Located on the Savannah River above the fall line, these sites contribute the bulk of evidence for a local lag in pottery adoption. Similar pre- or aceramic sites throughout the interior Savannah River Valley should likewise date to this interval. Two such examples in the sample are the Lewis-East and Moody sites. Concerning Lewis-East, hafted biface design and other lines of lithic artifact evidence suggest an occupation age in excess of 4500 B.P. (see Sassaman et al. 1990:95–96), while the Moody assemblage should predate 3700 B.P. based on the chronostratigraphic sequence of the nearby Stallings Island site. Because other means of dating the assemblages are lacking, even in a relative fashion, these estimates must be considered tentative.

The remaining two preceramic or aceramic components in the sample also contain evidence for ceramic period occupations, but they lack well-stratified deposits and radiometric dates. On the basis of stylistic and technological attributes that will be presented in later chapters of this study, I argue that the ceramic period occupations of Rucker's Bottom and 38AK158 are both late in the sequence, that is, post-3700 B.P. Although this supposition cannot be substantiated with independent data, it is nonetheless important to include the Rucker's Bottom and 38AK158 assemblages in the analysis because they bolster the sample size of interior sites at which pottery was eventually used.

In sum, the eight preceramic or aceramic components in my sample span a long interval of time, minimally 4700–3700 B.P. Pottery was eventually used and discarded during later occupations at three of the sites; a single radiocarbon assay shows that the earliest use of pottery at Stallings Island occurred at approximately 3700 B.P. Furthermore, the range of other available radiocarbon dates is evidence that 3700 B.P. is a reasonable estimate for the earliest use of ceramic vessels elsewhere in the Piedmont. The initiation of pottery use at many interior locations probably postdated 3700 B.P. by several centuries. Although this date cannot be substantiated with data from the pre- or aceramic sample at hand, the only dated fiber-tempered assemblage from the upper Savannah River Valley is late in the sequence (McCalla Bottom; 3410±80 B.P.), and ceramic vessels did not come into common use until after 2500 B.P.

Finally, my sample of pre- or aceramic components is restricted to sites in the interior Savannah River Valley. The lack of coastal sites in the sample is symptomatic of the effects of the rise of sea level on sites predating 4200 B.P. and, as argued here, of the widespread adoption of ceramic vessel technology on the coast shortly after 4500 B.P.

Ceramic Components

Twenty-nine sites in the sample contain ceramic components (Table 1). A few of these sites have deeply stratified ceramic deposits that have been correlated with radiometric dates. Unfortunately, most of the components lack chronostratigraphic data, being either surface collections from disturbed or poorly excavated sites or small samples of limited excavation. To build a chronological framework for these sites, a means of cross-dating sites is required. Thus a pottery sequence for the study area, based on some of the general trends for pottery surface treatment noted in Chapter 3, can be used to establish a component chronology in relative terms.

Two sites in the study area stand apart from all others in the depth and integrity of their stratigraphic sequences. Bilbo, at the mouth of the Savannah River, and Stallings Island, in the middle Savannah River Valley, form the backbone of fiber-tempered pottery chronology in the region. Some background material on these sites was presented in Chapter 3. In the following sections, detailed discussion of the stratigraphic sequences of these sites is presented in an attempt to derive chronologically sensitive sorting criteria for pottery from other sites in the sample.

Bilbo. In 1939 Antonio Waring excavated approximately 123 square meters of Bilbo to an average depth of around 140 centimeters below the surface (Stoltman 1972:42). Waring identified four zones in the sequence (Waring 1968b:155). The bottom zone (Midden Zone 1) consisted of a nearly uniform layer of oyster shell, 25 to 50 centimeters thick, lying on basal clays. Waring indicated that the "appearance was that of fresh, untrodden shell in which no ash or thick midden material was added" (Waring 1968b:155). The only artifacts recovered from this zone were a splinter awl, a perforated soapstone slab fragment, a perforated conch shell, and a baked clay object. Also present were "numerous animal bones" (Waring 1968b:155).

Overlying the oyster shell was a black, midden-stained river gravel 15 to 30 centimeters thick (Midden Zone 2). From this zone a small amount of fiber-tempered pottery, mostly plain, flaked stone artifacts, and bone were recovered. Several clay-lined pits were observed, one containing two bone awls and a bone pin, as were a few hearthlike features (Waring 1968b:156).

Above Midden Zone 2 was about 30 centimeters of lightly stained river gravel containing few artifacts. Midden Zone 3 consisted of dense mussel and oyster shell combined with sand and ash. Decorated and plain fiber-tempered pottery, flaked stone and bone tools, and bone refuse were recovered. The zone was arbitrarily terminated at 38 centimeters from the surface. The remaining surficial deposit (Midden Zone 4) contained artifacts of later cultural periods, including historic remains, as well as fiber-tempered pottery. Pits and hearths were found throughout Zones 3 and 4.

The vertical distribution of fiber-tempered pot sherds in Waring's stratigraphic block (n = 1,273) exhibits a predominance of plain wares in the lowest and uppermost levels, interrupted by a mode of linear punctate sherds centered on Level 8 (Figure 7). Random punctate and incised sherds are minor fractions of the assemblage in nearly all levels. Correlating this distribution with Waring's stratigraphic description, we find at least two distinct components: an early plain fiber-tempered component with an occasional decorated sherd concentrated in Midden Zone 2 (Levels 17–19) and a later plain and linear punctate component in Midden Zone 3 (Levels 6–10). Absolute sherd frequencies (Waring 1968b:179) support this interpretation. The upper 38 centimeters of mixed deposits (Midden Zone 4; Levels 1–5) might constitute a third fiber-tempered component in which the proportion of plain ware increases. Waring notes (1968b:160) that among plain sherds wedgelike lips were restricted to the deepest levels, indicating that the lip form of plain sherds may be used to define temporally distinct components of the sequence.

Bilbo was revisited in 1957 by William Haag, who opened 39.5 square meters to an average depth of 82 centimeters below the surface (Dye 1976). Only Unit 7 (1.5x3 m) penetrated the entire deposit. On the basis of the descriptions of this unit by David H. Dye (1976:41–51), Haag found a deeper, more complex stratigraphic sequence than Waring had. Ten zones were observed. The lowest, Zone 1, consisted

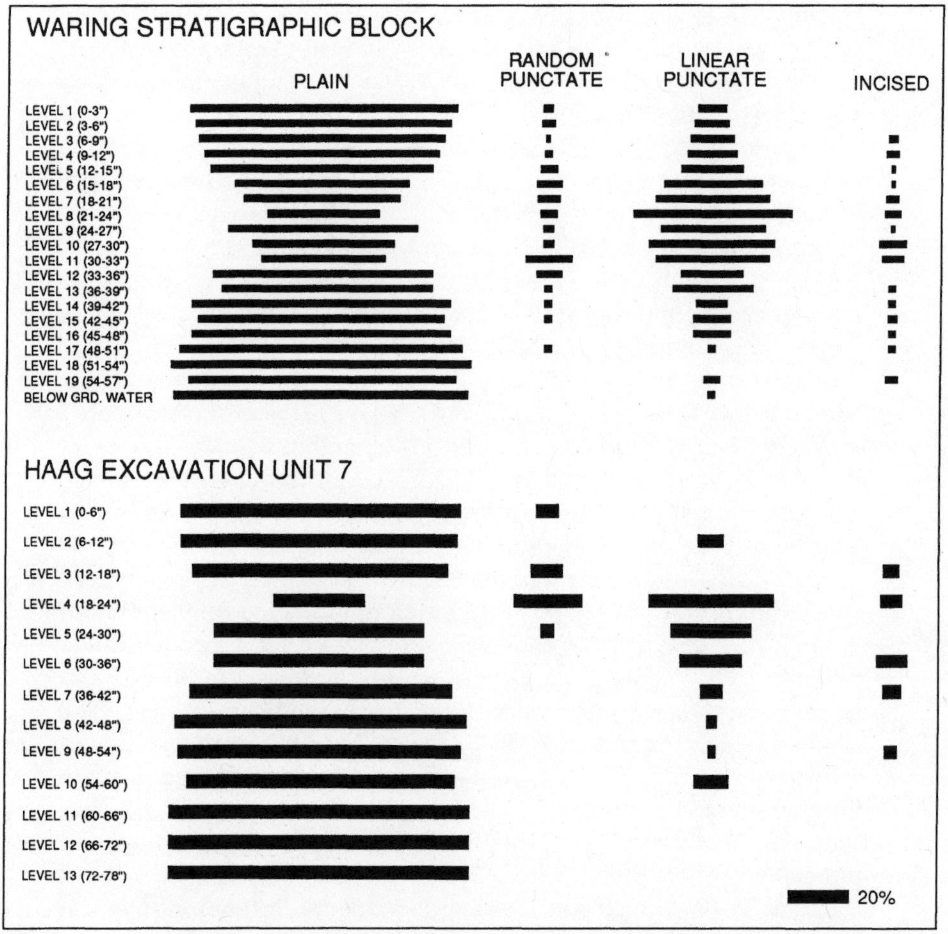

Figure 7. Relative distribution of fiber-tempered sherds by surface treatment and by excavation levels of Waring's (1968b) stratigraphic block (top) and Haag's (Dye 1976) Excavation Unit 7 (bottom) at Bilbo.

of sterile blue clay, excavated to a depth of 260 centimeters below the surface. From 183 to 198 centimeters below the surface, Zone 2 consisted of a mixture of blue clay, shell, and some wood and contained five plain fiber-tempered sherds and one baked clay object. Zone 3 was a thin (5 to 7.5 centimeters) lens of charcoal, wood roots, and nuts. The overlying stratum, Zone 4, consisted of nearly solid oyster shell along with two lithic tools, faunal remains, and thirty-nine plain fiber-tempered sherds. This zone corresponds with Waring's Midden Zone 1, though Waring recovered no pottery in his excavation of this stratum.

Above this initial shell midden was a 30-centimeter-thick layer of coarse sand with clay lenses (Zone 5). Numerous and diverse faunal remains, nut remains, bone and lithic tools, and plain, incised, and punctated fiber-tempered sherds were recovered. This zone seems to correspond with Waring's Midden Zone 2 (Dye 1976:45). The second shell midden in the sequence is represented by Zone 6. Lithic and bone tools, faunal remains, and plain, incised, and punctate fiber-tempered sherds were recovered. This zone cannot be reconciled within the Waring sequence, and it may represent an isolated shell lens at the site (Dye 1976:46).

Over the second shell midden was a mixed zone of dark earth and sand (Zone 7) about 30 centimeters thick containing lithic and bone tools, faunal material, plain, punctate, and incised fiber-tempered sherds, and a few Middle Woodland (Deptford) sherds. Above this was a thin upper shell midden (Zone 8), perhaps localized like Zone 6, with an assemblage similar to that in Zone 7. The upper 45 to 60 centimeters of deposits (Zones 9 and 10) contained a mixture of prehistoric and historic materials in a matrix of dark earth, ash, and minor shell.

It is evident that either Haag encountered a particularly complex portion of the site or Waring simplified the profile drawing provided in his report. Additional profiles of the Waring excavations were lost before his work was published (Waring 1968b:154–55) so we are left with only two limited sections. Haag's work establishes a fiber-tempered association for the earliest shell midden at the site, though it is hard to believe that Waring did not find a single sherd in the seemingly extensive exposures he made of this stratum. Nevertheless, Haag did define a seemingly pure plain fiber-tempered component in the lowest three levels of sherd-bearing deposits (Levels 11–13; Zones 2–4; Figure 7). Three radiocarbon dates were obtained on materials from Level 12, the lower portion of the first oyster shell layer in the sequence. The uncorrected dates are 3730±125, 3820±125, and 4125±115 B.P. (Appendix A). The subsequent shell layer (Zone 6) is associated primarily with plain and linear punctate sherds and yielded an uncorrected radiocarbon date of 3700±125 B.P. Linear punctate sherds increase in both relative and absolute frequency in Zone 8

(Levels 4–5), the third dense shell layer. Also in this zone is the first appearance of random (separate) punctate sherds. An anomalous date of 5500±115 B.P. from charcoal in Level 5 is attributed by Haag to the use of ancient wood out of the nearby marsh (Williams 1968c:330).

In sum, the Bilbo sequence provides at least two significant pieces of information for the development of a fiber-tempered pottery chronology. The first concerns plain pottery. An early occupation characterized by the exclusive use of plain pottery is apparent, and the predominance of plain sherds in upper levels of the sequence suggests that it may be difficult to separate early components from late components by the proportion of plain sherds alone. As discussed briefly in Chapter 3, the Daw's Island site has yielded a late assemblage (3400–3200 B.P.) dominated by plain pottery, and other coastal assemblages of plain pottery (e.g., Pagan Plum; DePratter 1979b) are suspected to be equally late in the sequence. Waring's comment on the occurrence of "wedgelike" lips in the lowest levels of Bilbo suggests that variation in the design of plain pottery will be chronologically sensitive. Quantitative data on the lip design of plain vessels were not published in the Waring or Haag excavation reports, nor has a stratigraphic analysis of plain vessel form been conducted on any assemblage in the region.

The second relevant aspect of the Bilbo sequence is the apparent trend in treatment of decorative surfaces. The documented increase in linear punctate at Bilbo has been a key element of the extant regional chronology. In addition, the occurrence of incising at Bilbo, albeit minor, seems to mimic that of linear punctate. Random (separate) punctation, in contrast, is characterized by less consistent patterning. Thus the relative percentages of linear punctate and incised sherds in an assemblage are potentially sound variables for relative chronology. Because these surface treatments decrease in frequency in the upper portion of the Bilbo sequence, the ordering of assemblages or levels on the basis of decorative sherds must also take into account the lip form of plain vessels.

Stallings Island. The first serious attempt to discern temporal variability in the stratigraphic sequence at Stallings Island was made by Bullen and Greene (1970). Their analysis was based on materials excavated in 1961 by Greene from eight test pits situated in the center of the mound between Claflin's earliest pits and the Cosgroves' largest trench. Stratigraphy in this portion of the site is described as "alternating layers of dirt, dirt and shell, shell and burnt shell" (Bullen and Greene 1970:10) up to 182 centimeters deep. Preceramic and ceramic strata were identified; pottery was confined to the upper midden zone, varying in thickness from 71 to 107 centimeters. Plain sherds were thought to be concentrated at the base of the ceramic zone, suggesting a gradual development of plain to decorated pottery. Three radiocarbon dates were obtained on charcoal and nut shell from the midden. Two samples from the basal portion of the midden gave uncorrected ages of 4450±150 and 4700±150 B.P. The base of the ceramic zone yielded an age of 3730±150 B.P.

The possibility of early manufacture of plain pottery at Stallings Island similar to that at Bilbo deserves detailed attention. Some writers have insinuated that a stratum containing plain fiber-tempered pottery was present at Stallings Island (Bullen and Greene 1970; Williams 1968c:331), though no data support this assertion. This problem can be traced to the presentation of radiocarbon dates from Stallings Island. The assay of 3730 B.P. derived from charcoal at 76 centimeters deep in Pit 4 is stated as probably dating the introduction of plain fiber-tempered pottery (Williams 1968c:331) or an "early phase of fiber-tempered ceramics, perhaps [a] plain period" (Bullen and Greene 1970:12). Ceramic data from Pit 4, however, were combined with those for three other excavation units in the report (Bullen and Greene 1970:17), and these figures show that nearly 30 percent of the sherds in the basal levels were punctated. Detailed and independent tabulations from two other excavation units (Bullen and Greene 1970:20) corroborate this pattern. Thus the basal date for fiber-tempered pottery at Stallings Island cannot be said to mark a period of plain pottery manufacture, though it does mark the onset of the use and discard of pottery at the site.

Despite the confusion about the earliest pottery at Stallings Island, the stratigraphic sequence has been used to infer developmental changes in fiber-tempered wares. From the Greene excavation data, Bullen and Greene (1970:16) suggest that simple (separate) punctation was being used shortly after pottery was introduced at the site. Subsequently, closely spaced linear punctation or the "stab-and-drag" (a.k.a. drag and jab) method became popular.

The vertical distribution of potsherds in units analyzed by Greene (Pits 1, 2, 4, 6; n = 888) clearly demonstrates the proposed trend (Figure 8), but units analyzed by Bullen (Pits 3 and 5) do not corroborate the seriation constructed by Greene. Pit 5 (n = 162), immediately to the east of Greene's units, only mildly supports the trend, while Pit

3, to the immediate west and consisting of the largest sherd sample from a single pit (n = 353), documents a continuous dominance of drag and jab punctation. These inconsistencies can probably be attributed to interanalyst bias and to horizontal stratification within the shell midden. Therefore, the proposed sequence of plain-separate punctation-drag and jab punctation must remain speculative, subject to further evaluation.

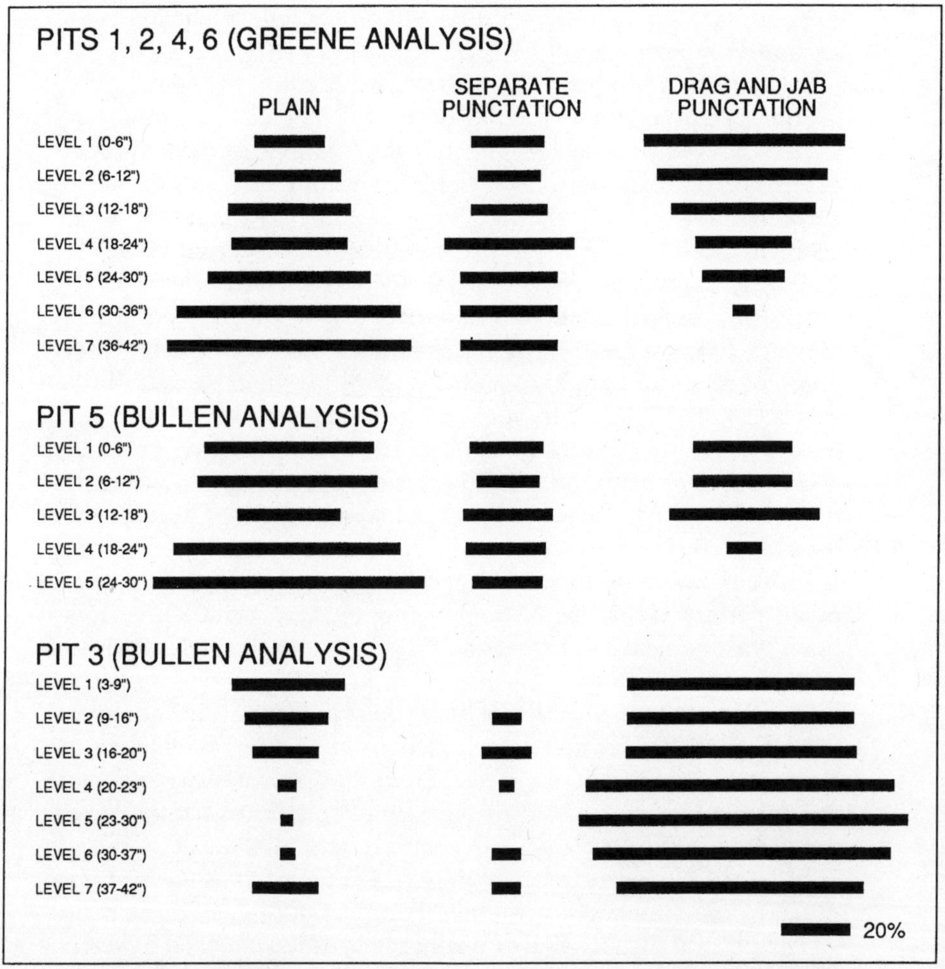

Figure 8. Relative distribution of fiber-tempered sherds by surface treatment and by excavation levels of Bullen and Greene (1970) excavation units at Stallings Island.

To summarize the Stallings Island sequence, we can be reasonably confident that the radiocarbon assay of 3730±150 B.P. accurately dates the onset of pottery use at the site, but this was not restricted to plain pottery. Instead, the earliest pottery at Stallings Island included both decorated and plain wares. The incidence of drag and jab (linear) punctation does appear to increase through time, though this is equivocal. Drag and jab punctation is present at the onset of pottery use, perhaps in only minor quantities. On the basis of this conclusion, we may infer that the regional appearance of this design technique may have occurred at or slightly before 3700 B.P. The Bilbo sequence discussed above supports this contention.

Other Stratigraphic Evidence. Based on stratigraphic evidence from Bilbo and Stallings Island, ceramic components in the site sample of this study can be classified into temporal groups. I begin with a review of stratigraphic evidence from sites in the sample. The review differs from the foregoing discussion of Bilbo and Stallings Island in its scales of analysis. Specifically, the analytical unit of pottery analysis from this point forward shifts from the sherd to the vessel. Because a vessel unit of analysis decreases the size of pottery samples, it is not possible to maintain a fine-grained stratigraphic analysis. The solution is to combine excavation levels to achieve acceptable sample sizes. If they are robust, temporal patterns in pottery form and surface treatment should continue to be apparent at a coarse-grained analytical scale.

Besides decreasing sample size, the use of a vessel level of analysis has the drawback of the problem of comparability discussed earlier. Because the Bilbo and Stallings Island sherd collections were not available for reanalysis or were otherwise incomplete, the stratigraphic patterns evident among sherds cannot be verified at a vessel unit of analysis. I therefore assume that stratigraphic patterns of vessel counts from these sites would be roughly comparable to those observed among sherds and look now to additional stratigraphic contexts for supporting evidence.

Three sites in the sample yielded large sherd assemblages from deep, stratified deposits. A. Busch Krick, Cane Patch, and Sapelo Ring No. 1 are shell middens of the Georgia coast that were tested through stratigraphic excavation. A fourth shell midden, Rabbit Mount in the Savannah River Valley, is shallow, but testing there yielded assemblage samples from distinct horizontal strata.

For the purposes of stratigraphic comparisons, I divided pottery from excavation contexts at each of the four sites into upper and lower, or older and younger, levels. For Rabbit Mount and Sapelo Ring No. 1, the divisions were made from visible stratigraphy: Rabbit Mount contained shell-midden and non-shell-midden deposits, the former documented as the older (Stoltman 1974), and Sapelo Ring No. 1 contained upper and lower shell middens separated roughly at Level 8 (Waring and Larson 1968:272). In the absence of visible stratigraphic separation within the A. Busch Krick and Cane Patch middens, excavation levels were arbitrarily separated into two equal subgroups representing the upper and lower portions of the deposits.

Beginning with plain vessels, the distribution of specimens with flanged or thickened (wedgelike) lips clearly documents the temporal precedence of this form over other plain vessel lip forms (Table 2). The two largest assemblages of plain vessels, from Rabbit Mount and Sapelo Ring No. 1, contain a relatively high proportion of flanged or thickened lips in the lower or older strata, and these values decrease

Table 2.
Stratigraphic Distribution of Flanged and Thickened Lipped Plain Vessels for Four Assemblages in Sample

	Number of plain vessels	*Thickened or flanged lip*	
		Number	*Percent*
A. Busch Krick			
Upper (0–76 cm)	2	0	0
Lower (76–152 cm)	5	1	20
Cane Patch			
Upper (0–91 cm)	2	0	0
Lower (91–183 cm)	9	1	11
Sapelo Ring No. 1			
Upper (Levels 1–8)	16	1	6
Lower (Levels 9–17)	19	5	26
Rabbit Mount			
Nonshell midden	19	4	21
Shell midden	103	41	40

Table 3.
Stratigraphic Distribution of Punctated and Incised Vessels for Four Assemblages in Sample

	Number of punctated and incised vessels	*Separate punctate*		*Drag and jab linear punctate*		*Incised*	
		Number	*Percent*	*Number*	*Percent*	*Number*	*Percent*
A. Busch Krick							
Upper (0–76 cm)	5	1	20	0	0	4	80
Lower (76–152 cm)	9	6	67	0	0	3	33
Cane Patch							
Upper (0–91 cm)	39	26	67	1	2	12	31
Lower (91–183 cm)	43	31	72	1	2	11	26
Sapelo Ring No. 1							
Upper (Levels 1–8)	5	3	60	0	0	2	40
Lower (Levels 9–17)	0	0	0	0	0	0	0
Rabbit Mount							
Nonshell midden	14	13	93	1	7	0	0
Shell midden	20	17	85	2	10	1	5

appreciably in subsequent strata. Assemblages from the other two sites include only isolated examples of this lip form, but both were recovered from the lower strata of the respective middens.

The incidence of drag and jab linear punctate on decorated vessels is too low in the assemblages to verify the Bilbo and Stallings Island sequences (Table 3), although the incidence of vessels with incised surfaces shows a proportional increase from lower to upper strata in each of the three Georgia coastal sites. This finding supports the observation made earlier about the Bilbo sequence regarding a simultaneous growth in the popularity of linear punctate and incised decorative techniques. The third major design technique, separate punctation, exhibits erratic values across strata and is hence not unlike the pattern evident among separate punctation in the Bilbo sequence.

The radiocarbon dates from Rabbit Mount, Sapelo Ring No. 1, and A. Busch Krick represent a time span of roughly 4500–3200 B.P. Dates for Cane Patch are not available, although the high proportion of decorated vessels in the assemblage (89 percent) strongly suggests that the site was occupied after 3700 B.P. Putting these sites into relative chronological order, it is apparent that the observed changes within the Stallings Island and Bilbo sequences have parallels in the sample of vessel assemblages. Moreover, the vessel samples lend support to the proposition that thickened, flanged, or wedgelike lips are common to early assemblages of plain fiber-tempered pottery. The combined data show that although plain vessel surfaces were never fully replaced by elaborate surface treatments, the incidence of thickened and flanged lips on plain vessels decreased through time and apparently disappeared by about 3700 B.P. Concomitant with the decrease in flanged or thick-lipped plain vessels, the incidence of linear punctation or incision increased. Stratigraphic data for both of these trends are unequivocal, and further support is found among available radiocarbon dates. Thus the observed patterns provide a strong foundation for the temporal classification of assemblages.

Temporal Classification of Vessel Assemblages. Temporal classification of vessel assemblages can now proceed with the help of the observed stratigraphic trends in pottery design discussed above and from a paradigmatic sorting of formal and stylistic attributes. For this purpose, I retain the stratigraphic divisions employed for Rabbit Mount, Sapelo Ring No. 1, Cane Patch, and A. Busch Krick. One additional subdivision is made for the Fish Haul assemblage to preserve distinct feature contexts (i.e., Features 21 and 18, large pits). In lieu of better contextual data at the other sites, the remaining vessel assemblages are each considered to be single components. Finally, six assemblages (9LI41, 9RI137, 9JF21, 38AK288, 38AK158, and 38BM4) are excluded for having fewer than ten vessels in the sample. For purposes of temporal classification, the final sample consists of twenty-eight assemblages with sherds representing 934 fiber-tempered vessels.

Temporarily ignoring radiometric and stratigraphic data, I isolated all assemblages that contained examples of vessels with flanged or thickened lips. I then examined these fifteen assemblages for decorative variability. Under the stratigraphic observations that thickened and flanged lips are most common to the earliest fiber-tempered vessel assemblages and that the incidence of these plain vessel lip forms decreases in conjunction with an increase in the use of linear punctate and incised designs, I expected that a further division of the subgroup might be made on the basis of the number of decorated vessels.

Toward this end I examined the percent distribution of decorated vessels with linear punctate or incised surface treatments (Figure 9). The results show that linear punctate or incised designs occur on less than 17 percent of the decorated vessels in nine of the assemblages and on more than 25 percent in the remaining six assemblages.

Using the apparent bimodality in decorative percentages to divide plain vessel assemblages further, we find the proportion of thickened and flanged lips is consistently distinct between assemblages of the two subgroups (Table 4). None of the assemblages with a high fraction of linear punctate or incised vessels contains a fraction of plain vessels with thickened and flanged forms exceeding 20 percent, while all of the assemblages with lesser percentages of the decorative designs have thickened and flanged lip fractions of at least 21 percent.

Further examination of the stylistic variability between the subgroups reveals some additional discriminating attributes. A few simple stamped vessels are present in five of the nine assemblages containing high fractions of plain vessels with thickened and flanged lips compared to only one of the six assemblages in the other sub-

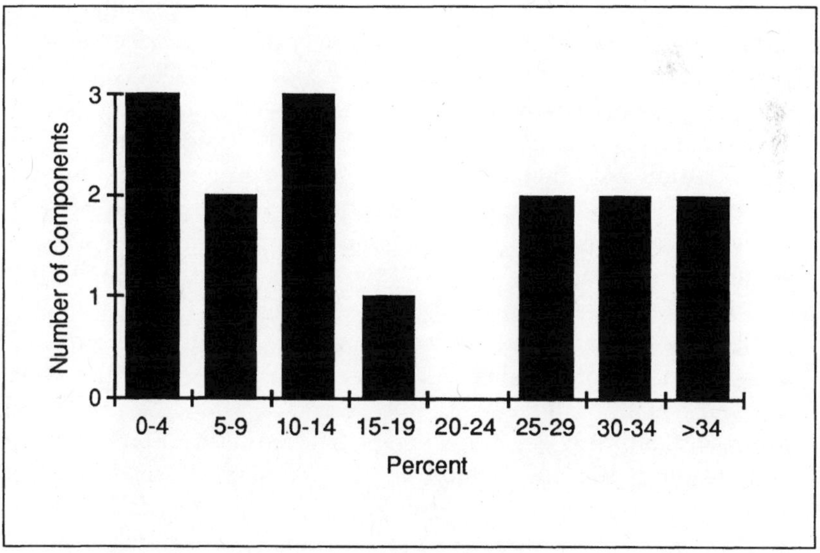

Figure 9. Percent distribution of decorated vessels with linear punctate and incised designs by component assemblage.

Table 4.
Summary Statistics on the Percentage of Plain Vessels with Thickened and Flanged Lips by Decorated Vessel Subgroup

	Proportion of decorated vessels with linear punctate and/or incised designs	
	<17 percent	*>25 percent*
Number of assemblages	9	6
Percentage of plain vessels with thickened or flanged lips		
mean	36	14
s.d.	12	5
minimum	21	6
maximum	55	20

group. Even more marked is the disparity in decorated vessels with regard to multiple design elements. All of the assemblages in the subgroup characterized by large fractions of linear punctate and incised vessels include examples of multiple designs, usually some combination of punctation and incision. These complex designs, ranging from 4 to 17 percent of all decorated vessels in an assemblage, are virtually absent from the other subgroup, with the exception of a multiple design vessel sherd in the lower stratum of Sapelo Ring No. 1.

Because of the apparent discriminating strength of the multiple design attribute, I divided assemblages lacking examples of thickened and flanged lip vessels into two groups by the presence or absence of multiple design elements. Under the assumption that the proportion of multiple design vessels covaries positively with the proportion of linear punctate and/or incised vessels, and under the stratigraphic observation that the incidence of linear punctate and/or incised vessels decreased late in the sequence after a peak of popularity, I expected that the subgroup of assemblages containing examples of multiple design would have a higher proportion of linear punctate and incised vessels than would the subgroup lacking specimens with multiple designs. The data uphold this expectation: all of the assemblages with multiple design vessels are characterized by linear punctate and/or incised vessel fractions of no less than 28 percent (mean = 45 percent), while half of the assemblages lacking multiple design vessels have linear punctate or incised vessel fractions less than 20 percent (mean = 31 percent). Two assemblages in the latter subgroup have linear punctate or incised percentages that exceed the maximum percent of the former subgroup. These exceptions exemplify the overall diversity of the subgroup, which is characterized by marked variation in the proportions of plain, separate punctate, linear punctate, and incised vessels. Also noteworthy is the abundance of simple stamped vessels in two of the seven assemblages in the subgroup. The lack of multiple design elements, erratic values among the punctated and incised vessels, and the reappearance of simple stamped vessels set this subgroup apart from the others.

To summarize, the sorting of assemblages on the basis of thickened and flanged-lip plain vessels, linear punctate and incised designs, and the incidence of multiple design elements yields three distinct assemblage groups. The sorting criteria employed to arrive at these groupings are summarized in Figure 10. A breakdown of site components by the groupings outlined in Figure 10 is provided in Table 5.

It remains now to evaluate the component breakdown with available radiocarbon dates and to establish absolute temporal parameters for the groups. A total of fifteen radiocarbon dates from nine components in the sample is available to evaluate the classification. As depicted in Figure 11, the dates lend supporting evidence to the temporal arrangement of groups deduced from stratigraphic data.

Among components in Group I, only the Rabbit Mount shell midden and Rae's Creek assemblages have been securely dated, although the latter yielded a series of dates that span nearly six centuries. Each of the samples from Rae's Creek was taken from different portions of a well-defined cultural stratum, and they produced dates that reflect their relative stratigraphic order (Crook 1990:38). The older dates, 4370±110 and 4100±110 B.P., were obtained from level-provenience charcoal samples at the base of the stratum, and a date of 3800±70 B.P. was obtained from a similar sample in the middle of the stratum. Because this stratum was overlain by a stratum containing later Woodland pottery, as well as Stallings material, it seems likely that some contamination from later occupations is reflected in the late date.

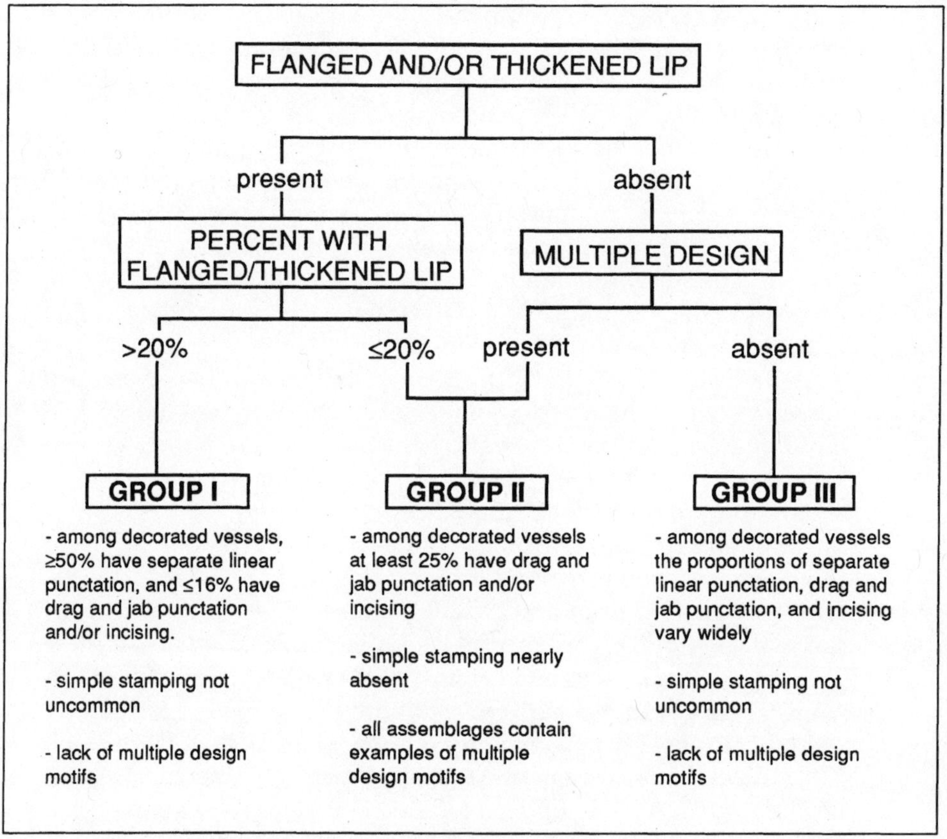

Figure 10. Paradigmatic classification of fiber-tempered pottery assemblages based on incidence of flanged/thickened lips and multiple designs.

The final date for Group I is from a shallow subsurface context outside Sapelo Ring No. 1. This date supports the conclusion that some Group I components postdate 4300 B.P. and may even be later than 3900 B.P. Two additional dates from Sapelo Ring No. 1 (3800±350 and 3600±350 B.P.) cannot be fully accepted because of the uncertainty of sample provenience (simply stated as being from "a late Archaic level with plain fiber-tempered pottery" [Williams 1968c:329]). If these assays date the onset of shell ring accumulation, their average of 3700±250 B.P. (Williams 1968c:329) would result in a span of 3950–3450 B.P. for this Group I component.

Table 5.
Component Groupings Based on Paradigmatic Classification

Group I	*Group II*	*Group III*
White's Mound	Chesterfield	9CH14a
Fennel Hill	McCalla Bottom	9CH114
Rabbit Mount—nonshell midden	38MC479	WV Site 23
Rabbit Mount—shell midden	Fish Haul—Feature 21	Daw's Island
9CH111	Cane Patch—Upper	Fish Haul—Feature 18
Rocky Ford	Cane Patch—Lower	Tinker Creek
Rae's Creek	Sapelo Ring No. 1—Upper	A. Busch Krick—Upper
Sapelo Ring No. 1—Lower	WV Site 14	
WV Site 18	Theriault	
	A. Busch Krick—Lower	
	Stallings Island	

Five components in Group II have radiocarbon dates. Dates for four of these fall within a six-hundred-year span from 3900 to 3300 B.P. Another date of 4290±120 B.P. on material from a shell-filled pit at WV Site 14 is especially early and would fit more comfortably within Group I. The sitewide assemblage of surface-collected pottery employed to characterize the WV Site 14 has few of the characteristics of Group I assemblages, however. Thus either the date or the assemblage is anomalous. At the other extreme, the basal date from A. Busch Krick of 3190±140 B.P. is later than any other component date in the sample. Because an earlier date of 3470±85 B.P. was obtained on material above the midden base, stratigraphy at the site may be disturbed. Lower and upper components of A. Busch Krick are split by the classification into Groups II and III, respectively. If the radiocarbon dates from this site approximate the entire span of occupation,

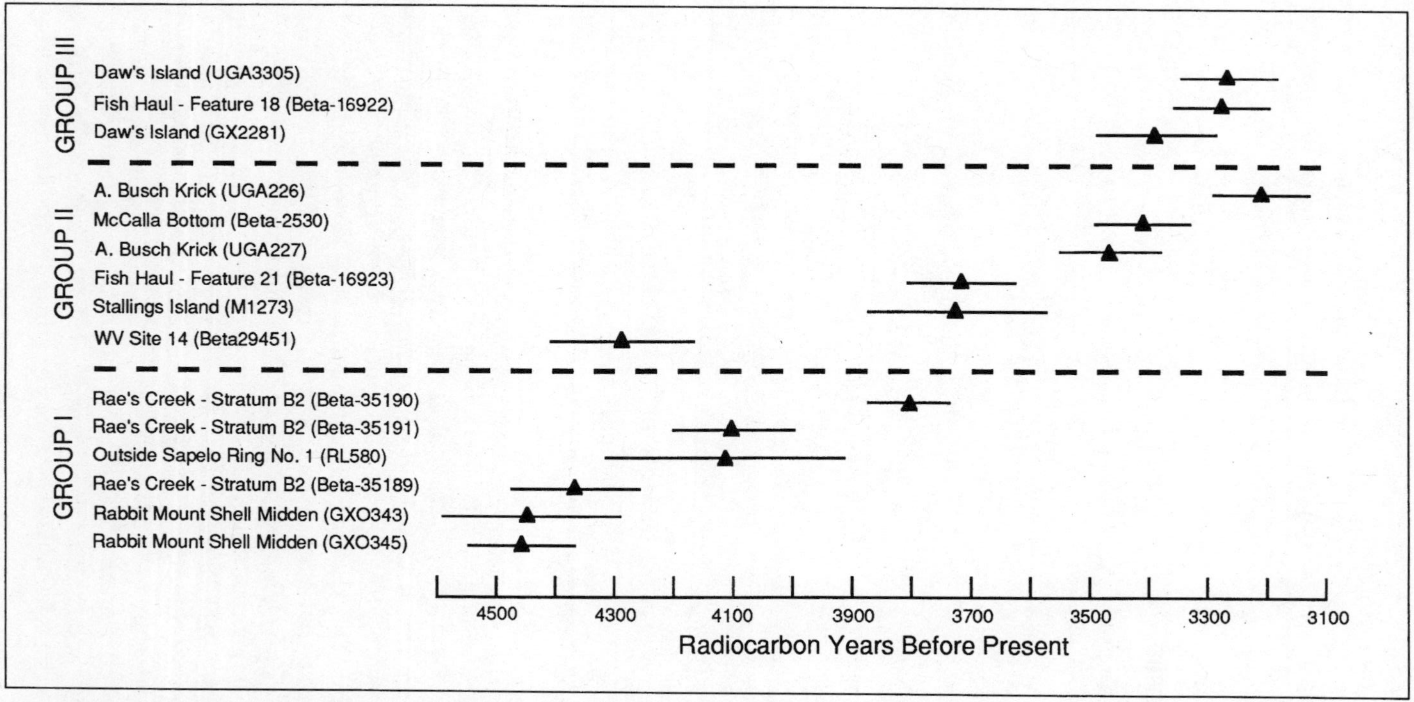

Figure 11. Radiocarbon dates and ranges (± one standard deviation) for sites in sample grouped by paradigmatic classes.

then the younger date adds support to the time span inferred from dates of other Group III components.

Three dates from two Group III components constitute a span of roughly three hundred years from 3500 to 3200 B.P. The oldest and youngest dates refer to one site, Daw's Island. The older date from Daw's Island has a range that overlaps with the date ranges of McCalla Bottom and A. Busch Krick from Group II. In the lack of thickened and flanged lips on plain vessels, Group III and late Group II assemblages are alike. Nonetheless, the lack of multiple design techniques on individual vessels of Group III sets these assemblages apart from their predecessors.

In sum, the paradigmatic classification provides an effective means of placing vessel assemblages into relative chronological order. The resultant groups (I–III) can therefore be related to temporal phases. Assemblages dating to the initial phase (Phase I), beginning by at least 4500 B.P., come primarily from Coastal Plain and Fall Zone locations. They are characterized by a high proportion of plain vessels, many with thickened and flanged lips. Decorative techniques are relatively simple, though each element of later techniques, with the exception of punctation over incision/grooving, is present. Examples of coastal sites with similar assemblages appear later (ca. 4200 B.P.) in this earliest phase and are characterized by a high incidence of plain vessels, also with a high proportion of thickened and flanged lips. Coastal sites dating to the early part of this phase may be buried beneath marsh sediment.

A terminal date for this initial phase is problematical because of the lack of early fourth-millennium radiocarbon ages. It may have continued as late as 3800–3700 B.P. in certain areas, as others have argued, but until more evidence is amassed, this remains speculative. If so, the interval described would encompass the Stallings II phase defined by Stoltman (1974) and the Bilbo/St. Simons I phases used on the Georgia coast (DePratter 1979a:114).

By about 3800 B.P., the accepted onset of the Stallings III and Bilbo/St. Simons II phases (DePratter 1979a:114; Stoltman 1974), vessel decoration began to dominate. Drag and jab linear punctation became common on the South Carolina coast and at the mouth of the Savannah River, while incising, sometimes with punctation, dominated assemblages from coastal Georgia. Some of the vessels from interior and coastal sites alike exhibit use of multiple decorative techniques. Thickened and flanged lips of the earlier centuries waned in popularity during the mid-fourth millennium and completely disappeared by 3400 B.P. The interval of 3800–3400 B.P. is defined as Phase II for the purposes of this study.

The final phase of fiber-tempered pottery in the study area began at or slightly before 3400 B.P. and is characterized by extreme variability among assemblages and the limited expansion of fiber-tempered pottery into the upper Piedmont. Few regularities in the types and proportions of vessel surface treatments are evident, but no assemblages contain examples of multiple design techniques. Certain assemblages contain high proportions of plain vessels, dispelling the belief that such assemblages are exclusively early in the sequence. These are distinguished from earlier assemblages of plain pottery by a complete lack of thickened or flanged lips. This final temporal interval, defined here as Phase III and spanning 3400–3000 B.P., has heretofore not been recognized as a distinct phase.

The classification duplicates many of the generalized trends implied or explicitly defined in previous attempts at cultural-historical reconstruction. It adds a new variable to the sequence—changes in the lip form of plain vessels—that allows for the relative dating of early assemblages. It also results in the recognition of a late phase of fiber-tempered pottery during which plain vessels were again common and many intraregional regularities in vessel surface finish disappeared.

On the basis of the documented stratigraphic patterns and supporting radiocarbon dates of the observed pottery changes, it may be possible to put components of each of the phases into relative order. I hesitate to do this, however, because of the lack of sample comparability across components, particularly the lack of intrasite stratigraphic control and radiocarbon dates for sites that were undoubtedly locations of repeated, long-term occupation. The need for better chronological control notwithstanding, the phase definitions and temporal classification presented in this chapter are more than sufficient as a foundation for the technofunctional and distributional analyses reported in the next two chapters.

CHAPTER 5

Innovations in Late Archaic Cooking Technology

Late Archaic cooking technologies in the Savannah River Valley have been described as alternative means of boiling foods (Anderson and Joseph 1988:201; Goodyear 1988). In general, boiling or other types of moist cooking such as simmering are argued to be techniques of food preparation that developed in conjunction with durable, fire-resistant containers. Moist cooking indeed represented a significant improvement over other techniques of cooking by permitting hunter-gatherers to include foods that were otherwise too costly or impractical (e.g., seeds, small gastropods; Goodyear 1988) and by increasing the nutritional value of traditional foods (e.g., bone grease; Waring 1968b). Pottery is cited as the innovation that enabled boiling techniques to be used (e.g., Loofs-Wissowa 1980) or replaced non-ceramic containers to improve the effectiveness of boiling (e.g., Cordell 1984:216). The presumed advantage of ceramic containers over most nonceramic alternatives is that pots can be set directly over fire or coals to heat the contents.

In their comparative study, Harold E. Driver and William C. Massey (1957:229) note that probably all North American Indian groups boiled foods, some more than others. Two major boiling techniques are known: "direct fire boiling, where a vessel containing liquid is set over or beside a fire; [and] stone-boiling, where stones are first heated in a fire and then immersed in the liquid" (Driver and Massey 1957:229). The use of ceramic vessels did not necessarily preclude the technique of stone boiling or stone cooking. Examples of stone cooking using low-fired clay containers are known from the American Northwest, leading Kenneth Reid (1989) to argue that indirect cooking techniques employing low-fired pottery may have been prevalent among prehistoric hunters and gatherers. This is an important observation for it suggests that although pottery may represent a substantial technological improvement over alternative containers for direct-heat moist cooking, not all cooking vessels were designed for this technique.

The Savannah River Valley region was home to innovations in stone cooking and ceramic vessel technology during the Late Archaic period. Perforated soapstone slabs or disks were manufactured for use and distribution in the valley before the advent of pottery, and this cooking stone technology persisted through a long period of pottery use. Direct-heat cooking with pottery eventually replaced stone cooking, but it is not yet clear whether pots were wholesale substitutes for other indirect cooking containers or were at times and in places used as containers for stone cooking. Direct evidence for the use of fiber-tempered vessels over fire (i.e., soot) has recently been observed in an assemblage of sherds from coastal Georgia (Skibo, Hally, and Schiffer 1988). The lack of similar evidence in an assemblage of sherds from Stallings Island (Skibo, Hally, and Schiffer 1988) suggests that stone cooking with ceramic vessels may have taken place. Further analyses are needed to document the regional incidence of alternative cooking technologies and to determine where and when innovations in such technologies took place. To foreshadow the results of my analysis, I provide evidence to show that the innovation of direct-heat cooking with pots and innovations to improve the effectiveness of this technique took place first on the coast, where the costs of alternative techniques were high because of the lack of lithic materials. Conversely, where soapstone was abundant, traditional techniques of stone cooking persisted long after pottery was adopted. These patterns of use have economic causes, but they also have social explanations, especially with regard to the persistence of traditional soapstone technology.

In this chapter I document innovations in Late Archaic cooking technology, using properties of mechanical performance, use alteration, and association to infer functions of various technologies. Functional parameters relevant to the Late Archaic innovations are established from ethnographic, experimental, and archaeological data. Unfortunately, local hunter-gatherer economies had vanished long before Europeans recorded accounts of native cooking so ethnohistorical data from the Southeast are of limited value to this study. As an alternative, the ethnographic literature on California tribes is pertinent because there are parallels between it and the Late Archaic record of the Savannah River Valley in soapstone, "baked clay," and ceramic cooking technologies and in ecology, demography, and socioeconomic organization (Anderson 1985).

Indirect Cooking with Stone

Most North American hunter-gatherer archaeological sites in stone-rich environments contain fragmented stone that archaeologists loosely refer to as "fire-cracked rock." Although this class of artifact appears to be present during all periods in the Eastern Woodlands, it is especially abundant at sites dating to the Late Archaic period (e.g., Chapman 1977:103; House 1975:68; Morse 1967:165; White 1982; Winters 1969:81–88). In these contexts, fire-cracked rock is attributed to hearths, earth ovens, and, most frequently, stone cooking (e.g., House 1975:68; Ozker 1982; Wobst 1968):

> The quantity of such stone seems to demonstrate the use of hot-rock cooking. Seemingly river pebbles of a wide variety of stone, and blocks of sandstone were placed in the fire for heating. When hot, these stones have been dropped into containers holding water. The water was boiled and the food cooked, perhaps by repeated operations. Such sudden cooling of the stones used for this purpose would eventually cause them to be broken and the fragments would be cast out in the debris. By some such process one may explain the considerable accumulation in the midden of broken sandstone and river pebbles showing fire action. [Webb 1946:242]

Experiments designed to explore possible functions of fire-cracked rock have been conducted by John H. House and James W. Smith (1975) and Paul Lorraine (1973). House and Smith (1975) attempted to define the types of use alteration produced under different cooking conditions (e.g., roasting vs. boiling), but the results were inconclusive. I am aware of no experimental work in North America that addresses the containers or techniques used in stone cooking or the foods being prepared this way. In lieu of such information, archaeologists most often depend on ethnographic descriptions of this cooking technique.

Ethnographic Descriptions of Stone Cooking

Ethnographic data on Native Americans indicates that stone cooking was the chief means of heating liquids in the western subarctic, Northwest coast and plateau, and California (Driver and Massey 1957:229, 232). Heating liquids with hot rocks was part of both food processing and food serving among many California groups. Acorn meal was usually leached in sand basins by repeated washes of cold and hot water (e.g., Gayton 1948:178). To prepare acorn mush, a staple food, for consumption, rocks were heated in a fire, lifted out with two sticks, and dropped into a basket containing acorn meal and water. Some accounts mention that hot rocks were quickly dipped in separate water to remove ash and dirt before being placed in cooking baskets (Ebeling 1986:216; Gayton 1948:178). Rocks had to be stirred to prevent them from burning holes in the basket and to ensure even heating (Gayton 1948:178–79; Kroeber 1925:87). Lila M. O'Neale's (1932:48) account of Yurok and Karok basketry indicates that cooking baskets usually broke where hot rocks partially burned through the walls.

In addition to its use for leaching and cooking acorn meal, stone cooking was the preferred way of cooking a variety of plant foods and a limited number of animal products in California (Ebeling 1986:123, 163–84). In the Northwest, nuts, animal bone, and fish were processed for oils and grease with the technique (Johnson 1969; Krause 1956; Reid 1989). In the Plains, Great Basin, and eastern subarctic both direct boiling and stone cooking were employed to prepare a variety of foods, and among some of the southern groups, stone cooking in baskets persisted long after pottery was available (Driver and Massey 1957:229).

Stone cooking with baskets may have been more laborious than direct fire boiling with pots, but if abundant stones were available, the process could be fairly quick (Driver and Massey 1957:231). An account of the preparation of Chuckchansi acorn mush supports this generalization:

> The fine meal which was cooked first was put in a cooking basket and some hot water was poured over it and stirred up; the mixture was quite thin like milk. The water was boiling hot: it took three hot stones to boil a basket of water. Then hot stones were put in this acorn gruel to cook it; they were stirred constantly to prevent burning the bottom of

> the basket. This process was continued for two to three minutes. Each time a cooking stone was lifted out the mush was scraped from it to prevent waste. The gruel became thicker in cooking. [Gayton 1948:178–79]

Cooking fish at a Kutenai festival took a similarly short time:

> Around a fire fifty feet long, partially overlaid with stones the size of turkey's eggs, eighty men range themselves; each man is provided with an osier vessel, cemented with gum and filled with water and fish. . . . Each one, armed with two sticks flattened at the extremity, makes use of them instead of tongs, to draw the stones from the embers, and put them in his kettle. This process is twice renewed, and in the space of five minutes the fish are cooked. [Johnson 1969:62–63]

Stone Cooking in the Savannah River Valley Region

The archaeological record of preceramic Late Archaic stone cooking in the Savannah River Valley region is limited to the remains of what are presumed to be cooking stones, for there is little that can be said about the containers used or methods of cooking. Fractured rock, typically quartz and quartzite, is abundant at sites across the Piedmont and Fall Zone (White 1982). Even in the relatively stone-poor Coastal Plain, Late Archaic sites often contain the fractured remains of quartz cobbles obtained from deeply buried, ancient marine deposits (e.g., Sassaman 1987). Elsewhere in the Coastal Plain and especially on the coast, clay alternatives to rock, so-called baked clay objects, are common items in Late Archaic assemblages. The extent to which fractured rock and baked clay objects reflect cooking activities remains unknown, but if only a small fraction of these materials was produced from stone cooking, we are safe to assume that the technique was important to Late Archaic subsistence.

Perforated Soapstone Slabs

That a stone-cooking technique was indeed central to Late Archaic subsistence technology is evident in the development of an important innovation around 5000 B.P. At this time in the Savannah River Valley we find the earliest use of perforated soapstone slabs or disks, items thought to have been used in moist cooking, among perhaps other cooking activities. Whole and fragmented examples of these artifacts are illustrated in Figure 12.

The Function(s) of Perforated Soapstone Slabs. That soapstone slabs served a stone cooking function is a relatively recent interpretation and is still shadowed by the traditional "net sinker" hypothesis. C. C. Jones referred to soapstone net sinkers in his compendium of prehistoric artifacts, noting two varieties in the Middle Savannah River Valley: perforated slabs such as those in Figure 12 and amorphous lumps encircled by a groove (Jones 1873:337). Commenting on the abundance of the perforated variety at Stallings Island, Claflin wrote: "That both of these classes of objects were used as net sinkers seems the most logical explanation of their existence in such large quantities, over 2500 of the flat perforated variety being found. In some cases considerable care was used in the manufacture of this latter type. . . . It seems strange that the Stalling's Island people preferred the perforated kind of net sinker, when the grooved variety needed much less work to make and presumably gave the desired results" (Claflin 1931:32). Because fishing was believed to be an important subsistence pursuit of the Stallings Island people (Claflin 1932:12; Wauchope 1966:192), the net sinker interpretation seemed a reasonable conclusion at a time when Late Archaic investigations were confined to riverine and coastal locations.

Presaged by Claflin's doubts about the function of perforated soapstone slabs, recent analyses and experiments have undermined the net sinker interpretation. It has been noted that although soapstone is soft and easy to carve, it is highly susceptible to fracture on impact, a property that would limit its usefulness as a tool subjected to the saltation or simple impact on channel beds (Dagenhardt 1972:66; Wood et al. 1986:324). It was also noted that most soapstone slabs are broken at one or more points of perforation, damage that would have resulted in their deposition in rivers, not habitation sites (Cook n.d.; Wood et al. 1986:324). Finally, appreciable numbers of soapstone slabs began to be found at upland sites far removed from streams sufficiently large for net fishing (Moody, Carter, and Beard 1985; Trinkley 1974).

As the credibility of the net sinker hypothesis diminished, several lines of argument were forwarded to support an interpretation that soapstone slabs were used as cooking stones. Johnny R. Dagenhardt (1972) conducted a preliminary experiment to document the superior

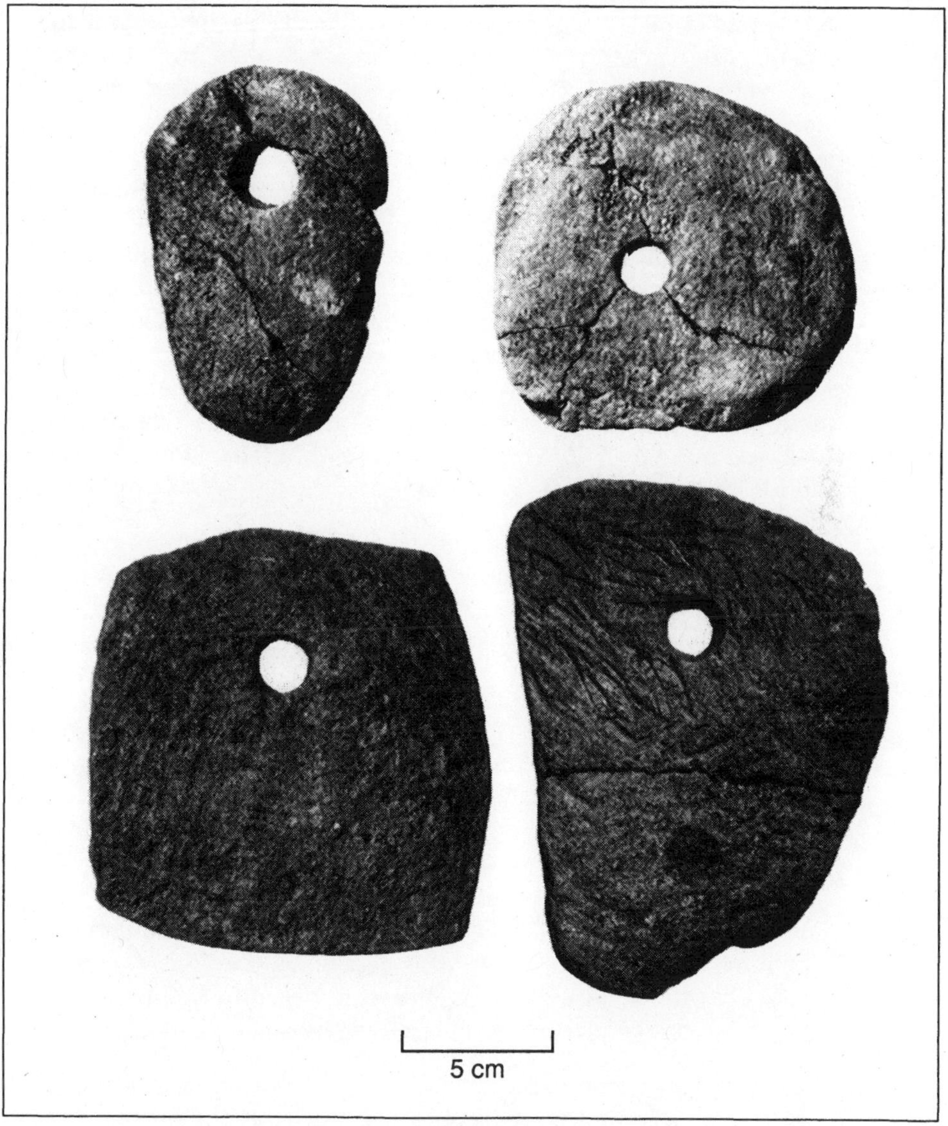

Figure 12. Examples of whole perforated soapstone slabs.

thermal shock resistance of soapstone. Unlike the raw materials in the generic "fire-cracked rock," soapstone, because of its low shrinkage and low thermal conductivity, is able to withstand repeated cycles of heating and cooling with little to no damage. Archaeological support for its use as a cooking stone has been found in the spatial association among soapstone slabs, fire-cracked rock, and hearth features (Anderson, Schuldenrein, and Cantley 1985:239; Anderson and Joseph 1988:200). Traces of thermal alteration in the form of discoloration and particle attrition are also common to slab fragments.

Further support for this interpretation is found in the ethnographic literature of certain California tribes. Most notable is the record of coastal Chumash material culture compiled by Hudson and Blackburn (1983). They draw from accounts by John P. Harrington (1942) and make the following observations about soapstone "boiling stones":

> Boiling stones were made of steatite [*soapstone*] on purpose, not from broken bowls. They were as thick as a board, some as big as a sheet of paper. There was a hole in them for a lifting stick to handle them with. They were also good for baking on.
>
> [*A boiling stone*] was a slab of stone with a little hole in it for putting the end of a stick in for handling when hot. Used these in boiling acorn mush in a cooking basket. When an olla [*soapstone vessel*] broke they sometimes made the boiling stone from the pieces.
>
> The stones Mrs. Richardson has are made for heating mush. Put the meal and water in a big *watik* [cooking basket] (2 feet high) and have these rocks heating in the fire till red hot and put in sometimes as many as four at a time to make it boil. Make ollas of the same kind of rock (steatite). [All quotes from Harrington 1942:9 cited in Hudson and Blackburn 1983:183–84; italicized bracketed al remarks mine.]

Soapstone was also exploited by interior California groups for cooking stones, as well as small vessels, ornaments, and other items. Boiling stones were made exclusively of soapstone among the Nisenan (Southern Maidu) of the north-central Sierra Nevada (Beals 1933:352). Soapstone was the preferred material for boiling stones among the Chuckchansi (Yokut) of the northern foothills of the Sierra because it did not fracture like other rocks and "spoil the food" (Gayton 1948:190).

Intensive use of soapstone cooking stones in ethnographic California appears to have been restricted to locations near sources of the material, primarily on and around Santa Catalina Island, the northern foothills of the Sierra Nevada, and minor interior locations of the south-central region. Unmodified soapstone, soapstone vessels, ornaments, and other items were exchanged throughout the region, but soapstone cooking-stone technology remained localized. The same might be said of soapstone slabs in the Savannah River Valley region. The key difference between the two regions, however, is that the geological distribution of soapstone in the East appears to have had little to do with the regional distribution of perforated slabs. In locations where soapstone was abundant and used for vessels and other items (Midsouth, western Georgia, the mid-Atlantic, and New England), a soapstone cooking-stone technology similar to that of the Savannah River Valley never emerged. The Savannah marks the center of a localized distribution that extends only as far west and south as the Oconee-Ocmulgee-Altamaha drainage of central Georgia and perhaps not much farther north and east than southern North Carolina. Nowhere within this area are soapstone slabs more abundant than in the Savannah River Valley.

The Distribution of Soapstone Slabs in the Savannah River Valley. Little is known about the function of soapstone slabs in the Savannah River Valley, but there has been some empirical support for broad spatial and temporal trends in the use of the technology. Two basic patterns have been inferred: first, that slabs were used before the advent of ceramic vessels and became obsolete or gradually declined after pots were adopted (Crusoe and DePratter 1976; Elliott and Doyon 1981:99; Wood et al. 1986:324); and second, that the frequency of soapstone slabs at archaeological sites decreases sharply the farther they are from quarries (Anderson and Joseph 1988:199; Stoltman 1972:46; Wood et al. 1986:324). I will return to the first of these inferences in the later section on pottery. Here I will explore the effects of quarry distance on soapstone use.

Twenty cases in the sample of thirty-seven assemblages contain a total of 3,406 soapstone artifacts and debris (Table 6). Slab or disklike pieces with a perforation or portion of one amount to 473 specimens, while another 590 pieces are fragments of slabs lacking traces of perforation. Most of the miscellaneous soapstone debris in these assemblages is probably weathered or reworked pieces of slabs, with

Table 6.
Soapstone Artifact Inventory Tabulated by Artifact Class and Assemblage

Site	*Soapstone w/ perf.*	*Slab/slab frag. w/o perf.*	*Vessel sherd*	*Atlatl weight*	*Other worked*	*Unident. fragment*	*Total*	*Weight (g)*
38AK158	3	0	1	0	0	64	68	771.6
38AK288	2	0	0	0	0	2	4	43.2
9JF21	1	1	0	0	0	0	2	151.4
9RI137	0	0	2	0	0	0	2	367.5
Cal Smoak	4	4	0	0	0	13	21	461.0
Daw's Island	6	3	1	0	0	1	11	902.0
Fennel Hill	17	18	0	0	0	1	36	1,173.2
Lewis-East	22	23	0	0	0	15	60	1,746.5
McCalla Bottom	5	2	37	0	0	529	573	2,466.3
Moody	56	31	0	7	4	28	126	8,660.4
Paris Island	78	387	0	0	0	1,225	1,690	14,457.0
Rabbit Mount	47	37	0	0	0	4	88	2,266.0
Rae's Creek	17	11	0	1	0	32	61	4,121.6
Rocky River	41	22	0	0	0	329	392	2,656.7
Sara's Ridge*	25	0	0	0	0	0	25	-
Stallings Island	59	6	1	2	2	0	70	8,836.0
Theriault	51	19	2	1	2	11	86	4,517.1
Tinker Creek	1	5	2	0	0	5	13	174.9
White's Mound	37	21	7	0	0	12	77	1,917.7
WV14	1	0	0	0	0	0	1	28.4
TOTAL	473	590	53	11	8	2,271	3,406	55,718.5

*Sample based on count of perfortated slabs only; weight not recorded.

two exceptions: McCalla Bottom, the only sample with a substantial number of soapstone vessel sherds, and Moody, the only sample with a large number of soapstone atlatl weights.

There are several means by which to compare the relative abundance of soapstone slabs at sites. The simplest is to calculate the amount of soapstone per unit area for each site. This requires some estimate of the area excavated at each site, a requirement that reduces the sample size to twelve assemblages. To this list two sites can be added for which total weight of soapstone and area excavated are available in the literature, 9RI86 and 9RI88 (Elliott and Doyon 1981). The necessary figures for each of the fourteen assemblages are provided in Table 7. Included here are measures of the linear distance between sites and the nearest documented location of soapstone procurement. The quarry used for calculations of Fall Zone and Coastal Plain sites is 9CB23; the Piedmont source is located three kilometers to the south of Paris Island.

In Figure 13 the sites are arranged from left to right in order of increasing linear distance from a quarry. Assuming that the relative abundance of soapstone is largely a function of distance from quarries (e.g., Elliott 1981), the shape of the soapstone histogram should be an inverse image of the distance curve. Generally this is true, but there is considerable variation in the abundance of soapstone independent of distance. Analytical and behavioral sources of this variation can be cited. Analytically, the comparison of soapstone abundance at sites suffers from biases in the samples. Artifact recovery techniques differed from site to site. Deposits that were passed through quarter-inch screens (all but two) yielded a greater number of small fragments than did those that were only troweled through (Fennel Hill and Rabbit Mount). Furthermore, excavation area at some sites, notably Lewis-East and White's Mound, exceeded the spatial limits of Late Archaic deposits, while others were restricted to dense deposits of Late Archaic refuse (e.g., Rabbit Mount and Rae's Creek). A different analytical problem is that additional sources of soapstone were probably exploited, and it is naive to assume that routes of transport or exchange were linear.

Conservation of soapstone at sources away from quarries has a large impact on the formation of soapstone assemblages. Elliott and Roy Doyon (1981:165) have noted that the incidence of multiple perforations on soapstone slabs (Figure 14) increases with distance from quarries (see also Wood et al. [1986:282]). Reperforation is

Table 7.
Data on Soapstone Slabs Used in Calculations of Histograms in Figures 13, 15–20

Assemblage	*Quarry distance (km)*	*Area excavated* (m^2)	*Soapstone weight (g)*	*Density* (g/m^2)	*% Slabs w/ multiple perforations*	*Mean # perforations per slab*	*Adjusted MNI per* m^2	*Mean wt. slab frag. (g)*	*Mean slab thk. (mm)*
Paris Island	3	109	14,457.0	132.6	0.0	1.00	0.7	-	19.97
Rocky River	5	88	2,656.7	30.2	4.0	1.04	0.3	88.73	14.90
McCalla Bottom	9	93	2,466.3	26.5	-	-	-	-	-
Stallings Island	18	-	8,836.0	-	6.8	1.07	-	145.18	19.10
Moody	19	-	8,660.4	-	7.1	1.07	-	104.94	19.14
Rae's Creek	24	18	4,121.6	229.0	5.9	1.06	0.9	243.18	19.13
9RI86	31	24	7,227.7	301.2	-	-	-	-	-
Sara's Ridge	32	369	-	-	4.0	1.04	0.1	-	16.45
9RI88	33	52	2,560.7	49.2	-	-	-	-	-
White's Mound	46	84	1,917.7	22.8	13.5	1.14	0.4	48.24	15.22
Lewis–East	61	348	1,746.5	5.0	22.7	1.23	0.1	72.57	15.96
38AK288	63	13	43.2	3.3	0.0	1.00	0.2	-	12.90
38AK158	64	142	771.6	5.4	0.0	1.00	0.0	215.07	28.37
Tinker Creek	67	56	174.9	3.1	-	-	-	-	-
Theriault	83	-	4,517.1	-	43.1	1.45	-	91.05	17.41
Fennel Hill	102	44	1,173.2	26.7	41.2	1.47	0.3	64.48	17.27
Rabbit Mount	124	51	2,266.0	44.4	22.6	1.26	0.5	85.17	17.58
Cal Smoak	132	37	461.0	12.5	0.0	1.00	0.1	130.47	20.70
WV14	168	-	28.4	-	-	-	-	28.40	-
Daw's Island	197	-	902.0	-	33.3	1.33	-	112.60	19.80

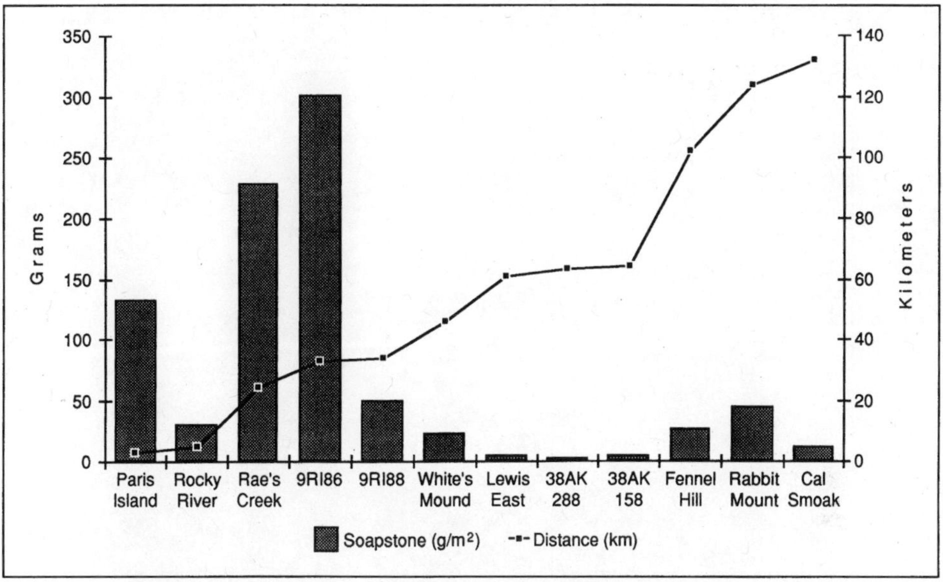

Figure 13. Soapstone weight (g) per square meter of excavation by distance from quarry (km).

argued to be a strategy for conserving soapstone at locations removed from sources (Elliott and Doyon 1981:165). Referring to the sample at hand, a positive relationship between distance and incidence of this conservation measure is apparent, whether measured by percent of perforated pieces with traces of additional perforation (Figure 15) or by mean number of perforations on pieces with perforations (Figure 16).

Conservation and recycling of soapstone slabs has the net effect of decreasing the size and weight of soapstone slab fragments that enter the archaeological record. For instance, many reperforated slab fragments have fracture planes that were ground to remove irregular edges. Material ground from these edges is, of course, irretrievable.

To obviate the biases of conservation on estimates of soapstone abundance, the minimum number of individual slabs (MNI) was calculated in several ways. Initially, this was attempted by finding all conjoins in an assemblage and then counting the number of slabs having more than one-half of a perforation (e.g., Wood et al. 1986:282). This approach proved to be conservative, as was especially

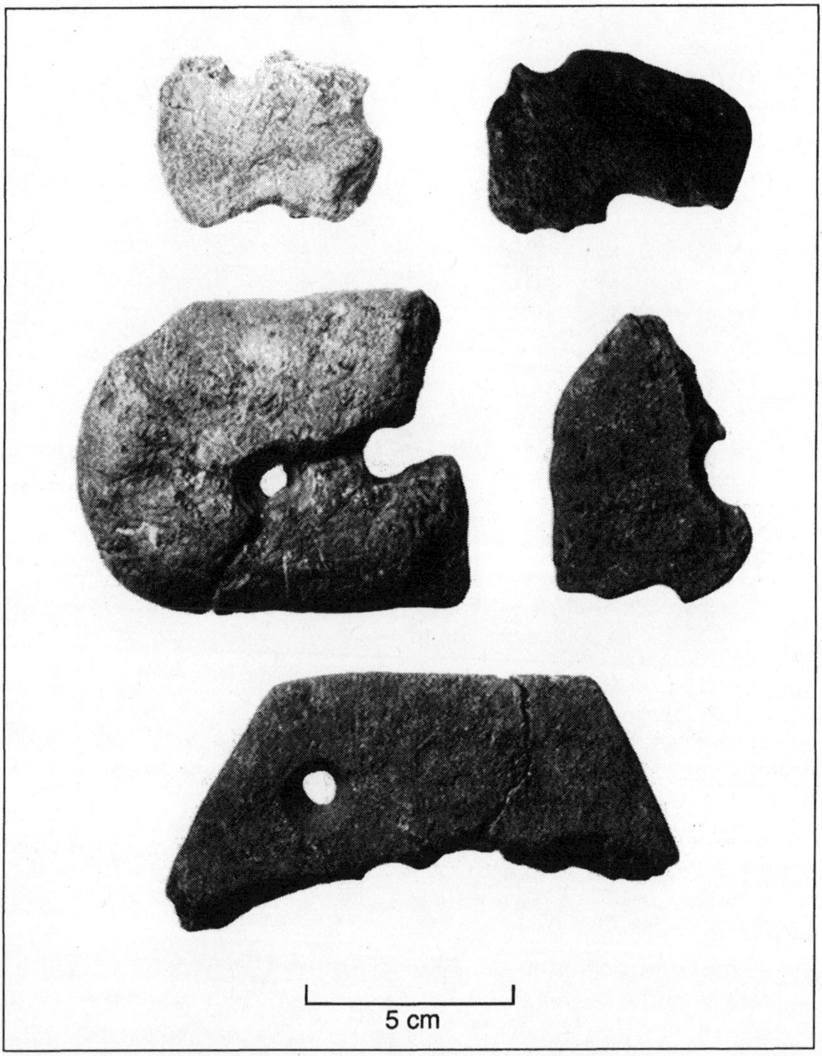

Figure 14. Examples of reperforated soapstone slabs.

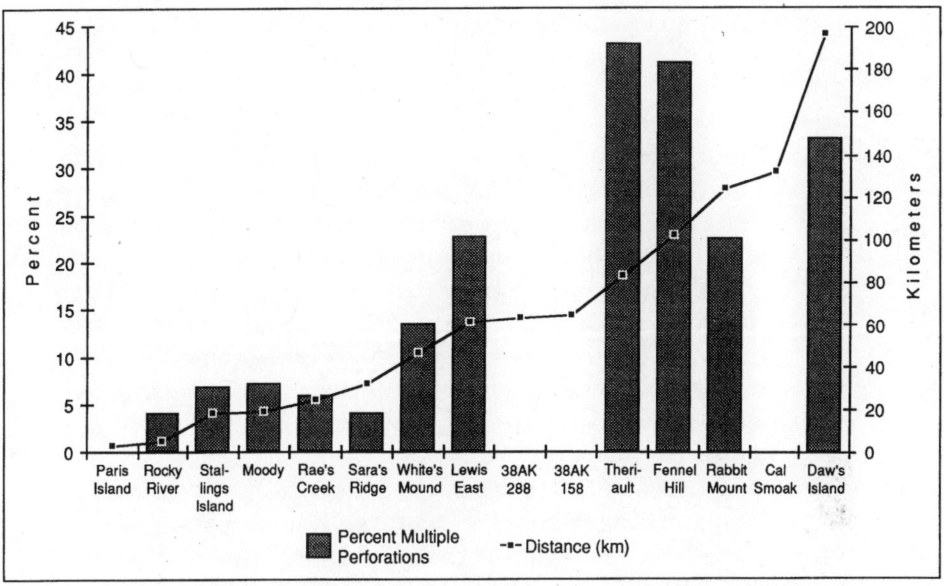

Figure 15. Percentage of soapstone slabs with multiple perforations by distance from quarry (km).

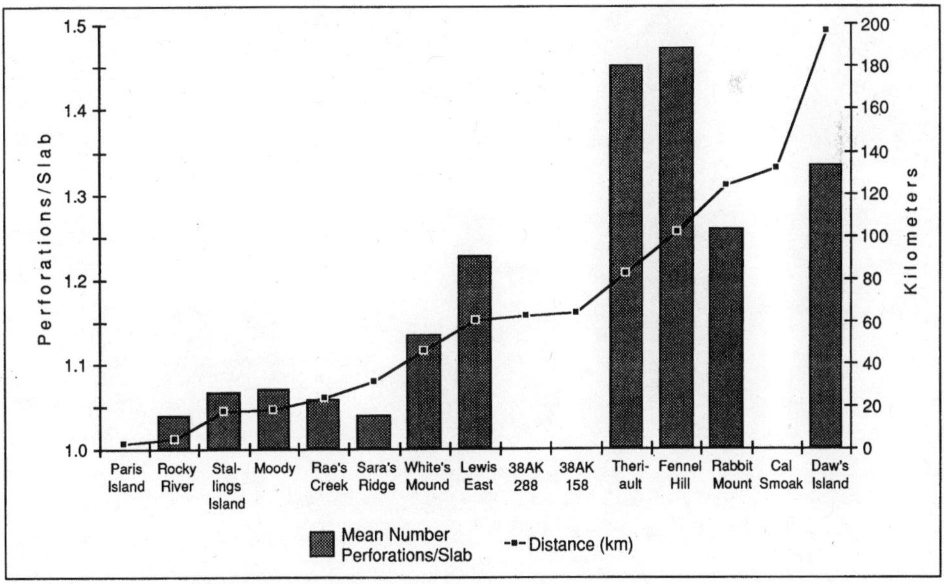

Figure 16. Mean number of perforations per slab by distance from quarry (km).

apparent within assemblages composed of diverse types of soapstone (i.e., from different outcrops) but which had few perforations over half complete. The alternative was to count all pieces with traces of perforation as individuals and then adjust by factoring in the incidence of reperforation. The logic here is that individual slabs include not only the original whole artifacts but also any fragment that can be reperforated and reused (i.e., a serviceable cooking stone). If a slab breaks at the perforation, which it usually does, the proposed MNI method would result in a count of two. Whether or not these hypothetical fragments were drafted into further use is a separate issue, but correction for inflation of the MNI in assemblages with reperforated slabs can be accomplished by dividing the mean number of perforations per perforated fragment into the total number of perforated fragments.

Soapstone slab densities based on adjusted MNIs show some interesting patterning (Figure 17). Predictably, sites closest to sources of soapstone have the highest density of slabs. The relatively high density of slabs at certain Coastal Plain sites, however, was unex-

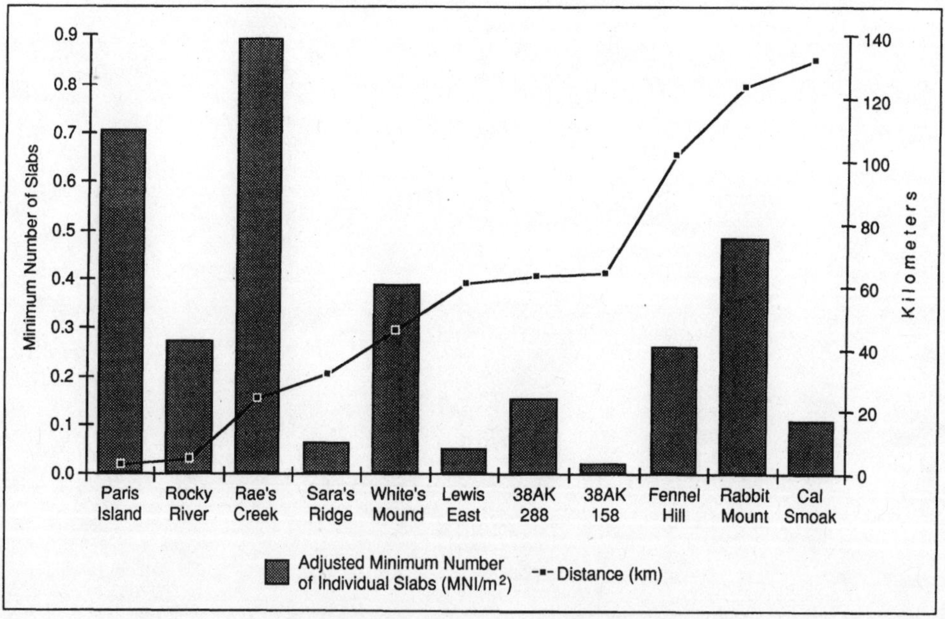

Figure 17. Minimum number of slabs per square meter of excavation by distance from quarry (km).

pected. Overall, the density of slabs is erratic, owing in part to the sample biases noted earlier, as well as possible temporal and functional differences between assemblages.

Taking a different tack, can the effect of distance on assemblages be discerned on the basis of the weight of slab fragments? The mean weight of all perforated pieces at least five centimeters long was calculated for each assemblage and plotted against distance (Figure 18). Fragments less than five centimeters were excluded to avoid the bias of differential recovery. The results show that mean slab fragment size at most Coastal Plain sites is not appreciably different from that at sites close to sources of soapstone. The three highest mean weights are from assemblages with unique biases: the Stallings Island sample consists of a high proportion (37 percent) of whole slabs; the Rae's Creek assemblage includes a cache of four exceptionally large, whole specimens; and the small sample (n = 3) from 38AK158 is skewed to the high end by one thick, whole specimen. Excluding these from consideration, the highest two mean values are from sites farthest removed from sources of soapstone, Cal Smoak and Daw's

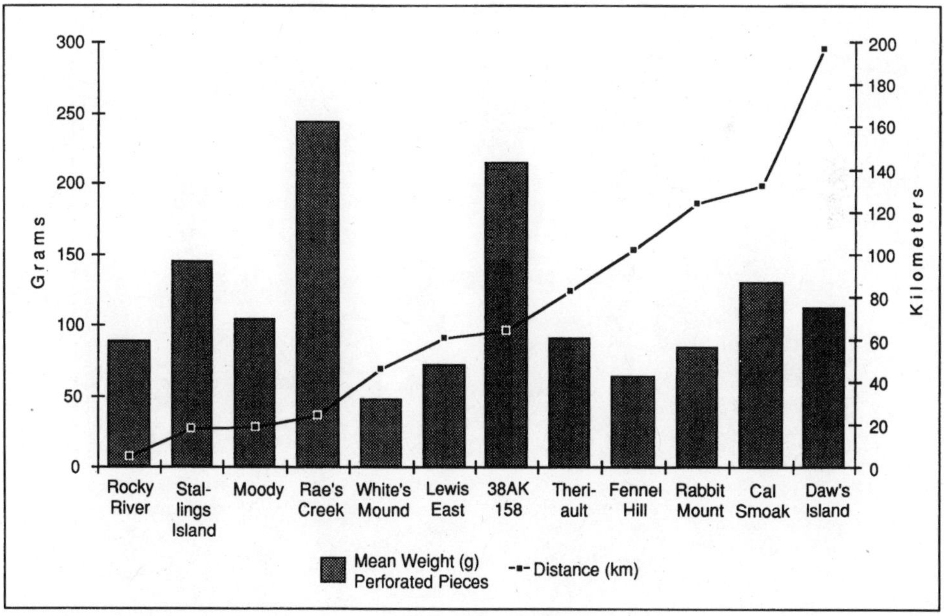

Figure 18. Mean weight (g) of perforated slab fragments by distance from quarry (km).

Island. There are potential biases because of recovery technique and sample size at these sites, but still Coastal Plain assemblages as a whole cannot be discriminated from those of the Piedmont and Fall Zone on the basis of the weight of slab fragments. What is more, adjustments of mean slab fragment weight based on incidence of reperforation (mean weight multipied by mean number perforations) suggest that within the Coastal Plain, mean slab weight actually increases with distance from the soapstone source (Figure 19). This may indicate that slabs brought into the Coastal Plain were larger on average than those used in the Piedmont and Fall Zone. These slabs, of course, broke and were often reperforated, but they appear to have entered the archaeological record at a weight that was on average larger than similarly broken though nonrecycled slabs close to soapstone sources. Accordingly, the design of slabs brought to the Coastal Plain seems to have incorporated the need and desire to conserve soapstone.

Anticipated conservation of soapstone could have been accommodated by slab design (as opposed to abundance) in several ways. One

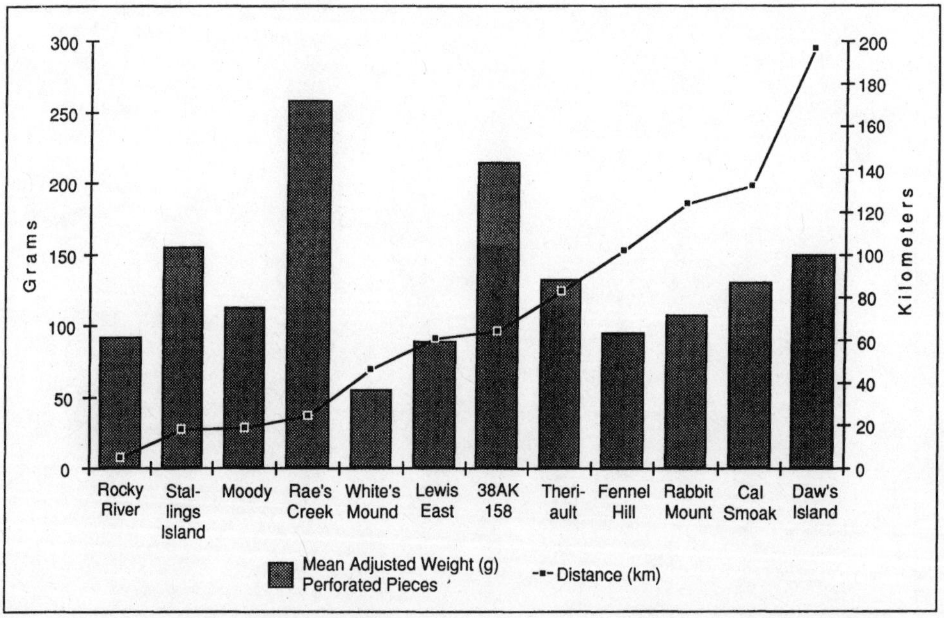

Figure 19. Mean adjusted weight (g) of perforated slab fragments by distance from quarry (km).

that can be readily examined is slab thickness. This variable, measured at the perforation (almost always the thickest portion of the slab), is least susceptible to sample biases so some of the assemblage samples excluded in earlier comparisons can be reintroduced into the analysis. If slab thickness was being manipulated to accommodate soapstone conservation, slab thickness should increase with distance from sources. This is not readily apparent in the sample at hand (Figure 20). It is nevertheless notable that three of the four largest means are from Coastal Plain sites, albeit ones with small sample sizes. Otherwise, the three middle Coastal Plain Savannah River sites in the sample (Rabbit Mount, Theriault, and Fennel Hill) have nearly identical means (17–18 mm thick), while the three Fall Zone assemblages (Stallings Island, Moody, and Rae's Creek) share values only slightly greater (ca. 19 mm) than the Coastal Plain examples. Compared to these modes, mean slab thickness is lower among other Piedmont assemblages (except Paris Island) and among those in the upper Coastal Plain (except 38AK158). Elliott and Doyon (1981:164) record a distinct difference between mean slab thickness at 9RI86 (18

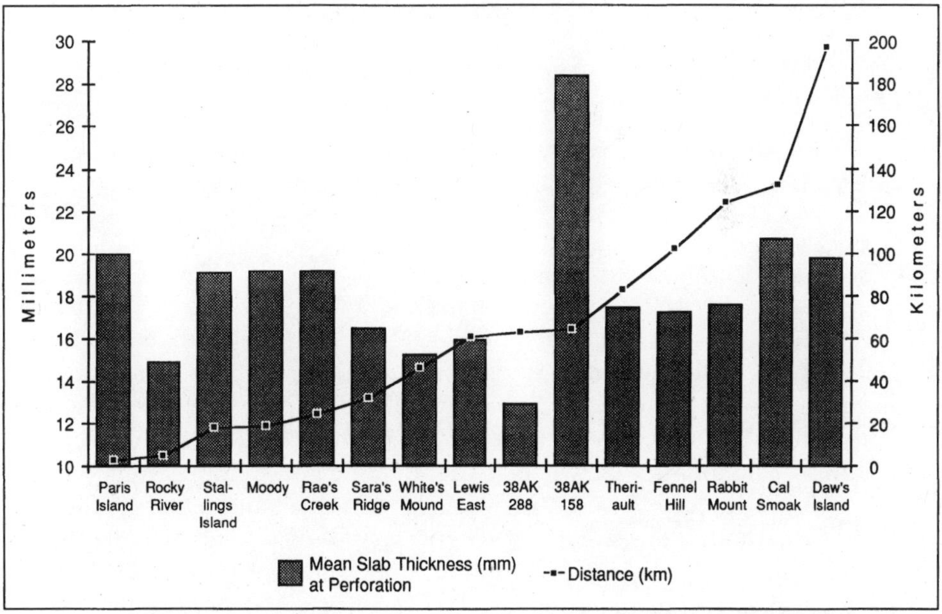

Figure 20. Mean thickness (mm) of slabs at perforation by distance from quarry (km).

mm) and at 9RI88 (12 mm), adjacent upper Coastal Plain sites. An explanation for this difference is not entertained, though temporal, functional, and social factors are mentioned. The present sample does not suggest a clear bimodal distribution between "thick" and "thin" slabs (Figure 20), though interassemblage differences are apparent.

A functional explanation for variation in slab thickness should not be overlooked. Properties of thermal retention and transfer may be especially relevant. In this regard, the ratio of surface area to mass will be critical to the rate of heat absorption and loss. Objects with a high surface area to mass ratio absorb and dissipate heat quicker than do objects with low ratios. Slab thickness may have been manipulated to achieve different rates of heating. If so, the remarkable uniformity of slab thickness across most assemblages in the sample suggests that an ideal design was achieved.

To summarize, a greater amount of soapstone is present in certain Coastal Plain assemblages than previously believed. Soapstone was conserved at locations away from sources, and this must be taken into account when comparing the volume of Coastal Plain and Piedmont assemblages. Larger and thicker slabs may have been purposefully designed for use away from sources of soapstone.

Baked Clay Objects

> Baked clay objects represent an invention, probably made more than once, in response to the household needs of a pottery-less people in a stone-less land.
>
> —Ford, Phillips, and Haag 1955:56

Baked clay objects consist of hand-molded lumps of fired clay that are often presumed to be the functional equivalent of cooking stones (Figure 21). The technology has been documented in at least three separate areas of North America: central California, the lower Mississippi Valley, and the south Atlantic Coastal Plain. In the western areas, baked clay objects were made and used long before pottery was widely adopted. This may also be true of the Savannah River Valley region, though the lack of preceramic coastal components limits the strength of this inference to minor evidence from interior Coastal Plain sites. As the quote above indicates, lithic raw material is limited or completely absent from areas where baked clay object technology developed. This is generally true of the Savannah River Valley region,

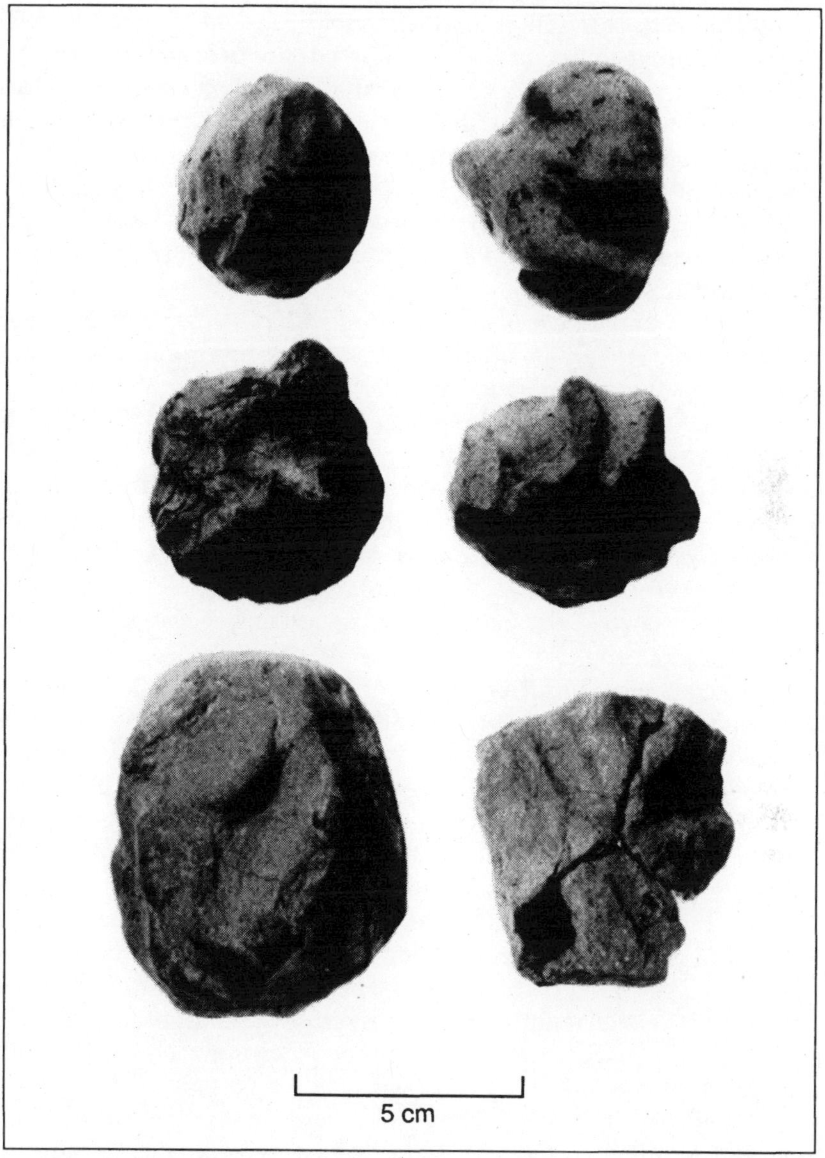

Figure 21. Examples of baked clay objects from Charles Towne (after South 1970:Figures 1, 5).

but an additional strategy for dealing with a lack of lithic raw material was the provisioning of Coastal Plain sites with soapstone. The two are not mutually exclusive; soapstone and baked clay objects have considerable geographical overlap at early sites in the Coastal Plain. This constitutes sufficient cause to question the "lithic substitute" argument for baked clay objects. Furthermore, the co-occurrence of baked clay objects and pottery in South Carolina and Georgia draws suspicion about the functional relationship between the two ceramic technologies.

Little is known about the function of baked clay objects. Those made in the stone-poor areas of central California seem to have filled a variety of needs that are usually met with lithic raw materials (Moratto 1984:171–73, 231–32; Schenck and Dawson 1929:359). The Plains Miwok, for instance, used baked clay as a lithic substitute for net weights, pipes, and cooking stones (Moratto 1984:173). Unfortunately, the ethnographic record does not indicate the cooking functions (i.e., boiling, roasting) baked clay objects served. Archaeological objects presumed to be used for cooking include a variety of shapes, though most were oblong spheroids measuring 75 x 40 x 30 millimeters (Schenck and Dawson 1929:362–64).

Baked clay objects from the lower Mississippi are less varied than those from California, being limited primarily to variations of the cooking stone ("ball") theme. Though less varied and generally smaller than the California types, those from Poverty Point and related sites conform to a well-defined set of morphological types (Ford, Phillips, and Haag 1955:39–43). Some types have grooves that presumably allowed for safe and easy transfer of the objects from the fire to the container or pit. Others lack grooving and some are quite small (3 cm diameter), suggesting that they were used in activities other than cooking (Ford, Phillips, and Haag 1955:56). Poverty Point objects have been reported from sites across the Gulf coastal plain and are often invoked as evidence for the extent of the Poverty Point interaction network.

Baked clay objects in South Carolina and Georgia lack the morphological specificity of the Poverty Point objects and hence are not usually described as such. Admittedly, few assemblages from South Carolina and Georgia contain sufficient numbers of intact baked clay objects to warrant typological studies. One exception is the assemblage of objects from Charles Towne (38CH1). Two basic types of objects are reported by Stanley A. South (1970), both differing from

Poverty Point objects in their massive size (i.e., up to 10 cm long and 7.5 cm thick) and in the use of perforations. The thicker, "melon-shaped" forms include some with grooves in addition to perforations, features similar to Poverty Point objects and perhaps related to their function as cooking stones. South (1970:6–7) posits an alternative function for these forms, that of an atlatl weight. He (1970:7) also describes one example of a perforated "biscuit" similar in form and size to perforated soapstone slabs, arguing that it may well have been a clay substitute for a cooking stone. Other assemblages from the Coastal Plain of South Carolina and Georgia contain examples of Charles Towne types (e.g., Anderson 1982:319–20; Southerlin 1989), but more typical is an amorphous lump of fired clay sometimes with traces of finger grooves and palm impressions and less often reed punctations.

Other than a few observations based on morphology, inferences about the function of baked clay objects center on context and association. The chief basis for functional inference is negative association: to paraphrase the quote above, baked clay objects are used in potteryless and stoneless contexts. Some of the Savannah River Valley data contradict this conclusion, though they are generally interpreted in its support. For example, stratigraphic evidence from Sapelo Ring No. 1 (Waring and Larson 1968:278) and Pagan Plum (DePratter 1979:44) indicates that baked clay objects were used less frequently over the course of occupation and apparently became obsolete by about 3700 B.P. Emphasis in interpreting these data is on the inference that pots replaced baked clay objects, an inference that implies functional equivalence between the two ceramic technologies. But many assemblages in the coast and Coastal Plain of South Carolina have baked clay objects and Thom's Creek or later pottery in direct association (Anderson n.d.; Anderson, Cantley, and Novick 1982; South 1970; Southerlin 1989; Trinkley 1980b), indicating that the former technology persisted late into the fourth millennium.

Similarly, baked clay objects and soapstone slabs are often described as having inverse geographic distributions (Anderson and Joseph 1988:200), a pattern that suggests they were nonoverlapping, functional equivalents. What is not generally appreciated is the wide geographic overlap of the two in the Coastal Plain (Table 8). Baked clay objects are common at Savannah River Valley Stallings sites as far inland as the Fall Zone (e.g., 9RI86, White's Mound, Rae's Creek), sites also noted for an abundance of soapstone slabs.

Table 8.
Presence or Absence of Soapstone Slabs and Baked Clay Objects at Late Archaic Sites by Physiographic Province

	Soapstone slabs	*Baked clay objects*
Piedmont sites		
Sara's Ridge	X	
McCalla Bottom	X	
Moody	X	
Rocky River	X	
Paris Island	X	
Stallings Island	X	
Coastal Plain sites		
Lewis-East	X	
Tinker Creek	X	
Rae's Creek	X	X
Lover's Lane	X	X
White's Mound	X	X
Fennel Hill	X	X
Rabbit Mount	X	X
WV14	X	X
Coastal sites		
Bilbo	X	X
Daw's Island	X	X
Fish Haul		X
9CH14a		X
9CH111		X
Sapelo Ring No.1		X

Speculation about the function of baked clay objects has not considered criteria of mechanical performance. For example, information on the thermal properties of baked clay objects would be helpful in determining their relative worth in moist cooking. Experiments designed to generate these data are beyond the scope of this study, but some preliminary observations on thermal shock resistance and heating effectiveness can be offered. First, we must consider the effects of various paste combinations on thermal shock resistance (e.g., Bronitsky and Hamer 1986; Rye 1981). Temper serves to impede cracking caused by the differential expansion and shrinkage of the ceramic body when subjected to rapid changes in temperature. This was recently documented in an experiment which showed that nontempered ceramics were less resistant to thermal shock than ceramics with sand or organic temper (Skibo, Schiffer, and Reid 1989:132–33). Because baked clay objects are generally temperless (Ford, Phillips, and Haag 1955:39; Schenck and Dawson 1929:362–64; South 1970:4; Trinkley 1986:210), they probably had low thermal shock resistance and would therefore be ineffective as substitutes for boiling stones. This property would, of course, be irrelevant under cooking conditions in which heat is dissipated slowly, such as pit roasting.

The heating effectiveness of baked clay objects in a stone-cooking function is also suspect. As is true for soapstone, heating effectiveness will vary with the ratio of surface area to mass. Most forms of baked clay objects, particularly those with grooves, have a low ratio of surface area to mass and presumably would be ineffective heating devices. Forms with high surface area to volume ratios, such as those resembling perforated soapstone slabs, were perhaps effective heating devices, but lacking temper, and thus lacking thermal shock resistance, it is doubtful they would have served as effective substitutes for soapstone slabs.

These preliminary observations on mechanical performance undermine the probability that baked clay objects were used in moist cooking. Pit roasting with baked clay objects seems much more likely. This alternative interpretation finds further indirect support from archaeological (DePratter 1979b:19; Southerlin 1989), experimental (Trinkley 1986:210–12), and ethnographic data (Ford, Phillips, and Haag 1955:56–57). This interpretation would also account for the on-site co-occurrence of baked clay objects and soapstone slabs and/or pottery: they simply did not serve the same functions.

Nonceramic Stone-Cooking Containers

Baskets were the most common containers used by ethnographic Native American Indians for indirect cooking (Driver and Massey 1957:231). Baskets were made watertight in a variety of ways. In the Great Basin, piñon resin was used to waterproof baskets as well as pots (Ebeling 1986:113). In California, closely woven baskets were watertight, and certain southern tribes made baskets impervious by coating them with asphalt (e.g., Chumash) or pine resin (e.g., Panamint) (Ebeling 1986:173). The Papago made coiled baskets from willow bark and cattail, materials that swelled when wet to become watertight (Crosswhite 1981). Northern Paiute cooking baskets are described as watertight by virtue of their close weave (Kelly 1932:124).

A variety of other containers were used for stone cooking. Bark containers were common in the subarctic and also on the Northwest coast and the plateau (Driver and Massey 1957:231). Wooden vessels were especially popular on the Northwest coast. One account of the Tlinget by Aurel Krause (1956) describes fish oil processing using a half-buried canoe and stones of fist and head size that were heated and cycled into the vessel filled with water and salmon to maintain boiling heat for several hours. The Flathead and Kutenai used hide-lined pits and baskets for stone cooking (Johnson 1969). The Kutenai and neighboring Northwest groups also used unfired clay vessels (Johnson 1969; Reid 1989). The Osage lined pits with an inch of clay, built fires within, then cleared them for filling with water and hot rocks (Burns 1984:122). Finally, the Paiute are said to have used concavities in bedrock as hot rock containers for processing bone grease (Kelly 1932:94).

Certain containers for stone cooking were used on a contingency basis. One account of the Northern Paiute indicates that the hide-lined cooking pits were not used for cooking, but in the winter when water was scarce a traveler might employ this technique to melt snow (Kelly 1932:91). Carcasses were used for stone cooking by Plains and Great Basin hunters on long-distance forays (Driver and Massey 1957:231).

Aceramic Late Archaic sites in the Piedmont portion of the Savannah River Valley typically contain shallow basins, devoid of artifacts or with only a few pieces of cracked rock and debitage. At Rocky River, six oval to circular-shaped basins 50–75 centimeters wide and 10–25 centimeters deep were mapped within the Late Archaic midden (Anderson, Cantley, and Schuldenrein 1985:227–30). Several similar features were recorded at Sara's Ridge (Wood et al. 1986:126–28; 140), and at least one was found at Paris Island (Wood et al. 1986:257–60). The Paris Island example was exceptional in that it contained charred hickory nut shell, debitage, and nearly two kilograms of cracked rock. There is general agreement that these features served some cooking function, perhaps nut oil extraction, using skins or other materials to line the pits (Anderson and Joseph 1988:161; Wood et al. 1986:126).

Clay-lined pits have been reported from sites in the middle Savannah River Valley (Bowen 1978; Claflin 1931). Examples from Stallings Island measured 45–55 centimeters in diameter and 25–30 centimeters deep. The sides of one pit "were plastered smooth with clay and were burned a brick red" (Claflin 1931:8). Another contained four large stones and fragments of perforated soapstone slabs (Claflin 1931:9).

Shallow basin features have also been recorded at an aceramic Coastal Plain site, Lewis-East. Two were found in the center of a dense concentration of lithic debitage, soapstone slab fragments, and fire-cracked quartz (Sassaman 1988). Discrete hearth features were not observed, though their presence nearby is suggested by the volume of fire-cracked rock.

All other Coastal Plain sites with pit features contained fiber-tempered pottery. Especially noteworthy are pits from the basal ceramic component at Bilbo. Waring (1968b:156) describes three pits lined with blue clay in Zone 2. Bone awls and a pin were recovered from one of the pits, suggesting to Waring that they were for storage. He also indicates that two hearths were found at the same level as the clay-lined pits. Shallow basins are reported from Fish Haul (Trinkley 1986:147), and pits of unspecified dimensions are reported from basal sands beneath the shell deposits at Sapelo Ring No. 1 (Waring and Larson 1968:271) and Pagan Plum (DePratter 1979b:44–45). Baked clay objects were found in some of the pits, suggesting to DePratter (1979b:45) that they were used for roasting. Others contained dense shellfish remains and probably represent infilled shellfish steaming pits similar to those described from Fish Haul (Trinkley 1986:140–41), Lighthouse Point, and Stratton Place (Trinkley 1980b). Most of these are large, deep features.

There is no evidence for organic containers in the Late Archaic archaeological record of the Savannah River Valley region. Basket technology was apparently known to mid-Holocene populations of the Eastern Woodlands (e.g., Milanich and Fairbanks 1980:155), but recovery of such materials requires exceptional preservation conditions. Marrinan (1975) considers the Late Archaic bone awl and pin technology to be indicative of a basket industry, an inference supported by a high degree of polish on such implements. DePratter (1979b:19) does not reject this inference but argues instead that bone pins were primarily netting needles. Because either function, as well as other uses such as piercing, could have resulted in polished bone surfaces, the existence of basket technology cannot be argued from this evidence alone. At the same time, there is no reason to dismiss the idea that baskets played a major role in Late Archaic cooking technology.

Ceramic Vessels

> As pottery became more and more common it tended to replace stone-boiling with direct fire boiling because the latter required less labor on the part of the housewife.
>
> —Driver and Massey 1957:229.

> It is often impossible to say whether a particular piece of pottery, found archaeologically, was used for boiling food or not, but it is relatively easy to determine whether it was suited for boiling.
>
> —Linton 1944:370.

That early pottery was used directly over a fire and that this technique, when adopted, represented an improvement over stone cooking are two assertions that have never been tested. One means of testing them is to examine the mechanical performance of early vessels as regards heating effectiveness, thermal shock resistance, and other properties related to use. Although Ralph Linton (1944) pointed archaeologists in this direction over four decades ago, it is only recently that studies of mechanical performance have become common in analyses of ceramic vessels (e.g., Braun 1983; Bronitsky and Hamer 1986; Hally 1986; Pauketat 1987; Schiffer and Skibo 1987, to name but a few). A second, more direct means of examining vessel function is the analysis of use alteration (e.g., Duma 1972; Hally 1983; Skibo 1992). Sooting, food residues, and abrasion are by-products of vessel usage and thus provide direct evidence of function as well as an important, independent set of data with which to test functional inferences derived from mechanical performance properties such as vessel form and paste composition.

There is a rich and growing body of literature of mechanical performance and use alteration of ceramic vessels (see Rice [1987] for a thorough review of this literature). Unfortunately, little of this material addresses the unique circumstances of early (i.e., initial) pottery technology or the economic needs and limitations of a nonsedentary, food-collecting, pot-making people. Before proceeding, then, some qualifying comments on the pottery and pot-using activities of hunter-gatherers must be raised.

The bulk of the literature on mechanical performance of pots focuses on horticulturalists or agriculturalists. But some of the basic economic assumptions about the pottery of sedentary, food-producing people may not apply to hunter-gatherer economies. For instance, heating effectiveness of cooking pots is an important concern of people who depend on foods that can be made palatable only through sustained boiling. Examples of such foods include domesticated starchy seeds (e.g., chenopodium), legumes (e.g., beans), and maize, which became important to prehistoric Native Americans only after pottery and a relatively sedentary settlement strategy were in place. Unless foods that required prolonged boiling were being used in the Late Archaic, it is doubtful that choices among alternative vessel technologies (pits, baskets, pots) depended solely, or even primarily, on heating effectiveness.

Further, there is good reason to suspect that boiling is a misnomer for much of the ethnographic and ethnohistorical description of hunter-gatherer pot cooking. On the basis of accounts of hunter-gatherer cooking in northwestern North America, Reid (1989) points out that a major function of moist-cooking technology involving pots was to render oil from seeds and nuts or grease from meat and bone. These tasks are accomplished most effectively through simmering, not boiling. Simmering temperatures (85–88° C) are ideal for reducing connective tissue or collagen to a gel, whereas at boiling temperature (100° C) protein coagulates, which toughens and shrinks the product (Lundberg and Kotshcevar 1968:5, 83, 115 cited in Reid 1989). Moreover, boiling produces a turbulent water surface that causes difficulty in skimming off the desired oils and fats (Leechman 1951:355–56 cited in Reid 1989).

Nothing definite is known about the foods that were processed in fiber-tempered vessels in the Savannah River Valley region, but if Reid's observations apply to this case, there is no reason to suspect that performance properties of early pottery were being manipulated to improve heating effectiveness. This is not to say that form and composition were not manipulated to adapt pots for use over fire, only that heating effectiveness may not have been an important concern if pot usage was limited to short-term, low-temperature moist cooking.

Further, pottery was adopted and used in the study area by hunter-gatherers who possessed a sophisticated stone-cooking technology. There is no evidence that a stone-cooking technique was immediately abandoned after pots were adopted, so the functional equivalency of pots and cooking stones is subject to question. Is it possible that early ceramic vessels were used as containers for stone cooking? The Kutenai, West Alaskan Eskimo, and other groups of the Northwest made unfired or low-fired clay vessels for the purpose of stone cooking (Reid 1989:Table 2; Wissler 1946:36 cited in Johnson 1969:76). From these ethnographic cases, Reid (1989) argues that pottery used in stone cooking embodied design properties that are very distinct from those of vessels used over direct heat. Accordingly, if early hunter-gatherer pottery in the Savannah River Valley region was being used for stone cooking, we cannot rely solely on the extant literature on mechanical performance of ceramic cooking vessels to interpret or predict the design of this pottery.

The analysis that follows begins by defining mechanical performance and use-alteration criteria to discriminate cooking pots that were used directly over fire from those that were not. This is a relatively straightforward task, based largely on the extant literature and Reid's (1989) provisions for hunter-gatherer pottery. Difficulty is anticipated, however, in applying these ideal criteria to an assemblage of early pottery because few of the relevant mechanical performance variables are readily observable in an assemblage of pot sherds. This problem can be partially circumvented by a multistaged analytical procedure that works from the most secure data set (i.e., complete vessels) to ones that are progressively less secure. Sample size increases through this procedure so that robust patterns in the data, however incomplete they may be with regard to relevant performance variables, might yet be detectable.

Mechanical Performance of Cooking Pots

Linton (1944:370) defined a cooking pot as "any pottery utensil which is structurally adapted to boiling food by the process of bringing the utensil into contact with fire." For the purpose of this research, the definition is expanded to include any vessel that is structurally adapted to simmering or boiling liquid (water or food) through direct contact with external heat (flame or coals) or through the process of stone cooking.

Mechanical performance criteria that can be used to distinguish between vessels used for direct and indirect cooking include heating effectiveness, vessel content heat loss, thermal shock resistance, and manipulation and removal of contents (Table 9).

Heating effectiveness is defined as the rate at which the temperature of the contents of a vessel is raised by the application of heat. For vessels heated by direct, external sources (flame or coals) vessel shape and paste composition can be manipulated to increase heating effectiveness. Thin vessel walls facilitate rapid heating (Braun 1983), as does the inclusion of inorganic temper (i.e., quartz) with a high level of thermal conductivity (Kingery 1960:499–508). Vessels with round bottoms permit air flow to the heat source, which increases combustion to generate more heat (Hally 1986:280). In contrast, designs of vessels used for indirect cooking must emphasize insulation over thermal conduction. Insulation is facilitated by thick vessel walls, a porous paste such as that provided by organic temper, and a flat, thick bottom for radiating the internal source of heat (Reid 1989; Schiffer and Skibo 1987:606).

Vessel content heat loss is defined as the rate at which the contents

Table 9.
Mechanical Performance Attributes of Direct- and Indirect-Heat Cooking Vessels

Attributes	*Direct heat*	*Indirect heat*
Heating effectiveness	thin vessel walls (conduct) sand temper round bottom	thick vessel walls (insulate) fiber temper flat bottom
Vessel content heat loss	reduce permeability constricted orifice low orifice:volume ratio	reduce permeability thick vessel walls (insulate)
Thermal shock resistance	temper smooth wall curvature uniform wall thickness	temper
Manipulation and removal of vessel contents		high orifice:volume ratio

of a vessel lose heat (Hally 1986:280). Heat can escape a vessel by radiation from the surface and by convection through the orifice. Radiation heat loss can be significant if vessel walls are permeable and thus permit surface evaporation (Schiffer 1988). Permeability can be reduced by decreasing the porosity of the paste and by applying a coating to the interior of vessels (Rye 1981:26). Designs of vessels for indirect heating overcome radiation loss through a combination of reduced permeability and thick vessel walls. Vessels intended for direct heating are likewise expected to have features that reduce permeability and therefore reduce heat loss through radiation. Increasing the thickness of the walls of such vessels, however, is an impractical solution to radiation heat loss because thick walls impair the transfer of external heat through the ceramic body.

More critical than radiation is convection heat loss. For direct-heat vessels, convection loss is most effectively reduced by decreasing the size of the orifice. Tightly constricted orifices are, however, unsuited to boiling because the steam produced becomes concentrated at the mouth, forcing contents to spill over (Linton 1944:370). In overall vessel shape, the critical value is the ratio of orifice area to vessel volume (Hally 1986:280). Low orifice:volume ratios limit convection loss. For indirect-heat vessels, reduction of convection loss through constriction of the orifice conflicts with the need to manipulate and remove vessel contents, including cooking stones (see below).

Thermal shock resistance is the ability of a ceramic body to withstand rapid changes in temperature. This property is vital to the long-term survival of direct-heat vessels but is probably not critical for indirect-heat vessels because temperature changes in the body of such vessels are relatively slow. Thermal shock resistance is affected by paste composition and structure and by vessel shape and uniformity. Rye (1981:27) states that organic temper is desirable because the pores left behind by burned fibers arrest cracks caused by thermal shock. Apparently, the inclusion of any type of aplastic in clay improves resistance to thermal shock over nontempered clay, but because tempers differ in thermal expansion properties, the degree of resistance varies (Bronitsky and Hamer 1986; Rye 1981:27). Quartz has a high degree of thermal expansion relative to most clays and is therefore probably not as beneficial for shock resistance as other tempers, including fiber. If quartz temper is selected to improve the performance of other thermal properties, then a combination of fiber and sand may provide an effective compromise for shock resistance.

Thermal shock resistance can be maximized by avoiding sharp angles in the shapes of vessel walls. Round-bottom pots with simple body contours are most resistant to shock (Rye 1976:27). Thermal shock resistance is likewise maximized by uniform thickness of vessel walls.

The manipulation and removal of vessel contents is important to both direct-heat and indirect-heat cooking vessels but is especially critical to the latter. Accounts of indirect-heat cooking mentioned earlier indicate that stones are repeatedly cycled from fire to container and have to be stirred to facilitate even cooking and prevent burning. The use of pots may alleviate the problem of burning, though the need repeatedly to insert and remove the source of heat remains critical. The ease with which vessel contents can be manipulated is determined by the size of the orifice and height of the vessel (Hally 1986:279–80). To maximize this property, indirect-heat vessels will have wide openings (Reid 1989; Schiffer and Skibo 1987:606) and be relatively shallow. The relationship between these two attributes can be expressed as the ratio of orifice area to vessel volume, which in this case will be high. A high orifice:volume ratio is poor for preventing convectional heat loss, but because the source of heat depends on the ability to cycle heated stones into a vessel, designs permitting efficient manipulation of stones can be considered effective thermal designs.

Use Alteration of Cooking Pots

Soot deposits constitute direct evidence for the heat source used in pot cooking. Hally (1983:7–10) provides a thorough discussion of the chemical and physical processes that lead to soot formation on vessels. One type of soot consists of distilled resins and solid carbon that yield a hard, indelible deposit on surfaces of vessels exposed above a fire (i.e., rims and upper portions of walls). The presence of this type of soot is evidence that a vessel was placed over an open fire during use. Conversely, with some exceptions, the absence of soot indicates that a vessel was not placed over an open fire (Hally 1983:9–10). The exceptions are that exterior vessel surfaces have been eroded, obliterating any traces of soot; soot was burned off by the user following use over open fire; and because soot is unevenly distributed across vessel surfaces, traces of soot may not be detected on small portions of large vessels. Moreover, cooking with direct heat would not result in soot formation when small vessels are placed in large, hot fires (Hally 1983:10) and when vessels are placed directly over beds of embers, a heat source lacking flaming combustion and therefore lacking the physical and chemical properties necessary for indelible soot deposition.

Mechanical Performance and Use Alteration of Late Archaic Ceramic Vessels in the Savannah River Valley Region

The analysis of early ceramic vessels for mechanical performance and use alteration begins with an examination of relatively complete specimens. Unfortunately, only eight vessels out of a sample of over twelve hundred could be reconstructed enough to enable accurate measures of height, girth, and basal and wall morphology. Profiles of these vessels, hereafter referred to as complete vessels, are depicted in Figure 22.

Despite the small sample of complete vessels, two distinct forms are evident. One group of four consists of shallow, wide-mouthed basins with flat to semi-flat bottoms (Figure 22e-h). These have orifices ranging from 32.0 to 45.0 centimeters in diameter and heights ranging from 13.5 to 18.3 centimeters (Table 10). A second distinct group of three vessels consists of round-bottomed bowls with orifice diameters ranging from 25.0 to 35.0 centimeters and heights from 18.5 to 22.3 centimeters (Figure 22a, c, d; Table 10).

One vessel in the sample stands apart from the others for its diminutive size (Figure 22b). In form it most closely resembles the basins. It remains to be seen whether it represents a distinct class of vessel (i.e., small basin) or is simply the low end of a normal range of basin sizes.

An additional vessel form not represented in the sample of complete vessels is represented in the larger sample by carinated and recurvate rim profiles (Figure 23). The carinated form is a fiber-tempered vessel known from the middle Savannah River Valley, and the recurvate form is typical of Thom's Creek assemblages and constitutes a minor element of fiber-tempered assemblages. These vessels are believed to be shallow, round-bottomed bowls. Recurvate and carinated profiles combined make up less than 5 percent of the total sample of vessels with rim sherds. Because of the small sample size and lack of complete examples, this form is excluded from the analyses that follow. It will be discussed in a later section of this chapter.

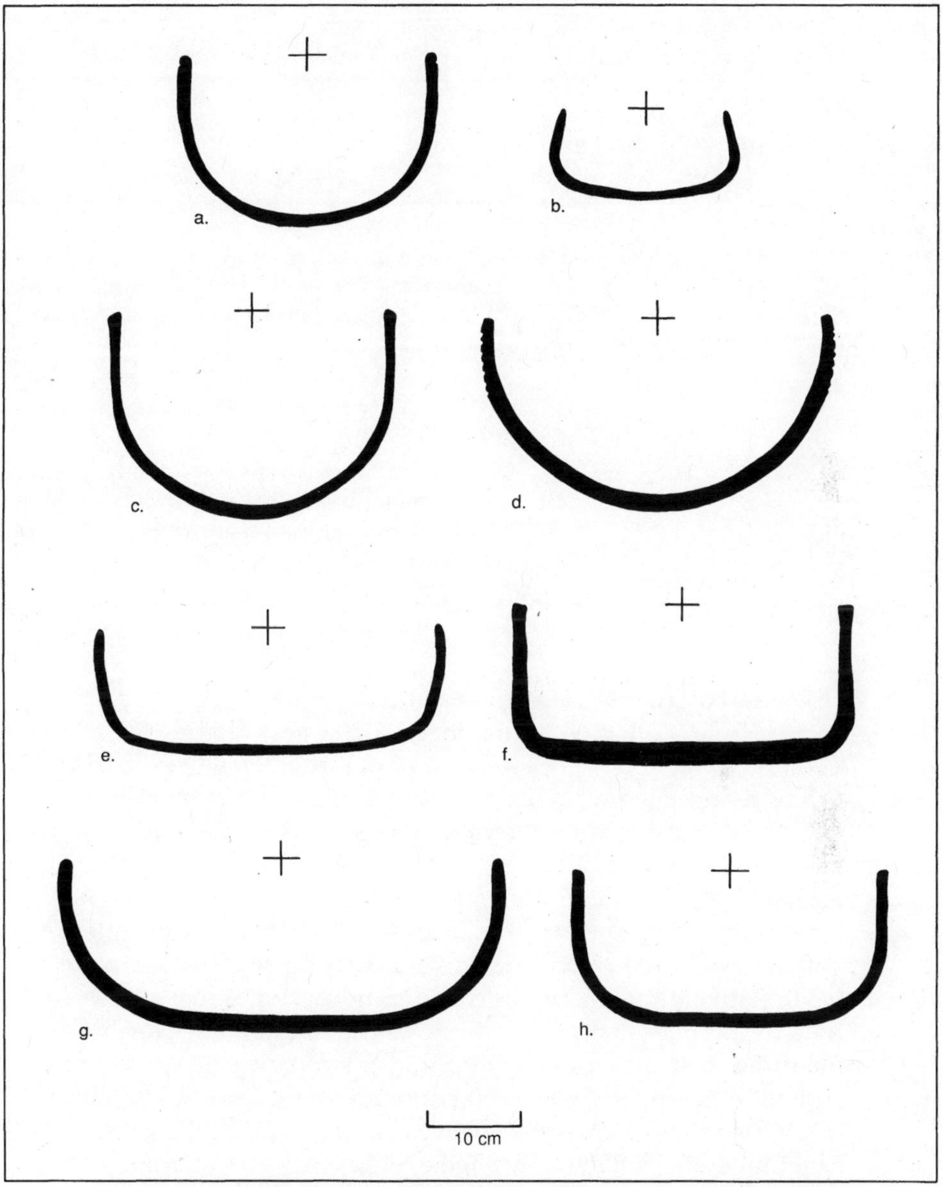

Figure 22. Profiles of partially reconstructed fiber-tempered vessels (a. 9JF21; b. Rabbit Mount; c. 38AK288; d. unrecorded site on the lower Savannah River; e. Rabbit Mount; f. 38MC479; g. WV Site 23; h. 9CH114).

Table 10.
Attributes of Complete Fiber-Tempered Vessels

	Orifice diameter (cm)	*Height (cm)*	*Ratio of orifice to height*	*Wall thickness (mm)*	*Temper*	*Base*	*Soot*
Basins							
	36.0	13.5	2.7:1	8.9	abundant fiber, no sand	semi-flat	absent
	32.0	17.0	1.9:1	12.3	abundant fiber with sand	flat	absent
	45.0	18.3	2.5:1	12.7	abundant fiber, no sand	semi-flat	absent
	32.0	16.5	2.0:1	12.3	abundant fiber, no sand	semi-flat	absent
mean	36.3	16.3	2.3:1	11.6			
Bowls							
	28.0	22.3	1.3:1	8.5	abundant fiber, no sand	round	present
	25.0	20.5	1.2:1	12.1	abundant fiber with grit	round	present
	35.0	18.5	1.9:1	10.9	abundant fiber with sand	round	absent
mean	29.3	20.4	1.5:1	10.5			

On the basis of form alone, none of the complete vessels appears to be particularly adapted to prolonged direct-heat cooking (cf. Hally 1986:283; Linton 1944:370). Relative to one another, however, basins exhibit many of the attributes of vessels designed for indirect heating, while bowls have rudimentary properties of vessels designed for use over fire. The most discriminating formal attributes between the two are basal configuration and ratio of orifice to height. (Height is substituted for vessel volume because of an inability to estimate volume for all the reconstructed vessels. Because all of the vessels have relatively straight profile configurations, height and volume are roughly proportional.) The ratio is consistently smaller for bowls, reflecting their increased height; in fact, two bowls are sufficiently high to be described as pots rather than bowls. Compared to basins, bowls also show a greater tendency for uniform wall thickness and have smoother wall curvature and a higher incidence of sand or grit in the paste. Other attributes listed among the performance criteria above are comparable for basins and bowls: all vessels contain abundant fiber so porosity is similar; vessel wall thickness is only slightly less among the bowls but still thick compared to Woodland cooking vessels; and accessibility to contents is not dramatically different,

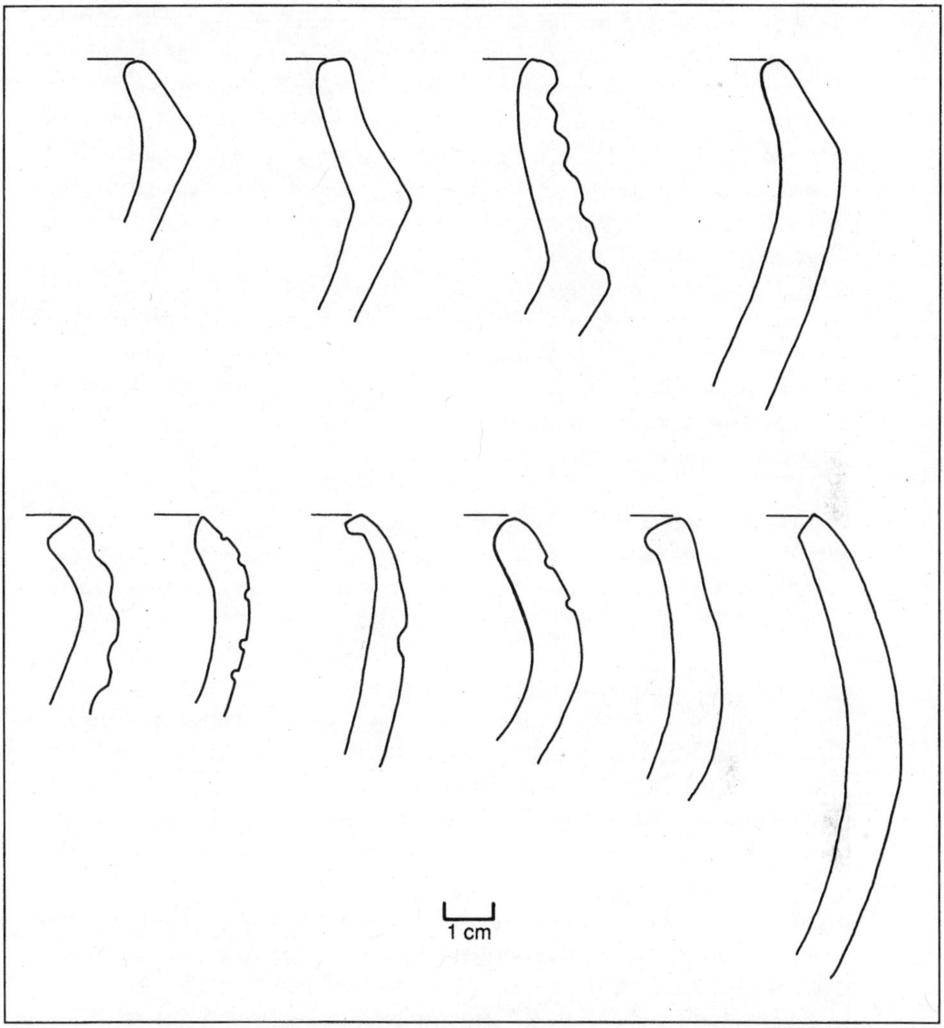

Figure 23. Vessel rim profiles of carinated and recurvate vessel forms.

though certainly better among the basins because of the shallow, wide-mouthed form.

Evidence for use alteration supports the functional distinction based on performance criteria. None of the basins exhibits external soot, though two of the three bowls have definite traces of soot on the external rim.

Thus two related functions are inferred from the limited sample of complete vessels—indirect-heat cooking basins and direct-heat cooking bowls or pots. Remaining to be seen is the degree to which this small sample reflects the larger population of Late Archaic vessels. Ultimately, it is desirable to determine when and where these distinct vessel forms were being used in the study area. To do this we must try to make sense of the larger data set based on the functions inferred from the complete vessels.

Of the formal properties that discriminate basins from bowls in the sample of complete specimens, only orifice diameter was observable across a relatively large sample of incomplete vessels. I will therefore attempt to use orifice diameter as a dependent variable against which the discrimination of basin and bowl forms can be tested with independent mechanical performance and use-alteration data.

Orifice Diameter and Vessel Function. Orifice diameter was recorded for ninety-nine vessels or 8 percent of the entire sample. Among complete vessels, mean orifice diameter of basins (36.3 cm) is appreciably greater than that of bowls (29.3 cm) so we might expect a bimodal distribution in the orifice diameters of the larger sample.

The plotted frequency distribution of ninety-nine orifice diameters (including the reconstructed vessel subset) indeed yields a bimodal distribution but not one consistent with the sample of complete vessels (Figure 24). The mean and range for large basins accounts for the upper end of the entire sample range (i.e., the larger mode), but bowl orifices overlap the low end of the basin orifice range and contribute to the shape of the large mode. What is more, the low end of the reconstructed bowl range straddles orifice values that, because of a small number of cases, appear to divide the larger sample into two modes. Among the cases in the low orifice mode is the small reconstructed basin/bowl, a form that may be more common than the small sample of complete vessels would lead one to believe.

Assuming that the apparent modes in orifice diameter reflect distinct vessel forms (whether or not these forms correspond to those identified among complete vessels), distributions of additional formal attributes of the vessels may reveal patterns of variation that will allow extrapolation to the larger data set. Three attributes observed across the larger data set are the form of the rim and lip and thickness of the vessel wall.

Rim form does not vary with orifice diameter among the complete

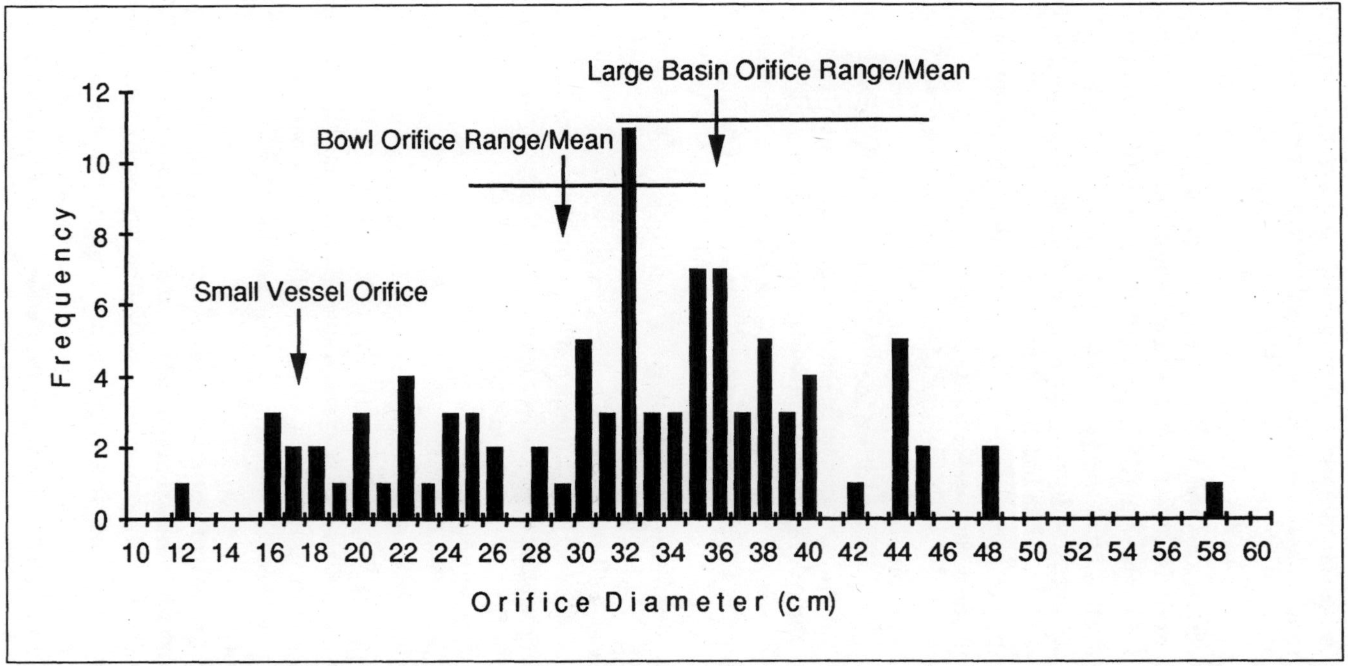

Figure 24. Absolute frequency of vessels by orifice diameter (cm).

vessels. The larger sample of orifice diameters duplicates this pattern (Figure 25). Rims are roughly equally divided between straight and (slightly) incurvate forms, with minor occurrences of excurvate and irregular forms. Mean orifice diameter for the two largest groups is nearly identical, and the frequency distribution of each is similar to the bimodal distribution of the entire (orifice) sample.

Lip design was not implicated in the performance criteria discussed earlier because no obvious connection between lip form and the cooking functions predicted for the vessels is envisioned. But thickened and flanged lips seemed to be common in plain vessel assemblages containing a high proportion of thick, flat basal sherds (Figure 26). Assuming that thickened and flanged lips are common to basin-shaped vessels, orifices of thick- or flanged-lipped vessels may reflect the predicted large size of basins. This expectation is supported by the data for orifices (Figure 27). Thick-lipped vessels are indeed among the widest in the sample, on average three centimeters wider than flat-lipped and over six centimeters wider than round-lipped vessels. Irregular, tapered, and beveled lips are minor types in the sample. The difference in orifice means between thick-lipped and round-lipped vessels is statistically significant. (A difference of means test yielded a t value of 2.80 with 57 degrees of freedom at $<.005$ level of significance.)

Vessel wall thickness is not appreciably different between complete basins and bowls. Mean thickness plotted by orifice diameter for the larger sample shows an equally poor correlation (Figure 28). Although vessel walls are consistently thick (>9 mm) among the widest vessels, narrower forms have walls ranging from thin (<7 mm) to thick (>11 mm).

Finally, the incidence of sooting (Figure 29) on vessels shows no nonrandom tendency as regards orifice diameter (Figure 30). The mean orifice size of sooted vessels is less than that of unsooted vessels, a difference in accord with the functional distinction predicted between bowls and basins but one that is not statistically significant.

To summarize, variation in vessel orifice diameter provides limited support for the functional classes inferred from the form and use alteration of reconstructed vessels. The strongest nonrandom tendency for formal attributes to vary with orifice diameter is found among lip forms. Performance criteria specified earlier made no predictions for lip form, and the association of thickened or flanged

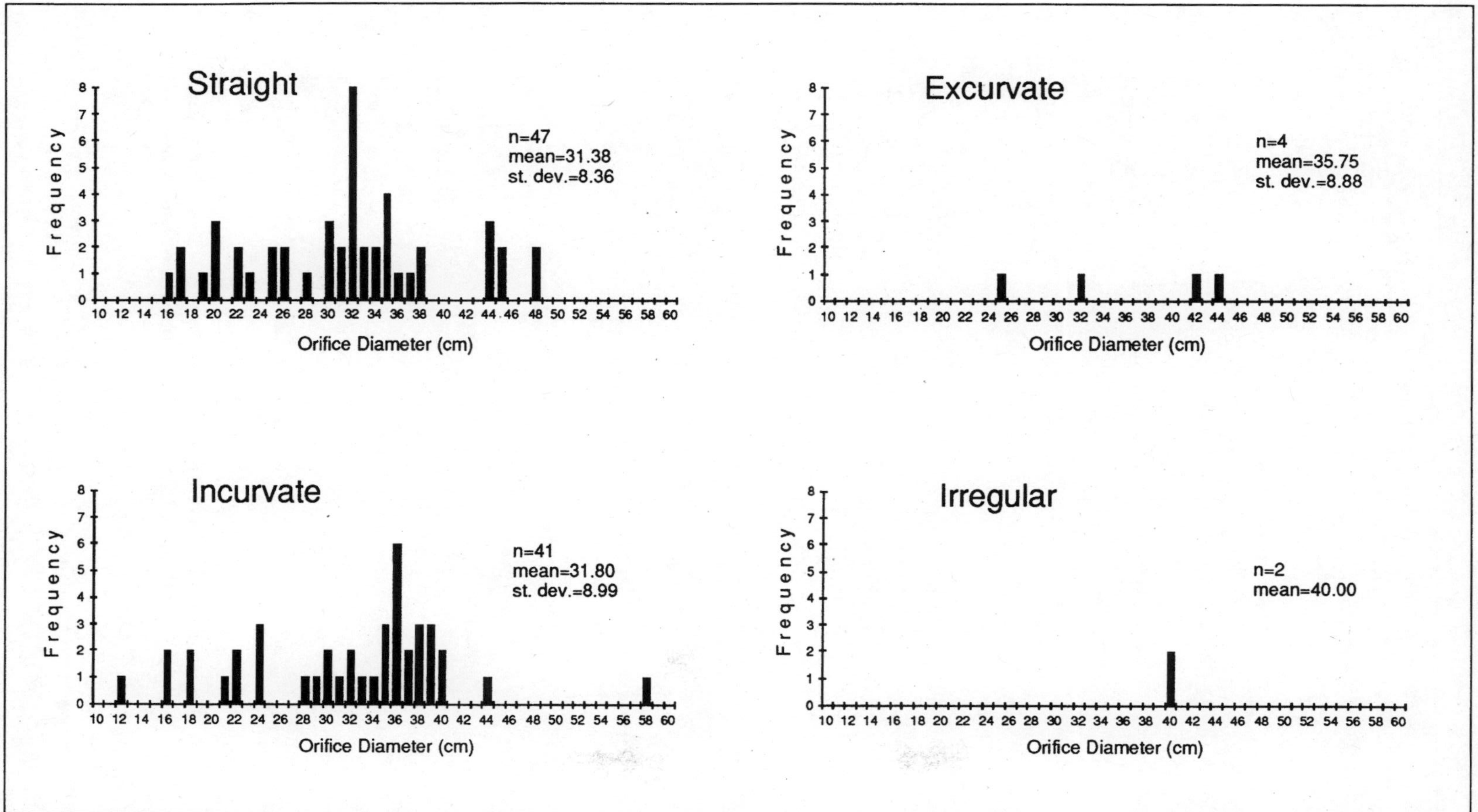

Figure 25. Absolute frequencies of vessels by rim form and by orifice diameter (cm).

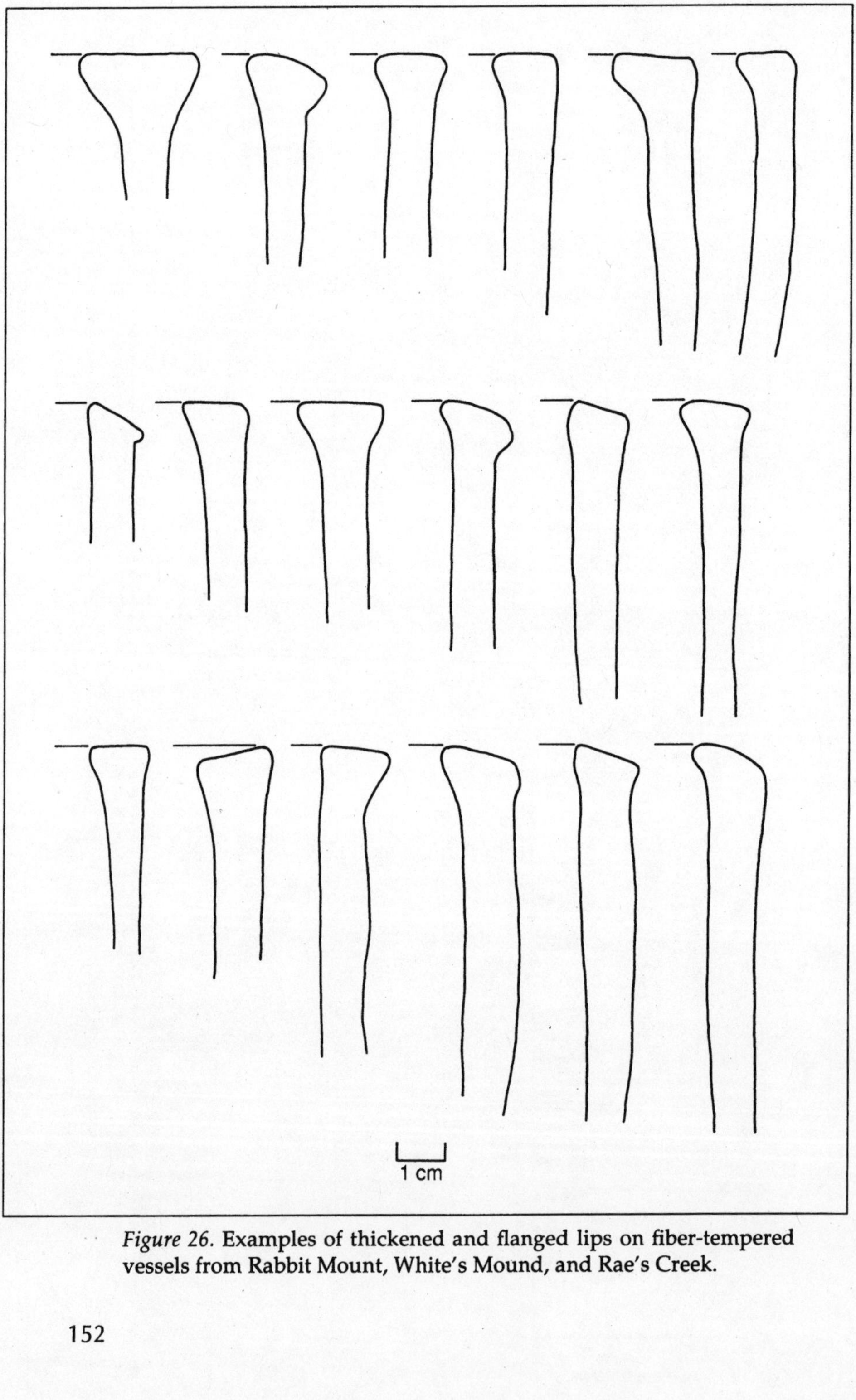

Figure 26. Examples of thickened and flanged lips on fiber-tempered vessels from Rabbit Mount, White's Mound, and Rae's Creek.

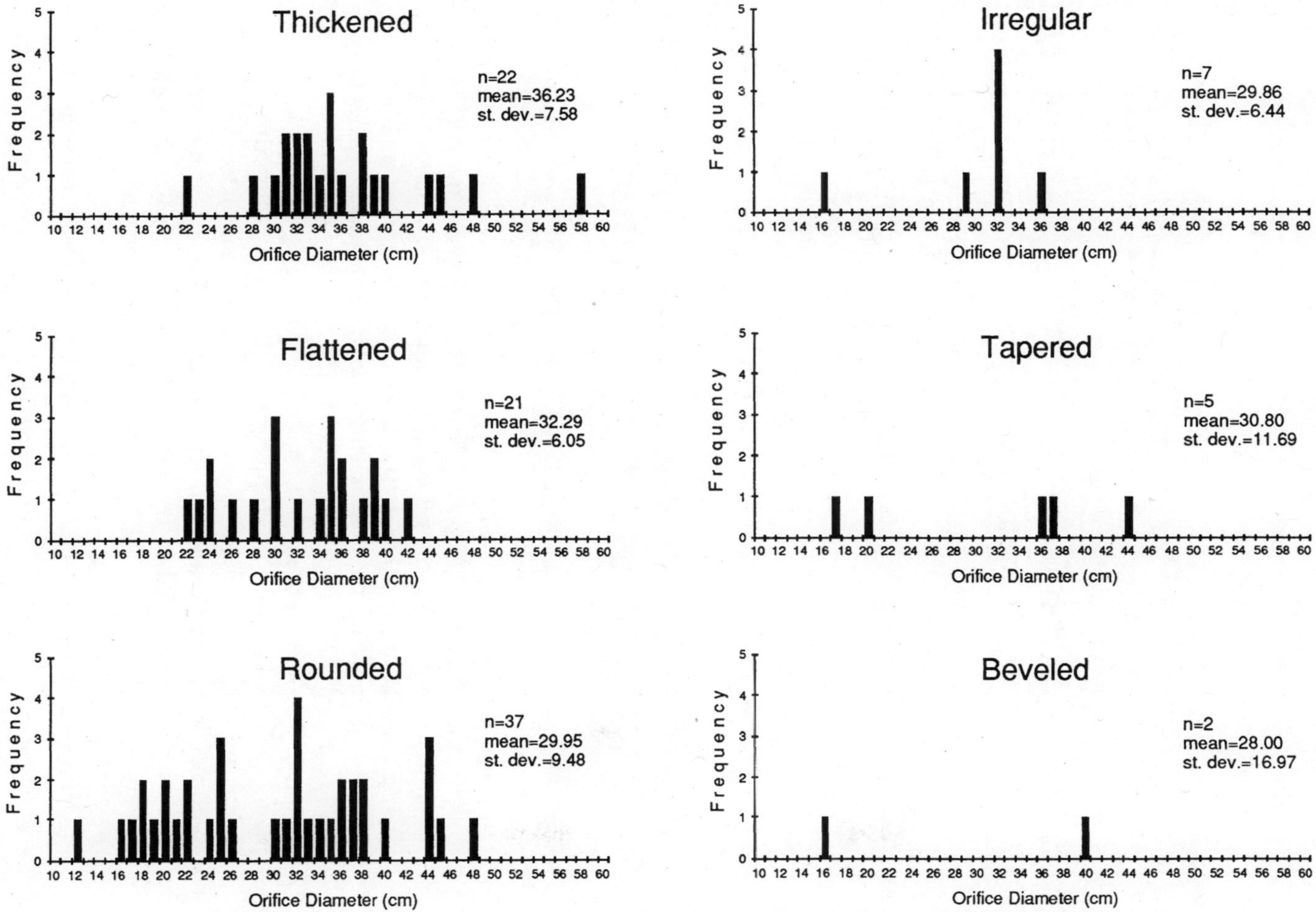

Figure 27. Absolute frequencies of vessels by lip form and by orifice diameter (cm).

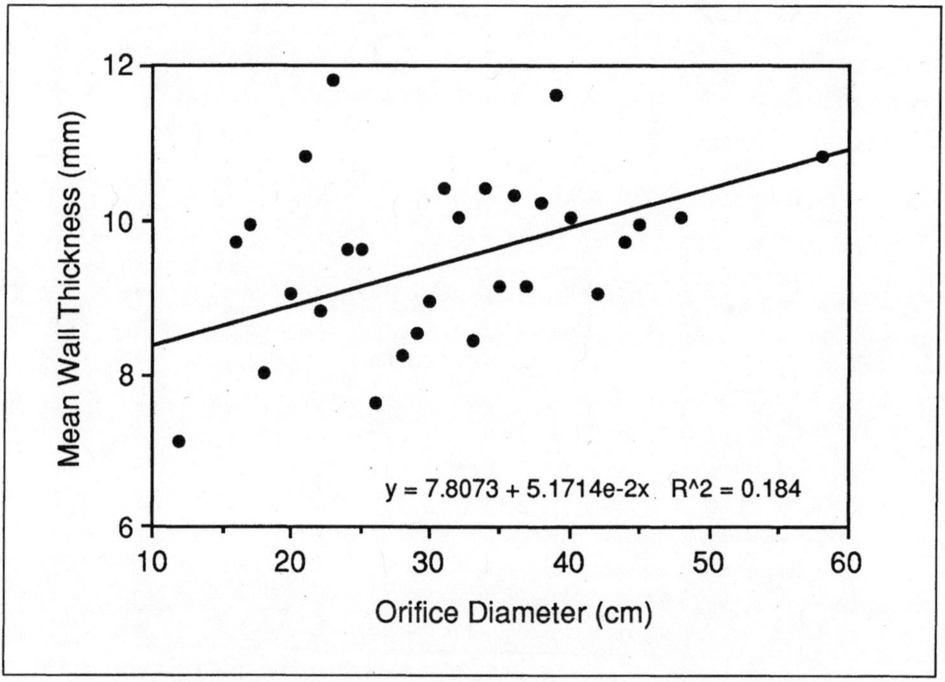

Figure 28. Mean vessel wall thickness (mm) by orifice diameter (cm).

lips with wide-mouthed vessels and rounded lips with small-mouthed vessels may be spurious in connection with vessel function. Nevertheless, because thick-lipped vessels tend to have wide orifices, and the proportion of sooted vessels is generally lower among wide-mouthed vessels than among small-mouthed vessels, many thick-lipped vessels may be basin-shaped containers used for indirect-heat cooking. Support for this assertion is found in the incidence of soot in the sample for which lip form is recorded. Only twelve, or 9 percent, of the vessels with thickened or flanged lips (n = 133) show traces of soot, while ninety-eight, or 22 percent, of the vessels with other lip forms (n = 447) have soot. (The association yields an x^2 value of 11.101 with 1 degree of freedom at <.01 level of significance.) If the majority of basins have thickened or flanged lips, an early temporal placement for this vessel form can be inferred from the pottery chronology presented in Chapter 4.

The lack of better discrimination between vessel forms on the basis

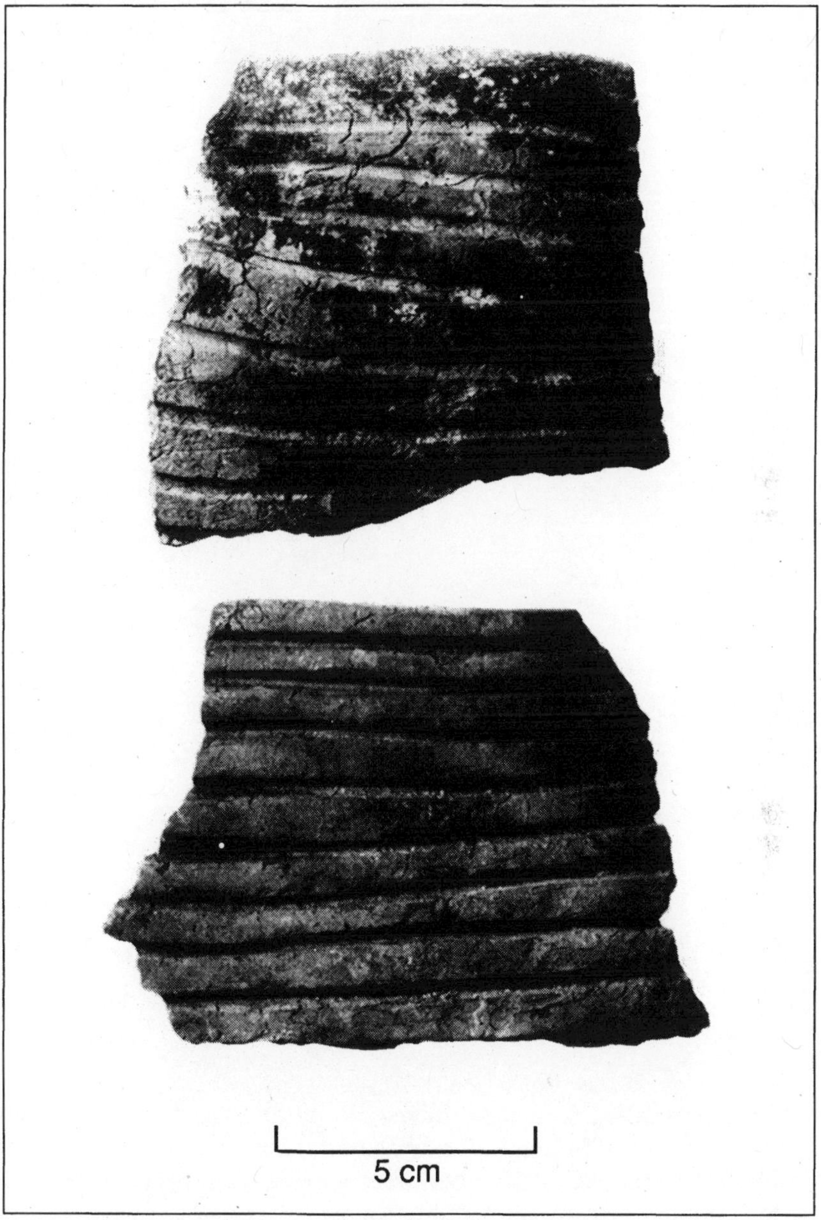

Figure 29. Examples of sooted sherds (top: Fish Haul; bottom: Cane Patch).

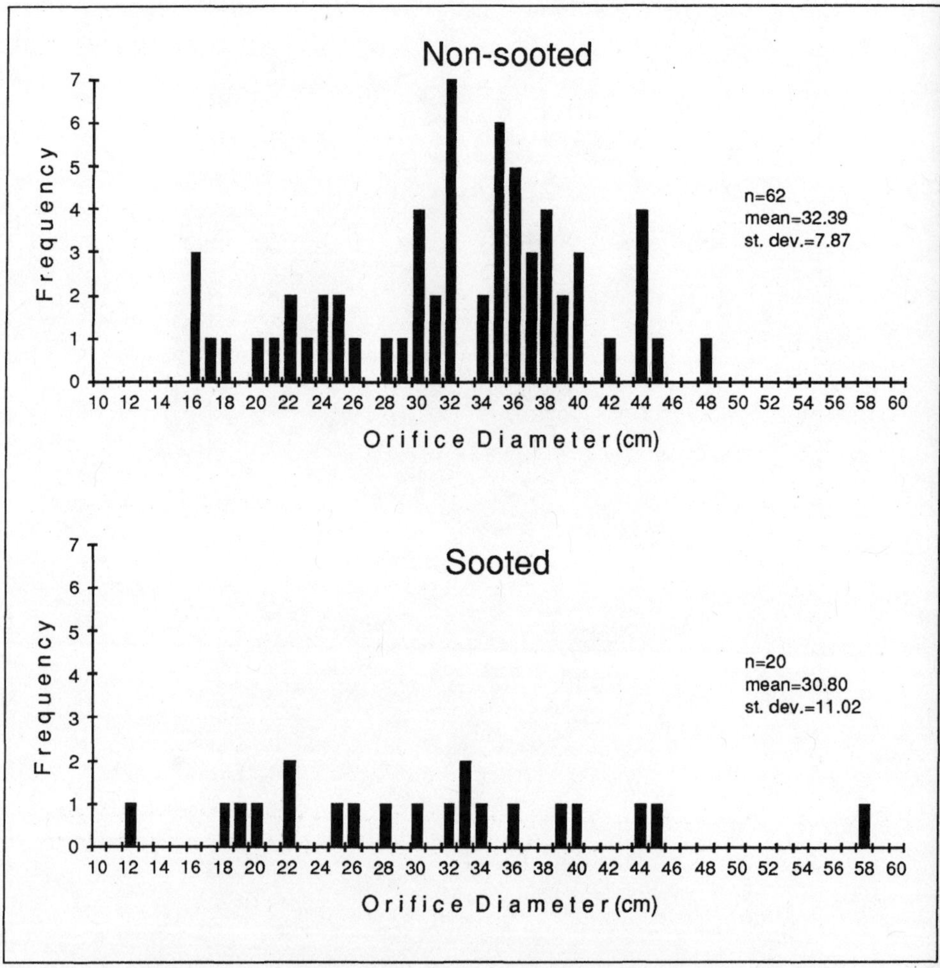

Figure 30. Absolute frequencies of vessels by absence (top) or presence (bottom) of soot by orifice diameter (cm).

of mechanical performance and use alteration suggests that there was little uniformity in the design and use of Late Archaic pottery. Either little attention was paid to performance factors or regularities in the data, if they exist, are masked by temporal and spatial variation in the manufacture and use of pots. To evaluate the latter possibility, analysis proceeds diachronically through use of the pottery chronology presented in Chapter 4. Recognizing that vessel form and function may have varied from place to place within the study area, the analysis that follows explores possible differences in the local design and use of fiber-tempered vessels.

Temporal and Spatial Variation in Vessel Form and Function

Two distinct vessel forms have been inferred from the foregoing analysis. Limited data on mechanical performance and use alteration suggest that the forms were used for different cooking functions. On the basis of knowledge that stone cooking was a significant technique of Late Archaic food preparation before the introduction of pottery, a trend from indirect-heat to direct-heat cooking might be discerned in the design of Late Archaic pottery. Further, because lithic materials for stone cooking were not widely available on the coast, and if we assume that baked clay objects were not functionally equivalent to stones used in moist cooking, the adoption of a direct-heat cooking vessel technology may have been more imperative on the coast than in the interior. I expect, then, that the innovation of direct-heat cooking, along with innovations to improve the use efficiency of direct-heat vessels, was first adopted on the coast. Conversely, temporal and spatial variation in the design of pottery from interior sites and in the association of soapstone slabs and pottery suggest that innovations of direct-heat cooking were more slowly adopted in the interior than on the coast.

In the subsections that follow, mechanical performance and use-alteration data are reexamined for evidence to test the temporal and spatial patterns hypothesized above. Tabulations of temper, rim form, mean thickness of vessel walls, and incidence of soot by component assemblage are provided in Tables 11–14. Components are grouped by the temporal phases inferred from the chronostratigraphic order of pottery attributes. A further subdivision within each phase group is made to elucidate relevant differences between coastal and interior pottery.

Soot. Strong temporal and spatial patterns in the incidence of sooted vessels are evident in the data presented in Table 11. The proportion of sooted vessels increases from a low of 6.7 percent in Phase I to a high of 30.7 percent in Phase III. This temporal trend differs for coastal and interior areas. The increase in sooted vessels is rapid on the coast but lags behind in the interior.

Table 11.
Absolute and Relative Frequencies of Noneroded Vessels with Soot by Temporal Phase and Location

	Noneroded vessels	*Definite soot*		*Probable soot*		*Total soot*	
	n	*n*	*%*	*n*	*%*	*n*	*%*
PHASE I							
Interior components							
Rabbit Mount —nonshell midden	39	0	0.0	0	0.0	0	0.0
Fennel Hill	44	0	0.0	5	11.4	5	11.4
Rabbit Mount —shell midden	125	0	0.0	0	0.0	0	0.0
Rae's Creek	25	1	4.0	0	0.0	1	4.0
White's Mound	44	0	0.0	2	4.5	2	4.5
Rocky Ford	20	1	5.0	5	25.0	6	30.0
WV Site 18	7	0	0.0	1	14.3	1	14.3
Subtotal	304	2	0.7	13	4.3	15	4.9
Coastal components							
Sapelo Ring —Levels 9–17	14	3	21.4	1	7.1	4	28.6
9CH111	10	0	0.0	3	30.0	3	30.0
Subtotal	24	3	12.5	4	16.7	7	29.2
Phase I Subtotal	328	5	1.5	17	5.2	22	6.7
PHASE II							
Interior components							
38MC479	6	0	0.0	1	16.7	1	16.7
McCalla Bottom	6	0	0.0	0	0.0	0	0.0
Theriault	79	0	0.0	2	2.5	2	2.5
Stallings Island	88	0	0.0	3	3.4	3	3.4
WV Site 23	7	0	0.0	3	42.9	3	42.9

Irrespective of rates of change, coastal assemblages in general have a much higher incidence of sooted vessels than do interior assemblages (Figure 31). With only two exceptions, vessels with definite traces of soot come from coastal sites. Vessels with probable traces of soot are present in interior assemblages but in a much lower proportion than those from the coast. Combining definite and probable cases

Table 11.
(Continued)

	Noneroded vessels	Definite soot		Probable soot		Total soot	
	n	n	%	n	%	n	%
WV Site 14	36	0	0.0	2	5.6	2	5.6
Subtotal	222	0	0.0	11	5.0	11	5.0
Coastal components							
A. Busch Krick 2.5–5'	12	1	8.3	5	41.7	6	50.0
Cane Patch 0–3'	51	1	2.0	16	31.4	17	33.3
Cane Patch 3–6'	58	11	19.0	11	19.0	22	37.9
Sapelo Ring—Levels 1–8	15	3	20.0	4	26.7	7	46.7
Fish Haul—Feature 21	4	3	75.0	0	0.0	3	75.0
Chesterfield	54	5	9.3	22	40.7	27	50.0
Subtotal	194	24	12.4	58	29.9	82	42.3
Phase II Subtotal	416	24	5.8	69	16.6	93	22.4
PHASE III							
Interior components							
Tinker Creek	14	0	0.0	2	14.3	2	14.3
Coastal components							
Fish Haul—Feature 18	19	4	21.1	6	31.6	10	52.6
9CH114a	7	0	0.0	2	28.6	2	28.6
Daw's Island	23	0	0.0	4	17.4	4	17.4
9CH14a	6	1	16.7	3	50.0	4	66.7
A. Busch Krick 0–2.5'	6	0	0.0	1	16.7	1	16.7
Subtotal	61	5	8.2	16	26.2	21	34.4
Phase III Subtotal	75	5	6.7	18	24.0	23	30.7
TOTAL	819	34	7.5	104	17.8	138	25.3

of sooting, 39.4 percent of coastal vessels (n = 279) are sooted, compared to only 5.2 percent of vessels from the interior (n = 540).

Comparing the incidence of sooted vessels to indirect cooking technology shows a strong inverse relationship between sooting and presence of soapstone slabs. Only one out of twenty vessels (5.4 percent) is sooted in assemblages containing soapstone slabs, while

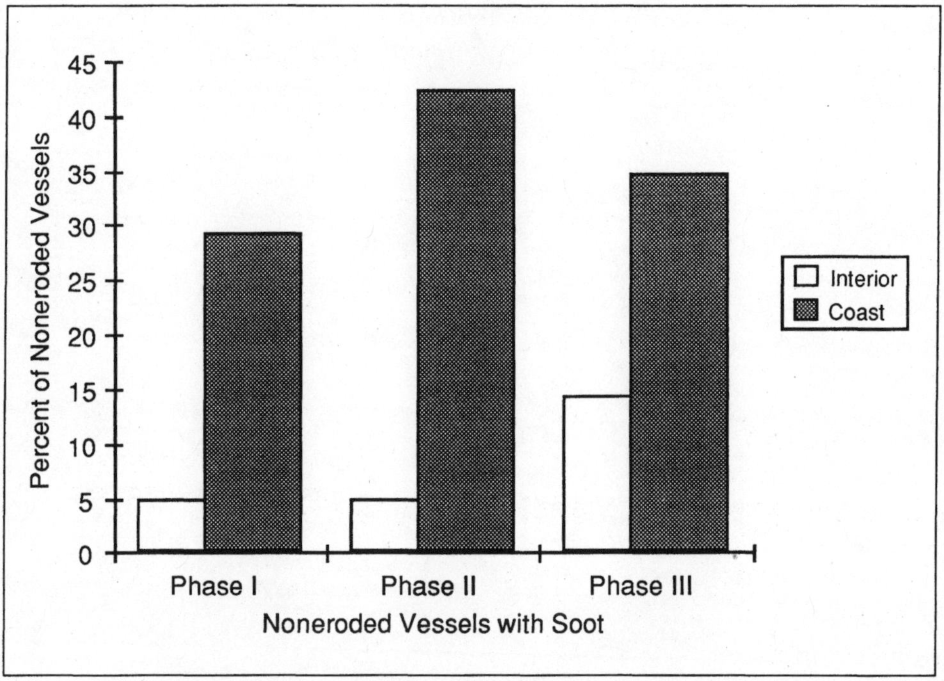

Figure 31. Relative frequency of noneroded vessels from interior and coastal assemblages with traces of soot by chronological phase.

eight of twenty vessels (40.0 percent) are sooted in assemblages lacking soapstone slabs. Sooted vessels are particularly rare among early Coastal Plain assemblages characterized by a high incidence of thickened and flanged lips on vessels (presumably basins), a high ratio of plain to decorated vessels, and an abundance of soapstone slabs. It is reasonable to conclude that the vast majority of vessels in these early assemblages was used as containers for indirect cooking with soapstone slabs.

A low incidence of sooted vessels is also found in later interior assemblages, which contain an abundance of soapstone slabs but have lower numbers of thickened- or flanged-lipped vessels and increased numbers of decorated vessels. The continued low incidence of sooted vessels in Phase II assemblages supports the notion that an indirect cooking technique continued to be used in the interior long after pottery was locally adopted and long after the pots were widely used over fire on the coast.

The incidence of soot on coastal assemblages indeed reflects a distinct technological history from that of the interior. Soot is apparent on vessels of the earliest documented coastal assemblage in the sample (lowest levels of Sapelo Ring No. 1), and the fraction of sooted vessels increases markedly in Phase II. Lower Coastal Plain sites lacking soapstone are perhaps the earliest assemblages with appreciable numbers of sooted vessels, but only on the coast is a consistent pattern of pot use over fire apparent. If the need or desire to use pots over fire led to technological innovations to improve the use efficiency of coastal pots, then differences in the performance properties of coastal and interior vessels should be evident.

Temper. Many assemblages from coastal and interior sites alike contain combinations of fiber-tempered (Stallings/Bilbo/St. Simons) and sand-tempered (Thom's Creek) vessels (Table 12). In general, coastal assemblages in the sample contain few non-fiber-tempered vessels. Also, relatively few fiber-tempered vessels from coastal sites have visible sand grains or grit in the paste, expect for certain late coastal sites which have higher fractions of inorganic inclusions. In contrast, fiber-tempered vessels from interior sites more often than not have either sand or grit in the paste, and the fraction of such vessels increases through time. Part of the geographical contrast may be attributed to differences in the composition of marine and interior fluvial clays (i.e., differences in the natural occurrence of aplastics), but some evidence suggests that paste was manipulated to improve thermal properties of coastal vessels.

The first evidence in support of this idea has to do with the relative amount of fiber added to clays (Figure 32). In Phase I, nearly all fiber-tempered vessels in coastal and interior assemblages alike have pastes consisting of abundant fiber. After this time the amount of fiber in pastes of interior vessels decreases and assemblages of coastal sites continue to contain high fractions of vessels with abundant fiber. The only coastal fiber-tempered vessel assemblage with pastes lacking abundant fiber is Daw's Island, which is exceptional as well for the low incidence of soot and occurrence of soapstone slabs. The persistence of fiber tempering on the coast in conjunction with direct fire usage may indicate that fiber continued to be added to clays for functional reasons. Fiber does little to improve the thermal conductivity of ceramics, but it does provide effective resistance to thermal shock. If the primary function of coastal pots was to process animal

Table 12.
Absolute and Relative Frequencies of Vessels with Sand/Grit Temper, Fiber Temper, and No Temper by Temporal Phase and Location

	Total vessels	*With Sand/Grit*		*Fiber only*		*Non-tempered*	
	n	*n*	*%*	*n*	*%*	*n*	*%*
PHASE I							
Interior components							
Rabbit Mount —nonshell midden	48	29	60.4	18	37.5	1	2.1
Fennel Hill	68	37	54.4	31	45.6	0	0.0
Rabbit Mount —shell midden	138	63	45.7	75	54.3	0	0.0
Rae's Creek	32	17	53.1	15	46.9	0	0.0
White's Mound	47	32	68.1	15	31.9	0	0.0
Rocky Ford	28	21	75.0	7	25.0	0	0.0
WV Site 18	13	6	46.2	7	53.8	0	0.0
Subtotal	374	205	54.8	168	44.9	1	0.3
Coastal components							
Sapelo Ring—Levels 9–17	20	0	0.0	20	100.0	0	0.0
9CH111	27	6	22.2	21	77.8	0	0.0
Subtotal	47	6	12.8	41	87.2	0	0.0
Phase I Subtotal	421	211	50.1	209	49.6	1	0.2
PHASE II							
Interior components							
38MC479	9	6	66.7	3	33.3	0	0.0
McCalla Bottom	23	16	69.6	7	30.4	0	0.0
Theriault	124	93	75.0	24	19.4	7	5.6
Stallings Island	-	-	-	-	-	-	-
WV Site 23	12	6	50.0	6	50.0	0	0.0
WV Site 14	48	28	58.3	20	41.7	0	0.0
Subtotal	216	149	69.0	60	27.8	7	3.2
Coastal components							
A. Busch Krick 2.5–5'	15	0	0.0	15	100.0	0	0.0
Cane Patch 0–3'	54	5	9.3	48	88.9	1	1.9
Cane Patch 3–6'	59	2	3.4	57	96.6	0	0.0

Table 12.
(Continued)

	Total vessels	With Sand/Grit		Fiber only		Non-tempered	
	n	*n*	%	*n*	%	*n*	%
Sapelo Ring—Levels 1–8	23	0	0.0	23	100.0	0	0.0
Fish Haul—Feature 21	7	0	0.0	7	100.0	0	0.0
Chesterfield	67	6	9.0	51	76.1	10	14.9
Subtotal	225	13	5.8	201	89.3	11	4.9
Phase II Subtotal	441	162	36.7	261	59.2	18	4.1
PHASE III							
Interior components							
Tinker Creek	23	23	100.0	0	0.0	0	0.0
Coastal components							
Fish Haul—Feature 18	22	1	4.5	21	95.5	0	0.0
9CH114a	21	8	38.1	13	61.9	0	0.0
Daw's Island	49	14	28.6	32	65.3	3	6.1
9CH14a	17	17	100.0	0	0.0	0	0.0
A. Busch Krick 0–2.5'	7	0	0.0	7	100.0	0	0.0
Subtotal	116	40	34.5	73	62.9	3	2.6
Phase III Subtotal	139	63	45.3	73	52.5	3	2.2
TOTAL	1,001	436	43.6	543	54.2	22	2.2

and vegetable foods for fat, the simmering temperatures involved would not require a great deal of heating efficiency. Accordingly, temper type and abundance would have been influenced more by the need to avoid thermal shock than by the need to transfer heat efficiently.

During Phase III the proportion of fiber-tempered vessels with sandy or gritty pastes increases in both interior and coastal assemblages (Figure 32). Limited to only one Phase III component, the interior vessel sample is too small to draw reliable conclusions about changing vessel functions. Increases in sand or grit, however, coupled

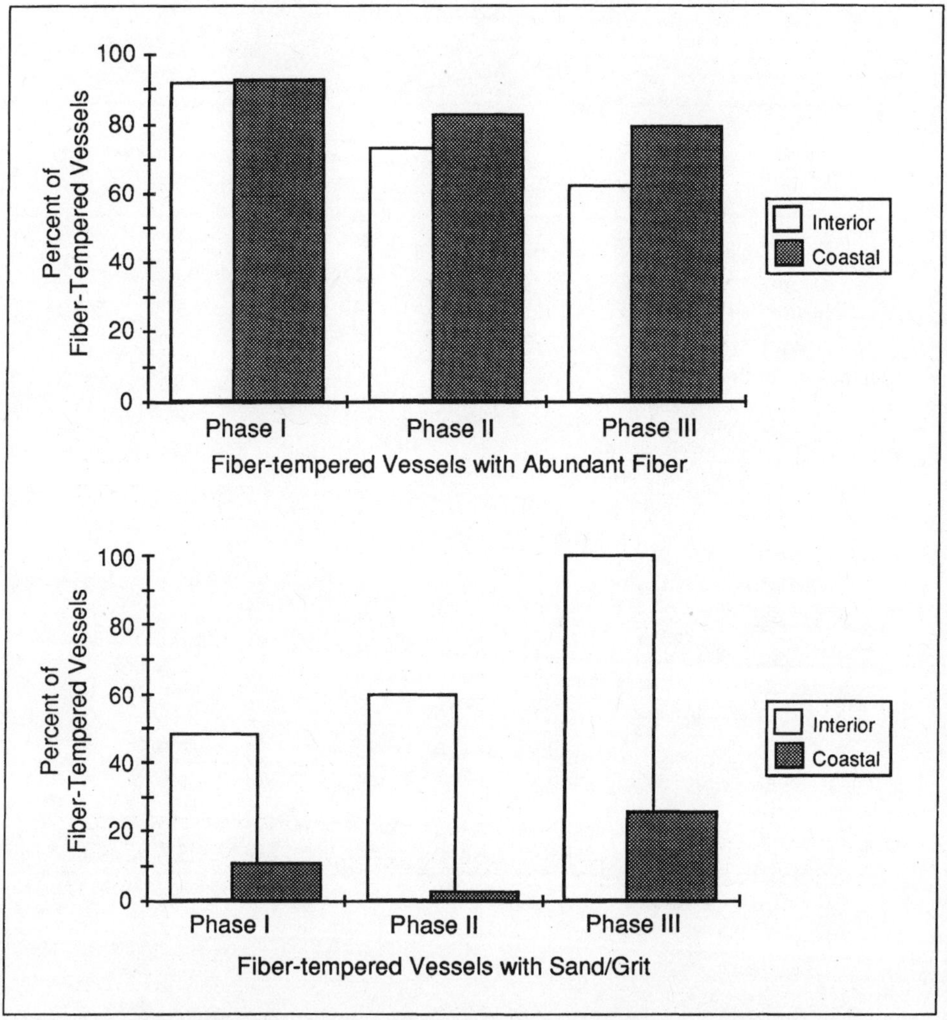

Figure 32. Relative frequency of interior and coastal vessels with abundant fiber temper (top) and with sand/grit temper (bottom) by chronological phase.

with decreases in fiber in pastes, have been noted in other interior assemblages thought to be late in the Stallings sequence (Chapter 4). Thus, combined with the increased incidence of soot on interior vessels dating to Phase III, the changes in temper may signify a late shift to a direct-heat vessel technology for which the efficiency of heat transfer was improved.

Simultaneously, coastal vessels continue to have abundant fiber in the paste, but at least two Phase III assemblages, 9CH14a and 9CH114, also contain examples with abundant sand or grit. These may simply reflect a local source of clay with unusually high fractions of aplastics, but it may also indicate that late in the sequence paste was altered to increase thermal conductivity. The evidence from 9CH14a is particularly relevant in this regard, as later discussion will reveal.

Rim Form. Straight and incurvate rim profiles dominate vessel assemblages in all phases, particularly those from the coast (Table 13). Among coastal assemblages, the fraction of straight rim profiles is consistently larger than that of incurvate profiles, though it is noteworthy that during Phase II the proportions are nearly equal (Figure 33a, b). Overall, there is no clear diachronic trend in coastal rim profiles. A tendency for increasing incurvate forms through time is suggested, but this is overshadowed by the persistent domination of straight profiles.

In contrast, the trend in rim form among interior assemblages is for increasing diversity. The majority of Phase I vessel profiles have straight rims (Figure 33a), but these decrease markedly in subsequent phases. The decreased proportion of straight rims is accounted for by increases in incurvate and especially recurvate and carinated rim forms (Figure 33b, c). The increase in vessels with constricted rim profiles suggests that a trend was under way to decrease the orifice: volume ratio and therefore improve heat retention properties of vessels. Although such a trend may signify a shift from indirect- to direct-heat cooking, the lack of supporting evidence from Phase II interior assemblages weakens this inference. Alternatively, vessels with recurvate and carinated rim profiles may have served functions other than cooking and thus cannot be explained by the performance criteria for cooking vessels.

Only seven assemblages in the sample contain examples of recurvate and/or carinated rim profiles. Examples are found in all but one interior assemblage postdating Phase I and only one coastal assemblage (Chesterfield). Limited measures of orifice diameter suggest that Phase II recurvate forms are smaller (20–30 cm) than Phase III ones (35–40 cm). Vessel wall thickness is highly variable among the entire group, ranging from 4.9 to 13.5 millimeters, with a mean of 9.4

Table 13.
Absolute and Relative Frequencies of Vessels by Rim Type, Temporal Phase, and Location

	Total vessels	*Straight*		*Excurvate*		*Incurvate*		*Recurvate*		*Carinated*	
	n	*n*	%	*n*	%	*n*	%	*n*	%	*n*	%
PHASE I											
Interior components											
Rabbit Mount—nonshell midden	13	7	53.8	0	0.0	6	46.2	0	0.0	0	0.0
Fennel Hill	33	23	69.7	2	6.1	8	24.2	0	0.0	0	0.0
Rabbit Mount—shell midden	96	38	39.6	3	3.1	55	57.3	0	0.0	0	0.0
Rae's Creek	23	19	82.6	0	0.0	4	17.4	0	0.0	0	0.0
White's Mound	26	15	57.7	1	3.8	10	38.5	0	0.0	0	0.0
Rocky Ford	10	4	40.0	1	10.0	5	50.0	0	0.0	0	0.0
WV Site 18	11	5	45.5	0	0.0	6	54.5	0	0.0	0	0.0
Subtotal	212	111	52.4	7	3.3	94	44.3	0	0.0	0	0.0
Coastal Components											
Sapelo Ring—Levels 9–17	10	7	70.0	0	0.0	3	30.0	0	0.0	0	0.0
9CH111	13	9	69.2	1	7.7	3	23.1	0	0.0	0	0.0
Subtotal	23	16	69.6	1	4.3	6	26.1	0	0.0	0	0.0
Phase I Subtotal	235	127	54.0	8	3.4	100	42.6	0	0.0	0	0.0

PHASE II											
Interior components											
38MC479	8	3	37.5	0	0.0	3	37.5	1	12.5	1	12.5
McCalla Bottom	5	1	20.0	0	0.0	2	40.0	2	40.0	0	0.0
Theriault	106	31	29.2	2	1.9	59	55.7	14	13.2	0	0.0
Stallings Island	70	26	37.1	0	0.0	38	54.3	5	7.1	1	1.4
WV Site 23	5	3	60.0	0	0.0	2	40.0	0	0.0	0	0.0
WV Site 14	18	9	50.0	0	0.0	8	44.4	1	5.6	0	0.0
Subtotal	212	73	34.4	2	0.9	112	52.8	23	10.8	2	0.9
Coastal components											
A. Busch Krick 2.5–5'	6	5	83.3	0	0.0	1	16.7	0	0.0	0	0.0
Cane Patch 0–3'	13	7	53.8	0	0.0	6	46.2	0	0.0	0	0.0
Cane Patch 3–6'	21	13	61.9	2	9.5	6	28.6	0	0.0	0	0.0
Sapelo Ring—Levels 1–8	14	8	57.1	0	0.0	6	42.9	0	0.0	0	0.0
Fish Haul—Feature 21	4	2	50.0	0	0.0	2	50.0	0	0.0	0	0.0
Chesterfield	61	24	39.3	2	3.3	31	50.8	4	6.6	0	0.0
Subtotal	119	59	49.6	4	3.4	52	43.7	4	3.4	0	0.0
Phase II Subtotal	331	132	39.9	6	1.8	164	49.5	27	8.2	2	0.6
PHASE III											
Interior components											
Tinker Creek	9	1	11.1	0	0.0	4	44.4	2	22.2	2	22.2
Coastal components											

Table 13.
(Continued)

	Total vessels	*Straight*		*Excurvate*		*Incurvate*		*Recurvate*		*Carinated*	
	n	*n*	%	*n*	%	*n*	%	*n*	%	*n*	%
Fish Haul—Feature 18	3	2	66.7	0	0.0	1	33.3	0	0.0	0	0.0
9CH114a	10	5	50.0	0	0.0	5	50.0	0	0.0	0	0.0
Daw's Island	30	25	83.3	0	0.0	5	16.7	0	0.0	0	0.0
9CH14a	7	2	28.6	0	0.0	5	71.4	0	0.0	0	0.0
A. Busch Krick 0–2.5'	6	2	33.3	1	16.7	3	50.0	0	0.0	0	0.0
Subtotal	56	36	64.3	1	1.8	19	33.9	0	0.0	0	0.0
Phase III Subtotal	65	37	56.9	1	1.5	23	35.4	2	3.1	2	3.1
TOTAL	631	296	46.9	15	2.4	287	45.5	29	4.6	4	0.6

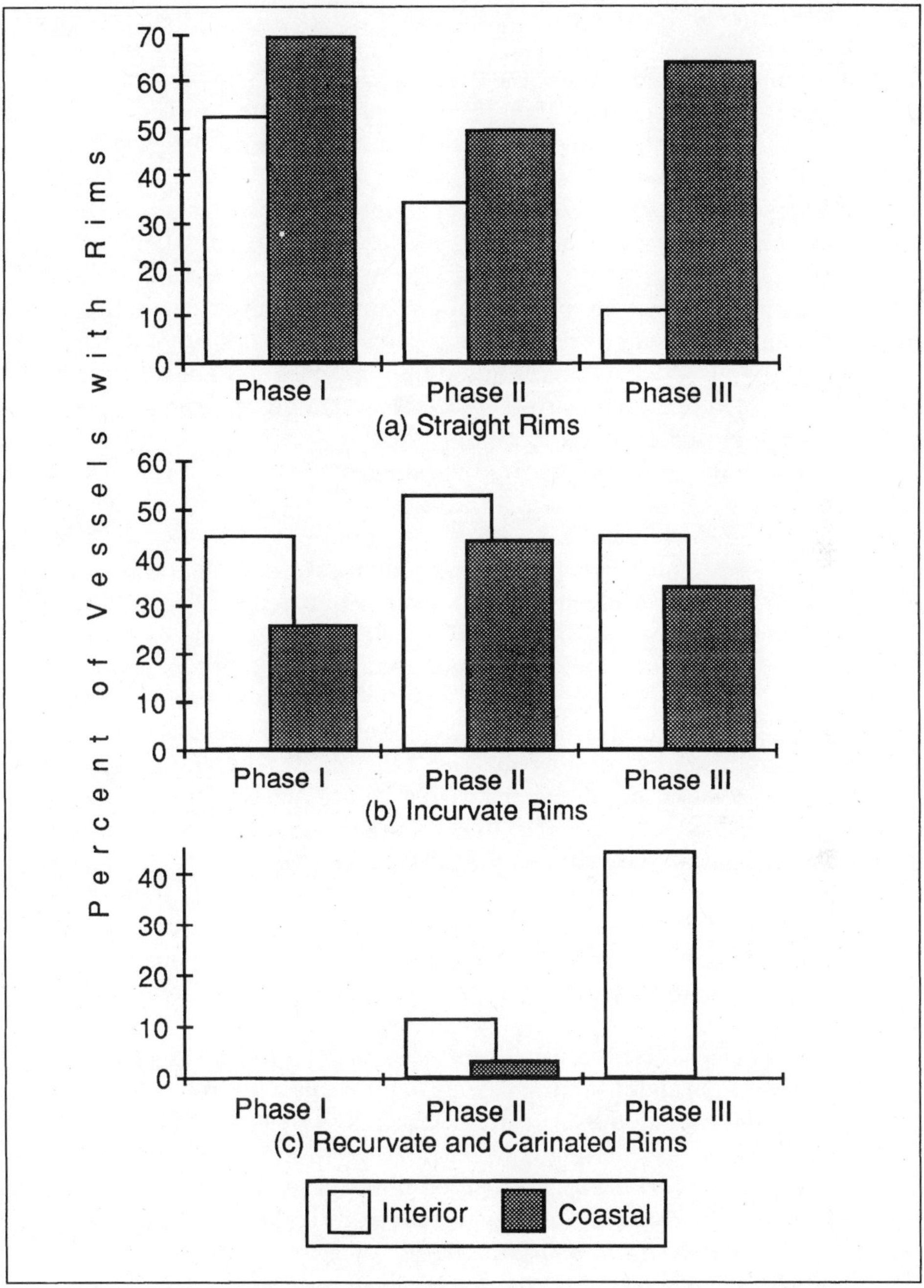

Figure 33. Relative frequency of interior and coastal vessels by rim form and chronological phase.

millimeters. All but one of the thirty-three examples in the sample are decorated, most with elaborate drag and jab motifs.

In consideration of the function of vessels with recurvate and carinated profiles, observations about similar Mississippian vessel forms are instructive. Two forms of carinated bowls—large (28–42 cm diameter) and small (15–25 cm)—are described by Hally (1986) in his analysis of Barnett phase vessels from northwest Georgia. Hally presents evidence on mechanical performance and use alteration to demonstrate that both forms were used to cook and serve foods of liquid consistency, which required minimal cooking. The form is not as adapted to cooking as other Mississippian vessel forms and was probably used to reheat foods that were already cooked. It typically has a high degree of decoration, suggesting to Hally (1986) and following Wobst (1977) that it was used in social contexts involving a large number of people.

There is good reason to suspect that Late Archaic varieties of recurvate and carinated vessels served a function similar to that of Mississippian carinated bowls. The Chesterfield examples demonstrate that some of the vessels were used directly over fire, while the more common interior versions, like their bowl and basin counterparts, were probably used with cooking stones. Despite the constricted design of the orifice, access to the vessel's contents is good so indirect heating was certainly feasible. Alternatively, recurvate forms are associated with sooted soapstone vessels at the late Piedmont and upper Coastal Plain sites so perhaps the ceramic vessels were used only to serve the heated contents of soapstone vessels (see the section below on soapstone vessels). The high incidence of decoration on Late Archaic recurvate and carinated bowls, like the Mississippian examples, suggests that they were used in highly social serving contexts.

The discussion of recurvate and carinated vessels raises an important question about serving vessels in the earliest assemblages in the sample. Recalling the reconstructed vessel sample described earlier, is it possible that the enigmatic small vessel form from Rabbit Mount was used for serving food prepared in the larger basins and bowls? The reconstructed example is plain, but many of the decorated vessels in other Phase I assemblages appear to represent similar small bowls or basins. One example from Rae's Creek is a thin-walled, twenty-two-centimeter- diameter vessel with hollow reed punctation. It is the only sooted vessel in the Rae's Creek assemblage. Similar examples from Fennel Hill and White's Mound have possible traces of soot. On the basis of this limited information, I suggest that decorated vessels in the earliest assemblages were primarily limited to small serving bowls. It must be stressed, however, that not all serving vessels in early assemblages were decorated; in fact, decoration seems to be exceptional. Whether decorated or plain, if thin-walled, small-orifice vessels functioned as serving bowls, then the earliest use of vessels over fire, as currently documented by this sample, was for reheating food in a serving (as opposed to cooking) context.

Vessel Wall Thickness. Data on vessel wall thickness are characterized by little regularity within phases or geographical subsets of phases (Table 14). Wall thickness means vary from 7.7 to 11.2 millimeters for all vessels and 7.8 to 11.2 for fiber-tempered vessels. Only within the Phase I subset of interior assemblages is the range of mean vessel wall thickness small (8.5–9.5 mm). Otherwise, values below this range are observed for assemblages from Stallings Island, Feature 18 at Fish Haul, and 9CH14a. Mean values exceeding the range are more numerous and include those from both portions of the Sapelo Ring No. 1 sequence, 38MC479, Theriault, WV Site 23, Feature 21 at Fish Haul, Tinker Creek, 9CH114a, and the upper portion of A. Busch Krick.

Aggregated by phase and geographical subdivision, mean values for vessel wall thickness are virtually identical (Table 15). When these are subdivided into smaller groups, contrasting temporal trends in wall thickness are evident. Specifically, mean vessel wall thickness among interior assemblages increases uniformly from a low of 8.9 millimeters in Phase I to a high of 10.3 millimeters in Phase III. The opposite trend is observed among coastal vessels: mean wall thickness is highest at 10.06 millimeters in Phase I and decreases to a low of 8.99 millimeters in Phase III.

The apparent trends in vessel wall thickness lend support to the argument that changes in pottery technology on the coast were responsive to the need or desire to improve the efficiency of direct-heat cooking, specifically thermal conductivity. If this indeed is the case, then the same trend should be evident among the subset of coastal vessels with traces of soot. As indicated in Table 16, this expectation is met. Similar to the larger vessel sample, the sooted vessel subset is characterized by a marked decrease in mean wall thickness from Phase I to Phase II, followed by a relatively similar mean and range in

Table 14.
Mean Vessel Wall Thickness (mm) by Vessel Type, Incidence of Soot, Temporal Phase, and Location

	All vessels	*Fiber-tempered vessels*	*Other vessels*	*All sooted vessels*	*All unsooted vessels*
PHASE I					
Interior components					
Rabbit Mount —nonshell midden	8.51	8.48	9.00	-	-
Fennel Hill	8.76	8.76	-	-	-
Rabbit Mount —shell midden	8.98	8.98	8.20	-	-
Rae's Creek	9.07	9.20	7.97	7.40	9.29
White's Mound	8.51	8.59	8.10	7.90	8.49
Rocky Ford	9.21	9.21	-	8.20	10.06
WV Site 18	9.49	9.49	-	9.20	9.72
Coastal components					
Sapelo Ring —Levels 9–17	11.01	11.01	-	12.35	10.55
9CH111	9.19	9.19	-	9.80	9.83

Phase III. Contributing to the sharp decrease in mean vessel wall thickness are the Chesterfield and Cane Patch assemblages. Included in both are sherds from thin (<6 mm), well-made vessels with definite traces of soot. They exemplify the achievement of highly effective direct-heat cooking technology on the coast by Phase II.

The trend of increasing mean values in the wall thickness of vessels from interior assemblages could be taken as evidence that thermal conductivity was irrelevant to pot design. This would support the argument for persistent indirect cooking technology in the interior, though I am reluctant to argue that pot design was trending toward increased thermal insulation (i.e., thicker walls) over the course of Phases II and III. Instead, the changes in mean vessel wall thickness among interior assemblages can partly be attributed to the diversification of vessel forms in Phase II, particularly the introduction of vessels with recurvate and carinated rim profiles.

Support for this inference is found in a cross-tabulation of wall thickness, rim form, and sooting. Sooted vessels in Phase I assem-

Table 14.
(Continued)

	All vessels	*Fiber-tempered vessels*	*Other vessels*	*All sooted vessels*	*All unsooted vessels*
PHASE II					
Interior components					
38MC479	10.61	11.24	6.20	-	-
McCalla Bottom	8.85	8.85	-	-	-
Theriault	9.87	9.42	10.37	10.10	9.62
Stallings Island	8.07	8.07	-	-	-
WV Site 23	10.21	10.21	-	9.50	11.80
WV Site 14	9.28	9.33	8.00	11.25	9.08
Coastal components					
A. Busch Krick 2.5–5'	9.46	9.46	-	9.88	8.77
Cane Patch 0-3'	8.53	8.53	-	8.50	8.57
Cane Patch 3-6'	9.24	9.33	7.30	9.12	8.96
Sapelo Ring—Levels 1–8	9.53	9.53	-	9.50	9.15
Fish Haul—Feature 21	11.00	11.00	-	-	-
Chesterfield	8.73	8.96	7.76	8.42	8.84
PHASE III					
Interior components					
Tinker Creek	10.35	11.93	9.64	10.00	10.65
Coastal components					
Fish Haul—Feature 18	8.27	8.27	-	9.00	7.90
9CH114a	9.79	9.79	-	-	-
Daw's Island	8.67	8.64	9.50	8.58	8.67
9CH14a	7.71	7.85	7.53	8.10	8.00
A. Busch Krick 0–2.5'	11.20	11.20	-	12.60	10.98

blages have consistently thinner walls than unsooted vessels. The sooted vessels are usually decorated, and those with intact or reconstructed rims have orifices of twenty-two centimeters or less in diameter. Although lacking the recurvate or carinated rim profile, these small sooted vessels are believed to be serving bowls in which food was reheated over direct heat but not cooked. In contrast, many assemblages (coastal, as well as interior) dating to Phases II and III are characterized by sooted vessels with walls that are as thick as or thicker than those of unsooted vessels. Sooted vessels in these assem-

Table 15.
Summary Statistics on Vessel Wall Thickness (mm) for All Specimens with Rims by Temporal Phase and Geographical Subdivision

	Interior	*Coastal*	*Total*
Phase I			
n	230	23	253
mean	8.91	10.06	9.02
s.d.	1.71	2.05	1.77
minimum	4.8	6.3	4.8
maximum	14.3	14.3	14.3
Phase II			
n	221	129	350
mean	9.31	9.01	9.20
s.d.	2.04	1.61	1.90
minimum	4.8	4.3	4.3
maximum	15.4	13.7	15.4
Phase III			
n	13	57	70
mean	10.35	8.99	9.24
s.d.	2.49	1.87	2.05
minimum	6.6	4.6	4.6
maximum	15.3	13.3	15.3
Total			
n	464	209	673
mean	9.14	9.12	9.13
s.d.	1.91	1.76	1.87
minimum	4.8	4.3	4.8
maximum	15.4	14.3	15.4

blages include combinations of serving bowls and cooking bowls and pots, the latter being substantially larger than the former and usually with thicker walls. That the walls of unsooted vessels are often thinner than those of sooted vessels suggests that small noncooking vessel forms prevailed during Phases II and III. If we can assume that many of the thinner unsooted vessels were indeed serving bowls, the need to reheat foods in serving bowls may have diminished by the time cooking vessels were being used over direct fire. This may be

Table 16.
Summary Statistics on Vessel Wall Thickness (mm) for All Sooted Specimens with Rims by Temporal Phase and Geographical Subdivision

	Interior	*Coastal*	*Total*
Phase I			
n	6	6	12
mean	8.18	11.50	9.84
s.d.	1.89	1.92	2.51
minimum	6.0	9.4	6.0
maximum	11.4	14.3	14.3
Phase II			
n	9	60	69
mean	9.54	8.91	8.99
s.d.	2.62	1.57	1.73
minimum	5.9	4.3	4.3
maximum	13.1	13.5	13.5
Phase III			
n	2	7	9
mean	10.00	9.14	9.33
s.d.	3.39	2.48	2.49
minimum	7.6	4.6	4.6
maximum	12.4	12.6	12.6
Total			
n	17	73	90
mean	9.12	9.14	9.14
s.d.	2.41	1.82	1.93
minimum	5.9	4.3	4.3
maximum	13.1	14.3	14.3

true not only because of changes in cooking techniques but because the cooking of food in pots may have increasingly become a social activity coupled with the immediate serving of foods.

Further Evidence for Improvements in the Mechanical Performance of Direct-Heat Cooking Vessels. To lend further support to the apparent improvements in direct-heat cooking technology noted above, I emphasize relevant data from certain coastal sites. I do this to reiterate evidence for improvements in vessel technology at stratified shell middens and to introduce ancillary evidence for technological changes that heretofore have gone unmentioned. Alternate strategies for improving the mechanical performance of direct-heat cooking vessels on the coast are exemplified by these data.

All three of the Georgia coastal sites with deep shell deposits have an increased incidence of incurvate vessel profiles through time, forms that may have helped to decrease convection heat loss (Table 17). Over half of the incurvate vessels in these assemblages have soot. Orifice diameters range from 21.0 to 57.5 centimeters so these vessels may include both serving and cooking vessels used over fire. Mean wall thickness of sooted vessels decreases through time in two of the three assemblages, corroborating the trend for improved thermal conductivity documented above. The assemblage from the upper stratum at A. Busch Krick includes few vessels with intact surfaces, only one of which was sooted. The wall thickness for this vessel is 12.6 millimeters.

Many of the profiles of sooted vessels from other coastal sites include straight-sided forms with a low orifice-to-volume ratio (Figure 34). A coiling technique of manufacture may have been used to achieve the deeper forms. A suggestion of coiling was noted on

Table 17.
Comparison of Lower and Upper Strata of Three Georgia Coastal Shell Middens for Variables Relevant to Mechanical Performance of Direct-Heat Cooking Vessels

	A. Busch Krick	*Sapelo Ring No.1*	*Cane Patch*
Relative frequency			
Incurvate rims			
Upper stratum	50.0%	42.9%	46.2%
Lower stratum	16.7%	30.0%	28.6%
Mean wall thickness (mm)			
of sooted vessels			
Upper stratum	-	9.50	8.50
Lower stratum	9.88	12.35	9.12

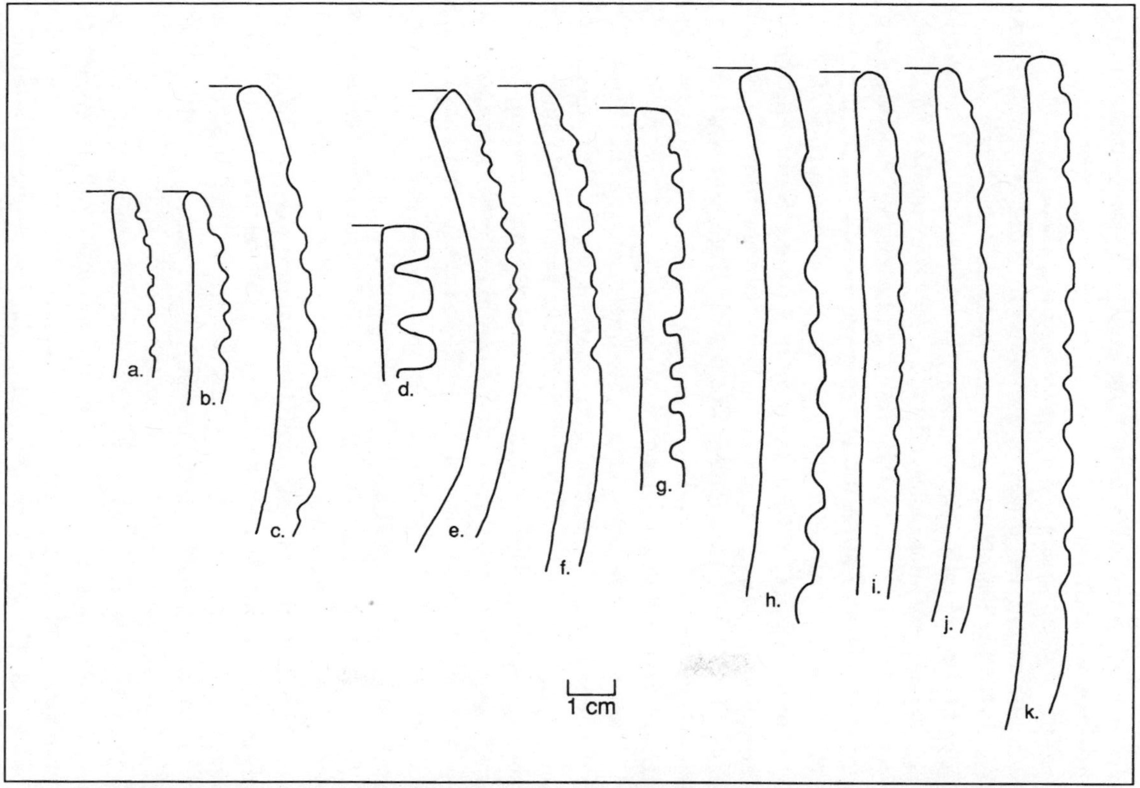

Figure 34. Vessel rim profiles of selected coastal vessels (a–c. 9CH14a; d–g. Cane Patch; h–k. Chesterfield).

Chesterfield sherds by Griffin (1942), and Trinkley (1986) has provided convincing evidence for coiling on sherds from Fish Haul. Whether the innovation of coiling started among coastal potters remains uncertain.

Walls of deep, straight-sided vessels are typically thin or, if thick, deep punctation and grooving provided increased external surface area. Whether deep punctations and grooves were intended to improve heating effectiveness can never be known, but it is certain that such surface treatment allowed for quicker transfer of heat through the ceramic body. Cane Patch grooving is especially notable for the excessive depth of punctations and grooves, so deep in some cases that styli nearly protruded through vessel walls (Figure 34d).

A combination of several performance properties for efficient direct-heat usage is evident in the small assemblage from 9CH14a. Like many of the coastal examples, the vessels have thin walls and are extensively punctated, and there is a high incidence of incurvate rim forms. Unlike other coastal assemblages in the sample, most of the 9CH14a specimens have paste consisting of even mixtures of fiber and sand or grit. This combination may have provided an effective compromise for the conflicting requirement of thermal shock resistance and heating effectiveness. Other vessels in the assemblage lack fiber altogether; these appear to represent the southernmost extent of Thom's Creek pottery on the Georgia-South Carolina coast. Minor decorative motifs in the assemblage parallel Thom's Creek designs from the Charleston area (see Chapter 6).

Finally, shell scraping marks on the interior and, sometimes, exterior of coastal vessels testify to the desires of potters to thin vessel walls or at least to achieve uniform wall thickness (Figure 35). Assemblages with many sooted vessels have several examples of shell scraping (e.g., Cane Patch, Chesterfield, Sapelo Island). The highest incidence of shell scraping (48 percent) in the sample is in the Daw's Island assemblage, noted also for the relatively low incidence of sooting. Because of the lack of sooting, increased heating effectiveness probably was not the sole intent of potters employing the technique. It is nonetheless noteworthy that of the few instances of sooted vessels in the Daw's Island assemblage, half were scraped with shell. Shell scraping is relatively common in Thom's Creek assemblages of the South Carolina coast, especially the finger-pinched series (roughly 12 percent; Trinkley 1980a:9). Use-alteration studies of this series have not been conducted, but my incidental observations of

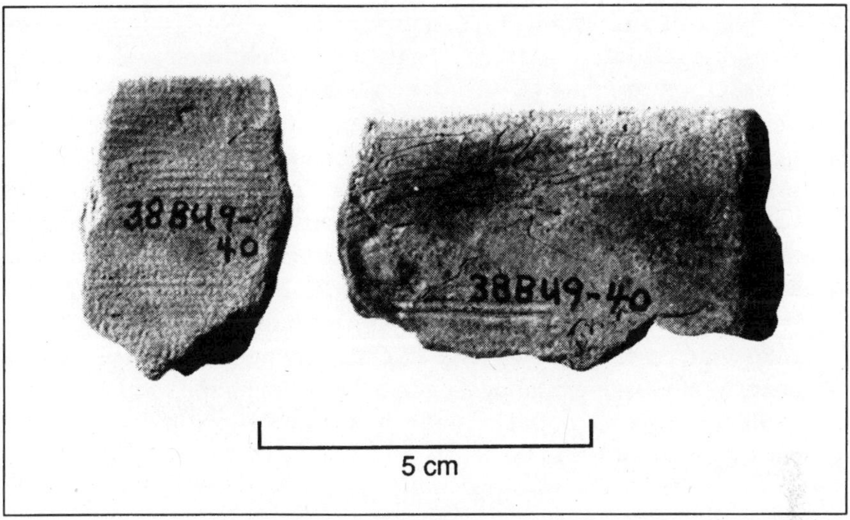

Figure 35. Examples of shell scraping on the interior of vessels from Daw's Island.

finger-pinched vessel sherds include some examples of exterior sooting.

Many of the traits that seemingly improved the thermal efficiency of pots for use over direct fire on the coast have coeval equivalents among interior assemblages. For instance, Stallings Island pottery is among the thinnest in the region, and there is a high incidence of incurvate rim forms. Information on paste was not available for the Stallings Island sample included in this study, but Claflin (1931:14) indicates that about 60 percent of the sherds he uncovered contained some type of aplastic. Despite these technological traits, very little of the interior pottery shows traces of soot. In the chief assemblages dating to around 3700 B.P.—Stallings Island and Theriault—fewer than 4 percent of the vessels have soot (see also Skibo, Hally, and Schiffer 1988, who detect a similarly low incidence of possible soot [3 percent] on a sample of 267 sherds from Stallings Island). As indicated earlier, these data, combined with the persistence of soapstone slabs, suggest that ceramic vessels continued to be used as containers for stone cooking at interior sites as late as 3700 B.P. What is more, this technique of cooking persisted even though certain innovations that seemingly improved the effectiveness of using vessels over fire were absorbed or perhaps even developed by interior potters.

By Phase III, ceramic vessels appear to have been regularly used over fire at interior sites. As discussion in Chapter 6 will show, the distribution of Phase III sites with fiber-tempered pottery contrasts sharply with earlier distributions. The chief difference is that pottery began to be used deep in the Piedmont and in the upland tributaries of the interior Coastal Plain. Soot is found on sherds from these sites, basin forms disappear completely, and there is a uniform increase in the amount of sand in the paste. The only late assemblage to lack sooted vessels, McCalla Bottom, includes the earliest large assemblage of soapstone vessels. Neighboring interior sites also contain soapstone vessel sherds, a large fraction of which have traces of soot. Soapstone vessel technology, once believed to be the local precursor to fiber-tempered pottery, is the final innovation of Late Archaic cooking technology to be discussed.

Soapstone Vessels

Soapstone was widely used by North American Indians north of Mexico for the manufacture of cooking vessels (Holmes 1912:635). Prehistorically, soapstone vessels were made by populations of the south Pacific coast, the Mid-Atlantic region, New England, and the Southeast. Soapstone vessel industries predated ceramic vessel technology in each of these areas, and among some California groups it survived through the contact period.

Although soapstone bowls are well documented in preceramic contexts in the greater Southeast (e.g., Webb and DeJarnette 1942), fiber-tempered pottery seems to have preceded soapstone vessels by several hundred years in certain parts of the South Atlantic Slope. Soapstone vessel sherds have never been found in preceramic contexts in the Savannah River Valley. On the basis of recent excavations in the Piedmont (Schuldenrein, Anderson, and Cantley 1985; Tippitt and Marquardt 1984), soapstone vessels probably were not manufactured or imported into the area until about 3500 B.P., a full millennium after fiber-tempered pottery appeared in the Coastal Plain. Some minor examples of sherds in early ceramic contexts (e.g., White's Mound) may point to a much earlier date for soapstone vessels, but there is nothing to suggest that they played more than a minor role in preceramic cooking technology.

Soapstone vessel technology in the study area never seems to have reached the level of utilitarian importance it did among the Chumash and Gabrielino of California. In California and the Southeast alike, however, exchange of soapstone vessels was significant to the regulation and maintenance of intersocietal relations (Elliott 1981:24–30; Hudson and Blackburn 1987:35; Webb 1944). The relevance of this exchange to changes in Late Archaic cooking technology and societal organization is addressed in Chapter 6.

There is little doubt that most, if not all, of the specimens in the Savannah River Valley sample were used directly over fire for cooking (Figure 36). Soapstone was not a widespread and common vessel alternative locally. Fragments of only fifteen vessels were observed from eight assemblages in the sample (Table 18). Six, or 40 percent, of the vessels have traces of soot, while another two are basal fragments lacking soot but with heavy thermal attrition. Both the absolute frequency of vessel sherds and the incidence of sooting are biased by the recycling of soapstone sherds at locations away from quarries. Coastal Plain examples of vessels (save one from White's Mound) are represented by relatively small sherds that have been sawn, ground, or otherwise modified. Examples of vessel sherds recycled into pendants, gorgets, and perhaps cooking stones are not uncommon. Such recycling often obliterates diagnostic traits of vessel sherds, including surficial deposits of soot. Nevertheless, the frequency of soapstone vessels in the Coastal Plain portion of the Savannah is well below the rate at which soapstone slabs entered the province.

A variety of vessel sizes and shapes can be inferred from the sherds, but only one vessel in the sample could be reconstructed to provide an accurate profile and orifice measurement (Figure 37g). The vessel, from White's Mound, is thirteen centimeters tall and roughly circular in plan with an inside orifice diameter of twenty-eight centimeters. Wall thickness is very uniform at slightly over one centimeter. The exterior is uniformly gouged from the shaping and thinning of the vessel, while the interior is highly polished. Examples of similar vessels are reported from a site in the Oconee Valley of Georgia (Hally 1982:23–25) and from a site on the Saluda River in South Carolina (Ryan 1972:177–78). Each of these vessels has definite soot deposits.

Rim sherds from McCalla Bottom, the only assemblage with more than one vessel, depict a thicker, less refined soapstone vessel form (Figure 37a–d). Wall thickness varies from 1.0 to 2.5 centimeters, and one example has a base at least 3.0 centimeters thick. One example consists of two rim sherds with different degrees of curvature, suggesting an oblong vessel shape. The form of the others is indeterminate.

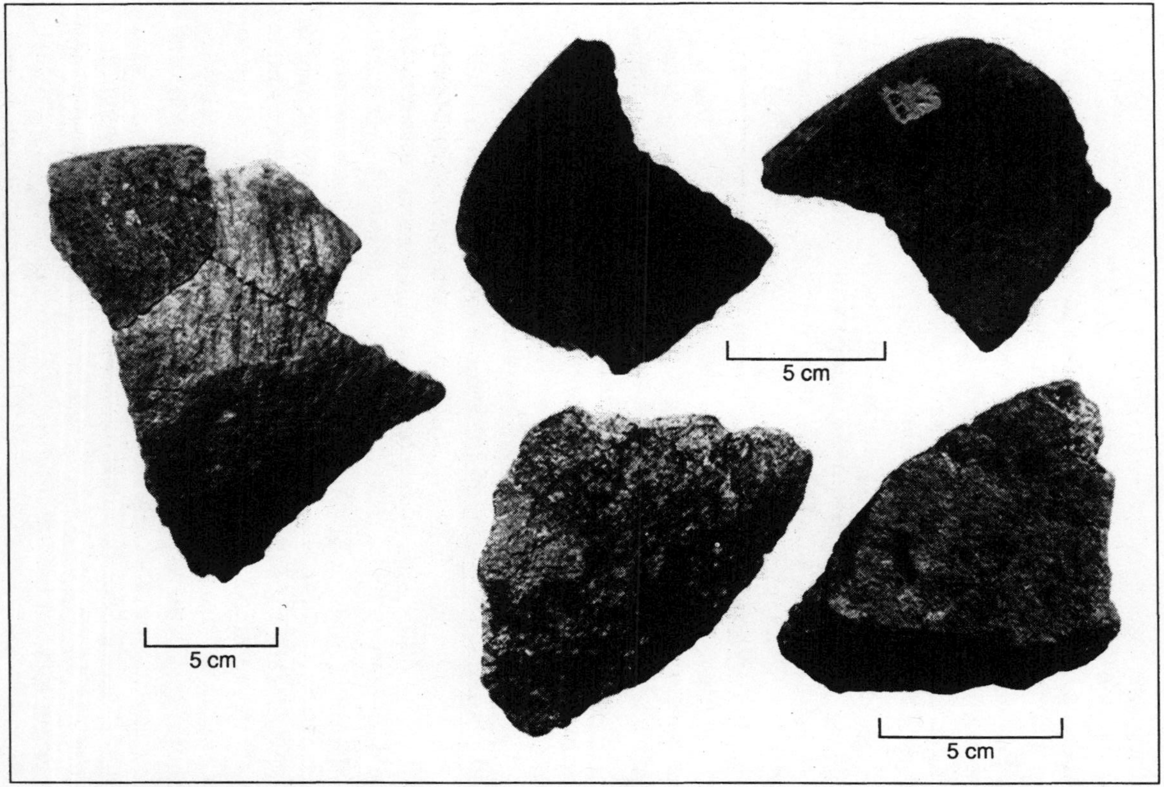

Figure 36. Examples of sooted soapstone vessel sherds. Interior and exterior of example from 9RI137 shown at upper right; interior and exterior of example from McCalla Bottom shown at lower right; exterior of example from White's Mound shown at left.

Table 18.
Tabulation of Soapstone Vessel Sherds, Vessel Count, Incidence of Sooting, and Sherd Weight Statistics for Eight Assemblages in the Sample

				Weight (g)		
Assemblage	*Sherd count*	*Vessel count*	*Sooted vessels*	*Minimum*	*Maximum*	*Mean*
McCalla Bottom	37	8	2	4.2	281.7	66.5
Stallings Island	1	1	0	55.4	-	-
9RI137	2	1	1	149.3	218.2	183.7
White's Mound	7	1	1	366.9	-	-
38AK158	1	1	0	27.5	-	-
Tinker Creek	2	1	1	50.9	-	-
Theriault	2	1	1	27.9	72.0	49.9
Daw's Island	1	1	0	28.2	-	-

Several soapstone outcrops in the Piedmont portion of the Savannah were quarried for bowls (Wauchope 1966:430; Daniel Elliott, personal communication 1989), but bowl manufacture seems to have been much more prevalent at Piedmont quarries in the adjacent watersheds (Dickens and Carnes 1983; Elliott 1981, 1986a; Ferguson 1976; Lowman and Wheatley 1970; Overton 1969).

A variety of vessel forms was produced at quarries in South Carolina and Georgia. Two styles of bowls are noted from quarry sites in Cherokee and Spartanburg counties, South Carolina: an oval bowl with a flat bottom and a circular bowl with a round bottom (Lowman and Wheatley 1970; Overton 1969:6). The dimensions of two abandoned circular preforms are roughly 42 to 47 centimeters wide and 25 to 28 centimeters tall (Lowman and Wheatley 1970:8). At Soapstone Ridge near Atlanta at least three forms were being made: a hemispherical bowl, a conical form with flat or pointed base, and an elongated bowl with rounded or squared ends and usually with lug handles (Dickens and Carnes 1983:86; Elliott 1986a).

Besides soapstone's superb thermal properties, there is nothing about the typical vessel forms in the Southeast to indicate that they were especially adapted to cooking over a direct flame. Contrast the open, shallow bowl form of the Southeast with the deep, hemispherical olla of coastal California populations. The Chumash olla was a round-bottomed vessel up to sixty centimeters wide but with a small,

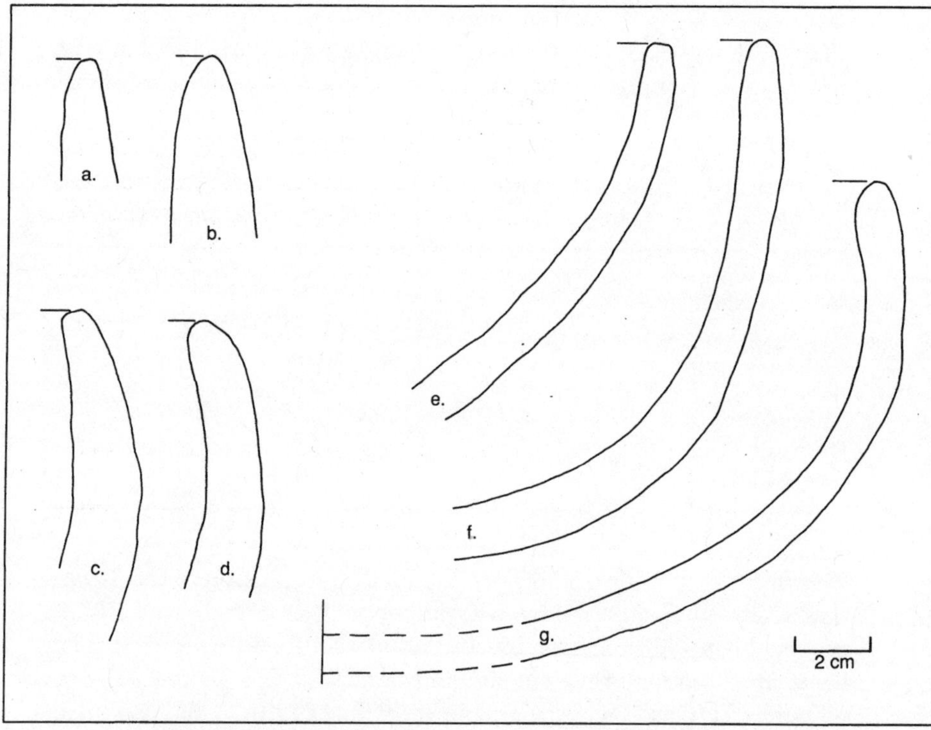

Figure 37. Profiles of soapstone vessels (a–d. McCalla Bottom; e–f. 9GE145; g. White's Mound).

constricted orifice and thin walls (Kroeber 1925:562). In these vessels the Chumash roasted seeds and boiled acorn mush. They used other open bowl forms for serving food or in religious ceremonies. Pottery was known to the historic Chumash, but they preferred to use soapstone to manufacture vessels for use over a direct flame (Ebeling 1986:280–81; Hudson and Blackburn 1983:207–10).

More similar to the soapstone bowls of the Savannah River Valley are those made by populations of the upper San Joaquin Valley (Gifford 1932; Kroeber 1925:527). Unlike those of their coastal neighbors, the soapstone vessels of San Joaquin groups were usually small, wide-mouthed, shallow cooking bowls. Rather than being substitutes for cooking baskets, soapstone vessels and occasionally pottery (e.g., Yokuts) were secondary containers that apparently were used for only a limited number of cooking functions (e.g., Kroeber 1925:527). Owing to the relatively poor and limited soapstone resources of the central valley area, a soapstone vessel technology limited to shallow, open bowls provided little advantage over basket cooking.

Because pottery and the innovation of using pots over fire were widely diffused in the Savannah River Valley at about the same time soapstone vessels appeared, there probably was little advantage to expending time and energy to produce shallow, open bowls as an alternative to pots that were adapted for use over fire. Soapstone vessels may have been labor-saving to use, but they were costly to obtain (i.e., raw material is limited in distribution and bowl manufacture is time-consuming and laborious). Moreover, raw soapstone and finished vessels alike were certainly more difficult to transport than other containers and would thus be impractical from the standpoint of portability.

Economic drawbacks notwithstanding, the Chumash and other California groups continued to use soapstone vessels long after pottery became available to them. The acquisition and distribution of soapstone were central to intersocietal relations of the southern California tribes, and the persistence of Chumash cooking traditions can be understood only in the context of this exchange. Late Archaic use of soapstone vessels in the Savannah River Valley pales in comparison to that of the Chumash, but at the time soapstone vessels were first being used in the valley, the Poverty Point exchange network was in full swing. The scale and complexity of Poverty Point exchange, which included soapstone vessels, easily rivaled, if not exceeded, the California networks. Distant though it may seem, Savannah River Valley soapstone vessel use (or lack thereof) was probably influenced by the surrounding commerce in vessels.

Summary and Conclusions

Four major innovations in cooking technology emerged in the Savannah River Valley region during the Late Archaic period. The first, soapstone slabs or cooking stones, appeared around 5000 B.P. and persisted for at least twelve hundred if not sixteen hundred years. These items were highly curated tools that were at times produced in large quantities for use by groups occupying both the soapstone-rich Piedmont and Fall Zone and the soapstone-free Coastal Plain. Because of the limited distribution of soapstone outcrops, these tools were expensive to obtain but relatively easy to transport, use, and maintain. They provided superior thermal efficiency compared to hard crystalline rocks. In lieu of replacement, soapstone slabs could be readily repaired when they broke, which led to their seemingly long use lives.

Soapstone slabs and other cooking stones were used long before pottery was available and thereafter by groups lacking pottery as well as by pot users themselves. In the absence of pottery, water and liquid foods were probably cooked in a variety of organic containers and pits. Examples of possible cooking pits have been reported, though the use of inorganic containers such as baskets or hides can only be inferred from indirect evidence.

The second major innovation in the study area was ceramic vessel technology. Data on the mechanical performance and use alteration of pottery dating roughly from 4500 to 4000 B.P. indicate that vessels were most often used as containers for stone cooking. This conclusion is supported by formal and use-alteration properties, which preclude the use of these vessels over direct fire, and by their association with soapstone slabs. The earliest vessels were shallow, flat-bottomed basins with thick walls and thickened or flanged lips. Emphasis in design was, by intention or default, on insulation of internal heat rather than conduction of external heat. In essence, these early vessels were portable, above-ground "pits."

The advantages of early pottery over other indirect cooking containers were probably limited. Ethnographic accounts of indirect cooking with pottery cited earlier indicate that ceramic vessels were sometimes considered superior to organic containers such as baskets because hot rocks could not burn through the bottoms of pots and therefore required less attention. The thermal insulation of thick ceramic vessels would certainly exceed that of baskets or bark vessels but would be less than that of clay-lined pits. Heat loss through convection is a factor independent of the container medium. Judging from the size and shapes of pits believed to have been used for indirect cooking, convection loss was lower in ceramic basins than in pits. Nevertheless, if indirect moist cooking in vessels emphasized short-term, low-temperature methods, as Reid (1989) suggests, then thermal advantages of pots over other containers may have been negligible.

Given the traditional stone-cooking technology into which pottery entered, the advantage of ceramic vessels over alternative forms of indirect cooking might be best understood in relation to soapstone availability. Limited access to soapstone may have placed a premium on the insulation of containers regardless of the thermal requirements of an indirect cooking technique. That is, an abundance of soapstone or other cooking rock mitigated excessive heat loss by allowing for rapid cycling of heated stones into containers. A lack of sufficient soapstone (i.e., small pieces or few pieces) may have led to strategies to increase thermal retention. One solution would be to increase the depth and decrease the aperture of pits. The sandy substrate of the Coastal Plain required that pits be lined with clay, treated hides, or some other impervious material. Under these conditions, a technological transition from subterranean fire-clay pits to self-contained ceramic containers is not hard to imagine. There is some support for this transition, but I do not rule out the possibility that the innovation of pottery came to the Savannah region from elsewhere. In either case, the choice of pottery over a more thermally efficient pit technology suggests that portability was desirable (Schiffer and Skibo 1987).

Innovations related to the development of pots for use over fire took place on the coast about three to five hundred years after pottery was available in the region. These innovations consisted of changes in the form and composition of vessels to improve the thermal conductivity (e.g., thinner vessel walls) and heat retention (e.g., lower orifice-volume ratio) of ceramic vessels. The innovations appear to have been precipitated by a decrease in the flow of soapstone to the coast (see Chapter 6) and perhaps associated with new cooking requirements (prolonged cooking). Baked clay objects may represent an initial attempt to offset the decreased availability of soapstone or other lithic materials, but the poor thermal shock properties of untempered clay combined with the widespread co-occurrence of baked clay objects and soapstone in the interior argue against this and instead point to another function for the objects.

During the time that fiber-tempered pots were used over fires on the coast, interior pottery underwent change in form and composition that suggests improved heating effectiveness, but pots were not regularly used over fire until late in the sequence. Until about 3500 B.P., soapstone cooking stones continued to be used in bowls and shallow pots. Carinated and recurvate bowls appear to have been serving vessels that were sometimes used directly over fire to reheat, but not cook, food. The eventual adoption in the interior of the direct-heat method of cooking coincides with the expansion of fiber-tempered pottery deep into the Piedmont and in the tributaries of the upper Coastal Plain. Soapstone vessels made their first substantial appearance at this time, but never seem to have gained much functional importance in the study area. The McCalla Bottom site is one exception. The relatively large number of soapstone vessels in the assemblage coupled with a lack of sooted ceramic vessels suggests that when the innovation of direct-fire cooking was adopted by the resident group it was grafted onto the traditional raw material for cooking technology.

The relationship between soapstone and ceramic cooking technologies cannot be fully understood without taking into consideration the social relations underpinning the production, distribution, and use of these alternatives. The innovations I have documented in this chapter may have arisen for reasons that are readily interpretable in economic (cost-benefit) terms alone, but the slow rate at which the innovations spread and the sometimes indirect pathways they took have much to do with social factors.

CHAPTER 6

Social and Economic Contexts of Early Ceramic Vessel Technology

In this chapter I present evidence for the distribution of Late Archaic sociocultural entities in the Savannah River Valley region and data on the flow of soapstone among them. Combined with the chronological and technofunctional evidence presented earlier, this information is then used to evaluate propositions presented in Chapter 2 about social factors in the development and spread of fiber-tempered pottery.

Stylistic Variation of Fiber-Tempered Pottery in the Savannah River Valley Region

Discrete sociocultural entities within Late Archaic populations of the Savannah River Valley region have been inferred by some researchers from patterned variation in the spatial distribution of fiber-tempered pottery (e.g., Anderson 1975; Waring 1968a; Widmer 1976). Discussion along these lines has been largely devoted to broad stylistic attributes such as random punctation, separate linear punctation, drag and jab punctation, incision, and the like. Other dimensions of variability, including lip form, incidence of multiple design techniques, and type of punctation stylus, have received little attention. This is perhaps not surprising because of the seemingly infinite variation such fine-grained analyses would entail. Taking into consideration variability of the more fine-grained attributes, one is hard-pressed to find two identical decorated pots in a particular assemblage. Given such fundamental diversity, which dimensions of variability might be sensitive to sociocultural boundaries or territories in the study area?

A recent study of southern African fiber-tempered pottery by C. Garth Sampson (1988) is instructive in detecting spatial patterns of stylistic variation. In its incidence and variety of punctation, southern African pottery has uncanny similarity to fiber-tempered pottery of the South Atlantic Slope. Sampson found that the type of stylus used to punctate pottery varied across subregions of his study area, and he combines several lines of evidence (including the distribution of raw materials) to suggest that the stylistic clusters represent sociocultural entities.

Within the Savannah region punctation was the chief form of pottery decoration. The technique is observed in all assemblages with decorated vessels, and it spans the entire duration of fiber-tempered pottery manufacture. Temporal trends in the use of punctation have been noted, of course, and these provide effective means of relative dating. That the type of stylus used to punctate pottery might reflect significant synchronic variation among potters, related to group signaling or bounding, has not been adequately considered (cf. Widmer 1976). There is some suggestion that differences in styli are fortuitous, reflecting more the local availability of materials than cultural preference for particular types of styli (Trinkley 1980b). Support for this assertion is drawn from the apparent exclusion of shell-punctated pottery from interior sites. Because most shell-punctated pottery on the coast is made with marsh periwinkle, the lack of this decoration within interior assemblages is argued to be the simple result of a lack of periwinkle in freshwater settings.

In contradiction to this argument stand a considerable number of shell-punctated pots among the earliest assemblages of the interior Savannah River Valley. These pots were decorated with freshwater gastropod shells, an example of which is depicted in Figure 38. That the use of freshwater gastropod shells did not persist in the interior during the fourth millennium was a cultural choice, not a matter of the availability of shell, because these species continued to be used during this time, presumably for food, by occupants of Stallings Island and the surrounding contemporaneous shell midden sites of the Fall Zone.

As for nonshell styli, there is some evidence to suggest that punc-

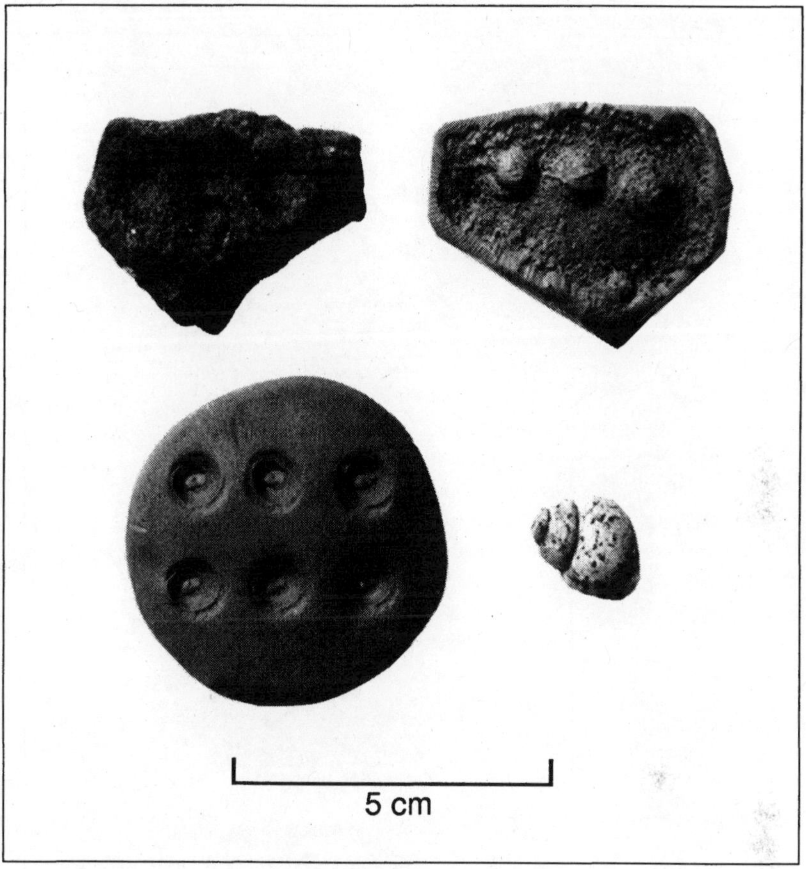

Figure 38. Shell point punctate sherd (upper left) and clay impression of design (upper right) made from freshwater gastropod shell (lower right), as exemplified by clay impression (lower left). Sherd and shell from Fennel Hill.

tation styli were sometimes formal, curated tools used over a long period of time, perhaps even passed down from generation to generation. An example of such a tool was found on the surface of Stallings Island by Daniel R. Robinson (personal communication 1988). The implement is a long bone fragment (presumably deer) with two distinct worked ends (Figure 39). One end was beveled to form a subtriangular, pointed tip. Obvious traces of polish on this end indicate that it was used to punch or groove relatively soft material. The

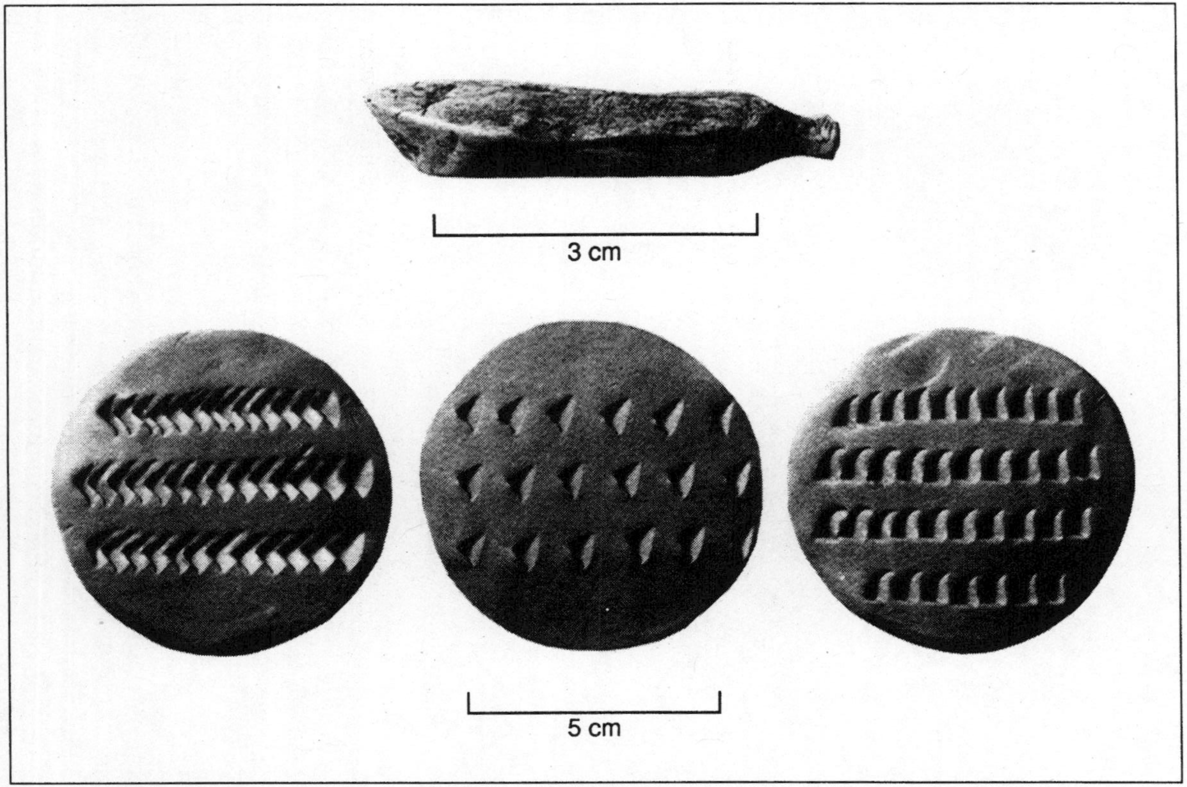

Figure 39. Bone tool from Stallings Island postulated to be stylus for making subtriangular pointed punctations on pottery and clay impressions of variation of the design.

opposite end has been carved to produce a constricted neck that may have served to haft the tool or to attach it to a thong. The subtriangular punctation that can be made with this tool is seen in many sherds from Stallings Island and vicinity. Variation in the angle, depth, and spacing of punctations produces distinct patterns (Figure 39) so the user could be creative or consistent depending on the manipulation of the tool. Despite variation in use, properties of the stylus should enable observers to identify the maker of a vessel.

I have identified at least eighteen distinct punctation styli among the decorated fiber-tempered vessels in my sample. These can be grouped into three categories: styli made from reed, wood, antler, or bone; shell styli; and fingernail. In the first group some minor types are recognized but not formally classified, and others could not be identified because of irregularities or poor preservation. A small minority of vessels were punctated with two types of styli, usually a combination of cylinder and shell. Table 19 provides a breakdown of vessel count and percentage of punctated vessels by type of stylus.

Before I review distributional patterns of various punctation styli, some qualifying comments regarding this classification are necessary. First, there is nothing particularly meaningful about the categories listed; they simply consist of classes that were intuitively distinct to me and, with the exception of shell styli, there is nothing in the literature to suggest that these categories have temporal or spatial significance.

Second, the reed categories are not mutually exclusive. In particular, it appears that a crescent punctation was often made by pressing a complete hollow cylinder into the vessel wall at an oblique angle. Also, among solid cylinders, the distinction between a pointed and rounded end could not always be upheld, especially when punctations were deep. Accordingly, in the analysis that follows, I have combined the hollow and crescent styli into one group and the pointed-end and rounded-end cylindrical styli into another. These combined groups constitute the largest subset of nonshell styli in the sample.

The final comment has to do with incising. The extant literature on incised decoration documents a wide distribution for the motif, but there is no information on possible temporal and spatial patterns in types of incisions, such as bold versus fine. Line width and cross-sectional shape are functions of the tool used so variation in incising can be dealt with in much the same way as punctation styli. Limited data on incisions were collected, but these nevertheless provide ancillary support for distributional patterns of punctation styli.

Specific Design Technique Distributions

In examining the spatial distribution of punctation styli and incised techniques, we must keep in mind certain suppositions from the extant literature and the classification in Chapter 4. Foremost is the delineation of subregional, localized pottery styles. Distinct Late Archaic groups along the coast and in the interior have been proposed (e.g., Anderson, Lee, and Parler 1979; Waring 1968a; Widmer 1976),

Table 19.
Count and Percentage of Fiber-Tempered Vessels by Type of Punctation Stylus

Types of Stylus	*Number*	*Percent*
Reed, Wood, Antler, and Bone		
Hollow cylinder	11	2.4
Crescent (hollow half cylinder)	52	11.3
Bifurcated hollow cylinder	6	1.3
Half-circle (solid half cylinder) with flat end	27	5.9
Solid cylinder with pointed end	50	10.9
Solid cylinder with rounded end	20	4.4
Solid cylinder with flattened end	7	1.5
Wedge	35	7.6
Triangular with flattened end	7	1.5
Subtriangular with pointed end	40	8.7
Square/rectangle with flattened end	4	0.9
Chevron	14	3.1
Fluted	2	0.4
Pinhole	5	1.1
Irregular/unknown	60	13.8
Other minor types	15	3.3
Shell		
Point	96	21.0
Side	1	0.2
Edge	1	0.2
Fingernail	6	1.3
Multiple styli	(11)	
Total	459	100.0

and to some extent this analysis is designed to provide empirical evidence to evaluate these propositions. At the same time, temporal trends in the use of certain styli and design techniques are also evident so we must control for time in examining spatial distributions of stylistic elements. To this end, I employ the phase parameters defined in Chapter 4 to examine distributional patterns at three separate times. The criteria used to classify sites temporally overlap a bit with the punctation and incision data, though the data sets are largely independent. To review the phase designations derived from the paradigmatic classification in Chapter 4, Phase I spans the interval 4500–3800 B.P. and is characterized in the early centuries by plain pottery with thickened or flanged lips and in the later centuries by plain and decorated vessels. Phase II, spanning 3800 to 3400 B.P., marks the period of abundant and elaborate decoration of pottery. Phase III encompasses all fiber-tempered pottery assemblages postdating 3400 B.P. and is characterized by a high degree of inter-assemblage variability.

Shell Point Punctate. Shell point punctation has a wider regional distribution than previously thought, being found in appreciable quantity at sites as far inland as White's Mound (Figure 40). The vast majority of shell punctate vessels at interior sites is attributed to Phase I assemblages. All of the Phase I examples consist of separate linear designs, with minor examples of random punctation. In the subsequent phase, shell point punctate is virtually restricted to coastal assemblages. Its absence at Stallings Island is especially notable. The shell stylus is common in coastal assemblages both north and south of the Savannah, where it is used to create separate linear designs. It is also found over incisions and grooves but only at sites on the Georgia coast. The only interior Phase II site with a large number of shell punctate vessels is Theriault, where the stylus is restricted to separate linear designs. Shell point punctation persists into Phase III but is restricted to the Georgia and Carolina coasts in the form of separate linear designs.

Incising and Grooving. The distinction between assemblages in coastal Georgia and Carolina with regard to shell punctation is indicative of the broader tendency for the punctation-over-incising technique to be restricted to Georgia coastal assemblages (Figure 41). The design is completely absent from Phase I assemblages. During

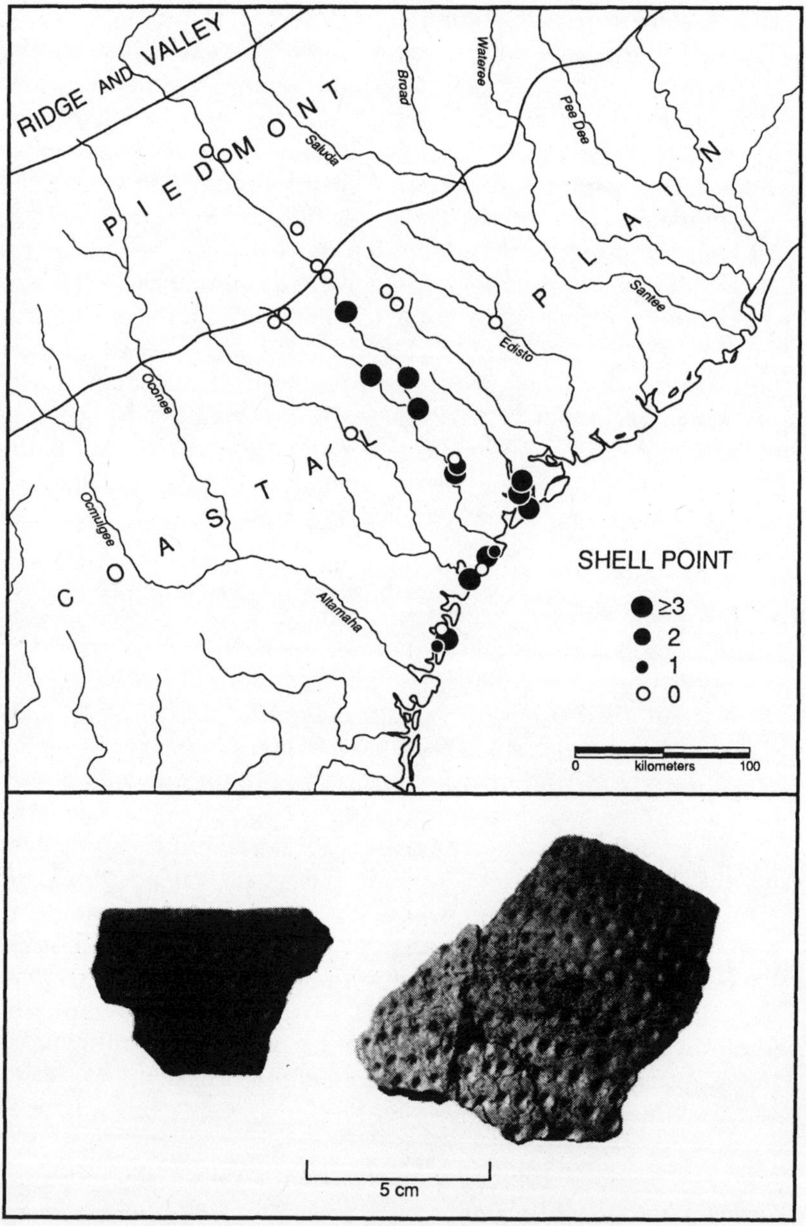

Figure 40. Distribution of shell point punctate vessels (sherd on left from Theriault; sherd on right from Cane Patch).

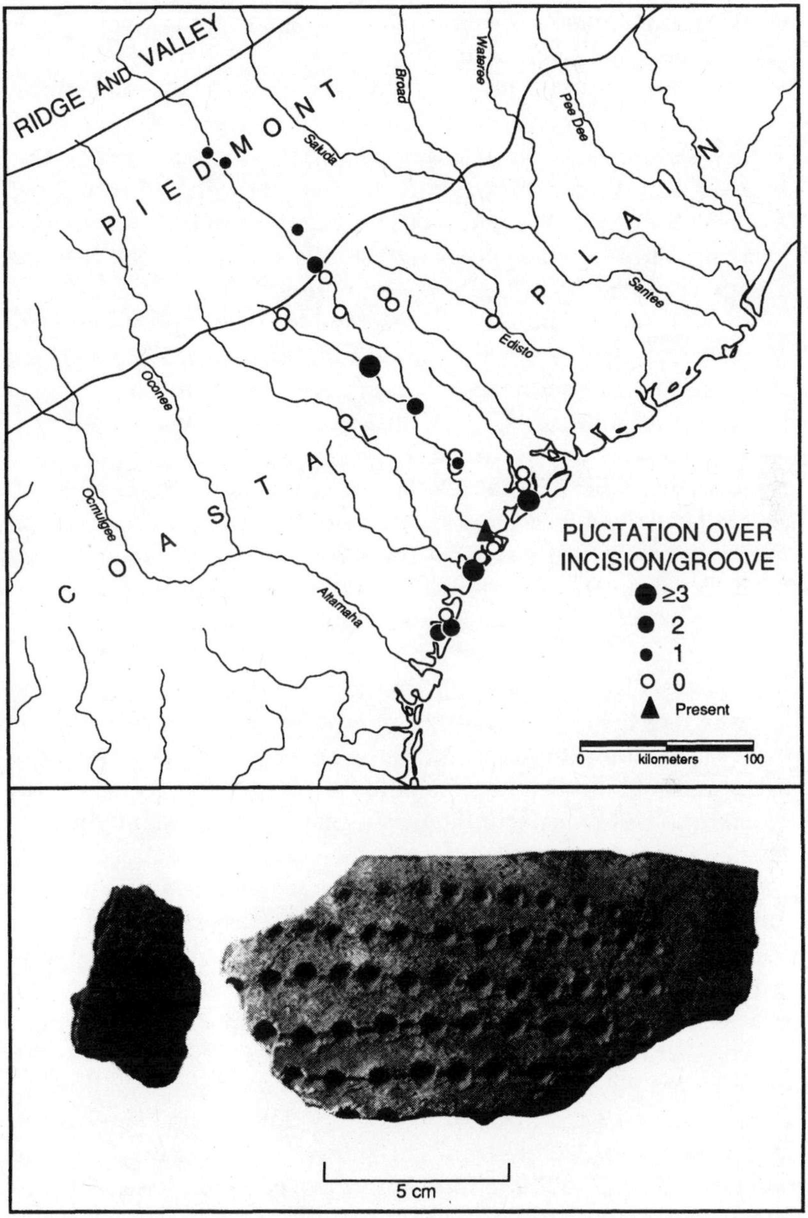

Figure 41. Distribution of vessels with punctation over incision/groove (sherd on left from Theriault; sherd on right from A. Busch Krick).

the subsequent phase, several Georgia coastal sites have examples of dowel/reed and shell punctation over incising or grooving. One coastal site north of the Savannah, Fish Haul, has Phase II examples of the technique (only with reed), but its absence from the large Chesterfield assemblage is more indicative of the local situation. Minor inland examples are observed during Phase II, with Theriault being the major exception for its abundance. Punctation over incising/grooving virtually disappears in Phase III, and what little remains is widely scattered from the Piedmont to the coast.

Incising lacking punctation has a wider distribution and longer history in the study area than does punctation over incision (Figure 42). Incised vessels are present in small numbers in Phase I assemblages throughout the Coastal Plain portion of the Savannah. The early incised examples are usually simple, often haphazard, and typically made up of fine, discontinuous lines. Phase II incising is much more diverse, being especially abundant and varied at Cane Patch and A. Busch Krick on the Georgia coast. These sites have multiple examples of bold incising, some deep, others shallow. Contemporaneous interior examples tend to have finer incisions. Hatched incised designs are emphasized at Stallings Island (Claflin 1931:Plates 13, 15), as are combinations of separate punctation and incising (see below). Most other interior examples of incising come from Phase III assemblages, but these are rare, generally sloppy, and never in combination with punctation. Overall, incising is primarily a coastal and Fall Zone technique, being especially abundant in certain coastal Georgia assemblages and decreasing in frequency up the coast. The northward decrease in incising makes sense with respect to the rarity of the technique in Thom's Creek assemblages from the South Carolina coast (Trinkley 1980a).

Having noted the tendency for Georgia coastal incising to be relatively bold compared to interior and Carolina coastal incising, we find further support in the distribution of vessel decoration classified as "grooved" (Figure 43). This treatment is defined as shallow incisions at least 0.5 centimeters wide. Only three assemblages contain examples of this decoration, all of which are located on the Georgia coast, two dating to Phase II, the other assigned to Phase III.

Hollow Cylinder. Hollow cylinder styli were used over a long period of time, but they are most common in Phase I assemblages from the fall line to the coast (Figure 44). Examples dating to this

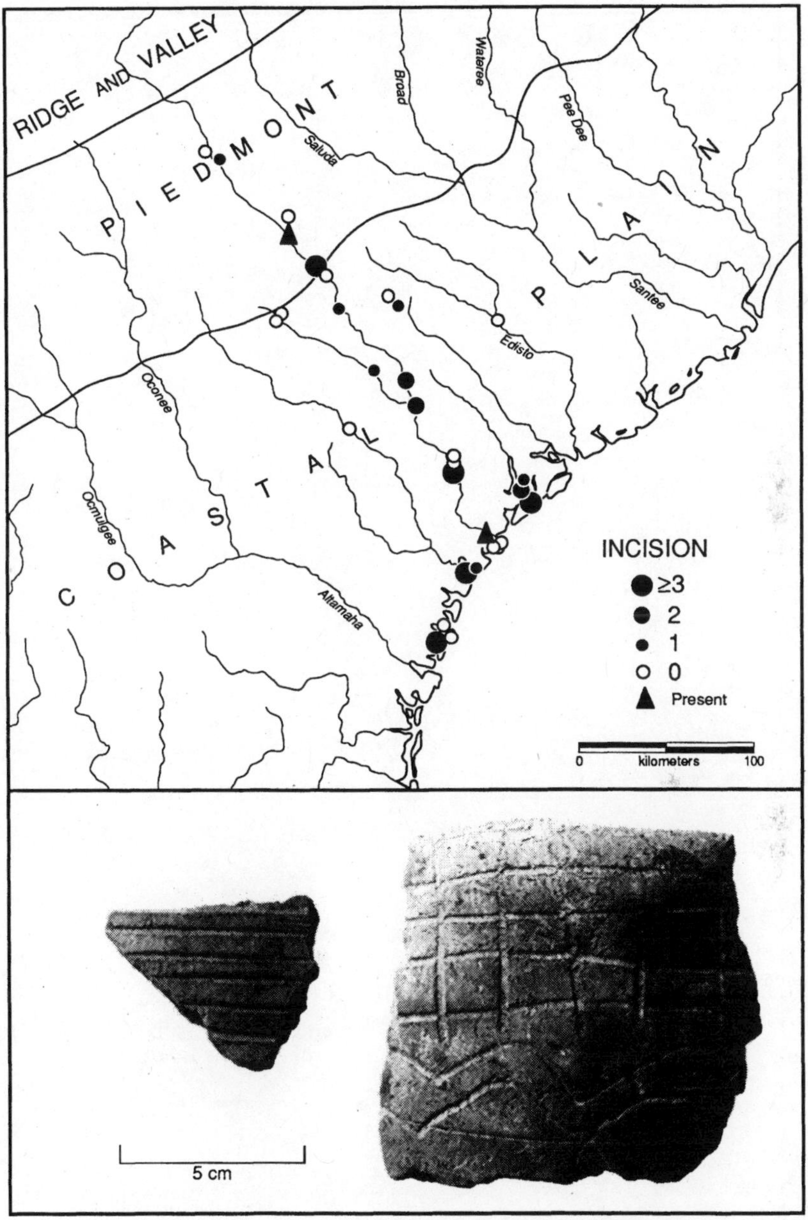

Figure 42. Distribution of incised vessels (sherd on left from Cane Patch; sherd on right from A. Busch Krick).

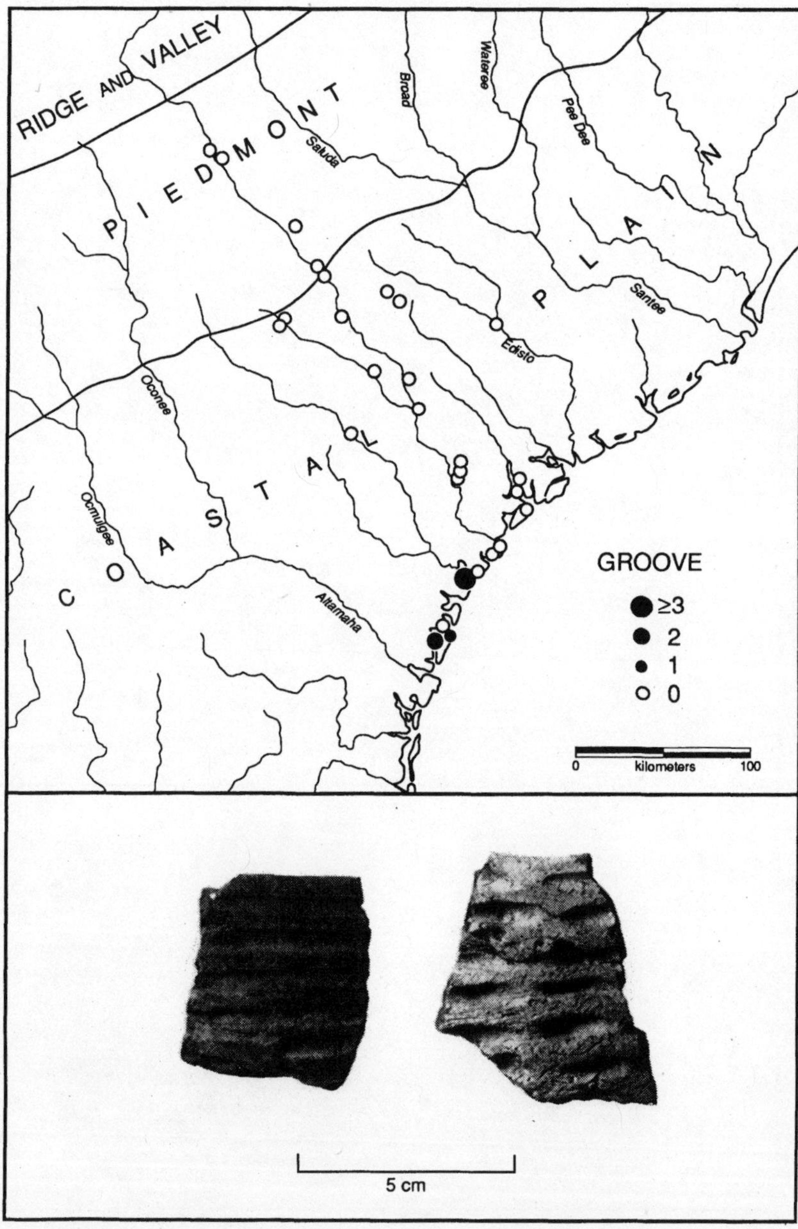

Figure 43. Distribution of grooved vessels (both sherds from Cane Patch).

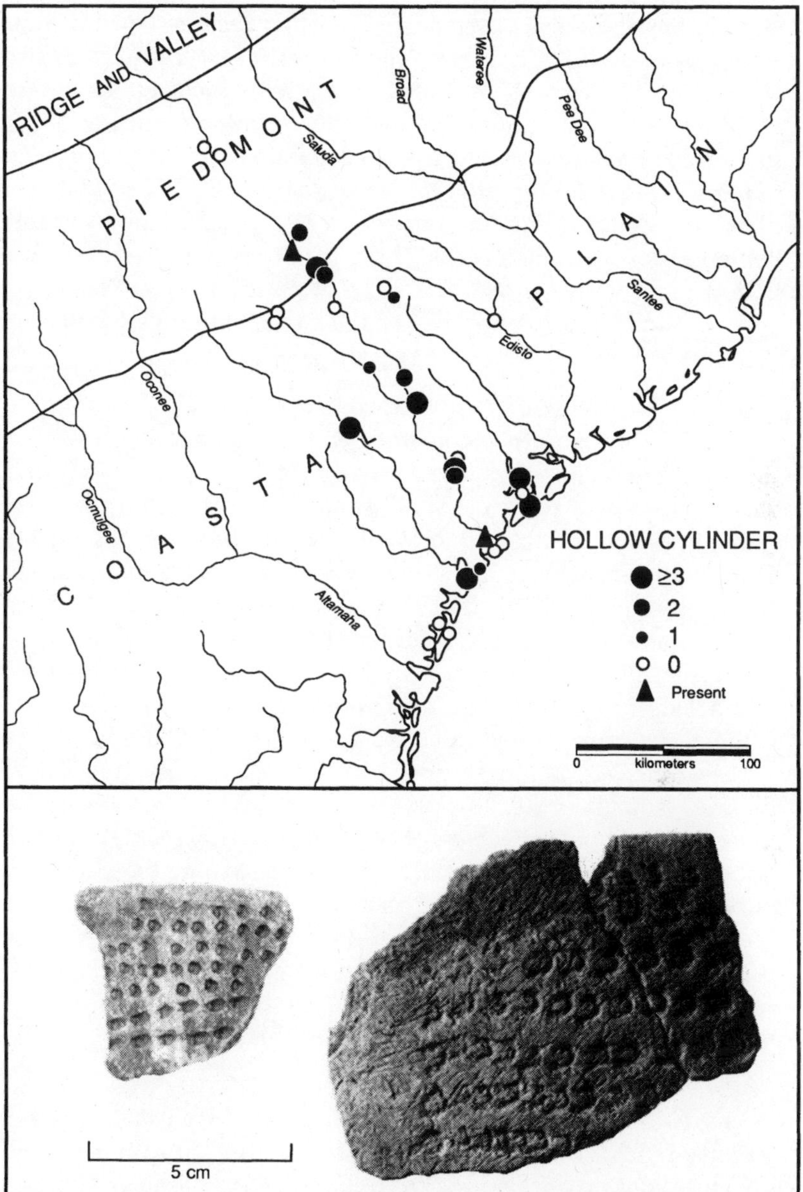

Figure 44. Distribution of vessels with hollow cylinder punctation (sherd on left from Rabbit Mount; sherd on right from Fish Haul).

period consist of separate linear and random designs. During Phase II hollow reed styli were used on the Georgia coast for separate linear punctations and rarely in conjunction with incising. In contrast, Stallings Island has examples of hollow cylinder punctation over incision, as well as drag and jab and separate linear techniques. Uses of the stylus at Chesterfield are similar to those at Stallings Island. In Phase III, hollow cylinder punctation is rare, the major exception being Feature 18 at Fish Haul. Throughout the time they were used, hollow reeds varied in size and angle of punctation, but there are no apparent spatial or temporal trends to either of these attributes.

Solid Cylinder. Cylindrical reeds or dowels with either pointed or rounded tips were perhaps the most widespread and long-lived styli used to decorate fiber-tempered pottery (Figure 45). Certain forms of these styli closely resemble shell punctation; except for the lack of spiral lines, antler tines are especially reminiscent of shell point styli. These may have been used to imitate shell punctation in the absence of shell, though it is likely that shell styli were intentionally curated if design consistency was important to the potter.

All Phase I sites with decorated pottery have examples of solid cylinder styli. Separate linear designs are prevalent, but a minority of random and geometric designs are also observed. Phase II examples of the stylus are common and widespread. Its low frequency at Stallings is noteworthy, however, especially given the large number of vessels in the sample. In contrast, the cylindrical stylus is common to the Theriault collection, where it is often used over lines of incision and closely resembles Georgia coastal vessels with shell punctation over incision. Few assemblages dating to the final phase include examples of solid cylinder styli. The major exception is 38MC479, where one example has punctations that are so deep as nearly to penetrate the interior vessel wall (Figure 45).

Subtriangular Pointed. Subtriangular pointed styli such as the one depicted in Figure 39 were used across the entire study area except at most locations on the Georgia coast (Figure 46). Phase I examples are limited to a few separate linear and drag and jab designs. The stylus is much more common in the subsequent phase, when it is primarily used for drag and jab designs. Stallings Island and Chesterfield have numerous examples of these designs. Use of subtriangular pointed

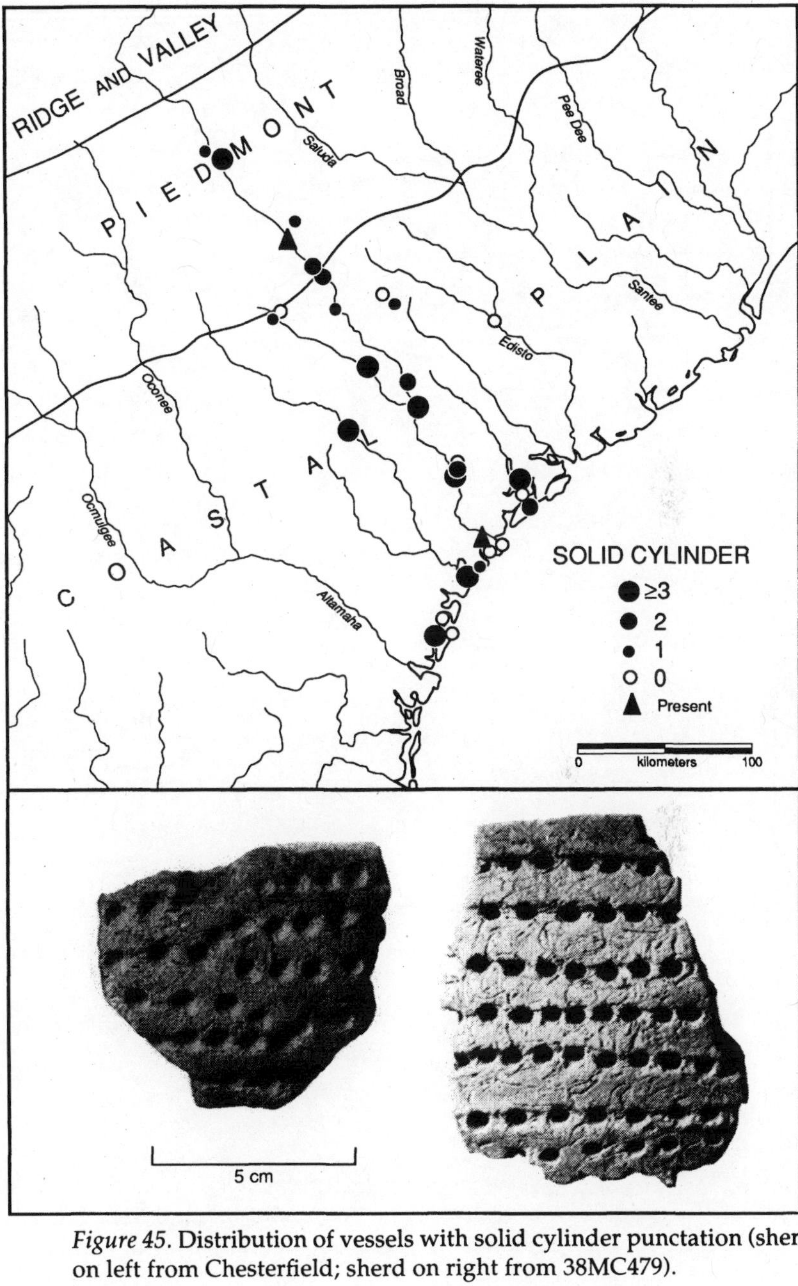

Figure 45. Distribution of vessels with solid cylinder punctation (sherd on left from Chesterfield; sherd on right from 38MC479).

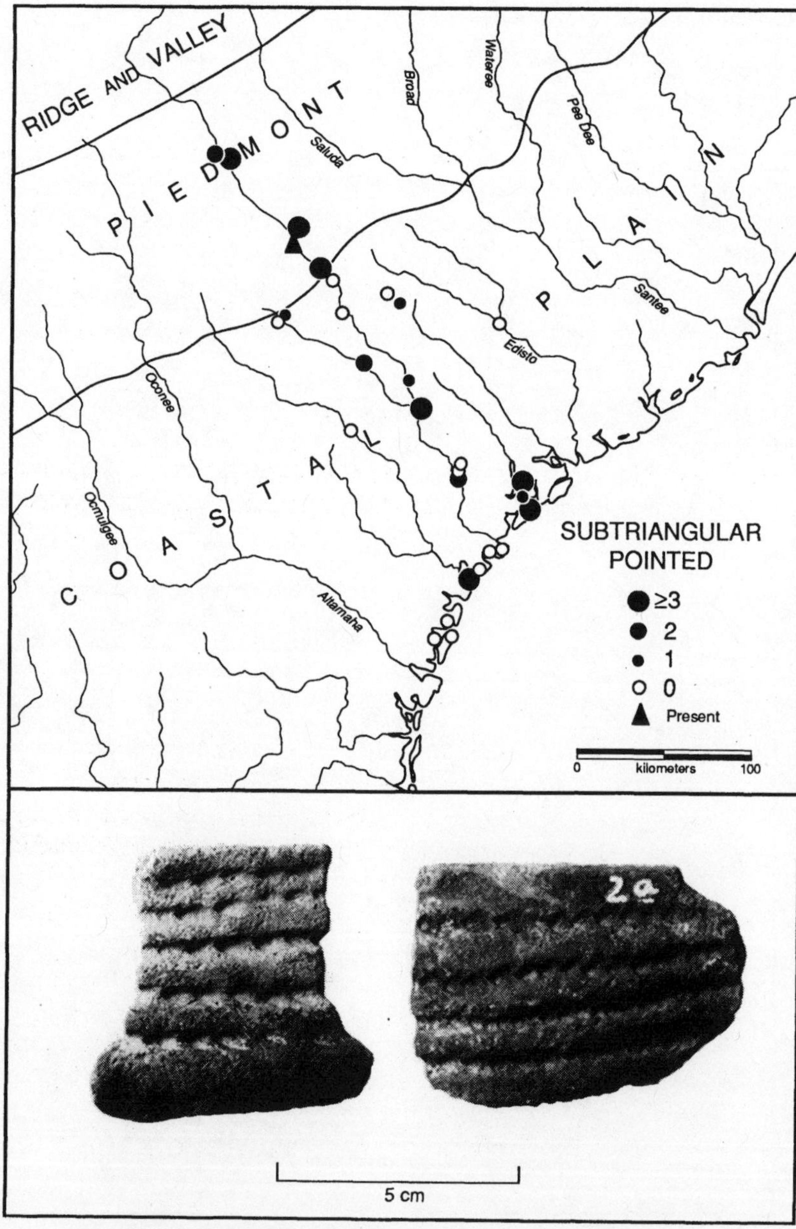

Figure 46. Distribution of vessels with subtriangular pointed punctation (sherd on left from 38MC479; sherd on right from Chesterfield).

styli continued into Phase III at Piedmont and South Carolina coastal sites. Drag and jab designs made with subtriangular pointed styli are common to Thom's Creek assemblages throughout South Carolina so the geographical and temporal tendencies seen within the fiber-tempered vessel sample are not unexpected. In other words, the subtriangular stylus is a trait that distinguished interior Savannah and coastal South Carolina assemblages from coastal Georgia assemblages.

Simple Stamped Lip. The incidence of simple stamped lips is another trait that is absent from coastal Georgia assemblages (Figure 47). The lip treatment on fiber-tempered vessels is rare in Phase I assemblages but common to Phase II and III assemblages in the interior and South Carolina coast, especially those containing Thom's Creek pottery. Like the drag and jab design described above, simple stamped lips are found on Thom's Creek vessels, particularly in the middle Savannah River Valley (Phelps 1968:26).

Fingernail Punctation and Finger Pinching. There are very few examples of fingernail punctation and finger pinching in the fiber-tempered vessel assemblages. Finger pinching is a popular design technique of Thom's Creek assemblages on the South Carolina coast between the Santee and Edisto rivers (Figure 48; Anderson 1975). Radiocarbon dates for these assemblages cluster between roughly 3400 and 3200 B.P., placing them in Phase III as defined here. An earlier date of 3770 B.P. is reported from Yough Hall, but it has met with repeated skepticism (Trinkley 1980a:14; Williams 1968c:330–31). That finger pinching was practiced this early is supported by the occurrence of a few finger-pinched (Thom's Creek) vessels at Chesterfield. What is more, sherds from at least two finger-pinched fiber-tempered vessels are present in the WV Site 14 assemblage dating to 4290±120 B.P. These data seem to indicate that finger pinching originated very early and to the south of the area where it eventually became an appreciable surface treatment. Regardless of its origin, the distribution of finger pinching during Phase III is without a doubt the most spatially discrete and well-defined of all decorative techniques used on Late Archaic pottery.

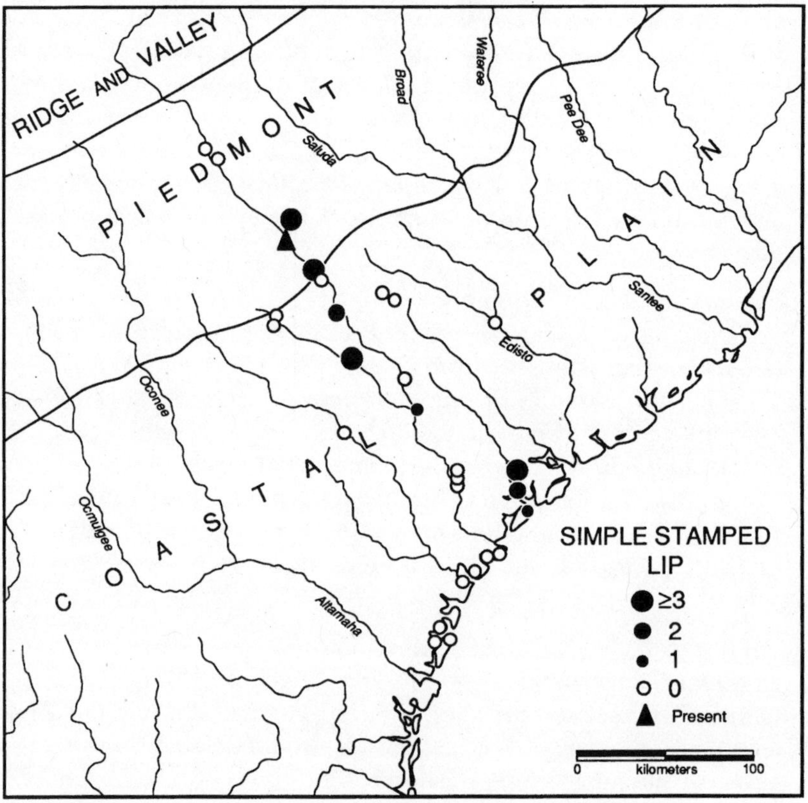

Figure 47. Distribution of vessels with simple-stamped lip.

Summary of Design Technique Distributions

With the exception of finger pinching on the coast of South Carolina and grooving on the Georgia coast, the decorative techniques examined above tend to be widely distributed in the study area. Certain types of styli, however, exhibit discrete distributions when broken into temporal phases. Shell punctation is found in minor frequency in assemblages from the fall line to the coast during Phase I and is subsequently restricted to coastal locations. Shell punctation is often used over lines of incision on the Georgia coast but not elsewhere. Incision is primarily a Georgia coastal trait; the grooved

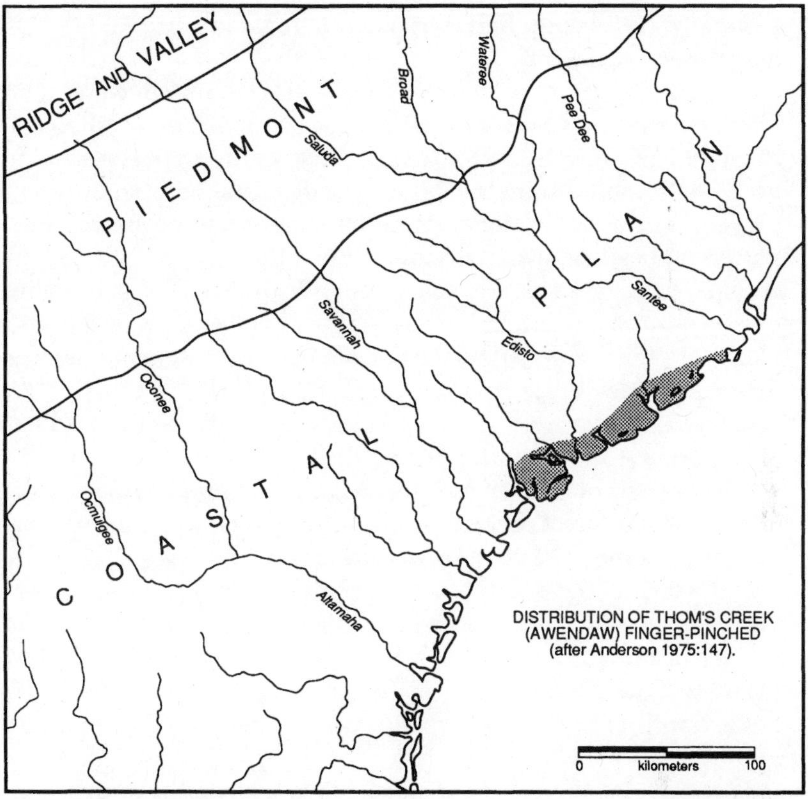

Figure 48. Distribution of finger-pinched pottery documented by Anderson (1975:147).

variety is restricted to this area. The distribution of hollow cylinder and solid cylinder styli in Phase I assemblages lends further support to the unity of sites from the fall line to the coast during this time. These styli continue to be widely distributed in Phase II, although solid cylinders, especially the pointed variety, are not as common on the coast as they are in the interior. Subtriangular pointed styli are most common to middle Savannah River Valley sites dating to Phase II, particularly Stallings Island, but a high incidence of this type is also found on vessels from the coastal site of Chesterfield. Simple stamped lips are also common to both locations during Phase II and continue into Phase III. Simple stamped lips are completely absent in coastal assemblages below the Savannah. Finally, Phase III assemblages defy generalization, being characterized by a tremendous amount of inter-assemblage variability.

In sum, the distributions of punctation styli, incising, and simple stamped lips suggest that distinct stylistic clusters are discernible during Phase II but not before or after that. In the earliest phase, traits are widely shared from the fall line to the coast with nothing in the ceramic artifact inventory other than the presence or absence of pottery to indicate spatial discontinuity within the study area. Phase II evidence suggests that at least three stylistic clusters can be defined: one on the coast south of the Savannah, another north of the Savannah, and a third centered on the middle Savannah River Valley. These distinct entities do not persist into Phase III, but a fourth cluster characterized by finger pinching is apparent north of the study area on the South Carolina coast during Phase III.

On the basis of the foregoing comparisons, I propose three models of the distribution of sociocultural entities which will serve as a basis for interpreting variation in the adoption and use of alternative cooking technologies in the Late Archaic period. I propose that during the early centuries of Phase I (ca. 4500–4200 B.P.), two sociocultural entities occupied the Savannah River Valley (Figure 49). The lower valley, or Coastal Plain, entity is distinguished from the upper valley, or Piedmont, entity by the exclusive use of ceramic vessels and by the exploitation of shellfish.

Probably by the time a coastal archaeological record becomes apparent, that is, by 4200 B.P., and certainly by 3800 B.P., three discrete sociocultural entities were present in the study area (Figure 50). I have given each of the entities place names for ease of communication and note that except for Edisto, the names have precedence in pottery typologies of the region. Aside from the stylistic traits that serve to discriminate between these entities, a suite of economic, sociopolitical, and especially technological differences are observed. I have alluded to some of these in Chapter 3 and provided specific data on technological differences between the interior and coast in Chapter 5. The coastal entity I refer to as Edisto in Figure 50 is divided into "Upper" and "Lower" subgroups on the basis of chronological data which suggest that the latter predates the former by several centuries or that there was a northward time-transgressive development in the processes that created the Edisto sociocultural entity.

Patterns indicative of discrete sociocultural entities generally disappear from the archaeological record of Phase III (Figure 51). I

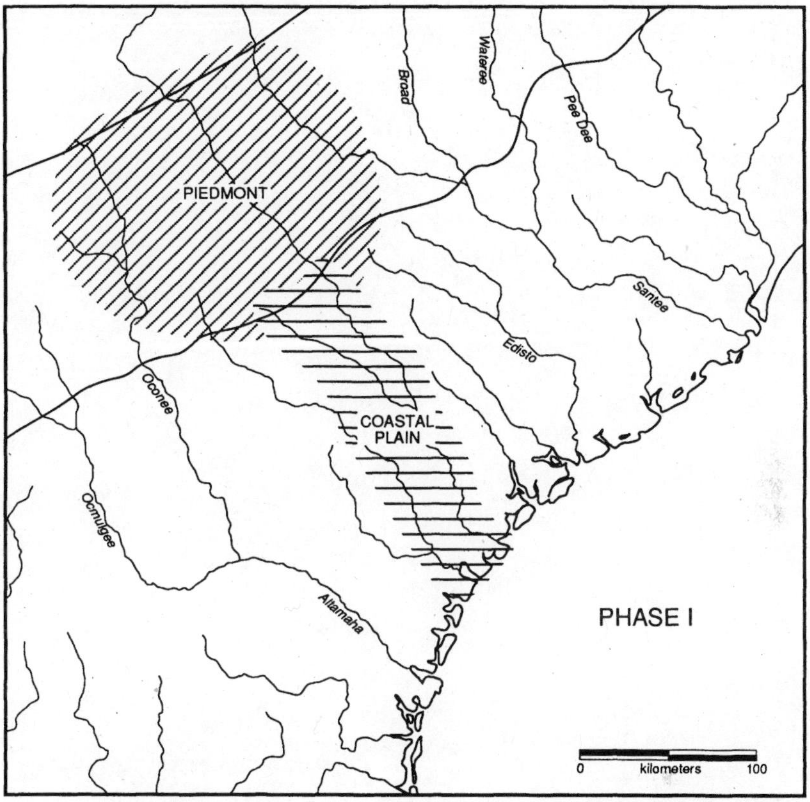

Figure 49. Model of Phase I sociocultural entities in the Savannah River Valley region.

suggest that these entities dissolved after 3400 B.P., though I do not wish to imply that the respective areas were abandoned. Simultaneous with the dissolution, a single discrete entity referred to as Awendaw emerged on the north coast, perhaps as a late manifestation of the time-transgressive trend noted above. Awendaw represents the only Phase III sociocultural entity in the study area that can be discerned on the basis of pottery design.

To conclude this section, I emphasize that the analysis of pottery design attributes is used here simply to delimit regularities and differences in the use of design options that might represent the formation and bounding of discrete sociocultural entities. I am obviously equating regularities in design choices with social and cultural

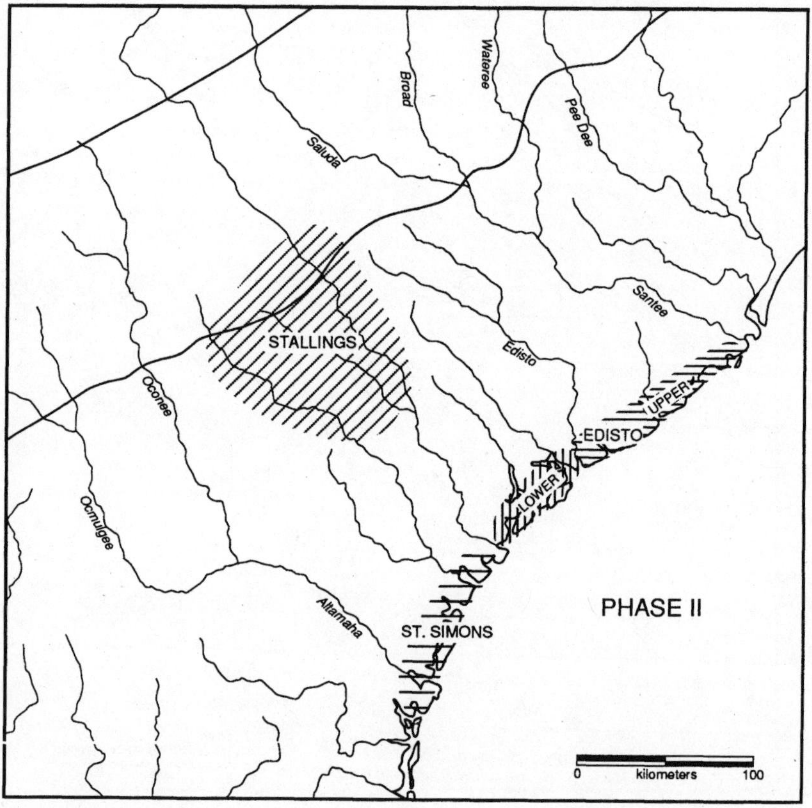

Figure 50. Model of Phase II sociocultural entities in the Savannah River Valley region.

regularities or similarities, but I do not wish to imply anything about the organization of inferred sociocultural entities. My only assumption here is that the interactions that led to regularities in the design of pottery would also be expected to lead to regularities in the technology and uses of pottery.

The Social and Economic Contexts of Alternative Cooking Technologies

The technofunctional and distributional analyses in Chapter 5 point to three key differences in the cooking technologies of interior and coastal Late Archaic groups. First, soapstone was widely used in the interior but not on the coast. Second, pottery was adopted early in

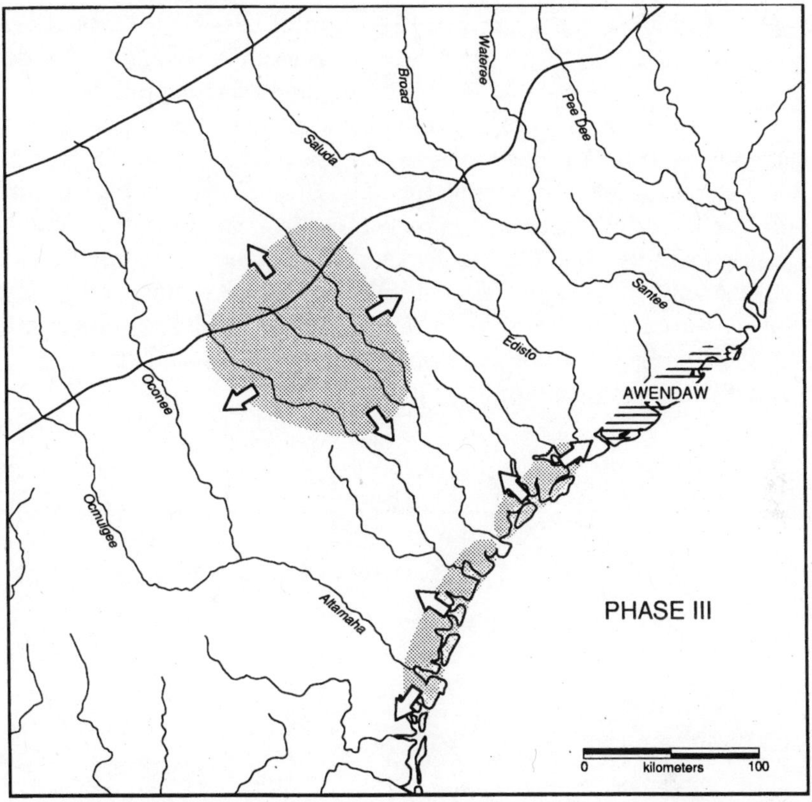

Figure 51. Model of Phase III sociocultural entities in the Savannah River Valley region.

the Coastal Plain and on the coast but not in the Piedmont. Third, the innovation of using pots directly over fire was widely and quickly adopted on the coast but not in the interior. Drawing from the sociocultural models proposed above, the theoretical concepts presented in Chapter 2, and the archaeological background in Chapter 3, I explore below the social and economic circumstances under which each of these technological developments unfolded.

Phase I and II Soapstone Exchange

In the previous chapter, I presented data to support the argument that soapstone slabs were imported into the Coastal Plain and that they were an important part of the cooking technology of Coastal

Plain residents. Apparently, this pattern of use in the Coastal Plain was short-lived. All Phase I assemblages in the valley, including contemporaneous aceramic ones in the Piedmont, contain perforated soapstone slabs (Figure 52), but Phase II assemblages of slabs are largely restricted to locations at and above the fall line (Figure 53). The decrease in use of soapstone in the Coastal Plain appears to have begun in the second half of Phase I; by 4200 B.P. soapstone was not being used below the upper Coastal Plain. Thus sometime between 4500 and 4200 B.P., a process was initiated which reduced the volume of soapstone moving out of the Piedmont and Fall Zone and into the lower valley. The emergence of distinct sociocultural entities on the coast dates to the end of this interval.

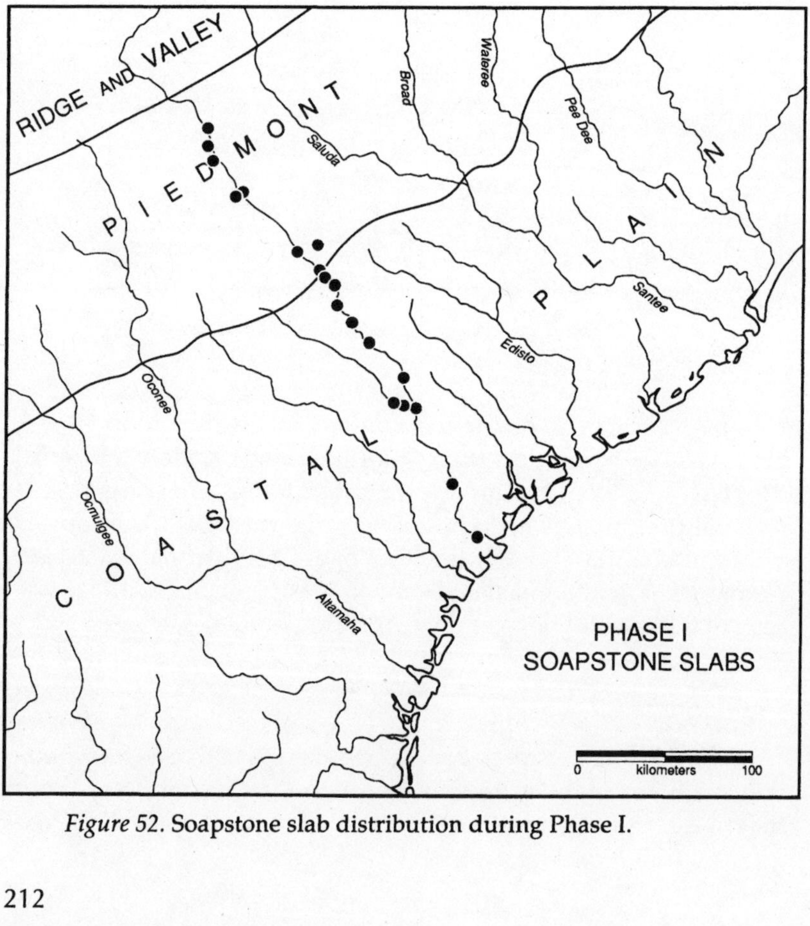

Figure 52. Soapstone slab distribution during Phase I.

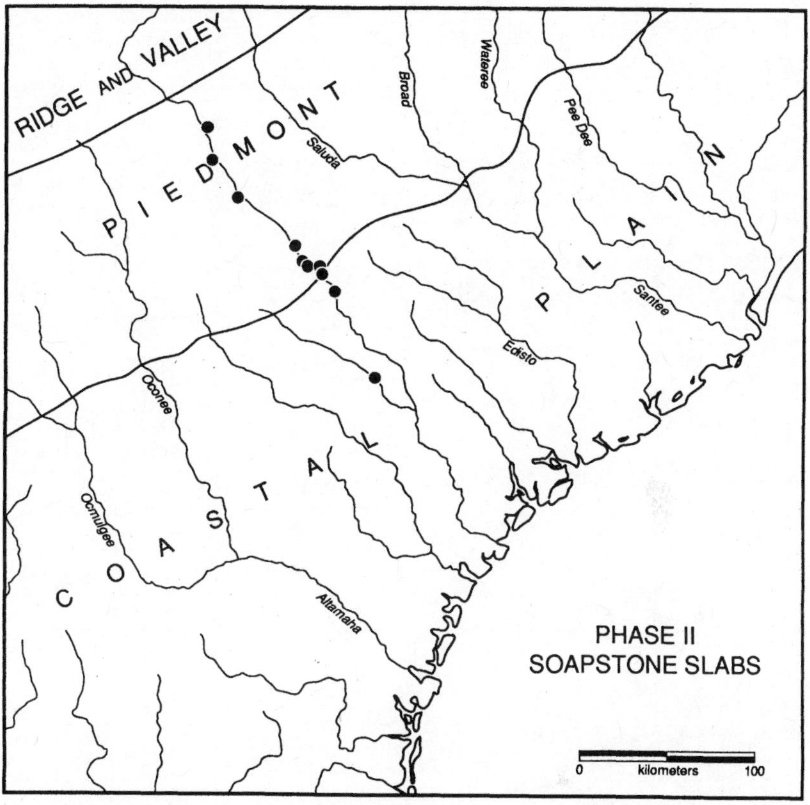

Figure 53. Soapstone slab distribution during Phase II.

I earlier suggested that soapstone was delivered into the Coastal Plain through exchange. Two pieces of evidence can be cited in support of this argument. For one, the frequency distribution of soapstone slabs plotted against distance (see Chapter 5) does not assume a normal falloff rate (e.g., Renfrew 1977) but instead is characterized by frequency modes at middle Coastal Plain sites such as Fennel Hill and Rabbit Mount. This pattern is distinct from the frequency distributions of raw materials used to make hafted bifaces (Figure 54). Within the Savannah River Valley, the movement of materials used to manufacture hafted bifaces has been shown to decrease over the course of the Holocene, a pattern believed to reflect a reduction in the mobility range of hunter-gatherer bands in the area (Sassaman, Hanson, and Charles 1988). The Late Archaic data reflect

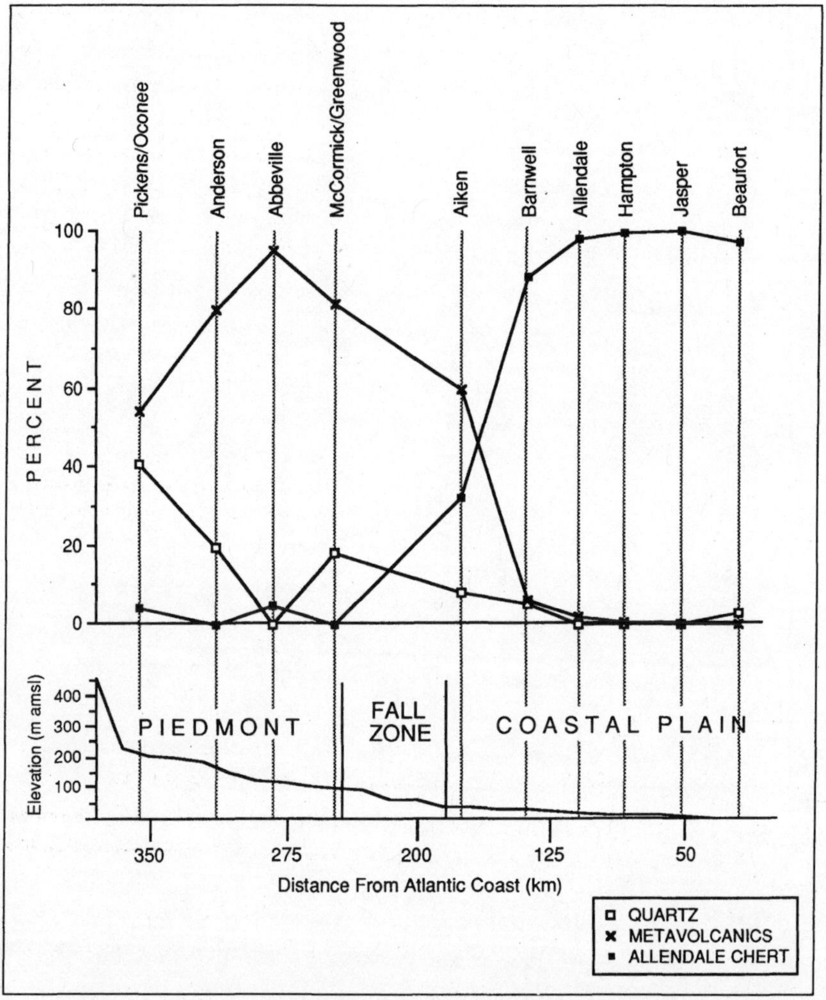

Figure 54. Late Archaic hafted bifaces by percent raw material and by South Carolina county (after Sassaman, Hanson, and Charles 1988).

distinct Piedmont and Coastal Plain patterns of procurement, with little to no interprovincial movement of flaked stone. Data for flaked stone therefore provide supporting evidence for discrete sociocultural entities above and below the fall line during Phase I, and soapstone appears to represent a medium through which the two articulated.

The second piece of evidence to support the argument for soapstone exchange is the diversity of soapstone in Coastal Plain assemblages. In contrast to the homogeneous composition of slab assemblages in the Piedmont and Fall Zone, those of the Coastal Plain include many different kinds of soapstone, which indicates that it was obtained from different sources, perhaps from different exchange partners. If procured directly from quarries, soapstone in a given assemblage would be relatively homogeneous.

The Adoption of Ceramic Vessel Technology

Fiber-tempered pottery was introduced to a preexisting soapstone cooking technology. The earliest pottery consisted of shallow basins used for indirect-heat cooking. In their form and function, the vessels did not represent a dramatic departure from traditional pit-based or basket-based stone-cooking technology, but the pots may have had some advantage over alternative containers. It is generally true that the innovation was adopted earliest in locations where individuals used, but could not produce, soapstone cooking slabs, that is, the Coastal Plain.

By the time soapstone exchange diminished in the Coastal Plain, pots were being used directly over fire on the coast and a series of innovations to improve the thermal efficiency of direct-heat cooking quickly emerged. The coincidence of these events may be more apparent than real, for we have little chronological control during the last centuries of Phase I. Nevertheless, I do not believe that the use of pots over fire was simply a response to the diminishing supply of soapstone. We have to consider also that the consolidation of sociopolitical entities on the coast was accompanied by economic responses that greatly increased social demands on individual labor.

One of the most significant developments on the coast was the formation of shell rings. These sites were occupied continuously or repeatedly over relatively long periods of time. Their form suggests that they were special places, perhaps locations of ritual or ceremony. The natural productivity of these locations was good; they apparently were the best estuarine locations for sustaining exploitation by humans. It might appear that the abundance and diversity of food resources alone explains the patterns of long-term settlement and reuse. Yet this argument is inadequate when we take into consideration that smaller-scale occupations could be sustained at innumerable other locations along the coast. The key difference is social, not ecological. There must have been binding obligations between individuals and groups occupying shell rings that constrained options for fissioning. Communal labor ventures (e.g., fish weirs), storage, and ceremonial activities are three possible factors that might have had such an effect.

The economic arrangements that I suspect characterized shell ring occupations could account for increased social demand on labor and thus the desire for new technology to meet these demands. Specific evidence to support this conclusion requires more archaeological data than are currently available. Nevertheless, I will briefly propose a scenario that illustrates how one economic activity at shell ring sites could have amplified social demands on labor and contributed to the adoption and development of pottery.

The activity I choose to highlight is shellfishing. Because early pottery is associated with shellfish remains, both locally and globally (Bullen 1972), the activity of shellfishing apparently had a direct bearing on the innovation of pottery. I would suggest that the relationship was not a functional one, that pots were not used to capture, process, or store shellfish. Instead, I believe that the innovation of pottery can be traced to labor constraints attributed to shellfishing. A recent paper by Claassen (1991) provides a useful launching point for this argument.

In her study of the Shell Mound Archaic, Claassen (1991) explores the issue of gender among shellfishers. Taking into consideration that women do most of the shellfishing in societies where shellfish are consumed (Waselkov 1982), Claassen suggests that the addition of shellfish to the Archaic diet posed a time management crisis for women. She cites alternative solutions to this crisis: substitution of tasks in which some activities were abandoned to accommodate shellfishing; reallocation of tasks in which priorities or responsibilities were reassigned to accommodate shellfishing; and specialization of tasks in which some women collected shellfish more than others or to the exclusion of others.

The vast amounts of shell in the coastal shell rings indicate that shellfishing was time-consuming, if not labor-intensive, and that it affected the work schedules of women. Any of the solutions Claassen cites to alleviate schedule conflicts could have created economic differentiation among women. As an example, individuals devoting more time to shellfishing had less time for other activities, while those spending little or no time shellfishing were able, through sharing, to provide shellfishers with the goods and services they could not produce for themselves. Given these possible arrangements, the use of pottery may have been adopted to reduce the time needed to process food or to expand the amount of food that could be processed in a given amount of time.

The simple addition of shellfish to the coastal diet could not have fueled this process, for, indeed, households in such productive environments could have easily produced shellfish for immediate consumption at minimal costs of time and labor. Instead, it seems likely that shellfishing on the coast was a large-scale, intensive activity that, at times, required large labor inputs. As Claassen (1991) has shown, there is evidence to suggest that shell mounding was a ritual or ceremonial activity not unlike earth mounding among Woodland and Mississippian societies. Such intensive activity no doubt required material provisioning that put demands on individual labor (Bender 1985b). I suggest that such ceremonial requirements were a major impetus for technological change. Interestingly, if we assume that women's increased contribution to diet accentuated their status, perhaps leading to leadership roles in ritual, then women would probably be the first to develop new technology (pottery) and to accelerate the adoption of innovations that enhanced their social position.

To summarize, the combination of decreased supply of soapstone and increased social demands on labor on the coast led to the rapid development and spread of direct-heat cooking with pots. Shellfishing on the coast exemplifies an economic activity that had the potential, because of the social organization of its production and the possible ritual contexts of its use, to contribute to the rapid and widespread use of pottery. These conditions were not enough, however, to assure the adoption of pottery or direct-heat cooking in the inland portion of the Savannah River Valley.

Resistance to the Adoption of Pottery Innovations

Between 4200 and 3700 B.P., when distinct sociocultural entities consolidated on the coast and in the middle Savannah River Valley, resistance to innovations in pottery was apparently very strong. Shellfishing was fully under way on the coast throughout this time and became important in the middle Savannah by 3700 B.P. The technological response on the coast was to develop and adopt innovations such as deeper vessel shapes, thinner walls, and slightly incurvate profiles for using pots over fire. These same innovations were later adopted by individuals in the Stallings sociocultural entity, but pots were not used directly over fire. Instead, the tradition of indirect-heat cooking persisted through the duration of Phase II, and it appears that soapstone continued to be used for this function. Although economic conditions similar to those on the coast, including shellfishing, were in place in the middle Savannah during Phase II, the development and use of pottery took a much different direction.

To understand why pottery innovations were not widely and rapidly adopted in the interior, the organization of soapstone production and exchange is relevant. Soapstone was a limited resource that was extracted and distributed over a fairly wide area of the Savannah River Valley. Direct access to soapstone afforded individuals opportunities for exchange and accumulation of prestige. There were probably no restrictions on access to soapstone during Phase I because there seems to be little evidence for constraints on group mobility or territorial boundaries. Constraints on fissioning that led to distinct sociocultural entities in Phase II changed this situation. All members of the Stallings entity may have had access to soapstone, but it is unlikely that everyone enjoyed direct access. Similarly, it is unlikely that all individuals could equally appropriate social labor through soapstone exchange to participate in outside (interregional) exchange. Thus if we can assume that participation in local soapstone exchange afforded certain individuals opportunities for extralocal exchange, then it is likely that these same individuals helped to perpetuate the use of soapstone cooking technology. It is also likely that roles in extralocal exchange and the use of soapstone were legitimated or mediated by parallel roles in ritual and leadership.

I suggest that ritual activities at places like Stallings Island were important contexts for resistance to innovations, and outside of these contexts a much greater range of responses might be expected. For instance, during periods of settlement dispersal into upland tributaries (see Chapter 3), individuals might have exercised greater autonomy over the adoption of innovations, which may account for the coincident dissolution of the Stallings entity and widespread adoption of direct-heat cooking in Phase III. Settlement patterns during this period reflect intensified use of upland tributary terraces by small, dispersed households. Evidence for large social aggregation and attendant ceremonialism disappears completely. Simultaneously, the St. Simons and Edisto entities on the coast dissolve, suggesting that the existence of all of the bounded sociocultural entities was dependent on regional exchanges between them. Other factors contributing to their dissolution, including especially environmental changes associated with fluctuations in the sea level, have to be considered with regard to coastal entities, but in the interior, there are no apparent environmental explanations for observed changes. I suggest that the inherent contradictions between tradition and innovation contributed to increased fissioning from the social obligations that held the Stallings entity together, with one result being that individuals on the periphery of Stallings society adopted pottery innovations to enhance their economic autonomy.

Finally, the issue of gender I introduced in considering the relationship between pottery and shellfish provides an interesting process for the resistance to pottery in the interior. I suspect that resistance to pottery innovation was in part manifested in male efforts to maintain exchange relationships. I base this theory on the conventional assumption that lithic production, including soapstone production, was under the purview of male labor. This assumption is itself suspect (Gero 1991), but apropos the argument for shellfishing presented earlier, a gender conflict between the systems of lithic production and exchange versus shellfishing provides an alternative set of circumstances for interpreting the permutations pottery innovations took in the middle Savannah River Valley.

Soapstone Production and Exchange after 3500 B.P.

Soapstone exchange during Phase III waned as the Stallings entity dissolved. Minor incidences of slabs are present in upland contexts across the Coastal Plain and at Daw's Island on the coast (Figure 55). Their presence in these locations suggests that what little movement of soapstone there was during this time was channeled through upland tributaries, not down the Savannah River. Overall, the examples are minor; some of the slab fragments were used simply as raw material for the manufacture of smaller, nonutilitarian items. The Daw's Island assemblage is somewhat exceptional because of its distance from soapstone sources and relative abundance compared to other Phase III sites. It is tempting to suggest that the process of soapstone exchange observed during Phase I was being revitalized

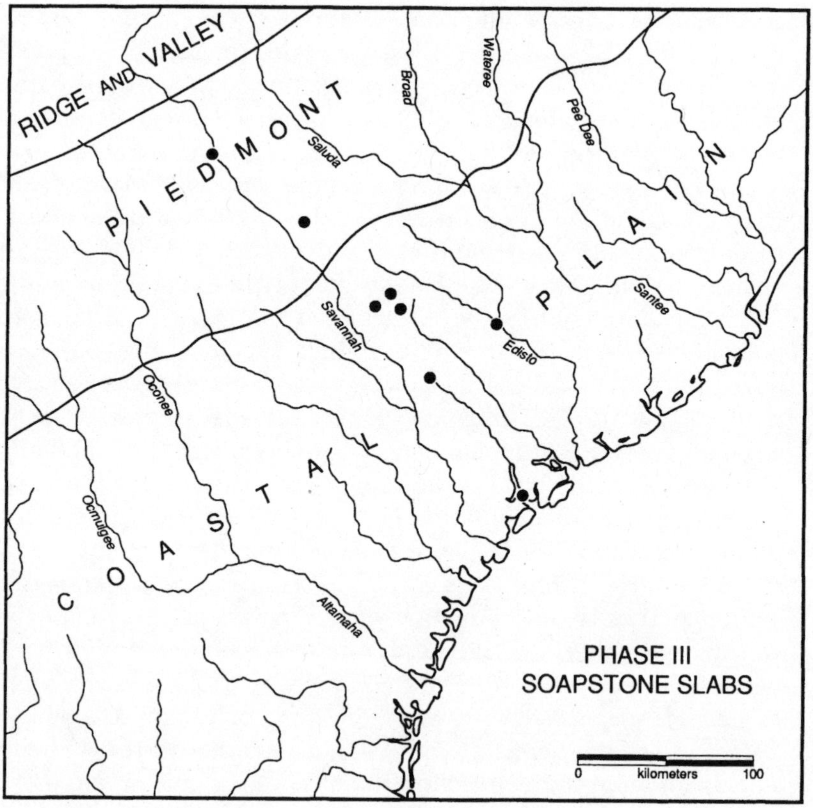

Figure 55. Soapstone slab distribution during Phase III.

on a smaller scale, this time through upland sources, but there are currently too few data to support this theory.

As the trade in soapstone slabs waned, soapstone began to be used in the region to make vessels. That soapstone vessels were being made in neighboring regions before Phase III is evidenced by a date of 4170±150 B.P. from the upper Flint River (Elliott 1989:51) and a date of 3890±250 B.P. from Gaston on the Roanoke River (Coe 1964:97–98). But as I discussed in Chapter 5, soapstone vessels were apparently not used in the Savannah River Valley region until after 3500 B.P. (Schuldenrein, Anderson, and Cantley 1985; Tippitt and Marquardt 1984); soapstone vessel sherds have not been reported from Stallings Island, and their absence suggests that the technology did not appear until after the Stallings sociocultural entity dissolved.

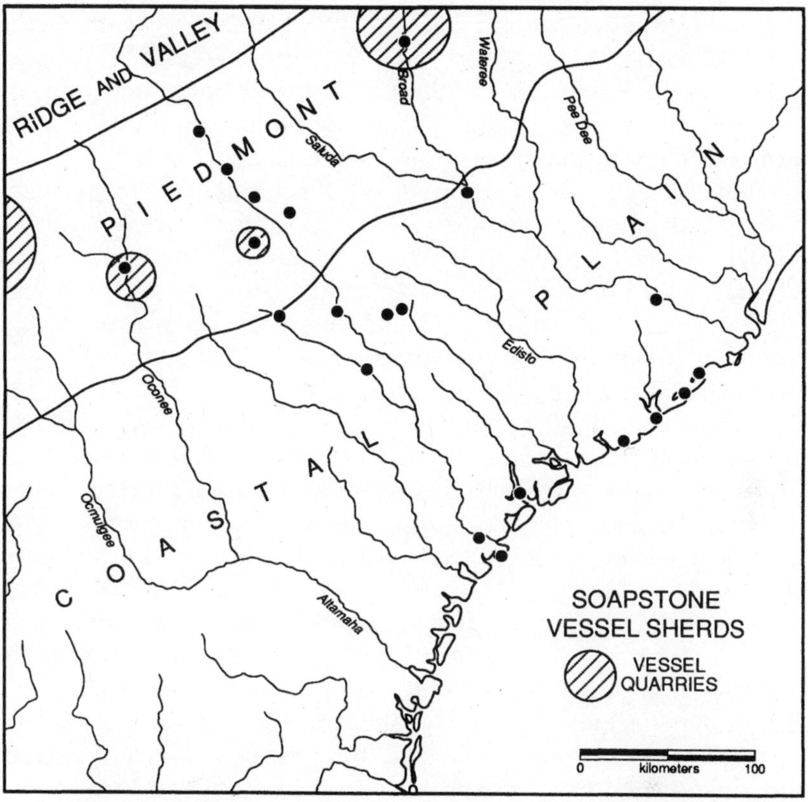

Figure 56. Soapstone vessel sherd distribution and locations of soapstone vessel quarries.

The distribution of bowl sherds in the Savannah River Valley shows a limited incidence of the artifact type below the Fall Zone (Figure 56). Like slab fragments, however, vessel sherds are not uncommon to upland tributary locations in the upper Coastal Plain (Sassaman 1988).

The relatively limited distribution of soapstone vessels in the Savannah region is peculiar when compared to the incidence of these items in adjacent regions. Late Archaic sites in the Piedmont portion of the Oconee River Valley contain a relatively high incidence of vessel fragments, many of which are associated with fiber-tempered pottery (Elliott 1981). Vessel sherds are found at low frequency in the Coastal Plain portion of the Ocmulgee-Oconee-Altamaha drainage (Snow 1977), though they are completely absent from coastal Georgia sites. Locations of production are well documented in the Oconee (Elliott 1981) and farther to the west at Soapstone Ridge (Dickens and Carnes 1983; Elliott 1986a). Moving south from Soapstone Ridge into the gulf draining the Chattahoochee and Flint rivers, we see a continuous distribution of soapstone vessels (Elliott 1989).

On the north side of the Savannah River Valley, soapstone vessel sherd distribution in the Broad-Congaree-Santee drainage is likewise more extensive than in the Savannah (Figure 56). The source of these vessels was probably the quarry areas of the upper Broad River Valley. Movement into the Awendaw area appears to have been directly down the Broad-Congaree-Santee throughway. Whether comparable numbers of soapstone sherds are present along upland tributaries on these rivers remains to be seen. In any event, the magnetic effect Awendaw individuals appear to have exerted on the flow of soapstone indicates that relatively strong alliances with interior residents were in place during Phase III. Nothing comparable to Awendaw is observed on the coast to the south or in the interior during Phase III.

The regional distribution of soapstone vessels reveals an interesting contrast to the distribution of early ceramic vessel technology. The Savannah River Valley marks the center of a developing and expanding pottery technology, while regions on either side of the Savannah generally lacked pottery for a long time and instead are noted for the production and use of soapstone vessels. Soapstone vessel production to the west was related, probably directly, to the Poverty Point interaction sphere. Poverty Point soapstone exchange has been cited by Jenkins and others as the means by which pottery diffused westward into the Midsouth (Jenkins 1982; Jenkins, Dye, and Walthall 1986; Walthall and Jenkins 1976). My reading of the Savannah River Valley situation offers an alternative perspective, which views Poverty Point exchange as a fetter to the adoption of pottery.

The Resistance to Innovation in the American Southeast

As summarized in Chapter 2, Jenkins and colleagues (1982; Jenkins, Dye, and Walthall 1986) have suggested that trading relationships within the Poverty Point sphere of interaction contributed to the westward diffusion of pottery (or the idea of making pottery) in the American Southeast. More specifically, the diffusion of fiber-tempered pottery is portrayed by Jenkins as a by-product of Poverty

Point soapstone vessel exchange. He implies that individuals participating in soapstone exchange were the primary sources of the diffusion of innovation and that the development and maintenance of such relationships were preconditions for the westward spread of pottery. The model does not aim to explain the slow rate of diffusion or why fiber-tempered pottery failed to be widely adopted throughout the geographical expanse of soapstone vessel exchange. Indeed, pottery was not widely used in the Poverty Point region although knowledge of the innovation, as well as pots themselves, were made available through long-distance exchange, and there was an obvious demand for durable, fire-resistant containers—soapstone vessels—that required a large amount of resources to acquire through exchange.

To be fair, the model proposed by Jenkins and his colleagues was designed to explain the origins of particular ceramic traits in the Midsouth, specifically the decorative and technological elements of the Wheeler series and the later (sand-tempered) Tchula Tchefuncte and Alexander complexes (Ned J. Jenkins, personal communication 1991). The Flint-Chattahoochee and Gulf coastal commerce in soapstone is the mechanism Jenkins cites (1982; Jenkins, Dye, and Walthall 1986) for the westward spread of these elements (Figure 57). His argument is based on the association of soapstone bowl sherds with Stallings-like (punctate) and St. Johns-like (incised) pottery at the Claiborne site and on sourcing analysis (Smith 1981), which shows that some Poverty Point soapstone originated in the Alabama-Georgia Piedmont. Also essential to the argument is the chronology of Gulf Coast and middle Tennessee assemblages with decorated fiber-tempered pottery, all of which date to the time when Poverty Point exchange was most extensive and most influential on regional dynamics.

The Jenkins model is a convincing account of the spread of punctated and incised decorative traits, but it does not adequately account for the widespread adoption of pottery because this did not occur until after the florescence of Poverty Point exchange. Might the production of soapstone vessels for exchange have inhibited the adoption of pottery in the Midsouth in much the same way the spread of pottery innovations in the Savannah basin was inhibited because of soapstone slab production and exchange?

Poverty Point traders probably viewed soapstone vessels and ceramic pots as functional equivalents, but they were technologically very different, particularly regarding access to raw materials. Soap-

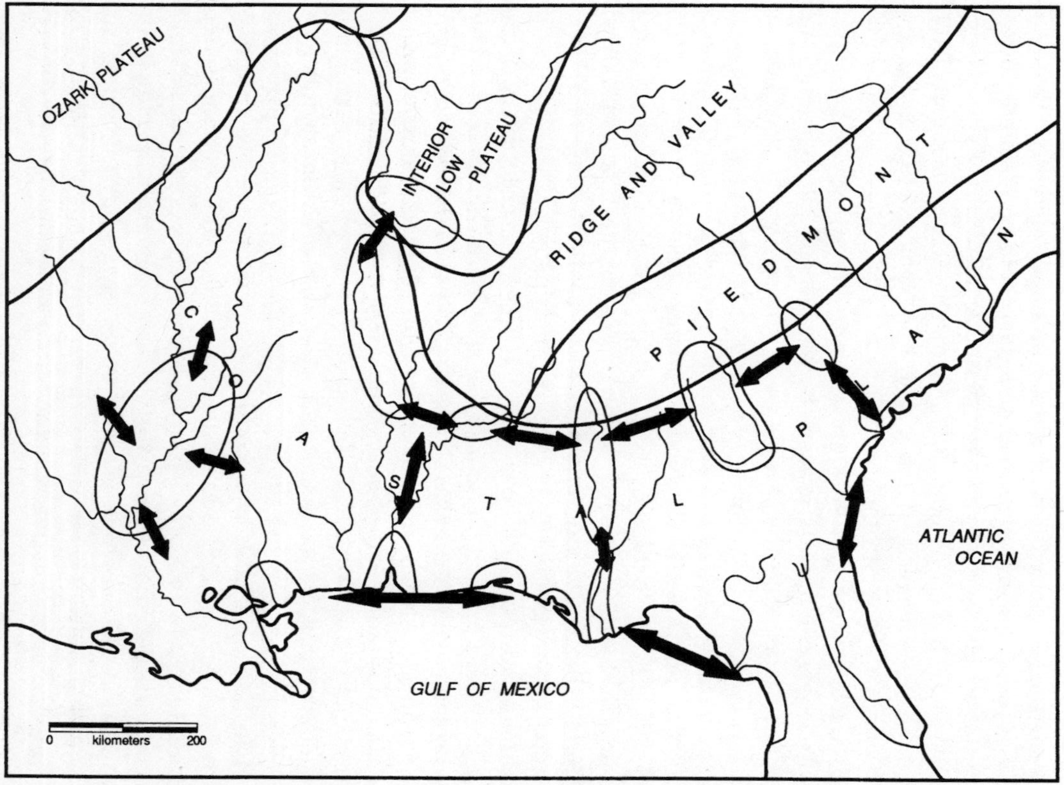

Figure 57. Patterns of interregional interaction circa 4500–3000 B.P.

stone was an "exotic" material whose access and flow may have been controlled by certain individuals, whereas it was undoubtedly difficult to control access to the resources needed to make pottery. It follows that soapstone exchange had the potential to create inequalities that were probably manifested in differential participation in ritual and ceremony and in opportunities to use prestige to influence the decisions of others. Furthermore, because Poverty Point exchange was apparently oriented along major river channels and along the Gulf Coast, participation engendered settlement patterns that created opportunities for individuals to regulate the flow of other resources. As in the Savannah River Valley, an innovation perceived to be a functional equivalent to traditional technology but incapable of being regulated was probably actively resisted by individuals who stood to lose power to appropriate social surplus.

Widespread Adoption of Pottery and the Demise of Poverty Point Exchange

If Poverty Point exchange did not facilitate the widespread acceptance of pottery, what did? I suggest that a viable alternative process can be traced to social variation within Late Archaic communities. For instance, individuals or groups peripheral to Poverty Point exchange may have adopted pottery for use in contexts outside the direct influence and control of traders. Seasons of dispersed settlement along upland tributaries of the Coastal Plain and Piedmont provided the greatest opportunity for exercising individual prerogative. Dendritic tributary morphology of the upper Coastal Plain is especially conducive to dispersed settlement. Households occupying small ridge noses and terraces would have been limited to a few families, and intergroup interaction above the level of household visiting is not expected. Thus dispersed settlement, probably in the fall and winter, afforded opportunities to experiment with new technologies without being subjected to social pressures and ritual conformance that characterized seasons of floodplain or coastal aggregation.

Although seasons of dispersed settlement relieved individuals from the pressures of social conformity, it would be inaccurate to view this as a time of social isolation or rebellion. Spread out among the many stems of upland tributaries, individuals had access to a wide, decentralized pool of reciprocal trading partners. Exchange across tributary divides would have facilitated the rapid spread of material and ideas "against the grain" of the Fall Zone and upper Coastal Plain (Figure 57). It is this form of interaction, I argue, that accounts for much of the westward expansion of fiber-tempered pottery. Assemblages of fiber-tempered pottery are documented from sites throughout the Fall Zone and interior Coastal Plain of Alabama and southwest Georgia (Chase 1966; DeJarnette 1975; Futato 1973; Jenkins 1978; McMichael and Kellar 1960; Snow 1977; Walthall 1980; Worth 1988:119), all apparently postdating 3300 B.P. (Chase 1966; Snow 1977:14; Walthall 1980:68). Although the amount of pottery at these sites is not great, there appears to be as much, if not more, than at sites along the entire Gulf coastal route of the Poverty Point exchange network. I hasten to add, however, that there is little decorated pottery in these interior areas and virtually none at sites along the middle Alabama River (Ned J. Jenkins, personal communication 1991).

The lack of decorated fiber-tempered pottery in the interior portions of the Gulf Coastal Plain deserves further discussion. It is apparent that plain and decorated fiber-tempered wares have distinct distributions in the Gulf Coast region and presumably resulted from distinct processes of social interaction. That only plain varieties of the ware spread westward across the interior Coastal Plain supports an argument for local or decentralized interaction. The resurgence of plain fiber-tempered pottery in the Savannah River Valley after 3400 B.P. (Phase III) provided a basis for the westward flow of undecorated wares. This time period marks the dissolution of the Stallings sociopolitical entity and the concomitant dispersal of households into upland portions of the upper Coastal Plain. Pottery assemblages lacking elaborate decorative motifs are perhaps one indication of this diminished level of social integration and complexity.

Recent survey and testing at sites along the Gulf Coast is showing that plain fiber-tempered pottery was locally available as early as 3600 B.P. Included among these are local manifestations of Poverty Point culture, such as those of the Elliott's Point complex around Choctawhatchee Bay in Florida (Thomas and Campbell 1988), as well as the more mundane Gulf formational sites in the Mobile Bay area (e.g., New World Research 1988; Read Stowe, personal communication 1991). An early date for one of the latter sites, 1Wn35 (3630±80 B.P.; New World Research 1988:10–13), suggests that some local process was effective in spreading innovations long before the Poverty Point exchange network reached its zenith. On balance, however, most of the evidence reflects a later time period for the local adoption of fiber-tempered pottery (Read Stowe, personal communication 1991), and pottery was obviously not widely used in the Gulf coastal region until after 3000 B.P.

As pottery began to gain acceptance across the greater Southeast, the abilities of individuals to influence the settlement and technological decisions of others probably diminished. In a sense, the adoption of pottery may have been one way that individuals (women) resisted such influences. Eventually, the widespread use of pottery increased the abilities of individuals to sustain long-term occupations of upland tributary sites and thus to exercise options to disengage from the social obligations of riverine aggregations. Similarly, the increased functional efficiency of food processing enabled Late Archaic households to be more economically self-sufficient and less reliant on intergroup alliances (cf. Muller [1986:148] for a similar case in the Late Woodland period of the Midwest).

With this set of circumstances in place in the South Atlantic Slope, the dissolution of riverine-based sociopolitical entities probably unfolded as an east-to-west time-transgressive process. This process would have weakened the bonds of soapstone exchange and other male-dominated interaction while simultaneously catalyzing the westward spread of pottery technology.

In contrast, a much different process was apparently operating to deliver decorated ceramic traits to the Midsouth, and the model of Jenkins and his colleagues is certainly a viable explanation. The distribution of decorated sherds along the Gulf Coast is truly discontinuous, owing perhaps to the directed nature of Poverty Point exchange. And it is not surprising that the decorated assemblages of fiber-tempered pottery are found at Poverty Point-related sites because these occupations undoubtedly involved complex social interactions that would engender elaborate forms of material communication (e.g., Wobst 1977).

As Jenkins and colleagues suggest, decorated pottery of the Stallings and St. Johns series apparently influenced the development of Midsouth pottery during the Middle Gulf Formational period. But we cannot equate the spread and adoption of specific decorative elements with the processes that led to the widespread use of pottery as a cooking technology. By whatever means, the processes leading to widespread adoption of pottery technology were either a product of or a precedent for the demise of long-distance exchange and regional integration during the Late Archaic period. I suggest that the adoption of pottery on the peripheries of soapstone exchange effectively undermined the abilities of certain individuals to appropriate social surplus and to channel that surplus into long-distance exchange. With the potential to affect not only patterns of settlement and subsistence but also access to resources, prestige, and power, the adoption of pottery may have indeed been revolutionary in a social or political sense.

Summary and Conclusions

From a historical standpoint, the innovation and diffusion of pottery cannot be understood without reference to the economic and social contexts of its technological precedents. In the Savannah River Valley, the production and distribution of soapstone slabs was an important means of intergroup integration when pottery appeared. The innovation was not adopted by members of communities having direct access to soapstone. Communities on the receiving end of soapstone exchange were the first to use pottery but only as containers for indirect-heat cooking. When pottery was later adopted for use at locations of soapstone production, the traditional method of indirect-heat cooking persisted in the highly social contexts of aggregation and ceremony.

The innovation of using pots over fire, as well as improvements in the thermal efficiency of pottery, all took place first on the coast, well outside the sphere of Savannah River soapstone exchange. Intensive shellfishing on the coast created social demands on labor that in turn placed a premium on the development of technological innovations. Social contexts in which prestige leaders exerted influence facilitated the rapid adoption of innovations. As shellfishers and potters, women may have enjoyed greater prestige on the coast than in the interior, and I suspect that activities involving communal feasting with pots were probably important arenas for women's power and influence.

Shellfishing was practiced when pottery was first used in the middle Savannah River Valley, as well as in the St. Johns and Midsouth regions. But in the middle Savannah, indirect-heat cooking with soapstone persisted for several centuries, whereas in the other areas, shellfishing predated pottery by a millennium or more. I argue that soapstone exchange inhibited the adoption of direct-heat cooking with pottery because pottery was perceived as a threat to the continuation of social relations based in soapstone exchange. I suggest that prestige accrued through control over the production and distribution of soapstone, and this prestige was converted to power and influence over individuals to resist the innovation of direct-heat cooking.

The insights gained from analysis of soapstone and pottery in the Savannah River Valley allow for a reevaluation of the regional process of innovation diffusion. I maintain that relations of producing and distributing soapstone vessels west of the Savannah inhibited the flow of pottery into the Gulf Coastal Plain. Instead, I believe that upland tributary sites along the upper Coastal Plain and Fall Zone constituted peripheral contexts in which innovations could quickly diffuse along chains of reciprocal exchange. The difference between the two paths is much more than geographic. The routes and mechanisms of soapstone vessel exchange were tightly controlled and channelized, and they involved few individuals. In contrast, reciprocal exchange at times of settlement dispersal was decentralized, impossible to regulate, and open to more individuals. I suspect that the eventual widespread adoption of pottery by small, dispersed households undermined the networks of interregional exchange by decreasing the demand for soapstone vessels and by enabling individuals to disengage from social obligations that required them to participate in large-scale social aggregation.

The major theoretical contribution of this study is its emphasis on social variation as a factor in the development and spread of technological innovation. I identify aspects of the organization of production and exchange which created differences in the needs and motives of individuals to adopt innovations. I specifically cite social demands on labor stemming from the formation and maintenance of exchange alliances as a cause of technological change, but I also show that similar relations can serve to impede innovation. Furthermore, by considering gender roles in the introduction of pottery, I implicate a whole new set of social relations that are useful in modeling the variation evident in the early ceramic record.

The methodological contributions of the study are twofold. First, I have succeeded in documenting considerable technofunctional variation in the manufacture, design, and use of early pottery in the Savannah River Valley region. That indirect-heat and direct-heat techniques of cooking were used simultaneously in the region is a significant find, especially when related to the production and use of soapstone slabs. Attention not only to mechanical performance criteria of pot design but also to use alteration allows me to show that vessels were not always used in functions for which they were designed. I am able to relate much of the variation in pot design and use to the availability of alternative cooking technologies and especially to social constraints and opportunities that underwrote their production and distribution.

The second methodological contribution of this study is its chronology for fiber-tempered pottery. Building on existing efforts at chronology, I document variation in the use of specific lip and surface designs and propose a third phase to account for the resurgence of plain pottery late in the period. My effort in this regard is enhanced through a vessel unit of analysis and the application of a large sample of vessels to the problem. The chronology enables me to view technofunctional variation of the vessel sample in its temporal and spatial contexts, ultimately relating it theoretically to the social variation inferred from other lines of evidence.

I use the results of my Savannah River case study to model processes of innovation diffusion elsewhere in the Southeast. My effort in this regard must be considered preliminary. Our knowledge about the temporal, spatial, and technofunctional variation of Orange and Wheeler pottery is limited. There are currently sufficient samples of Orange pottery to address technofunctional issues, but the chronology and distribution of the ware are not adequately documented. Variation in Wheeler pottery is even more poorly documented, owing largely to the limited samples currently available. If and when more detailed studies of Orange and Wheeler pottery are conducted, it should come as no surprise to find more variation in the design and use of these vessels than we presently observe. It should also come as no surprise that temporal, spatial, and technofunctional variation among these wares cannot be fully explained in simple economic or adaptational terms. I have provided in this study some alternative perspectives on early pottery that I hope will not only help to explain patterns of early pottery use in Florida and the Midsouth but also to compel other researchers to collect the data, design methods, and formulate theory to prove me wrong.

Afterword

Since 1990, when research for this book was completed, several projects in the middle Savannah River Valley have yielded data that are relevant to the interpretations I propose herein. In fact, results from two large-scale excavation projects were compared directly to my findings. In one case the results were corroborative, in the other contradictory.

One of the projects was undertaken in 1990 by R. Jerald Ledbetter and colleagues of Southeastern Archaeological Services at two sites near the headwaters of Brier Creek in Warren County, Georgia (Ledbetter 1991). The project entailed over 1,100 square meters of machine-stripping and hand excavation in deposits dating largely to the Late Archaic period. Late Archaic occupations spanning roughly 4000 to 3500 B.P. in age were delineated in three areas of the sites. Excavations in one area uncovered a pit house dated to about 3900 B.P. The fill of this feature yielded a large number of perforated soapstone slab fragments, large metavolcanic bifaces, and a few fiber-tempered sherds. A subsequent component dated to approximately 3700 B.P. lacked evidence for architecture or other well-defined features, but included an appreciable sample of fiber-tempered sherds, mostly plain, and a small number of soapstone slab fragments. A final Late Archaic occupation dated to about 3550 B.P. involved the increasing use of pottery, again mostly plain, and fewer soapstone slabs. Data on vessel form and decoration were compared to the criteria I established for chronological purposes. The comparisons were largely favorable; the limited number of basin-shaped vessels with thickened lips was particularly encouraging given the lack of evidence for a Phase I occupation.

The other project entailed the excavation of three sites near Augusta, Georgia, for the extension of the Bobby Jones Expressway. Headed by Daniel T. Elliott for Southeastern Archaeological Services, the excavations uncovered what has proved to be a complicated array of Late Archaic architectural and related features spanning seven centuries from roughly 3900 to 3200 B.P. (Elliott et al. 1992). The richest Late Archaic remains came from the Lover's Lane site (9RI86), one of several locations previously tested by Elliott and Doyon (1981), and a source of soapstone data employed in my analysis. An early Late Archaic occupation was isolated in a hand-excavated block at Lover's Lane, but the bulk of the feature assemblage was located in an area of repeated occupation. The magnitude of reoccupation obviously hampered efforts to identify changes in the technology or style of ceramic assemblages from feature contexts. Nonetheless, the assemblage as a whole was characterized by technological and stylistic traits that I attributed chiefly to Phase I assemblages. In particular, the Lover's Lane sample was dominated by plain vessels with thickened lips. Elliott suggests that these traits persisted into Phase II, presumably for indirect stone cooking, though he also notes that the use of perforated soapstone slabs diminished quickly after 3800 B.P.

Despite the lack of clarity in the Lover's Lane feature assemblage, the apparent persistence of basin forms and indirect-heat cooking lends support to the interpretations I advance in this book. What is brought to question by the Lover's Lane data are the chronological significance of certain ceramic traits and the relationship between soapstone slabs and pottery after 3800 B.P.

However, before these new findings are used to reinterpret middle Savannah River Valley prehistory, we must continue to seek and examine feature and stratigraphic contexts that provide greater clarity than Lover's Lane. Three of the seven dated features from the large block at Lover's Lane were contaminated, all by relatively recent materials. There is reason to suspect that dates from other features were likewise affected. Apart from difficulties in dating, the four features yielding "acceptable" Late Archaic dates contained very few diagnostic artifacts. Thus, the interpretation of technological trends hinges on associations within features and midden deposits that formed over a long period of time and that cannot be disentangled from provenience alone. This is not to detract from the exceptionally good research Elliott and his colleagues conducted on the Lover's Lane materials, but only to point out that sites such as Lover's Lane are particularly subject to alternative interpretation. Many of the site collections that I used in this study—Stallings Island, White's Mound, and Theriault, to name but a few—are also prone to such biases.

My effort at regional modeling and comparative analysis alleviates some of the problems that mixed contexts and long-term site use impose on any archaeological interpretation. Such efforts are, of course, built upon the careful, detailed analysis of individual sites and assemblages. The work of Ledbetter and Elliott is indeed exemplary in this regard, and I commend them for their efforts to regionalize their results. Other, smaller projects in the middle Savannah River Valley are also adding to the body of comparative evidence. Mims Point in Edgefield County, South Carolina, and Midden Point in Burke County, Georgia, are two Stallings phase sites that have been recently tested (Sassaman 1991b, 1991c). Preserved organic remains at these sites have been submitted for radiocarbon dating, and the analysis of artifact and feature assemblage is under way. As a small affiliate of the Stallings Island site, Mims Point promises to offer the temporal clarity that large midden sites lack. Similarly, Midden Point has stratigraphy conducive to diachronic analyses that are impossible to achieve with the neighboring Theriault site.

It is sad to note that all of the recent fieldwork on Late Archaic sites in the middle Savannah River Valley was prompted by destructive activities. Fortunately, field projects initiated by federal activity were successful not simply because the laws and regulations protecting sites are effective, but because Elliott and Ledbetter turned compliance initiatives into solid research programs. Other field efforts have been launched to salvage information from looted sites, a strategy that amounts to little more than a band-aid solution to a tourniquet-sized problem. The level of destruction in the region is overwhelming, and shell middens continue to be especially vulnerable targets (Sassaman 1992). I venture to guess that by the year 2000, no Late Archaic shell middens will remain on private or state lands; only a few survive today under federal protection.

Appendix

RADIOCARBON DATES FOR LATE ARCHAIC SITES IN THE SAVANNAH RIVER VALLEY REGION

Site no. ■ *Site name* ■ *Sample no.* ■ *C14 BP* ■ *Material* ■ *Reference*

38CH217 ■ Venning Creek ■ DIC-2514 ■ 2050±95 ■ hickory nutshell ■ Anderson n.d.

ash lens in single component shell midden containing Thom's Creek plain, punctated, and finger-pinched sherds; rejected as too late by D. G. Anderson (personal communication 1988)

KBS12 ■ Kings Bay ■ UM-1429 ■ 2330±180 ■ carbonized wood ■ Calvert et al. 1979:109

Feature 4; FS #116, KBS 12 (trash pit, ca. 60–62 cm BS), cultural affiliation uncertain

38BR383 ■ Pen Point ■ Beta-24764 ■ 2730±110 ■ hickory nutshell ■ Sassaman n.d.

Feature 14, lithic production feature containing MALA-Benton hafted bifaces; rejected as too late by K. E. Sassaman

9GN57 ■ Canon's Point ■ UM-519 ■ 2770±90 ■ wood ■ Marrinan 1975:49; Stipp et al. 1976:212

area south of shell ring, 3.55 m below marsh surface, thought to represent "transition" from fiber-tempered ceramics to Deptford

Site no. ■ *Site name* ■ *Sample no.* ■ *C14 BP* ■ *Material* ■ *Reference*

9GN57 ■ Canon's Point ■ UM-518 ■ 2780±80 ■ wood ■ Marrinan 1975:49; Stipp et al. 1976:212

area south of shell ring, 3.36–3.47 m below marsh surface, thought to represent "transition" from fiber-tempered ceramics to Deptford

38CH12 ■ Lighthouse Point ■ UGA-2904 ■ 2885±175 ■ charcoal ■ Trinkley 1980b:191–92

Feature 34, containing Thom's Creek sherds

38JA5 ■ Refuge ■ M-267 ■ 2920±200 ■ clam shell ■ Crane and Griffin 1958:1122; Williams 1968:329

"clambake" (i.e., Feature) 36 into midden, containing Refuge sherds

SoCv236 ■ Venning Creek (II) ■ UGA-3116 ■ 2930±160 ■ animal bone ■ Trinkley 1980b:287

context unreported; Thom's Creek finger impressed sherd association

9LI45 ■ Cunningham Mound C ■ UGA-1686 ■ 3010±80 ■ charcoal ■ Thomas and Larson 1979:20, 58, 64

Feature 2, human cremation, with plain fiber-tempered sherds

38BU7 ■ Sea Pines Shell Ring ■ I-2847 ■ 3110±110 ■ conch shell ■ Calmes 1968; Buckley and Willis 1969:79

top of shell deposits (0–6" BS) containing fiber-tempered and Thom's Creek sherd associations

38BU8-1 ■ Large Ford Shell Ring ■ I-2849 ■ 3120±110 ■ oyster shell ■ Calmes 1968; Buckley and Willis 1969:79

30" above charcoal (I-2850) in periwinkle layer and 27" BS, with fiber-tempered sherd association

38CH12 ■ Lighthouse Point ■ UGA-2903 ■ 3180±65 ■ charcoal ■ Trinkley 1980b:191–92

Feature 33, containing Thom's Creek sherds

38CH12 ■ Lighthouse Point ■ UGA-2901 ■ 3190±70 ■ charcoal ■ Trinkley 1980b:191–92

Level 2 of unit 23OR60, containing Thom's Creek sherds

Site no. ■ *Site name* ■ *Sample no.* ■ *C14 BP* ■ *Material* ■ *Reference*

9EB21 ■ Paris Island South ■ Beta-3763 ■ 3190±140 ■ charcoal ■ Wood et al. 1986:286
Level C fill of preceramic Late Archaic midden

9McI87 ■ A. Busch Krick ■ UGA-226 ■ 3215±80 ■ conch shell ■ Brandau and Noakes 1972:494
Base of midden (1.7–1.8 m BS), Pit 1, with plain and decorated fiber-tempered sherds

38CH12 ■ Lighthouse Point ■ UGA-2902 ■ 3275±55 ■ charcoal ■ Trinkley 1980b:191–92
Level 2 of unit 23OR70, containing Thom's Creek sherds

38BU805 ■ Fish Haul ■ Beta-16922 ■ 3280±80 ■ charcoal ■ Trinkley 1986:140
Feature 18, reused shellfish steaming pit; 129–141 block, with plain, shell punctate, and reed punctate fiber-tempered sherds and one Thom's Creek punctate sherd

38CH45 ■ Sewee Shell Ring ■ GX-2279 ■ 3295±110 ■ unpublished ■ Trinkley 1980a:14
context unreported, but "probably dates Awendaw finger-pinched" (Trinkley 1980a:14)

38CH12 ■ Lighthouse Point ■ UGA-2905 ■ 3345±70 ■ charcoal ■ Trinkley 1980b:191–92
Feature 37, containing Thom's Creek sherds

9BU9 ■ Daw's Island ■ GX-2281 ■ 3395±100 ■ shell ■ Michie 1973
from eroding shell midden containing fiber-tempered and Thom's Creek sherds

38BU7 ■ Sea Pines Shell Ring ■ I-2848 ■ 3400±110 ■ clam shell ■ Calmes 1968; Buckley and Willis 1969:79
base of shell deposits, Level 4, 20–26" BS, with fiber-tempered and Thom's Creek sherds

38AB288 ■ McCalla Bottom ■ BETA-2530 ■ 3410±80 ■ unpublished ■ Glander et al. 1981; Anderson and Schuldenrein 1985:8
Block 1, Feature 7, in association with fiber-tempered punctate sherds and soapstone vessel fragments

Site no. ■ *Site name* ■ *Sample no.* ■ *C14 BP* ■ *Material* ■ *Reference*

9McI23 ■ Sapelo Island ■ UGA-73 ■ 3430±65 ■ oyster shell ■ Noakes and Brandau 1974:133

1 m depth in ring 50 m diam, 2–3 m high; cultural affiliation unreported

9McI23 ■ Sapelo Island ■ UGA-74 ■ 3430±70 ■ oyster shell ■ Noakes and Brandau 1974:133

2 m depth in ring 50 m diam, 2–3 m high; cultural affiliation unreported

SN-13 ■ none ■ unpublished ■ 3450±80 ■ hickory nutshell ■ Joseph 1985:9

Feature 4, 30 cm deep pit originating 36 cm BD; cultural affiliation uncertain

9McI87 ■ A. Busch Krick ■ UGA-227 ■ 3470±85 ■ oyster shell ■ Brandau and Noakes 1972:495

30–40 cm above base of midden (1.4 m BS), Pit 1, with plain and decorated fiber-tempered sherds

38CH61 ■ none ■ unpublished ■ 3505±100 ■ oyster shell ■ Mark J. Brooks, personal communication 1988

base of shell midden containing plain and simple-stamped sherds, some with minor fiber

9McI23 ■ Sapelo Island ■ UGA-75 ■ 3545±65 ■ oyster shell ■ Noakes and Brandau 1974:133

2 m depth in remnant of ring neighboring one with UGA-73, 74 assays; cultural affiliation uncertain

38BU8-1 ■ Large Ford Shell Ring ■ I-2850 ■ 3585±115 ■ charcoal ■ Calmes 1968; Buckley and Willis 1969:79

Level 9, 56–57" BS; bottom half of shell deposits containing fiber-tempered and Thom's Creek sherds

9GN76 ■ Canon's Point ■ UM-523 ■ 3600±110 ■ oyster shell ■ Marrinan 1975:49; Stipp et al. 1976:212

West shell ring test 1, 12–20 cm BS (Level 2), dates last occupation of ring with plain and decorated fiber-tempered sherds

9MI1-1 ■ Sapelo Shell Ring 1 ■ M-39 ■ 3600±350 ■ shell ■ Crane 1956:665; Williams 1968:329

general shell level fill containing plain fiber-tempered sherds

Site no. ■ *Site name* ■ *Sample no.* ■ *C14 BP* ■ *Material* ■ *Reference*

38AN29 ■ Sara's Ridge ■ BETA-2737 ■ 3680±60 ■ charcoal ■ Wood et al. 1986:159

XU 2, near Feature 125 in preceramic Late Archaic midden

38BU805 ■ Fish Haul ■ Beta-16924 ■ 3680±60 ■ charcoal ■ Trinkley 1986:147

Feature 23, shellfish steaming pit; 1982 block, containing plain and reed punctate fiber-tempered sherds

9Ch4 ■ Bilbo ■ M-1109 ■ 3700±125 ■ charcoal ■ Crane and Griffin 1968:239–40; Williams 1968:330; Dye 1976:45

3–3.5' (Haag Zone 6) nearly solid shell within middle shell zone containing plain, puntated, and incised fiber-tempered sherds

38BU805 ■ Fish Haul ■ Beta-16923 ■ 3720±90 ■ charcoal ■ Trinkley 1986:147

Feature 21, pit; 1982 block, with plain, incised, drag and jab, and reed punctate fiber-tempered sherds

9Ch4 ■ Bilbo ■ M-1112 ■ 3730±125 ■ bone ■ Crane and Griffin 1968:239–40; Williams 1968:330; Dye 1976:43–44

5.5–6' (Haag Zone 3–4) at or just below nearly solid oyster in basal shell midden with plain fiber-tempered sherds

9Cb1 ■ Stallings Island ■ M-1278 ■ 3730±150 ■ charcoal ■ Crane and Griffin 1965:134; Williams 1968:331; Bullen and Greene 1970

Pit 4; basal depth of 30" BS with plain and decorated fiber-tempered sherds

9GN57 ■ Canon's Point ■ UM-521 ■ 3760±90 ■ oyster shell ■ Marrinan 1975:48; Stipp et al. 1976:212

Marsh shell ring at 18N3E, 13 cm BS Level 3; dates last occupation of ring with plain fiber-tempered sherds

9Ch54 ■ Dulaney ■ M-236 ■ 3770±200 ■ oyster shell ■ Crane and Griffin 1958:1122; Williams 1968:329

18" above base of shell midden containing plain fiber-tempered sherds

38CH41 ■ Yough Hall Plantation ■ M-1209 ■ 3770±130 ■ oyster shell ■ Crane and Griffin 1964:9–10; Waddell 1965; Williams 1968:330–31

general shell ring midden containing Thom's Creek punctate and finger-pinched sherds

Site no. ■ *Site name* ■ *Sample no.* ■ *C14 BP* ■ *Material* ■ *Reference*

9MI1-1 ■ Sapelo Shell Ring 1 ■ M-39 ■ 3800±350 ■ shell ■ Crane 1956:665; Williams 1968:329

general shell level fill with plain fiber-tempered sherds

9RI327 ■ Rae's Creek ■ Beta-35190 ■ 3800±70 ■ charcoal ■ Crook 1990:38

90–100 cm BS in Stratum D2 with plain fiber-tempered sherds, soapstone slabs, and minor Thom's Creek sherds

38CH62 ■ Spanish Mount ■ UGA-583 ■ 3820±185 ■ charcoal ■ Sutherland 1974; Brandau and Noakes 1975:107

basal stratum of shell midden containing Thom's Creek sherds; extracted from profile of cut bank

9Ch4 ■ Bilbo ■ M-1111 ■ 3820±125 ■ charcoal ■ Crane and Griffin 1968:239–40; Williams 1968:330; Dye 1976:43–44

5.5–6' (Haag Zone 3–4) at or just below nearly solid oyster; initial shell midden with plain fiber-tempered sherds

9CB15 ■ Uchee Creek ■ UM-341 ■ 3860±75 ■ shell ■ Eldridge et al. 1975:407

Pit 6; cultural affiliation unreported

9GN76 ■ Canon's Point ■ UM-522 ■ 3860±90 ■ oyster shell ■ Marrinan 1975:49; Stipp et al. 1976:212

West shell ring test 1, 45–55 cm BS (Level 4); dates initial occupation of ring with plain and decorated fiber-tempered sherds

38BU8-2 ■ Small Ford Shell Ring ■ I-3047 ■ 3890±110 ■ charcoal ■ Calmes 1968; Buckley and Willis 1969:79

base of midden; Level 4, 18–24" with Thom's Creek sherds that Calmes (1968) refers to as sand-tempered Stallings pottery

Hxv7 ■ Gaston ■ M-524 ■ 3894±250 ■ charcoal ■ Coe 1964:97–98, 118

combined charcoal from 3 hearths in stratum containing Savannah River Stemmed bifaces (and perhaps soapstone vessel fragments)

9CB15 ■ Uchee Creek ■ UM-340 ■ 3915±85 ■ shell ■ Eldridge et al. 1975:407

Pit 2; cultural affiliation unreported

38AN29 ■ Sara's Ridge ■ BETA-2735 ■ 3950±80 ■ charcoal ■ Wood et al. 1986:126

XU1, Feature 21 in preceramic Late Archaic midden

Site no. ■ *Site name* ■ *Sample no.* ■ *C14 BP* ■ *Material* ■ *Reference*

9EB21 ■ Paris Island South ■ Beta-3762 ■ 4070±70 ■ charcoal ■ Wood et al. 1986:286

Level X fill in preceramic Late Archaic midden

9EB21 ■ Paris Island South ■ Beta-3761 ■ 4090±70 ■ charcoal ■ Wood et al. 1986:260, 286

Feature 10 in preceramic Late Archaic midden

9RI327 ■ Rae's Creek ■ Beta-35191 ■ 4100±110 ■ charcoal ■ Crook 1990:38

90–100 cm BS in Stratum D2 with plain fiber-tempered sherds, soapstone slabs, and minor Thom's Creek sherds

9MI1-1 ■ Sapelo Shell Ring 1 ■ RL-580 ■ 4120±200 ■ hickory nutshell ■ Simpkins 1975

refuse pit 80–135 cm BS of unit approximately 30 m south of Shell Ring 1; plain fiber-tempered sherd association

9Ch4 ■ Bilbo ■ O-1047 ■ 4125±115 ■ charcoal ■ Williams 1968:330; Dye 1976:43–44

5.5–6' (Haag Zone 3–4) at or just below nearly solid oyster; initial shell midden with plain fiber-tempered sherds

38CH62 ■ Spanish Mount ■ UGA-584 ■ 4170±350 ■ charcoal ■ Sutherland 1974; Brandau and Noakes 1975:107

basal stratum of shell midden containing Thom's Creek sherds; extracted from profile of cut bank

9EB21 ■ Paris Island South ■ Beta-3759 ■ 4170±100 ■ charcoal ■ Wood et al. 1986:286

Level C fill of preceramic Late Archaic midden

9GN57 ■ Canon's Point ■ UM-520 ■ 4190±90 ■ oyster shell ■ Marrinan 1975:48; Stipp et al. 1976:212

Marsh Ring; base of midden deposit 1.47 m BS; initial occupation of shell ring with plain fiber-tempered sherds

38AN29 ■ Sara's Ridge ■ BETA-2736 ■ 4200±90 ■ charcoal ■ Wood et al. 1986:159

XU2, Feature 37 of preceramic Late Archaic midden

Site no. ■ *Site name* ■ *Sample no.* ■ *C14 BP* ■ *Material* ■ *Reference*

38AN29 ■ Sara's Ridge ■ BETA-2737 ■ 4210±60 ■ charcoal ■ Wood et al. 1986:159

XU 2, Feature 63 of preceramic Late Archaic midden

9Cam167 ■ Kings Bay ■ UM-1433 ■ 4260±100 ■ carbonized wood ■ Calvert et al. 1979:109

Feature 2, FS #60, KBS 8(hearth 24 cm BS) with fiber-tempered sherds

Hxv7 ■ Gaston ■ M-522 ■ 4274±350 ■ charcoal ■ Coe 1964:96, 118

combined charcoal from 2 hearths in stratum containing Halifax hafted bifaces

none ■ WV14 ■ Beta-29451 ■ 4290±120 ■ charcoal/nutshell ■ Brooks and Sassaman n.d.

Feature 1, Prov. 6; shell-filled refuse pit with shell punctate fiber-tempered sherd

9RI327 ■ Rae's Creek ■ Beta-35189 ■ 4370±110 ■ charcoal ■ Crook 1990:38

100–110 cm BS in Stratum D2 with plain fiber-tempered sherds, soapstone slabs, and minor Thom's Creek sherds

38AB91 ■ Rocky River ■ BETA-4307 ■ 4400±70 ■ unpublished ■ Anderson and Schuldenrein 1985:8

EU 77 midden with Small Savannah River hafted bifaces and soapstone slabs

38AL15 ■ Rabbit Mount ■ GXO-343 ■ 4450±135 ■ charcoal ■ Stoltman 1966, 1974

level provenience charcoal from square 18, Level B2 with plain fiber-tempered sherds and soapstone slabs

9Cb1 ■ Stallings Island ■ M-1277 ■ 4450±150 ■ charcoal/nutshell ■ Crane and Griffin 1965:134; Williams 1968:331; Bullen and Greene 1970

Pit 2; basal depth of 70" BS in preceramic Late Archaic midden

38AL15 ■ Rabbit Mount ■ GXO-345 ■ 4465±95 ■ charcoal ■ Stoltman 1966, 1974

level provenience charcoal from square 15, Level B2 with plain fiber-tempered sherds and soapstone slabs

Site no. ■ *Site name* ■ *Sample no.* ■ *C14 BP* ■ *Material* ■ *Reference*

9EB76 ■ Rufus Bullard ■ UGA-3612 ■ 4500±135 ■ unpublished ■ Flint and Suggs 1980; Anderson and Schuldenrein 1985:8

30S10W, Feature B with indirect association of fiber-tempered sherds; Anderson and Joseph 1988 interpret as "doubtful/early?"

9Cb1 ■ Stallings Island ■ M-1279 ■ 4700±150 ■ charcoal/nutshell ■ Crane and Griffin 1965:134; Williams 1968:331; Bullen and Greene 1970

Pit 5; basal depth of 70" BS in preceramic Late Archaic midden

SN-13 ■ none ■ Beta-14423 ■ 4860±130 ■ hickory nutshell ■ Espenshade 1986:74

Feature 6A, hearth 110–37 cm in plan, 23 cm deep, first recognized in Level 5; cultural affiliation uncertain

9Cam167 ■ Kings Bay ■ UM-1432 ■ 5000±180 ■ carbonized wood ■ Calvert et al. 1979:109

Feature 2, FS #56, KBS 8 (hearth 24 cm BS) with fiber-tempered sherds

none ■ Puerto Hormiga ■ UGA-311 ■ 5090±80 ■ oyster shell ■ Noakes and Brandau 1974:140

context unreported; sand-tempered and fiber-tempered sherd associations

38AN29 ■ Sara's Ridge ■ BETA-2737 ■ 5200±280 ■ charcoal ■ Wood et al. 1986:159

XU 2, near Feature 125 in preceramic Late Archaic midden

Hxv7 ■ Gaston ■ M-523 ■ 5434±350 ■ charcoal ■ Coe 1964:96, 99, 118

combined charcoal from 4 hearths in stratum containing Halifax hafted bifaces

9Ch4 ■ Bilbo ■ O-1046 ■ 5500±115 ■ charcoal ■ Williams 1968:330

Haag Zones 7–8 and Waring Zone 3; possibly with decorated fiber-tempered sherds (Haag in Williams 1968:330 rejects as too early)

SN-03 ■ none ■ Beta-13290 ■ 5740±90 ■ hickory nutshell ■ Elliott 1986:71

Level 5, Block 2; six samples combined from Level 5 fill; ca. 55–65 cm BS; cultural affiliation uncertain

Site no. ■ *Site name* ■ *Sample no.* ■ *C14 BP* ■ *Material* ■ *Reference*

SN-09 ■ none ■ unpublished ■ 5760±125 ■ unpublished ■ Wise 1986
Level 6 (62–72 cm BS); Middle-Late Archaic bifaces and soapstone slabs; overlain with plain fiber-tempered sherds

38BU805 ■ Fish Haul ■ Beta-16925 ■ 6060±110 ■ charcoal ■ Trinkley 1986:141
Feature 28, probable tree hole, originally thought to be hearth containing plain and decorated fiber-tempered sherds

References

Alterman, Michael C.

1987 A Reassessment of Late Archaic Settlement and Subsistence along the Upper Savannah River Valley: A View from the Richard B. Russell Reservoir. Ph.D. dissertation, Department of Anthropology, Columbia University.

Anderson, David G.

1975 Inferences for Distributional Studies of Prehistoric Artifacts in the Coastal Plain of South Carolina. *Southeastern Archaeological Conference Bulletin* 18:180–94.

1979 *Excavation at Four Fall Line Sites: The Southeastern Columbia Beltway Project*. Commonwealth Associates, Report No. R-2008, Jackson, Michigan. (Jointly released by South Carolina Department of Highways and Public Transportation.)

1982 The Mattassee Lake Ceramic Artifact Assemblage. In *The Mattassee Lake Sites: Archaeological Investigations along the Lower Santee River in the Coastal Plain of South Carolina*, assembled by D. G. Anderson, C. E. Cantley, and A. L. Novick, pp. 207–322. Archeological Services Branch, National Park Service, Special Bulletin 1.

1985 Why California? The Relevance of California Archaeology and Ethnography to Eastern Woodlands Prehistory. Manuscript in possession of the author.

N.d. Analysis of the Venning Creek Collection. Data in possession of the author.

Anderson, David G., Charles E. Cantley, and Andrea Lee Novick, assemblers

1982 *The Mattassee Lake Sites: Archaeological Investigations along the Lower Santee River in the Coastal Plain of South Carolina*. Archeological Services Branch, National Park Service, Special Bulletin 1.

Anderson, David G., Charles E. Cantley, and Joseph Schuldenrein

1985 The Rocky River Site (38AB91) Archaeological Record. In *Prehis-*

toric Human Ecology along the Upper Savannah River: Excavations at the Rucker's Bottom, Abbeville and Bullard Site Groups, assembled by D. G. Anderson and J. Schuldenrein, pp. 215–49. Atlanta: Interagency Archaeological Services Division, National Park Service, Russell Papers.

Anderson, David G., and Glen T. Hanson
1988 Early Archaic Settlement in the Southeastern United States: A Case Study from the Savannah River Basin. *American Antiquity* 53:262–86.

Anderson, David G., and J. W. Joseph
1988 *Prehistory and History along the Upper Savannah River: Technical Synthesis of Cultural Resource Investigations, Richard B. Russell Multiple Resource Area*. Atlanta: Interagency Archaeological Services Division, National Park Service, Russell Papers.

Anderson, David G., Sammy T. Lee, and A. Robert Parler
1979 *Cal Smoak: Archaeological Investigations along the Edisto River in the Coastal Plain of South Carolina*. Occasional Papers 1, Archeological Society of South Carolina.

Anderson, David G., and Joseph Schuldenrein (assemblers)
1985a *Prehistoric Human Ecology along the Upper Savannah River: Excavations at the Rucker's Bottom, Abbeville and Bullard Site Groups*. Atlanta: Interagency Archaeological Services Division, National Park Service, Russell Papers.

Anderson, David G., and Joseph Schuldenrein
1985b The Rucker's Bottom Site (9EB91) Archaeological Record. In *Prehistoric Human Ecology along the Upper Savannah River: Excavations at the Rucker's Bottom, Abbeville and Bullard Site Groups*, assembled by D. G. Anderson and J. Schuldenrein, pp. 251–590. Atlanta: National Park Service, Archaeological Services Branch, Russell Papers.

Anderson, David G., Joseph Schuldenrein, and Charles E. Cantley
1985 The Rufus Bullard Site (38EB76) Archaeological Record. In *Prehistoric Human Ecology along the Upper Savannah River: Excavations at the Rucker's Bottom, Abbeville and Bullard Site Groups*, assembled by D. G. Anderson and J. Schuldenrein, pp. 149–74. Atlanta: National Park Service, Archaeological Services Branch, Russell Papers.

Arnold, Dean E.
1985 *Ceramic Theory and Cultural Process*. Cambridge: Cambridge University Press.

Barnett, Homer G.
1953 *Innovation: The Basis of Cultural Change*. New York: McGraw-Hill.

REFERENCES

Barry, J. M.

1980 *Natural Vegetation of South Carolina*. Columbia: University of South Carolina Press.

Beals, Ralph L.

1933 Ethnology of the Nisenan. *University of California Publications in American Archaeology and Ethnology* 31:335–413.

Bender, Barbara

1981 Gatherer-Hunter Intensification. In *Economic Archaeology*, edited by A. Sheridan and G. Bailey, pp. 149–57. BAR International Series 96. Oxford: BAR.

1985a Prehistoric Developments in the American Midcontinent and in Brittany, Northwest France. In *Prehistoric Hunter-Gatherers: The Emergence of Cultural Complexity*, edited by T. D. Price and J. A. Brown, pp. 21–57. Orlando: Academic Press.

1985b Emergent Tribal Formations in the American Midcontinent. *American Antiquity* 50:52–62.

Bense, Judith A., ed.

1987 *The Midden Mound Project*. Report of Investigations 6. Pensacola: Office of Cultural and Archaeological Research, University of West Florida.

Binford, Lewis R.

1962 Archaeology as Anthropology. *American Antiquity* 28:217–25.

1968 Archaeological Perspectives. In *New Perspectives in Archaeology*, edited by S. R. Binford and L. R. Binford, pp. 5–32. Chicago: Aldine.

Blanton, Dennis B.

1979 An Archaeological Survey of the Upper Satilla Basin. *Early Georgia* 7(2):43–63.

Blanton, Dennis B., and Christopher Espenshade

1986 Archaeological Data Recovery at Cultural Property GP-SN-05, in Screven County, Georgia, on the 500 KV Vogtle-Effingham-Thalman Electric Transmission Line Corridor. Atlanta: Garrow and Associates.

Blanton, Dennis B., Christopher T. Espenshade, and Paul B. Brockington, Jr.

1986 An Archaeological Study of 38SU83: A Yadkin Phase Site in the Upper Coastal Plain of South Carolina. Contract Report F-117(99), South Carolina Department of Highways and Public Transportation. Atlanta: Garrow and Associates.

Blitz, John H.

1988 Adoption of the Bow in Prehistoric North America. *North American Archaeologist* 9:123–45.

Bowen, William R.
1979 Archaeological Testing at 9Ri(DOT)3: An Archaic Camp Site in the Central Savannah River Valley. *Southern Indian Studies* 30:18–32.

Boyce, James K.
1987 *Agrarian Impasse in Bengal: Institutional Constraints to Technological Change*. Oxford: Oxford University Press.

Braley, Chad O.
1992a Cultural Resource Survey of Agricultural Lease Lands, Fort Gordon, Richmond County, Georgia. Athens, Ga.: Southeastern Archaeological Services.
1992b Cultural Resource Survey of Selected Fiscal Year 1991 Timber Sales, Fort Gordon, McDuffie and Richmond Counties, Georgia. Athens, Ga.: Southeastern Archaeological Services.

Brandau, Betty Lee, and John E. Noakes
1972 University of Georgia Radiocarbon Dates II. *Radiocarbon* 14:486–97.
1975 University of Georgia Radiocarbon Dates IV. *Radiocarbon* 17:99–111.

Braun, David P.
1983 Pots as Tools. In *Archaeological Hammers and Theories*, edited by J. A. Moore and A. S. Keene, pp. 107–34. New York: Academic Press.
1987 Coevolution of Sedentism, Pottery Technology, and Horticulture in the Central Midwest 200 B.C.–A.D. 600. In *Emergent Horticultural Economies of the Eastern Woodlands*, edited by W. F. Keegan, pp. 153–81. Occasional Paper 7. Carbondale: Center for Archaeological Investigations, Southern Illinois University.

Brockington, Paul B.
1971 A Preliminary Investigation of an Early Knapping Site in Southeastern Georgia. South Carolina Institute of Archeology and Anthropology, University of South Carolina, Columbia, *Notebook* 3:34–46.

Bronitsky, Gordon, and Robert Hamer
1986 Experiments in Ceramic Technology: The Effects of Various Tempering Materials on Impact and Thermal Shock Resistance. *American Antiquity* 51:89–101.

Brooks, Mark J., and Glen T. Hanson
1989 Late Archaic-Late Woodland Adaptive Stability and Change in the Steel Creek Watershed, South Carolina. Report submitted to Savannah River Operations Office, U.S. Department of Energy.

Brooks, Mark J., and Kenneth E. Sassaman
1988 Environmental and Social Circumscription of Late Mid-Holocene Hunter-Gatherers in the Upper Coastal Plain Portion of the Savan-

nah River Valley. Manuscript on file at the Savannah River Archaeological Research Program, South Carolina Institute of Archaeology and Anthropology, University of South Carolina, Columbia.

N.d. Notes and records from survey and testing at sites in Jasper County, South Carolina, on file at the Savannah River Archaeological Research Program, South Carolina Institute of Archaeology and Anthropology, University of South Carolina, Columbia.

Brooks, Mark J., Donald J. Colquhoun, and Kenneth E. Sassaman

1990 Buried Sites in South Carolina's Estuaries: Possibilities and Implications. *COSCAPA Newsletter* 11(1):5.

Brooks, Mark J., Peter A. Stone, Donald J. Colquhoun, Janice G. Brown, and Kathy B. Steele

1986 Geoarchaeological Research in the Coastal Plain Portion of the Savannah River Valley. *Geoarchaeology* 1:293–307.

Brown, James A.

1989 The Beginnings of Pottery as an Economic Process. In *What's New? A Closer Look at the Process of Innovation,* edited by S. E. van der Leeuw and R. Torrence, pp. 203–24. London: Unwin Hyman.

Brown, James A., and Robert K. Vierra

1985 What Happened in the Middle Archaic? Introduction to an Ecological Approach to Koster Site Archaeology. In *Archaic Hunters and Gatherers in the American Midwest,* edited by J. L. Phillips and J. A. Brown, pp. 165–96. New York: Academic Press.

Brown, Lawrence A.

1981 *Innovation Diffusion: A New Perspective.* London: Methuen.

Broyles, Bettye J., and Clarence H. Webb, eds.

1970 The Poverty Point Culture. *Southeastern Archaeological Conference, Bulletin* 12.

Buckley, James D., and Eric H. Willis

1969 Isotope's Radiocarbon Measurements VII. *Radiocarbon* 11:53–105.

Bullen, Ripley P.

1954 Culture Changes during the Fiber-Tempered Period of Florida. *Southern Indian Studies* 6:45–48.

1955 Stratigraphic Tests at Bluffton, Volusia County, Florida. *Florida Anthropologist* 8:1–16.

1959 The Transitional Period of Florida. *Southeastern Archaeological Conference, Newsletter* 6:43–53.

1972 The Orange Period of Peninsular Florida. In *Fiber-Tempered Pottery in Southeastern United States and Northern Colombia: Its Origins,*

Context and Significance, edited by R. P. Bullen and J. B. Stoltman, pp. 9–33. Florida Anthropological Society Publications 6.

1974 The Origins of the Gulf Tradition as Seen from Florida. *Florida Anthropologist* 27:77–88.

Bullen, Ripley P., and Adelaide K. Bullen

1961 The Summer Haven Site, St. Johns County, Florida. *Florida Anthropologist* 14:1–15.

Bullen, Ripley P., and H. Bruce Greene

1970 Stratigraphic Tests at Stallings Island, Georgia. *Florida Anthropologist* 23:8–23.

Bullen, Ripley P., and James B. Stoltman, eds.

1972 *Fiber-Tempered Pottery in Southeastern United States and Northern Colombia: Its Origins, Context and Significance.* Florida Anthropological Society Publications 6.

Burns, Louis F.

1984 *Osage Indian Custom and Myths.* Fallbrook, Calif.: Ciga Press.

Cable, John S., and Charles E. Cantley

1979 *An Intensive Archaeological Survey of the South Carolina 151 Highway Widening Project.* Research Manuscript Series (no number). Columbia: South Carolina Institute of Archaeology and Anthropology, University of South Carolina.

Cable, John S., Charles E. Cantley, James L. Michie, and Stephen M. Perlman

1978 *An Archaeological Reconnaissance of the Bobby Jones Expressway Corridor, Aiken County, South Carolina.* Research Manuscript Series 124. Columbia: South Carolina Institute of Archaeology and Anthropology, University of South Carolina.

Caldwell, Joseph R.

1958 *Trend and Tradition in the Prehistory of the Eastern United States.* American Anthropological Association Memoir 88, Scientific Papers 10. Springfield: Illinois State Museum.

Caldwell, Joseph, and Catherine McCann

1941 *Irene Mound Site, Chatham County, Georgia.* Athens: University of Georgia Press.

Caldwell, Joseph R., and Antonio J. Waring, Jr.

1939 Some Chatham County Pottery Types and Their Sequence. *Southeastern Archaeological Conference, Newsletter* 1:5–6.

Calmes, Alan

1968 Test Excavations at Three Late Archaic Shell-Ring Mounds on Hilton Head Island, Beaufort County, South Carolina. *Southeastern Archaeological Conference Bulletin* 8:45–48.

Calvert, P. M., D. S. Introne, and J. J. Stipp
1979 University of Miami Radiocarbon Dates XIV. *Radiocarbon* 21:107–12.

Campbell, Janice L., Carol S. Weed, and Prentice M. Thomas, Jr.
1981 Archaeological Investigations at the Fort Gordon Military Reservation, Georgia. Final Contract Report C-55088(79) for Atlanta Interagency Archaeological Services Division, National Park Service. Report of Investigation 33, New World Research.

Canouts, Veletta, and Albert C. Goodyear
1985 Lithic Scatters in the South Carolina Piedmont. In *Structure and Process in Southeastern Archaeology,* edited by R. S. Dickens, Jr., and H. T. Ward, pp. 180–94. University, Ala.: University of Alabama Press.

Chagnon, Napoleon
1977 *Yanomamö: The Fierce People.* 2d ed. New York: Holt, Rinehart and Winston.

Chapman, Jefferson
1977 *Archaic Period Research in the Lower Little Tennessee River Valley—1975, Icehouse Bottom, Harrison Branch, Thirty Acre Island, Calloway Island.* Report of Investigations 18. Knoxville: Department of Anthropology, University of Tennessee.

Chase, D. W.
1966 A Stratified Archaic Site in Lowndes County, Alabama. *Florida Anthropologist* 19:91–101.

Childe, V. Gordon
1925 *The Dawn of European Civilization.* New York: Knopf.
1944 *Archaeological Ages as Technological Stages.* Huxley Lecture of the Royal Anthropological Institute of Great Britain and Ireland, London. *Man* 65:19–20.
1951 *Man Makes Himself.* New York: Mentor.

Claassen, Cheryl
1986 Shellfishing Seasons in the Prehistoric Southeastern United States. *American Antiquity* 51:21–37.
1988 New Hypotheses for the Demise of the Shell Mound Archaic. Paper presented at the Forty-fifth Southeastern Archaeological Conference, New Orleans.
1991 Gender, Shellfishing, and the Shellmound Archaic. In *Engendering Archaeology: Women in Prehistory,* edited by J. M. Gero and M. W. Conkey, pp. 276–300. Oxford: Basil Blackwell.

Claflin, William H., Jr.
1931 The Stalling's Island Mound, Columbia County, Georgia. *Peabody Museum of American Archaeology and Ethnology Papers* 14(1):1–47.

Coe, Joffre L.
1964 The Formative Cultures of the Carolina Piedmont. *Transactions of the American Philosophical Society* 54: pt. 5, 1–130.

Colquhoun, Donald J., and Mark J. Brooks
1986 New Evidence for the Southeastern U.S. for Eustatic Components in the Late Holocene Sea Levels. *Geoarchaeology* 1:275–91.

Colquhoun, Donald J., and H. S. Johnson
1968 Tertiary Sea-Level Fluctuations in South Carolina. *Palaeogeography, Palaeoclimatology, Palaeoecology* 5:105–26.

Connaway, John M., Samuel O. McGahey, and Clarence H. Webb
1977 *Teoc Creek: A Poverty Point Site in Carroll County, Mississippi.* Archaeological Report 3. Jackson: Mississippi Department of Archives and History.

Cook, Fred C.
N.d. Perforated Steatite Slabs: A Preliminary Study of Steatite Artifacts from Southeastern Georgia. Manuscript on file with author.

Cooke, C. Wythe
1936 Geology of the Coastal Plain of South Carolina. *U.S. Geological Survey Bulletin* 867.

Cordell, Linda S.
1984 *Prehistory of the Southwest.* Orlando: Academic Press.

Crane, H. R.
1956 University of Michigan Radiocarbon Dates I. *Science* 124:664–72.

Crane, H. R., and J. B. Griffin
1958 University of Michigan Radiocarbon Dates III. *Science* 128:1117–23.
1963 University of Michigan Radiocarbon Dates VIII. *Radiocarbon* 5:228–53.
1964 University of Michigan Radiocarbon Dates IX. *Radiocarbon* 6:1–24.
1965 University of Michigan Radiocarbon Dates X. *Radiocarbon* 7:123–52.

Crook, Morgan R., Jr.
1990 Rae's Creek: A Multicomponent Archaeological Site at the Fall Line along the Savannah River. Atlanta: Department of Anthropology, Georgia State University.

Cross, John R.
1983 Organizational Options for Non-Subsistence Production in the Late Archaic. Paper presented at the Forty-eighth Annual Meeting of the Society for American Archaeology, Pittsburgh.
1990 Craft Specialization in Non-Stratified Society: A Late Archaic Example from the Northeast. Ph.D. dissertation, Department of Anthropology, University of Massachusetts, Amherst.

Crusoe, Donald L.
1972 Interaction Networks and New World Fiber-Tempered Pottery. Ph.D. dissertation, Department of Anthropology, University of Georgia.

Crusoe, Donald L., and Chester B. DePratter
1976 A New Look at the Georgia Coastal Shellmound Archaic. *Florida Anthropologist* 29:1–23.

Dagenhardt, Johnny R.
1972 Perforated Soapstone Discs: A Functional Test. South Carolina Institute of Archaeology and Anthropology, University of South Carolina, Columbia. *Notebook* 4:65–68.

Davis, Dave D.
1983 Investigating the Diffusion of Stylistic Innovations. In *Advances in Archaeological Method and Theory,* vol. 6, edited by M. B. Schiffer, pp. 53–89. New York: Academic Press.

DeJarnette, David L.
1975 *Archaeological Salvage in the Walter F. George Basin of the Chattahoochie River in Alabama.* University Ala.: University of Alabama Press.

Delcourt, Paul A., and Hazel R. Delcourt
1987 *Long-term Forest Dynamics of the Temperate Zone.* New York: Springer-Verlag.

DePratter, Chester B.
1976 The 1974–75 Archaeological Survey in the Wallace Reservoir, Greene, Hancock, Morgan, and Putnam Counties, Georgia. Final Report on file at the Department of Anthropology, University of Georgia, Athens.
1979a Ceramics. In *The Anthropology of St. Catherine's Island: The Refuge-Deptford Mortuary Complex,* edited by D. H. Thomas and C. S. Larsen. *Anthropological Papers of the American Museum of Natural History* 56(1):109–32.
1979b Shellmound Archaic on the Georgia Coast. *South Carolina Antiquities* 11(2):1–69.

DePratter, Chester B., and James D. Howard
1980 Indian Occupation and Geologic History of the Georgia Coast: A 5000 Year Summary. In *Excursions in Southeastern Geology: The Archaeology-Geology of the Georgia Coast,* edited by J. D. Howard, C. B. DePratter, and R. W. Frey, pp. 1–65. Georgia Geological Society Guidebook 20.

Dickens, Roy S., Jr., and Linda R. Carnes
1983 Preliminary Investigations at Soapstone Ridge, DeKalb County,

Georgia. *Southeastern Archaeological Conference, Bulletin* 20 & 21:81–97.

Dickson, D. Bruce
1988 Anthropological Utopias and Geographical Epidemics: Competing Models of Social Change and the Problem of the Origins of Agriculture. In *The Transfer and Transformation of Ideas and Material Culture,* edited by P. J. Hugill and D. B. Dickson, pp. 45–72. College Station: Texas A&M University Press.

Dragoo, Don W.
1976 Some Aspects of Eastern North American Pre-History: A Review 1976. *American Antiquity* 41:3–27.

Driver, Harold E., and William C. Massey
1957 Comparative Studies of North American Indians. *Transactions of the American Philosophical Society* 47:165–456.

Duma, G.
1972 Phosphate Content of Ancient Pots as Indication of Use. *Current Anthropology* 13:127–29.

Dye, David H.
1976 The Bilbo Site Revisited: Archaeological Investigations from Chatham County, Georgia. M.A. thesis, Department of Geography and Anthropology, Lousiana State University.

Ebeling, Walter
1986 *Handbook of Indian Foods and Fibers in Arid America.* Berkeley: University of California Press.

Edwards, William
1965 Preliminary Report on Excavations at Sewee Indian Mound. Manuscript on file, South Carolina Institute of Archaeology and Anthropology, University of South Carolina, Columbia.

Eldridge, K. L., J. J. Stipp, J. Hattner, and E. McDougal
1975 University of Miami Radiocarbon Dates IV. *Radiocarbon* 17:407–12.

Elliott, Daniel T.
1981 *Soapstone Use in the Wallace Reservoir.* Wallace Reservoir Project Contribution 5. Athens: Department of Anthropology, University of Georgia.
1986a The Live Oak Soapstone Quarry, DeKalb County, Georgia. Atlanta: Garrow and Associates.
1986b Two Years before the Bear: The Savannah River Watershed. Paper presented at the Twelfth Annual Conference of the Archaeological Society of South Carolina, Columbia.
1986c CRM: Vogtle-Effingham-Thalman 500 kv Electrical Transmission

Line. GP-SN-08: Data Recovery. Report submitted to Georgia Power Company by Garrow and Associates, Atlanta.

1989 *Falcon Field and Line Creek: Two Archaic and Woodland Period Sites in West Central Georgia.* Athens, Ga.: Southeastern Archaeological Services.

Elliott, Daniel T., and Roy Doyon
1981 *Archaeological and Historical Geography of the Savannah River Floodplain Near Augusta, Georgia.* Laboratory of Anthropology Series Report 22. Athens: University of Georgia.

Elliott, Daniel T., R. Jerald Ledbetter, and Elizabeth A. Gordon
1992 Golf, Transportation, and the Late Archaic Period: Archaelogy for the Bobby Jones Expressway Extension Project. Draft report submitted to the Georgia Department of Transportation. Athens, Ga.: Southeastern Archaeological Services.

Elliott, Daniel T., and Lisa D. O'Steen
1987 Anatomy of the Brier Creek Archaic. Paper presented at the Forty-fourth Annual Meeting of the Southeastern Archaeological Conference, Charleston, South Carolina.

Espenshade, Christopher T.
1986 CRM: Vogtle-Effingham-Thalman 500 kv Electric Transmission Line. GP-SN-13: Data Recovery. Atlanta: Garrow and Associates.

Fairbanks, Charles F.
1942 The Taxonomic Position of Stallings Island, Georgia. *American Antiquity* 7:223–31.

Fawcett, William B.
1984 Communal Bison Hunting among Hunter-Gatherers on the High Plains. Ph.D. dissertation, Department of Anthropology, University of Massachusetts, Amherst.

Fenneman, Nevin M.
1938 *Physiography of Eastern United States.* New York: McGraw-Hill.

Ferguson, Leland G., and Randolph J. Widmer
1976 *Archaeological Examination of a Transect through the Middle Savannah River Valley, the Bobby Jones Expressway.* Research Manuscript Series 89. Columbia: South Carolina Institute of Archaeology and Anthropology, University of South Carolina.

Ferguson, T. A.
1976 Prehistoric Soapstone Procurement in Northwestern South Carolina. M.A. thesis, Department of Anthropology, University of Tennessee, Knoxville.

Filios, Elena L.

1984 Work and the Hunter and Gatherer Economy: A Statement of Field. Manuscript on file, Department of Anthropology, University of Massachusetts, Amherst.

1990 Thresholds to Group Fissioning among Hunters and Gatherers: An Archaeological Perspective. Ph.D. dissertation, Department of Anthropology, University of Massachusetts, Amherst.

Fish, Paul R.

1976 *Patterns of Prehistoric Site Distribution in Effingham and Screven Counties, Georgia.* Laboratory of Anthropology Series Report 11. Athens: University of Georgia.

Flannery, Regina

1943 Some Notes on a Few Sites in Beaufort County, S.C. *Bureau of American Ethnology Bulletin* 133:147–53.

Flint, Lawrence L., and Robert C. Suggs

1980 An Archaeological Investigation of the Bullard Group Sites 9EB76 and 9EB348, Richard B. Russell Multiple Resource Area, Elbert County, Georgia. Contract C-54044(80). Final report on file at the Atlanta Interagency Archaeological Services Division, National Park Service.

Ford, James A.

1966 Early Formative Cultures in Georgia and Florida. *American Antiquity* 31:781–99.

1969 *A Comparison of Formative Cultures in the Americas.* Smithsonian Contributions to Anthropology 11. Washington, D.C.: Smithsonian Institution.

Ford, James A., Phillip Phillips, and William G. Haag

1955 The Jaketown Site in West-Central Mississippi. *American Museum of Natural History, Anthropological Papers* 45.

Ford, James A., and Clarence H. Webb

1956 Poverty Point, A Late Archaic Site in Louisiana. *American Museum of Natural History, Anthropological Papers* 46, pt. 1.

Ford, Richard I.

1974 Northeastern Archaeology: Past and Future Directions. *Annual Review of Anthropology* 3:385–413.

Friedman, Jonathan

1974 Marxism, Structuralism and Vulgar Materialism. *Man* n.s., 9:444–69.

Futato, Eugene M.

1973 I-65 Highway Salvage: The Position of Twelve Archaeological

Sites in Central Alabama Prehistory. M.A. thesis, Department of Anthropology, University of Alabama.

Gagliano, Sherwood M., and Clarence H. Webb
1970 Archaic-Poverty Point Transition at the Pearl River Mouth. *Southeastern Archaeological Conference, Bulletin* 12:47–72.

Gardner, Paul S.
1986 Carbonized Plant Remains from Paris Island South (9EB21), Sara's Ridge (38AN29), and Simpson's Field (38AN8). In *Prehistory in the Richard B. Russell Reservoir: The Archaic and Woodland Periods of the Upper Savannah River*, edited by W. D. Wood et al., pp. 387–92. Russell Papers 1986, Archaeological Services. Atlanta: National Park Service.

Garrow, Patrick, and Ishmael Williams
1980 An Initial Investigation of the Archaeological and Historic Resources Which Would Be Affected by the Continued Operation and Maintenance of the Atlantic Intercoastal Waterway, Little River to Port Royal Sound, South Carolina. Marietta, Ga.: Soil Systems.

Gayton, A. H.
1948 Yokuts and Western Mono Ethnography, II: Northern Foothill Yokuts and Mono Ethnography. *University of California Anthropological Records* 10:143–301.

Gero, Joan M.
1991 Genderlithics: Women's Role in Stone Tool Production. In *Engendering Archaeology: Women in Prehistory*, edited by J. M. Gero and M. W. Conkey, pp. 163–93. Oxford: Basil Blackwell.

Gifford, E. W.
1932 The Northfork Mono. *University of California Publications in American Archaeology and Ethnology* 31:15–65.

Glander, W., G. Barber, and P. Brockington
1981 A Report of Archaeological Testing at Sites 38AB22, 38AB91, and 38AB288 in the Richard B. Russell Reservoir, Abbeville County, South Carolina. Contract C-54051(81). Final Report submitted to the Atlanta Interagency Archaeological Services Division, National Park Service.

Goodyear, Albert C.
1988 On the Study of Technological Change. *Current Anthropology* 29:320–23.

Goodyear, Albert C., and Tommy Charles
1984 *An Archaeological Survey of Chert Quarries in Western Allendale*

County, South Carolina. Research Manuscript Series 195. Columbia: South Carolina Institute of Archaeology and Anthropology, University of South Carolina.

Goodyear, Albert C., John H. House, and Neal W. Ackerly
1979 *Laurens-Anderson: An Archaeological Study of the Inter-riverine Piedmont*. Anthropological Studies 4. Columbia: South Carolina Institute of Archaeology and Anthropology, University of South Carolina.

Goodyear, Albert C., William Montieth, and Michael Harmon
1983 *Testing and Evaluation of the 84 Sites and Reconnaissance of the Islands and Cleveland Property, Richard B. Russell Dam and Lake, Savannah River, Georgia and South Carolina*. Research Manuscript Series 189. Columbia: South Carolina Institute of Archaeology and Anthropology, University of South Carolina.

Griffin, James B.
1943 An Analysis and Interpretation of the Ceramic Remains from Two Sites Near Beaufort, South Carolina. *Bureau of American Ethnology, Bulletin* 133:155–68.
1945 Ceramic Collections from Two South Carolina Sites. *Papers of the Michigan Academy of Science, Arts and Letters* 30:465–76.
1952 Culture Periods in Eastern United States Archaeology. In *Archaeology of Eastern United States,* edited by J. B. Griffin, pp. 352–64. Chicago: University of Chicago Press.
1967 Eastern North American Archaeology: A Summary. *Science* 156:175–91.

Griffin, John W.
1972 Fiber-Tempered Pottery in the Tennessee Valley. In *Fiber-Tempered Pottery in Southeastern United States and Northern Colombia: Its Origins, Context and Significance,* edited by R. P. Bullen and J. B. Stoltman, pp. 34–36. Florida Anthropological Society Publications 6.

Haag, William G.
1939 Type Descriptions. *Southeastern Archaeological Conference, Newsletter* 1(1).

Hägerstrand, Torsten
1967 *Innovation Diffusion as a Spatial Process* (orig. 1953). Chicago: University of Chicago Press.

Hall, Edwin S., Jr.
1978 Technological Change in Northern Alaska. In *Archaeological Essays in Honor of Irving B. Rouse,* edited by R. C. Dunnell and E. S. Hall, Jr., pp. 209–29. The Hague: Mouton.

Hally, David J.

1982 *Report of Archaeological Investigations at 9GE145.* Athens: Laboratory of Anthropology Series, University of Georgia.

1983 Use Alterations of Pottery Vessel Surfaces: An Important Source of Evidence for the Identification of Vessel Function. *North American Archaeologist* 4:3–26.

1986 The Identification of Vessel Function: A Case Study from Northwest Georgia. *American Antiquity* 51:267–95.

Hanson, Glen T.

1980 Excavations at Tinker Creek: A Stratified Late Archaic/Early Woodland Site. Paper presented at the Thirty-seventh Annual Meeting of the Southeastern Archaeological Conference, Columbia, South Carolina.

1982 The Analysis of Late Archaic-Early Woodland Adaptive Change along the Middle Savannah River: A Proposed Study. South Carolina Institute of Archaeology and Anthropology, University of South Carolina, Columbia, *Notebook* 14:5–38.

Hanson, Glen T., Richard D. Brooks, and John W. White

1981 *The Human Occupation along the Steel Creek Floodplain: Results of an Intensive Survey for the L-Area Reactivation Project, Savannah River Plant, Barnwell County, South Carolina.* Research Manuscript Series 173. Columbia: South Carolina Institute of Archaeology and Anthropology, University of South Carolina.

Hanson, Glen T., Rachel Most, and David G. Anderson

1978 *The Preliminary Archaeological Inventory of the Savannah River Plant, Aiken and Barnwell Counties, South Carolina.* Research Manuscript Series 132. Columbia: South Carolina Institute of Archaeology and Anthropology, University of South Carolina.

Hanson, Glen T., and Kenneth E. Sassaman

1984 Recent Investigations of Archaic Period Typology and Technology in the Upper Coastal Plain of South Carolina. Paper presented at the Forty-first Annual Meeting of the Southeastern Archaeological Conference, Pensacola, Florida.

Harrington, John P.

1942 Culture Element Distribution: XIX, Central California Coast. *University of California Anthropological Records* 7(1).

Hemmings, E. Thomas

1969 An Early Ceramic Site Near Beaufort, South Carolina. South Carolina Institute of Archaeology and Anthropology, University of South Carolina, Columbia, *Notebook* 1(6–9):6–7.

1970a Preliminary Report of Excavations at Fig Island, South Carolina. South Carolina Institute of Archaeology and Anthropology, University of South Carolina, Columbia, *Notebook* 2:9–12.

1970b *Emergence of Formative Life on the Atlantic Coast of the Southeast.* Research Manuscript Series 7. Columbia: South Carolina Institute of Archeology and Anthropology, University of South Carolina.

Hemmings, E. Thomas, and Eugene Waddell
N.d. Notes from the Shell Rings Survey. Notes on file at the South Carolina Institute of Archaeology and Anthropology, University of South Carolina, Columbia.

Hodder, Ian
1982 *Symbols in Action.* Cambridge: Cambridge University Press.

Holder, Preston
1938 Excavations on Saint Simons Island and Vicinity (Winter 1936–37). *Proceedings of the Society for Georgia Archaeology* 1:8–9.

Holmes, William Henry
1912 Steatite. In Handbook of American Indians, edited by Frederick Webb Hodge. *Bulletin of the Bureau of American Ethnology* 30:635–36.

House, John H.
1975 A Functional Typology for Cache Project Surface Collections. In *The Cache River Archaeological Project: An Experiment in Contract Archaeology,* assembled by M. B. Schiffer and J. H. House, pp. 55–73. Arkansas Archaeological Survey, Research Series No. 8. Fayetteville: Arkansas Archaeological Survey.

House, John H., and David L. Ballenger
1976 *An Archaeological Survey of the Interstate 77 Route in the South Carolina Piedmont.* Research Manuscript Series 104. Columbia: South Carolina Institute of Archaeology and Anthropology, University of South Carolina.

House, John H., and James W. Smith
1975 Experiments in the Replication of Fire-Cracked Rock. In *The Cache River Archaeological Project: An Experiment in Contract Archaeology,* assembled by M. B. Schiffer and J. H. House, pp. 75–80. Arkansas Archaeological Survey, Research Series No. 8. Fayetteville: Arkansas Archaeological Survey.

Hudson, Travis, and Thomas C. Blackburn
1983 *The Material Culture of the Chumash Interaction Sphere. Vol. 2: Food Preparation and Shelter.* Menlo Park, Calif.: Ballenna Press.

Ikawa-Smith, Fumiko
1976 On Ceramic Technology in East Asia. *Current Anthropology* 17:513–15.

Jenkins, Ned J.
1975 The Wheeler Series and Southeastern Prehistory. *Florida Anthropologist* 18:17–26.

1978 Prehistoric Chronology of the Lower Chattahoochee Valley: A Preliminary Statement. *Journal of Alabama Archaeology* 24:73–91.

1982 Archaeology of the Gainesville Lake Area: Synthesis. In *Archaeological Investigations in the Gainesville Lake Area of the Tennessee-Tombigbee Waterway*. Vol. 5. Report of Investigations 23. University, Ala.: Office of Archaeological Research, University of Alabama.

Jenkins, Ned J., David H. Dye, and John A. Walthall

1986 Early Ceramic Development in the Gulf Coastal Plain. In *Early Woodland Archaeology*, edited by K. B. Farnsworth and T. E. Emerson, pp. 546–63. Kampsville Seminars in Archaeology No. 2. Kampsville, Ill.: Center for American Archaeology Press.

Jenkins, Ned J., and Richard A. Krause

1986 *The Tombigbee Watershed in Southeastern Prehistory*. University, Ala.: University of Alabama Press.

Jochim, Michael A.

1983 Optimization Models in Context. In *Archaeological Hammers and Theories*, edited by J. A. Moore and A. S. Keene, pp. 157–72. New York: Academic Press.

Johnson, Douglas

1942 *The Origin of Carolina Bays*. New York: Columbia University Press.

Johnson, Olga Wetdemeyer

1969 *Flathead and Kootenay: The Rivers, the Tribes and the Region's Traders*. Glendale, Calif.: Arthur H. Clark.

Jones, Charles C., Jr.

1873 *Antiquities of the Southern Indians, Particularly of the Georgian Tribes*. New York: Appleton.

Joseph, J. W.

1985 CRM: Vogtle-Effingham-Thalman 500 KV Electric Transmission Line. GP-SN-13, GP-SN-15, and GP-SN-22: Resource Testing and Data Recovery Planning. Atlanta: Garrow and Associates.

Keel, Bennie C.

1976 *Cherokee Archaeology: A Study of the Appalachian Summit*. Knoxville: University of Tennessee Press.

Keene, Arthur S.

1983 Biology, Behavior, and Borrowing: A Critical Examination of Optimal Foraging Theory in Archaeology. In *Archaeological Hammers and Theories*, edited by J. A. Moore and A. S. Keene, pp. 137–55. New York: Academic Press.

1986 Stories We Tell: Gatherer-Hunters as Ideology. Paper presented at the Fourth International Congress on Hunter-Gatherers, London.

Kehoe, Alice B.

1962 A Hypothesis on the Origin of Northeastern American Pottery. *Southwestern Journal of Anthropology* 18(1):20–29.

1978 The Dominance of Diffusion and Its Decline in American Archaeology. In *Diffusion and Migration: Their Role in Cultural Development*, edited by P. G. Duke, J. Ebert, G. Langemann, and A. P. Buchner, pp. 22–29. Proceedings of the Tenth Annual Chacmool Conference. Calgary: Archaeological Association of the University of Calgary.

Kelly, Isabel T.

1932 Ethnography of the Surprise Valley Paiute. *University of California Publications in American Archaeology and Ethnology* 31:67–209.

King, Adam, and Chad O. Braley

1992 Cultural Resource Survey of Selected Fiscal Year 1992 Timber Sales, Fort Gordon, McDuffie and Richmond Counties, Georgia. Athens, Ga.: Southeastern Archaeological Services.

Kingery, W. D.

1960 *Introduction to Ceramics*. New York: Wiley.

Krause, Aurel

1956 *The Tlinget Indians: Results of a Trip to the Northwest Coast of America and the Bering Straits*. Seattle: University of Washington Press.

Kroeber, A. L.

1925 *Handbook of the Indians of California*. Smithsonian Institution, Bureau of American Ethnology Bulletin 78.

Küchler, A. W.

1964 *Potential Natural Vegetation of the Coterminus United States*. Special Publication 36. New York: American Geographical Society.

Langley, T. M., and W. M. Marter

1973 *The Savannah River Plant Site*. U.S. Atomic Energy Commission Report DP-1323. Aiken, S.C.: E. I. DuPont de Nemours, Savannah River Laboratory.

Larson, Lewis H., Jr.

1980 *Aboriginal Subsistence Technology of the Southeastern Coastal Plain during the Late Prehistoric Period*. Ripley P. Bullen Monographs in Anthropology and History 2. Gainesville: University Presses of Florida.

Lathrap, Donald W.

1987 The Introduction of Maize in Prehistoric North America: The View from Amazonia and the Santa Elena Peninsula. In *Emergent Horticultural Economies of the Eastern Woodlands*, edited by W. F. Keegan, pp. 345–71. Occasional Paper 7. Carbondale: Center for Archaeological Investigations, Southern Illinois University.

Lawrence, David
1986 Oysters from the Fish Haul Site. In *Indian and Freedman Occupation at the Fish Haul Site (38BU805), Beaufort County, South Carolina,* edited by M. B. Trinkley, pp. 328–33. Research Series 7. Columbia, S.C.: Chicora Foundation.

Ledbetter, R. Jerald
1988 The Pig Pen Site: Archaeological Investigations at 9RI158, Richmond County, Georgia. Report submitted to Georgia Department of Transportation by Southeastern Archaeological Services, Athens.
1991 Archaeological Investigations at Mill Branch Sites 9WR4 and 9WR11, Warren County, Georgia. Report submitted to J. M. Huber Corporation, Wrens, Georgia, by Southeastern Archaeological Services, Athens.

Ledbetter, R. Jerald, Stephen A. Kowalewski, and Lisa O'Steen
1984 Chert of Southern Oconee County, Georgia. *Early Georgia* 9:1–13.

Lee, Richard B.
1968 What Hunters Do for a Living, or How to Make out on Scarce Resources. In *Man the Hunter*, edited by R. B. Lee and I. DeVore, pp. 30–48. Chicago: Aldine.
1969 !Kung Bushman Subsistence: An Input-Output Analysis. In *Environment and Cultural Behavior,* edited by A. P. Vayda, pp. 47–79. Garden City, N.Y.: Natural History Press.

Levins, Richard, and Richard Lewontin
1985 *The Dialectical Biologist*. Cambridge, Mass.: Harvard University Press.

Lewis, Thomas M. N., and Madeline Kneberg Lewis
1961 *Eva: An Archaic Site*. Knoxville: University of Tennessee Press.

Linton, Ralph
1944 North American Cooking Pots. *American Antiquity* 9:369–80.

Loofs-Wissowa, H. H. E.
1980 Diffusion of Early Pottery in Southeast Asia: Some Suggestions. In *Diffusion of Material Culture,* edited by H. H. E. Loofs-Wissowa, pp. 1–17. Asian and Pacific Archaeology Series 9. Manoa: Social Science Research Institute, University of Hawaii.

Lorraine, Paul H.
1973 Some Observations on Stone Boiling. *Dallas Archaeological Society, Record* 29(3):2–3.

Lowman, D. W., and S. L. Wheatley
1970 Archaic Soapstone Quarries in Upper South Carolina. Institute of Archaeology and Anthropology, University of South Carolina, *Notebook* 2(6–7):6–12.

Marrinan, Rochelle

1975 Ceramics, Molluscs and Sedentism: The Late Archaic Period on the Georgia Coast. Ph.D. dissertation, Department of Anthropology, University of Florida, Gainesville.

1979 The Cultural Resources of Savannah National Wildlife Refuge, South Carolina and Georgia. Contract A5591(78). Final report submitted to the Atlanta Interagency Archaeological Services Division, National Park Service.

Marquardt, William H.

1985 Complexity and Scale in the Study of Fisher-Gatherer-Hunters: An Example from the Eastern United States. In *Prehistoric Hunter-Gatherers: The Emergence of Cultural Complexity,* edited by T. D. Price and J. A. Brown, pp. 59–98. Orlando: Academic Press.

Martin, Debra K., Glen T. Hanson, and Richard D. Brooks

1985 *An Intensive Archaeological Survey of Potential Cooling Ponds for Pen Branch and Four Mile Creek, Savannah River Plant, Aiken and Barnwell Counties, South Carolina.* Research Manuscript Series 198, South Carolina Institute of Archaeology and Anthropology, University of South Carolina, Columbia.

McKern, W. C.

1937 A Hypothesis for the Asiatic Origin of the Woodland Culture Pattern. *American Antiquity* 3:138–43.

McMichael, Edward V., and James H. Kellar

1960 *Archaeological Salvage in the Oliver Basin.* Laboratory of Archaeology Series 2. Athens: University of Georgia.

Meggers, Betty J., Clifford Evans, and Emilia Estrada

1965 *Early Formative Period of Coastal Ecuador: The Valdivia and Machalilla Phases.* Smithsonian Contributions to Anthropology, Vol. 1. Washington, D.C.: Smithsonian Institution.

Michie, James L.

1973 Archaeological Indications for Sea Level 3,500 Years Ago. *South Carolina Antiquities* 5(1):1–11.

1974 A Second Burial from Daw's Island Shell Midden, 38BU9, Beaufort County, South Carolina. *South Carolina Antiquities* 6(1):37–47.

1979 *The Bass Pond Site: Intensive Archaeological Testing at a Formative Period Base Camp on Kiawah Island, South Carolina.* Research Manuscript Series 154, South Carolina Institute of Archaeology and Anthropology, University of South Carolina, Columbia.

1980 *An Intensive Shoreline Survey of Archaeological Sites in Port Royal Sound and the Broad River Estuary, Beaufort County, S.C.* Research Manuscript Series 167, South Carolina Institute of Archaeology and Anthropology, University of South Carolina, Columbia.

Milanich, Jerald T., and Charles H. Fairbanks
1980 *Florida Archaeology*. New York: Academic Press.

Miller, Carl F.
1949 The Lake Spring Site, Columbia County, Georgia. *American Antiquity* 15:254–58.

Moody, W. C., E. E. Carter, and B. S. Beard
1985 The Moody Site: An Archaic Culture Site in Edgefield County. Paper presented at the Annual Conference of the Archaeological Society of South Carolina, Columbia.

Moody, W. C., E. E. Carter, E. Deason, and B. S. Beard
1979 The Moody Site: An Archaic Culture Site in Edgefield County. Manuscript on file at the South Carolina Institute of Archaeology and Anthropology, University of South Carolina, Columbia.

Moore, Clarence B.
1897 Certain Aboriginal Mounds of the Georgia Coast. *Journal of the Philadelphia Academy of Natural Sciences* 2:71–73.
1899 Certain Aboriginal Mounds of the Coast of South Carolina. *Journal of the Philadelphia Academy of Natural Sciences* 11:146–62.

Moore, Josselyn F.
1985 Archaeobotanical Analyses at Five Sites in the Richard B. Russell Reservoir, Georgia and South Carolina. In *Prehistoric Human Ecology along the Upper Savannah River: Excavations at the Rucker's Bottom, Abbeville and Bullard Site Groups*, assembled by D. G. Anderson and J. Schuldenrein, pp. 673–94. Atlanta: National Park Service, Archaeological Services Branch, Russell Papers.

Moratto, Michael J.
1984 *California Archaeology*. Orlando: Academic Press.

Morse, Dan F.
1967 The Robinson Site and Shell Mound Archaic in the Middle South. Ph.D. dissertation, Department of Anthropology, University of Michigan.

Morse, Dan F., and Phyllis A. Morse
1983 *Archaeology of the Central Mississippi Valley*. New York: Academic Press.

Muller, Jon
1986 *Ohio Archaeology*. Orlando: Academic Press.

New World Research
1988 Cultural Resource Testing on the Mobile Bay Pipeline Project, Choctaw, Washington, and Mobile Counties, Alabama. New World Research, Report of Investigations 167.

Noakes, John E., and Betty Lee Brandau
1974 University of Georgia Radiocarbon Dates III. *Radiocarbon* 16:131–41.

Oliver, Billy C.
1981 The Piedmont Tradition Refinement of the Savannah River Stemmed Point Type. M.A. thesis, Department of Anthropology, University of North Carolina, Chapel Hill.
1985 Tradition and Typology: Basic Elements of the Carolina Projectile Point Sequence. In *Structure and Process in Southeastern Archaeology*, edited by R. S. Dickens, Jr., and H. T. Ward, pp. 195–211. University, Ala.: University of Alabama Press.

Oliver, Billy C., Stephen R. Claggett, and Andrea Lee Novick
1986 Lithic Analysis. In *Indian and Freedman Occupation at the Fish Haul Site (38BU805), Beaufort County, South Carolina*, edited by M. B. Trinkley, pp. 183–207. Research Series 7. Columbia, S.C.: Chicora Foundation.

O'Neale, Lila M.
1932 Yurok-Karok Basket Weavers. *University of California Publications in American Archaeology and Ethnology* 32:1–184.

Osborn, Alan
1988 Limitations of the Diffusionist Approach: Evolutionary Ecology and Shell-Tempered Ceramics. In *The Transfer and Transformation of Ideas and Material Culture*, edited by P. J. Hugill and D. B. Dickson, pp. 23–44. College Station: Texas A&M University Press.

Overstreet, W. C., and Henry Bell III
1965 *The Crystalline Rocks of South Carolina.* United States Geological Survey Bulletin 1183.

Overton, J. M.
1969 A Survey of Soapstone Quarry Sites. Institute of Archaeology and Anthropology, University of South Carolina, *Notebook* 1:6–7.

Ozker, Doreen
1982 *An Early Woodland Community at the Schultz Site 20SA2 in the Saginaw Valley and the Nature of the Early Woodland Adaptation in the Great Lakes Region.* Anthropological Papers 70. Ann Arbor: Museum of Anthropology, University of Michigan.

Parmalee, Paul W., and Walter F. Klippel
1974 Freshwater Mussels as a Prehistoric Food Resource. *American Antiquity* 39:421–34.

Pauketat, Timothy R.
1987 A Functional Consideration of a Mississippian Domestic Vessel Assemblage. *Southeastern Archaeology* 6:1–15.

Peterson, Drexel

1971a The Cultural Excuses for Fiber-Tempered Pottery. Paper presented at the Twenty-eighth Southeastern Archaeological Conference, Macon, Georgia.

1971b Time and Settlement in the Archaeology of Groton Plantation. Ph.D. dissertation, Department of Anthropology, Harvard University.

1980 The Introduction, Use and Technology of Fiber-Tempered Pottery in the Southeastern United States. In *Early Native Americans,* edited by D. L. Browman, pp. 363–72. The Hague: Mouton.

Phelps, David S.

1965 The Norwood Series of Fiber-Tempered Ceramics. *Southeastern Archaeological Conference, Bulletin* 2:65–69.

1968 Thom's Creek Ceramics in the Central Savannah River Locality. *Florida Anthropologist* 21:17–30.

1983 Archaeology of the North Carolina Coastal Plain: Problems and Hypotheses. In *The Prehistory of North Carolina: An Archaeological Symposium,* edited by M. A. Mathis and J. J. Crow, pp. 1–51. Raleigh: North Carolina Division of Archives and History.

Phelps, David S., and Rebekah Burgess

1964 A Possible Case of Cannibalism in the Early Woodland Period in Eastern Georgia. *American Antiquity* 30:189–202.

Plog, Stephen

1978 Social Interaction and Stylistic Similarity: A Reanalysis. In *Advances in Archaeological Method and Theory,* Vol. 1, edited by M. B. Schiffer, pp. 143–82. New York: Academic Press.

Prentice, Guy

1986 Origins of Plant Domestication in the Eastern United States: Promoting the Individual in Archaeological Theory. *Southeastern Archaeology* 5:103–19.

Price, T. Douglas, and James A. Brown, eds.

1985 *Prehistoric Hunter-Gatherers: The Emergence of Cultural Complexity.* Orlando: Academic Press.

Price, T. Jeffrey, and Chad O. Braley

1990 Cultural Resource Survey of Selected Fiscal Year 1990 Timber Sales, Fort Gordon, Columbia and Richmond Counties, Georgia. Athens, Ga.: Southeastern Archaeological Services.

Reichel-Dolmatoff, Gerardo

1965 *Excavaciones arqueologicas en Puerto Hormiga.* Anthropologia 2. Bogota: Ediciones de la Universidad de los Andes.

Reid, Kenneth C.
1984 Fire and Ice: New Evidence for the Production and Preservation of Late Archaic Fiber-Tempered Pottery in the Middle-Latitude Lowlands. *American Antiquity* 49:55–76.
1989 A Materials Science Perspective on Hunter-Gatherer Pottery. In *Pottery Technology: Ideas and Approaches,* edited by G. Bronitsky, pp. 167–80. Boulder: Westview.

Renfrew, Colin
1977 Alternative Models for Exchange and Spatial Distribution. In *Exchange Systems in Prehistory,* edited by T. K. Earle and J. E. Ericson, pp. 71–90. New York: Academic Press.

Rice, Prudence M.
1987 *Pottery Analysis: A Sourcebook.* Chicago: University of Chicago Press.

Rodeffer, Michael J., Stephanie Holschlag, and M. K. Cann
1979 *Greenwood County: An Archaeological Reconnaissance.* Greenwood, S.C.: Lander College.

Rogers, Everett M.
1962 *Diffusion of Innovations.* New York: Free Press.

Rogers, Everett M., and F. F. Shoemaker
1971 *Communication of Innovations: A Cross-Cultural Approach.* 2d ed. New York: Free Press.

Root, Dolores
1983 Information Exchange and the Spatial Configurations of Egalitarian Societies. In *Archaeological Hammers and Theories,* edited by J. A. Moore and A. S. Keene, pp. 193–219. New York: Academic Press.
1984 Material Dimensions of Social Inequality in Non-Stratified Societies—An Archaeological Perspective. Ph.D. dissertation, Department of Anthropology, University of Massachusetts, Amherst.

Rostlund, Erhard
1952 *Freshwater Fish and Fishing in Native North America.* Berkeley: University of California Press.

Rowley-Conwy, Peter
1983 Sedentary Hunters: The Ertebolle Example. In *Hunter-Gatherer Economy in Prehistory,* edited by G. Bailey, pp. 111–26. Cambridge: Cambridge University Press.

Ryan, Thomas M.
1972 Archaeological Survey of the Columbia Zoological Park, Richland and Lexington Counties, South Carolina. South Carolina Institute of Archaeology and Anthropology, University of South Carolina, *Notebook* 4:141–86.

Rye, O. S.
1981 *Pottery Technology*. Taraxacum Manuals in Archaeology 4. Washington, D.C.: Taraxacum.

Sahlins, Marshall
1972 *Stone Age Economics*. Chicago: Aldine.
1976 *Culture and Practical Reason*. Chicago: University of Chicago Press.

Saitta, Dean J.
1987 Economic Integration and Social Development in Zuni Prehistory. Ph.D. dissertation, Department of Anthropology, University of Massachusetts, Amherst.

Saitta, Dean J., and Arthur S. Keene
1985 Concepts of Surplus in Primitive Economy: A Critique and Reformulation. Paper presented at the Fiftieth Annual Meeting of the Society for American Archaeology, Denver.
1990 Polities and Surplus Flow in Prehistoric Communal Societies. In *Evolution of Political Systems: Sociopolitics in Small-Scale Sedentary Societies*, edited by S. Upham, pp. 203–24. Cambridge: Cambridge University Press.

Sampson, C. Garth
1988 *Stylistic Boundaries among Mobile Hunter-Foragers*. Washington, D.C.: Smithsonian Institution Press.

Sassaman, Kenneth E.
1983 Middle and Late Archaic Settlement in the South Carolina Piedmont. M.A. thesis, Department of Anthropology, University of South Carolina, Columbia.
1985 The Middle Archaic Period in the Savannah River Valley: Patterns of Adaptive Flexibility. Paper presented at the Forty-second Annual Meeting of the Southeastern Archaeological Conference, Birmingham, Alabama.
1987 Report of Archaeological Investigations at 38AK158 and 38AK159, Aiken County, South Carolina. Report submitted to the Savannah River Operations Office, U.S. Department of Energy.
1988 The Mid-Holocene Archaeological Record of the Middle Savannah River Valley. Manuscript in possession of the author.
1991a Economic and Social Contexts of Ceramic Vessel Technology in the American Southeast. Ph.D. dissertation, Department of Anthropology, University of Massachusetts, Amherst.
1991b Interim Report on Archaeological Testing at the Midden Point Site (9Bk113), Burke County, Georgia. Manuscript on file, Savannah River Archaeological Research Program. Columbia: South Carolina Institute of Archaeology and Anthropology, University of South Carolina.

1991c Proposal for Archaeological Testing at the Mims Point Site (38ED9), Sumter National Forest, South Carolina. Manuscript on file, Savannah River Archaeological Research Program. Columbia: South Carolina Institute of Archaeology and Anthropology, University of South Carolina.

1992 The Second Fall of the Stallings Culture: Shellmidden Looting in South Carolina and Georgia. In *Site Destruction in the Southeast: A South Carolina Perspective*, edited by D. G. Anderson. Atlanta: Interagency Archaeological Services, National Park Service.

Sassaman, Kenneth E., Mark J. Brooks, Glen T. Hanson, and David G. Anderson

1990 *Native American Prehistory in the Middle Savannah River Valley: A Synthesis of Archaeological Investigations on the Savannah River Site, Aiken and Barnwell Counties, South Carolina*. Savannah River Archaeological Research Papers 1. Columbia: South Carolina Institute of Archaeology and Anthropology, University of South Carolina.

Sassaman, Kenneth E., Glen T. Hanson, and Tommy Charles

1988 Raw Material Procurement and the Reduction of Hunter-Gatherer Range in the Savannah River Valley. *Southeastern Archaeology* 7:79–94.

Schenck, W. Egbert, and Elmer J. Dawson

1929 Archaeology of the Northern San Joaquin Valley. *University of California Publications in American Archaeology and Ethnology* 25(4):289–413.

Schiffer, Michael B.

1988 The Effects of Surface Treatment on the Heating Effectiveness of Cooking Vessels. Paper presented at the Fifty-second Annual Meeting of the Society for American Archaeology, Phoenix.

Schiffer, Michael B., and James M. Skibo

1987 Theory and Experiment in the Study of Technological Change. *Current Anthropology* 28:595–622.

Schuldenrein, Joseph, David G. Anderson, and Charles E. Cantley

1985 The McCalla Bottom Site (38AB288) Archaeological Record. In *Prehistoric Human Ecology along the Upper Savannah River: Excavations at the Rucker's Bottom, Abbeville and Bullard Site Groups*, assembled by D. G. Anderson and J. Schuldenrein, pp. 175–214. Atlanta: Atlanta Interagency Archaeological Services Division, National Park Service, Russell Papers.

Sears, William H.

1977 Seaborne Contacts between Early Cultures in the Lower Southeastern United States and Middle through South America. In *The Sea in the Pre-Columbian World,* edited by E. P. Benson, pp. 1–13. Washington, D.C.: Dumbarton Oaks Research Library and Collections.

1982 *Fort Center: An Archaeological Site in the Lake Okeechobee Basin.* Gainesville: University Presses of Florida.

Sears, William H., and James B. Griffin

1950 Fiber-Tempered Pottery of the Southeast. In *Prehistoric Pottery of the Eastern United States,* edited by J. B. Griffin, pp. 2–20. Ann Arbor: Museum of Anthropology, University of Michigan.

Sharp, Lauriston

1952 Steel Axes for Stone Age Australians. In *Human Problems in Technological Change: A Casebook,* edited by E. H. Spicer, pp. 69–90. New York: Sage.

Shelford, Victor E.

1963 *The Ecology of North America.* Urbana: University of Illinois Press.

Simpkins, Daniel L.

1975 A Preliminary Report on Test Excavations at the Sapelo Island Shell Ring, 1975. *Early Georgia* 3(2):15–37.

Simpkins, Daniel L., and Dorothy J. Allard

1986 Isolation and Identification of Spanish Moss Fiber from a Sample of Stallings and Orange Series Ceramics. *American Antiquity* 51:102–17.

Simpkins, Daniel L., and Alan E. McMichael

1976 Sapelo Island: A Preliminary Report. *Southeastern Archaeological Conference, Bulletin* 19:95–99.

Skibo, James M.

1992 *Pottery Function: A Use-Alteration Perspective.* New York: Plenum.

Skibo, James M., David J. Hally, and Michael B. Schiffer

1988 The Manufacture and Use of Fiber-Tempered Pottery from the Southeastern United States. Paper presented at the Fifty-third Annual Meeting of the Society for American Archaeology, New Orleans.

Skibo, James M., Michael B. Schiffer, and Kenneth C. Reid

1989 Organic-Tempered Pottery: An Experimental Study. *American Antiquity* 54:122–46.

Smith, Brent W.

1981 The Late Archaic-Poverty Point Steatite Trade Network in the Lower Mississippi Valley: Some Preliminary Observations. *Florida Anthropologist* 34:120–25.

Smith, Bruce D.
1986 The Archaeology of the Southeastern United States: From Dalton to de Soto, 10,500–500 B.P. *Advances in World Archaeology* 5:1–92.

Smith, Eric A.
1979 Human Adaptation and Energetic Efficiency. *Human Ecology* 7:53–74.

Smith, Richard L.
1974 The Archaic Period in the Central Savannah River Area: A Study of Cultural Continuity and Innovation. Manuscript on file, Laboratory of Anthropology, University of North Carolina, Chapel Hill.

Snow, Dean R.
1980 *The Archaeology of New England*. New York: Academic Press.

Snow, Frankie
1977 *An Archaeological Survey of the Ocmulgee Big Bend Region*. Occasional Papers from South Georgia No. 3. Douglas: South Georgia College.

South, Stanley A.
1959 A Study of the Prehistory of the Roanoke Basin. M.A. thesis, Department of Anthropology, University of North Carolina, Chapel Hill.
1970 Baked Clay Objects from the Site of the 1670 Settlement at Charles Towne, South Carolina. South Carolina Institute of Archaeology and Anthropology, University of South Carolina, *Notebook* 2:3–16.

Southerlin, B. G.
1989 Baked Clay Objects along the South Carolina Coast. In *An Archaeological Study of the Minim Island Site: Early Woodland Dynamics in Coastal South Carolina*, edited by C. T. Espenshade and P. E. Brockington, Jr., pp. 265–71. Atlanta: Brockington and Associates.

Stevenson, A. E.
1982 Geomorphic History of a Portion of the Savannah River Flood Plain, Barnwell County, South Carolina. M.S. thesis, Department of Geology, University of South Carolina, Columbia.

Stipp, J. J., K. L. Eldridge, and R. Cadwell
1976 University of Miami Radiocarbon Dates VI. *Radiocarbon* 18:210–20.

Stoltman, James B.
1966 New Radiocarbon Dates for Southeastern Fiber-Tempered Pottery. *American Antiquity* 31:872–74.
1972 The Late Archaic in the Savannah River Region. In *Fiber-Tempered Pottery in Southeastern United States and Northern Colombia: Its Origins, Context and Significance*, edited by R. P. Bullen and J. B.

Stoltman, pp. 37–62. Florida Anthropological Society Publications 6.

1974 *Groton Plantation: An Archaeological Study of a South Carolina Locality*. Monographs of the Peabody Museum 1. Cambridge, Mass.: Harvard University.

1978 Temporal Models in Prehistory: An Example from Eastern North America. *Current Anthropology* 19:703–28.

Sutherland, Donald R.

1973 Preliminary Analysis of Ceramic Materials Recovered from the Spanish Mount Site, Edisto Island, S.C. *South Carolina Antiquities* 5:46–50.

1974 Excavations at the Spanish Mount Shell Midden, Edisto Island, S.C. *South Carolina Antiquities* 6:25–36.

Taylor, Richard L., and Marion F. Smith, assemblers

1978 *The Report of the Intensive Survey of the Richard B. Russell Dam and Lake, Savannah River, South Carolina and Georgia*. Research Manuscript Series 142, South Carolina Institute of Archaeology and Anthropology, University of South Carolina, Columbia.

Testart, Alain

1982 The Significance of Food Storage among Hunter-Gatherers: Residence Patterns, Population Densities and Social Inequalities. *Current Anthropology* 23:523–37.

1988 Some Major Problems in the Social Anthropology of Hunter-Gatherers. *Current Anthropology* 29:1–31.

Thomas, David Hurst, and Clark Spencer Larson

1979 The Anthropology of St. Catherines Island 2: The Refuge-Deptford Mortuary Complex. *Anthropological Papers of the American Museum of Natural History* 56(1).

Thomas, Prentice M., and L. Janice Campbell

1988 The Elliot's Point Complex: New Data Regarding the Localized Poverty Point Expression on the Northwest Florida Gulf Coast, 2000 B.C.–500 B.C. Paper presented at the Southeastern Archaeological Conference, New Orleans.

Tippitt, V. Ann, and William H. Marquardt

1984 *Archaeological Investigations at Gregg Shoals, a Deeply Stratified Site on the Savannah River*. Atlanta: Atlanta Archaeological Services Branch, National Park Service, Russell Papers.

Trimble, Stanley Wayne

1974 *Man-Induced Soil Erosion on the Southern Piedmont, 1700–1970*. Ankeny, Iowa: Soil Conservation Society of America.

Trinkley, Michael B.
1974 Report of Archaeological Testing at the Love Site (SoC240), South Carolina. *Southern Indian Studies* 26:3–18.
1975 Cox Site Report and Analysis. Manuscript on file at South Carolina Institute of Archaeology and Anthropology, University of South Carolina, Columbia.
1976 Paleoethnobotanical Remains from Archaic-Woodland Transitional Middens along the South Carolina Coast. *Southeastern Archaeological Conference, Bulletin* 19:64–67.
1980a A Typology of Thom's Creek Pottery for the South Carolina Coast. *South Carolina Antiquities* 12:1–35.
1980b Investigation of the Woodland Period along the South Carolina Coast. Ph.D. dissertation, Department of Anthropology, University of North Carolina, Chapel Hill.
1983 Ceramics of the Central South Carolina Coast. *South Carolina Antiquities* 15:43–54.
1985 The Form and Function of South Carolina's Early Woodland Shell Rings. In *Structure and Process in Southeastern Archaeology*, edited by R. S. Dickens and H. T. Ward, pp. 102–18. University, Ala.: University of Alabama Press.

Trinkley, Michael B., ed.
1986 *Indian and Freedman Occupation at the Fish Haul Site (38BU805), Beaufort County, South Carolina*. Research Series 7. Columbia, S.C.: Chicora Foundation.

Upchurch, Sam
1984 Petrology of Selected Lithic Materials from the South Carolina Coastal Plain. In *An Archaeological Survey of Chert Quarries in Western Allendale County, South Carolina*, by A. C. Goodyear and T. Charles, pp. 125–60. Research Manuscript Series 195, South Carolina Institute of Archaeology and Anthropology, University of South Carolina, Columbia.

Waddell, Eugene
1963 Thom's Creek Punctate. *Southeastern Archaeological Conference, Newsletter* 9:3–5.
1965 A C14 Date for Awendaw Punctate. *Southeastern Archaeological Conference, Bulletin* 3:82–85.

Walthall, John A.
1980 *Prehistoric Indians of the Southeast: Archaeology of Alabama and the Middle South*. University, Ala.: University of Alabama Press.

Walthall, John A., and Ned J. Jenkins
1976 The Gulf Formative Stage in Southeastern Prehistory. *Southeastern Archaeological Conference, Bulletin* 19:43–49.

Ward, Trawick
1983 A Review of Archaeology in the North Carolina Piedmont: A Study of Change. In *The Prehistory of North Carolina: An Archaeological Symposium,* edited by M. A. Mathis and J. J. Crow, pp. 53–81. Raleigh: North Carolina Division of Archives and History.

Waring, Antonio J., Jr.
1968a Fiber-Tempered Pottery and Its Cultural Affiliations on the Georgia-Carolina Coast (orig. 1952). In *The Waring Papers: The Collected Works of Antonio J. Waring, Jr.*, edited by Stephen Williams, pp. 253–55. Papers of the Peabody Museum of Archaeology and Ethnology, Harvard University, Vol. 58.
1968b The Bilbo Site, Chatham County, Georgia (orig. 1940). In *The Waring Papers: The Collected Works of Antonio J. Waring, Jr.*, edited by Stephen Williams, pp. 152–97. Papers of the Peabody Museum of Archaeology and Ethnology, Harvard University, Vol. 58.
1968c The Refuge Site, Jasper County, South Carolina (orig. 1940). In *The Waring Papers: The Collected Works of Antonio J. Waring, Jr.*, edited by Stephen Williams, pp. 198–208. Papers of the Peabody Museum of Archaeology and Ethnology, Harvard University, Vol. 58.
1968d The Cultural Sequence at the Mouth of the Savannah River (orig. 1955). In *The Waring Papers: The Collected Works of Antonio J. Waring, Jr.*, edited by Stephen Williams, pp. 216–21. Papers of the Peabody Museum of Archaeology and Ethnology, Harvard University, Vol. 58.

Waring, Antonio J., Jr., and Lewis H. Larson, Jr.
1968 The Shell Ring on Sapelo Island (orig. 1955–60). In *The Waring Papers: The Collected Works of Antonio J. Waring, Jr.*, edited by Stephen Williams, pp. 263–78. Papers of the Peabody Museum of Archaeology and Ethnology, Harvard University, Vol. 58.

Waselkov, Gregory
1982 Shellfish Gathering and Shell Midden Archaeology. Ph.D. dissertation, Department of Anthropology, University of North Carolina, Chapel Hill.

Wauchope, Robert
1966 *Archaeological Survey of North Georgia with a Test of Some Cultural Hypotheses.* Society for American Archaeology, Memoirs 21.

Webb, Clarence H.
1944 Stone Vessels from a Northeast Louisiana Site. *American Antiquity* 4:386–95.
1968 The Extent and Content of Poverty Point Culture. *American Antiquity* 33:105–14.

1982 The Poverty Point Culture. 2d ed. School of Geoscience, Louisiana State University, *Geoscience and Man* 17.

Webb, William S.
1946 *Indian Knoll* (rpt. 1974). Knoxville: University of Tennessee Press.

Webb, William S., and David L. DeJarnette
1942 *An Archaeological Survey of the Pickwick Basin in the Adjacent Portions of the States of Alabama, Mississippi and Tennessee.* Bureau of American Ethnology, Bulletin 129.

Whipple, Stephen A.
1978 Report for 1978 on the Research Project: A Gradient Analysis of Bottomland and Swamp Forests of the Savannah River Plant, South Carolina. Report by the Department of Botany, Louisiana State University.

Whipple, Stephen A., Lynn H. Wellman, and Bill J. Good
1981 *A Classification of Hardwood and Swamp Forests of the Savannah River Plant, South Carolina.* Report 6. Aiken, S.C.: Savannah River Plant, National Environmental Research Park Program, U.S. Department of Energy.

White, John W.
1982 An Integration of Late Archaic Settlement Patterns for the South Carolina Piedmont. M.A. thesis, Department of Anthropology, University of Arkansas, Fayetteville.

Widmer, Randolph J.
1976 *Archaeological Investigations at the Palm Tree Site, Berkeley County, S.C.* Research Manuscript Series 103, South Carolina Institute of Archaeology and Anthropology, University of South Carolina, Columbia.

Wiessner, Polly
1977 Hxaro: A Regional System of Reciprocity for Reducing Risk among the !Kung San. Ph.D. dissertation, Department of Anthropology, University of Michigan.
1982 Risk, Reciprocity and Social Influences on !Kung San Economics. In *Politics and History in Band Societies,* edited by E. B. Leacock and R. B. Lee, pp. 61–84. Cambridge: Cambridge University Press.

Williams, Stephen
1968a Editor's Introduction: Part II. In *The Waring Papers: The Collected Works of Antonio J. Waring, Jr.,* edited by Stephen Williams, pp. 101–6. Papers of the Peabody Museum of Archaeology and Ethnology, Harvard University, Vol. 58.
1968b Epilogue: Some Thoughts on Georgia Prehistory. In *The Waring*

Papers: The Collected Works of Antonio J. Waring, Jr., edited by Stephen Williams, pp. 315–25. Papers of the Peabody Museum of Archaeology and Ethnology, Harvard University, Vol. 58.

1968c Appendix: Radiocarbon Dates from the Georgia Coast. In *The Waring Papers: The Collected Works of Antonio J. Waring, Jr.*, edited by Stephen Williams, pp. 329–32. Papers of the Peabody Museum of Archaeology and Ethnology, Harvard University, Vol. 58.

Wilson, Jack H., Jr., and Homes Hogue Wilson

1986 Faunal Remains. In *Indian and Freedman Occupation at the Fish Haul Site (38BU805), Beaufort County, South Carolina*, edited by M. B. Trinkley, pp. 282–312. Research Series 7. Columbia, S.C.: Chicora Foundation.

Wimberly, Steve B.

1960 *Indian Pottery from Clarke County and Mobile County, Southern Alabama*. Alabama Museum of Natural History, Museum Paper 36.

Winters, Howard D.

1969 *The Riverton Culture: A Second Millennium Occupation in the Central Wabash Valley*. Illinois Archaeological Survey Monograph 1 and Illinois State Museum Reports on Investigations 13.

Wise, Robert P.

1986 CRM: Vogtle-Effingham-Thalman 500 kv Electric Transmission Line. GP-SN-09: Data Recovery. Atlanta: Garrow and Associates.

Wobst, H. Martin

1968 The Butterfield Site. University of Michigan, Museum of Anthropology, *Anthropological Papers* 32:173–275.

1977 Stylistic Behavior and Information Exchange. In *Papers for the Director: Research Essays in Honor of James B. Griffin*, edited by C. E. Cleland, pp. 317–42. Anthropological Papers 61. Ann Arbor: University of Michigan, Museum of Anthropology.

Wolf, Eric R.

1984 Culture: Panacea or Problem? *American Antiquity* 49:393–400.

Wood, W. Dean, Dan T. Elliott, Teresa P. Rudolph, and Dennis B. Blanton

1986 *Prehistory of the Richard B. Russell Reservoir: The Archaic and Woodland Periods of the Upper Savannah River*. Atlanta: Atlanta Interagency Archaeological Services Division, National Park Service, Russell Papers.

Woodburn, James

1968 Stability and Flexibility in Hadza Residential Groupings. In *Man the Hunter*, edited by R. B. Lee and I. DeVore, pp. 103–10. Chicago: Aldine.

1980 Hunters and Gatherers Today and Reconstruction of the Past. In *Soviet and Western Anthropology*, edited by E. Gellner, pp. 95–117. London: Duckworth.

1982 Egalitarian Societies. *Man* 17:431–51.

Worth, John E.

1988 Mississippian Occupation of the Middle Flint River. M.A. thesis, Department of Anthropology, University of Georgia.

Index